African American
Entertainers in Australia
and New Zealand

African American Entertainers in Australia and New Zealand

A History, 1788–1941

BILL EGAN

McFarland & Company, Inc., Publishers
Jefferson, North Carolina

ISBN (print) 978-1-4766-7795-8
ISBN (ebook) 978-1-4766-3743-3

Library of Congress and British Library
Cataloguing data are available

Library of Congress Control Number 2019047355

Front cover image: Sonny Clay band arrives in Sydney on *SS Sierra*.
Back row: (trumpet) Ernest Coycault, (saxophone) probably William Griffin,
(crouching) possibly Sonny Clay; center: (trombone) Luther Craven,
(banjo) Rupert Jordan; front, from left, Florence Covan, Ivy Anderson and
Herman Hoy (tuba) (photographer Sam Hood; courtesy Mitchell Library,
State Library of New South Wales; Hood Collection)

Printed in the United States of America

*McFarland & Company, Inc., Publishers
Box 611, Jefferson, North Carolina 28640
www.mcfarlandpub.com*

To the Aboriginal and Torres Strait Islander people of Australia, and the Maori people of New Zealand, who welcomed African American entertainers to their ancestral lands

Table of Contents

Acknowledgments

Inevitably, with a time span of over 150 years and more than 350 performers covered, many people and sources have contributed material and information for this book. I can only hope I have not accidentally omitted anyone who should be acknowledged. I will deal with people first before moving on to institutions and the highly valuable online sources.

At the top of the list has to be my wife, Jean, not only as a rigorous proofreader and editor, but also as a Photoshop wizard with old images. My wonderful granddaughters, Ruby and Frankie, provided valuable distraction from the tyranny of the book.

People

Thanks to the following people, who all contributed material or ideas:

Lynn D. Abbott (co-author of *Out of Sight* and *Ragged but Right*, both invaluable sources)
David Bergin (BoxingTreasures.com)
Mark Berresford (author of *That's Got 'Em!*)
Chris Bourke (for information on R.B. Williams)
Stephen Bourne (biographer of Nina Mae McKinney)
Gabriel Boyers (Schubertiade Music)
Mark Cantor (comprehensive expert on jazz and black film)
Professor Clare Corbould (prolific researcher on African American topics)
Noel Day (re: Mattie Lawrence Thrift)
Dr. Clay Djubal (creator of theatre archive web site OZVTA.com)
Simon Drake (Australian National Film and Sound Archive)
Lynette Dries (Niece and dedicated caregiver for Gracie Le Brun)
David Gleason (owner of Americanradiohistory.com website)
Steve Goldstein (author *L.A.'s Graveside Companion*, re: Jolly John Larkins)
The late Delilah Jackson (friend, and supplier of the U.S. Thompson interview tapes)
Green Jeffrey (expert on black Americans in Victorian Britain)
Bill Haesler (notable Australian jazz researcher)
Ian Heads (prolific sports writer, for Jack Johnson image)
Alaina Hebert (Associate Curator, Graphics, Hogan Jazz Archive, Tulane University)
The late Bill Hill, from Duke-LYM list (for the copy of his Ivie Anderson interview)

Professor Bruce Johnson (notable Australian author, jazz and social researcher)
Professor Marvin Keenze (information on Todd Duncan)
Nina Gamble Kennedy (assistance with Fisk Singers)
Steven Lasker (American expert on Duke Ellington and jazz)
The late Gracie Le Brun (for her friendship and memories of her career)
Gary Le Gallant (owner Nugrape website, for help with images)
Mitch Mader (for help with Cassie Walmer images)
Mark Miller (author *Some Hustling This!*)
Cynthia Millman (co-author *Frankie Manning: Ambassador of Lindy Hop*)
Deirdre O'Connell (Sonny Clay info and other help)
Clair Orbell (Otago Museum) for Ferry the Human Frog image
David Palmquist (creator of the amazingly comprehensive www.ellingtonweb.ca)
Marcello Piras (musicologist extraordinaire and jazz expert)
Rebecca Phillips-Vasilescu (for information on her ancestor Jolly John Larkins)
Professor Cassandra Pybus (whose book *Black Founders* was inspirational)
Tracy Rae (for information on her ancestor Sam Keenan)
Carolyn Rolls (for help with Jubilee Singers in Echuca)
Howard Rye (notable UK researcher on jazz, for help on many topics)
Gabor Toth (Local and NZ History Specialist, Wellington City Libraries)
Richard Thrift (re: Mattie Lawrence Thrift)
Ken Steiner (Ellington researcher par excellence)
The late June Strike (née Allen) (for memories of her U.S. trip)
Frank Van Straten (noted author and Tivoli expert)
Dr. Aleisha Ward (New Zealand jazz researcher).

Libraries and Institutions

National Archives of Australia (Pamela Barnetta)
National Library of Australia (including Natalie Clough for help with images)
Australian National Film and Sound Archive
State Library of Victoria
State Library of New South Wales
Echuca Historical Society Museum (Heather Rendle and Karen Bristol, researchers, for help with Jubilee Singers in Echuca)
National Library of New Zealand (Alexander Turnbull Library)
Wellington City Libraries (New Zealand)
Hogan Jazz Archive (Tulane University), Louisiana (U.S.)
New York Public Library and affiliated Schomburg Institute Public Library (U.S.)
UK National Jazz Archive (for online access to *Storyville* jazz magazine)
U.S. Library of Congress
Beinecke Library, Yale University (Anne Marie Menta)

Online Sources

Most important of the many online sources used were the Australian National Library's *Trove* catalogue and the New Zealand National Library's *Papers Past* catalogue.

Full text search of the following newspapers and journals was very useful:

California Eagle (Los Angeles); *Indianapolis Freeman*; *Pittsburgh Courier.*
Valuable search of multiple U.S. papers was gained through the website http://fulton history.com/Fulton.html.
Valuable search of the *New York Clipper*, *Broadax*, and *Vaudeville News* was gained through the website http://idnc.library.illinois.edu/.
Other valued online sources were Wikipedia.org; IMDb.com (the movie database); IBDb.com (the Broadway show database); Boxrec.com (the boxing database); OZVTA.com (Dr. Djubal Clay's Australian theatre database); http://www. jeffreygreen.co.uk/ (the website of historian Jeffrey Green); http://www.nugrape. net/ (Blues and Gospel website of Gary Le Gallant), and the Jazz Research email list and its founder, Michael Fitzgerald.

Preface

The need for a history of African American entertainers in Australia and New Zealand became apparent to me as a result of 10 years spent researching the life of Florence Mills, a forgotten international star, whose life spanned the period from the 1890s to the late 1920s. Meeting survivors of that era gave me a deep empathy for the experiences of generations of African American entertainers. This particularly related to how they patiently subverted and undermined the restrictions of their world of segregation and prejudice, in ways that are often not appreciated by contemporary generations. Aspects of that era may seem distasteful today, with its gross stereotypes, but that is all the more reason for sympathetically assessing the gradual evolutionary process that led to a world where a Beyoncé can be entertainment royalty and a Meghan Markle can be real royalty.

The world of contemporary African Americans is not yet the dream that Martin Luther King dreamed but it's a long way from the blackface buffoonery that was forced on earlier generations. Kudos for much of the successes of that long evolution can fairly be credited to generations of entertainers who stoically endured the indignities of earlier times, while slowly enlarging their horizons. It seems extraordinary today to realize that, in 1921, when the all-black show *Shuffle Along* opened on Broadway, there were fears of riots because it featured something hitherto unthinkable—a tender love scene between a black man and a black woman.

Before I became aware of the wider world of black entertainment in its myriad forms, I was already a lifetime jazz fan, with my heroes including the likes of Duke Ellington, Louis Armstrong, Bessie Smith, Charlie Parker, and Billie Holiday. I had also discovered other major African American cultural figures like Langston Hughes, Paul Robeson, James Reese Europe, and William Grant Still. Delving into the wider entertainment world, I became aware that over many years African American entertainers had been visiting the shores of my own homeland, Australia. Thanks to the brilliant research of Professor Cassandra Pybus (*Black Founders*, UNSW Press, Sydney 2006) I became aware that the African American presence in Australia was as old as European settlement via the founding First Fleet, even including one arrival who could be considered an "entertainer."

The story of the African American entertainers who came to Australasia is a microcosm of the wider world of black entertainment throughout the 19th and 20th centuries. I have chosen to delimit the scope of the narrative with the entry of the U.S. into World War II, following the attack on Pearl Harbor in December 1941. Thereafter, the nature and dynamics of the African American presence changed dramatically with the arrival of large numbers of U.S. troops. It continued to change after the war.

While the majority of the entertainers covered here were from mainland U.S., I have also included those who came from the wider African American diaspora, including the West Indies, and some born in countries like England with North American ancestry. There has always been a close affiliation across this wider context; the great Bert Williams was born in Antigua, while Shelton Brooks (composer of "The Darktown Strutters' Ball") was born in Canada, but each had a major impact on U.S. black culture.

I have also used a wide interpretation of what constitutes an "entertainer," summarized as "anyone the public will pay money to see perform." This includes sporting figures like boxers, and world champion cyclist Major Taylor, as well as minstrels, jubilee singers, vaudeville acts, dancers, jazz musicians and many others. My objective has been to provide a comprehensive history of all African American entertainers who came to Australasia during the reference period. In the early years these tended to be large troupes (minstrels and jubilee singers) who stayed for long periods of time, visiting rather remote parts of the region and sometimes returning over a number of years. Later, a more structured approach emerged, with local theatrical entrepreneurs engaging individual acts or small troupes for fixed engagements at the major theatrical centers. This was the era of vaudeville, which lasted many years, blending into the jazz era.

Some of those who came were household names, at least in their time. These include Jack Johnson, world heavyweight boxing champion; Major Taylor, world champion sprint cyclist; the Fisk Jubilee Singers (in many manifestations); glamorous film star Nina Mae McKinney; the Mills Brothers (harmony songsters); Billy Kersands, the dean of black minstrels; Eva Taylor and Ivie Anderson, both notable jazz singers, and Tim Moore, who would achieve later fame as the Kingfish in the *Amos 'n' Andy* TV show. Others were established performers who, though less known today, were highly regarded in their time. Some of the performers attracted attention for reasons beyond their strictly entertainment role, most notably in the case of Sonny Clay and his *Colored Idea* show, because of the appalling racism they faced. Jack Johnson similarly attracted attention beyond his prowess in the ring.

In all, more than 350 African Americans are identified as having performed in Australasia during the period covered. Some became permanent or long-term residents, much loved on the local scene, like Irving Sayles and Charles Pope in Australia, and R.B. Williams and the Hamilton Hodges in New Zealand. The memory of some is still recalled by many descendants.

Decades before the first genuine black minstrel troupes arrived in Australasia, regional towns and villages had their amateur blackface minstrels, performing syncopated music with whose origins they had no direct contact or knowledge. By contrast, the early jubilee singers presented an image of dignified respectability that belied the gross caricatures of minstrelsy, and even influenced some of the native Australian Aboriginal people and New Zealand Maoris.

With the arrival of vaudeville, ragtime, and jazz, the region experienced what Professor Robert O'Meally has labeled "the jazz cadence of American culture," based on the protean forms of black music that came out of the African American experience. Despite official government disapproval of African American performers in the early 20th century, local musicians and entertainers eagerly absorbed the technical skills and styles that the visitors brought, a process that continues to this day. A good example is the 1960s Indigenous female soul group the Sapphires, subject of a movie of that title, whose musical roots can be traced back through the Yorta Yorta people, to the 1886 visit by Frederick J. Loudin's Fisk Jubilee Singers to the Maloga Mission in NSW.

It would not be until the 1960s, and the Civil Rights era, that the worst aspects of the White Australia policy would be swept away. Today, Australasia is a multicultural region, welcoming people of all nationalities and ethnic backgrounds. One of the most potent symbols of that change is the video image coverage of Paul Robeson singing to the workers on the Sydney Opera House building site in 1960.

Introduction

The general structure of this book is a chronological historical account of the arrivals and activities of the many African American entertainers who visited the shores of Australia and New Zealand from 1788 to 1941. In some instances, where there was more than one visit by an individual or a group, it seemed better to deal with the later visits contiguously with the original ones, and therefore out of strict chronological sequence. In the case of the many boxers and the later manifestations of alleged "Fisk Jubilee" troupes, corralling them into chronologically organized appendices avoided a confusing fragmentation of the main narrative.

In dealing with the historical era involved, it is inevitable that many terms considered deeply offensive, racial slurs and demeaning epithets, occur. Even more disturbing for many modern-day readers will be the degree to which some of the entertainers themselves colluded in such usage. This was not so with the particularly offensive N-word, though their promoters and employers sometimes used it. I have not shielded the reader from these offensive terms, as they were part of the currency of the era and relevant to understanding the times. I am also well aware of the hard-fought battle by Lester Walton, against powerful opposition like the *New York Times*, for the capitalization of the word Negro, but I have left the contemporary usage stand in period quotations. Apart from the more offensive terms, the local media persistently portrayed the well-educated and articulate performers as speaking in a crude patois which I have generally not reproduced unless to make a point.

It is also worth noting that, though the offensive language that was commonplace in America could also be found in Australia and New Zealand, it was generally used in a less nasty fashion, typified by ignorance more than by venom. This changed significantly in Australia with the emergence of the racist White Australia policy at the beginning of the 20th century. Until then, African Americans had been viewed quite benevolently, the racial animus being directed towards Chinese immigrants on the gold fields, and the hijacked black indentured laborers in the Queensland cane fields. New Zealand, though not free of prejudice, did not have a direct equivalent of the White Australia policy, perhaps due to the influence of the large Maori population and their affinity with the other island peoples of the South Pacific region.

In quoting media coverage I have tried to give an objective assessment of how successful the performers were in their Australasian ventures, but one needs to "read between the lines" to some extent, as the media of the time was generally inclined to be kind to those who helped fill their advertising columns.

There has been a (perhaps inevitable) tension between providing a comprehensive chronological history of the entertainers' complete activities, and the maintenance of a free-flowing narrative of interest for general readers. How well this has been achieved readers must judge for themselves.

Abbreviations

"Australasia" has been used as a convenient shorthand for "Australia and New Zealand." The following abbreviations have been used frequently throughout the text:

NZ (New Zealand); Australian states: NSW (New South Wales), Vic (Victoria), Qld (Queensland), SA (South Australia), WA (Western Australia), Tas (Tasmania).

Newspapers: SMH (*Sydney Morning Herald*); Evening News (*Sydney Evening News*), NMH (*Newcastle Morning Herald*); Age (*Melbourne Age*); Argus (*Melbourne Argus*); Courier (*Brisbane Courier*), Freeman (*Indianapolis Freeman*), Eagle (*California Eagle*).

1

In the Beginning

The First African American Entertainer

Conventional wisdom portrays the European settlement that started in Australia with the First Fleet's arrival in 1788 as being by white Anglo-Celtic people. This was reinforced by a White Australia policy that existed well into the 20th century, with the original Aboriginal population marginalized as primitives, believed to be destined to die out or be assimilated. As always with history, the truth is much more complex. The popular slogan of recent times, "White Australia has a Black history," is literally true in more than one sense, as was demonstrated by Professor Cassandra Pybus in her book *Black Founders*.[1] The black people she referred to were African Americans, originally from the United States or the West Indies, who arrived in Australia from England on the First Fleet or later convict ships. Professor Pybus explains in considerable detail the events that led to black volunteers on the English side of the American War of Independence being taken to England to spare them the wrath of the colonial victors. Some subsequently fell afoul of the law in their new homeland, resulting in transportation to Australia, or more correctly, the penal colony of NSW.

The First Fleet included 11 black men, with more following on later ships. Australia's first bushranger was a black man known as Caesar, referred to probably inaccurately as being from Madagascar and more likely to have been from Virginia in the U. S.[2] Many Sydneysiders are amazed to learn that Blues Point on the North Shore is named after a black man, William (Billy) Blue. He arrived on a later ship and ran the first ferry service across Sydney Harbour.

Interesting as these early arrivals are, the theme of this book relates to African American entertainers who performed in Australia, so can we also find links there from First Fleet and similar arrivals? Today, a ferry ride on Sydney Harbour could be considered "entertainment," but back in the days before Luna Park smiled cheerfully from the North side, William Blue's activities would have been considered purely commercial. However, one of the First Fleeters was a John Randall, who arrived on the convict ship *Alexander* on January 20, 1788, having been in custody for several years for allegedly stealing a watch-chain. Randall was born in Connecticut around 1764 and had probably been a drummer boy in a British regiment before the War of Independence. He was described as being able to play "the flute and tambour" (a kind of drum).[3] He found employment initially as a game shooter for a prominent colonial official. An early marriage soon ended in the death of his first wife, Esther, but in 1790 he married an Irish woman, Mary Butler, who had arrived on a Second Fleet ship, the *Neptune*. She presented him with three children before dying in childbirth in 1802. By 1800, Randall's musical skills had enabled him to enroll in the NSW Corps and gain a place in the regimental band, formed in September 1801. Apart from its regular regimental functions, including concerts every morning on the parade grounds, the band offered entertainment for the community and the officers' mess—"The most important diversion for the officers was the formal mess dinner, where they and their guests would eat, drink and carouse, while the regimental band entertained."[4]

Randall enjoyed a life of relative prosperity and privilege as a bandsman until he was discharged in 1810. His later life, until his death (probably around 1822), was a tale of poverty and tragedy (including the loss by drowning of two sons from a later common law marriage to Fanny Randall). However, on the basis of his prosperous years as a bandsman, he can fairly be declared the first African American entertainer in Australasia.

Perry the Black

Many more African Americans probably arrived in the early years of colonization, but they didn't find their way into public notice. The next to attract public interest was in the field of boxing, commonly called "pugilism" at the time. John "Black" Perry was born in Dublin, Ireland, in 1819, of a Jamaican mother and a black U.S. father, known as Black Charley. Like Randall, Charley was a drummer in a military band. Due to his father's military travels, young John spent some of his formative years in Canada before being apprenticed as a ship's carpenter. In this capacity he ended up in England, where he became a protégé of the famous bare-knuckle English champion boxer, Jem Ward, who convinced him to take up a career in boxing.

From 1842 to 1847, Perry the Black (as he would sign himself in public notices) achieved significant success on the English boxing scene, interspersed with periods as a publican. His luck ran out in 1847, when he was accused of providing forged currency as part of his stake for a fight. A sympathetic account in *Bell's Life in Sydney* suggests he was "stitched up" by an envious rival. He was transported to Tasmania, where he gained a Ticket of Leave for good behavior after three years. Boxing opportunities being limited in Tas, he arrived in Sydney in 1849, ready for business.[5]

It didn't take long for Perry to make

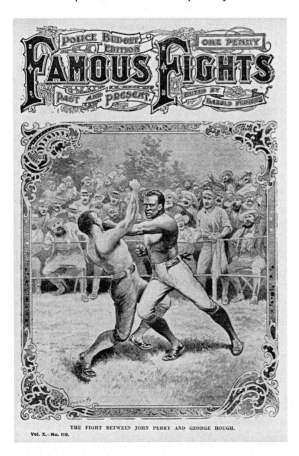

THE FIGHT BETWEEN JOHN PERRY AND GEORGE HOUGH.
Vol. X.—No. 119.

The fight between Black Perry and George Hough, 10 October 1849. Courtesy David Bergin, *www.boxingtreasures.com*.

a mark on the Australian scene. He challenged the reigning Australian heavyweight champion George Hough to a title bout, which took place on October 10, 1849, with stakes at £100 a side. The event caused great interest, but, as bare-knuckle fighting was illegal, it had to be staged at a point safe from police detection. After some false starts, it became known to all and sundry (with the exception of the police) that it would take place at a remote spot known as Cummings Point (Rocky Point), near Sydney. Spectators converged from afar by a variety of transport means, including boats. The event was something of an anticlimax, as Perry quickly disposed of his slightly heavier opponent, the champion's corner "throwing in the towel" during the fifth round. *Bell's Life* (October 13, 1849) commented: "With respect to Perry, no one will question his claim to being a scientific pugilist. He is a powerful hitter, a quick getter-away and the best out-fighter that was ever seen in the colony."

Perry the Black thus became the Australian heavyweight champion, and the first African American boxer to win a national title anywhere in the world. His reign as champion was largely unchallenged but did not gain him great wealth. His invitations to all comers went unheeded, or when bouts were arranged they fell through, presumably because the outcome was predictable. Apart from two fights in 1858, he fell back on his other vocation of publican, running a hotel at Windsor, where he gave boxing exhibitions and offered training for hopeful contenders. He was also at one time reported as entering the wider field of entertainment, playing Othello in a local production. Falling on hard times, he was charged with vagrancy in January 1859 and bound over on a good behavior bond.

While little is known of his later life, he did leave a legacy in Australian boxing history, as around the mid–1860s he was a trainer and mentor for Australian great Larry Foley (1849–1917). Foley in turn was a mentor for Hugh D McIntosh, whose name will feature later as a major promoter of boxing in Australia. Foley is considered the most likely contender to have been the Larry of "Happy as Larry" fame.[6] Perry the Black was the first of a long list of African Americans who made a career for themselves in boxing in Australasia.

Hackett Coulthurst

After Perry the Black, the next African Americans to attract attention in Australia were two dramatic actors, though with very different impact and success. First was Hackett Coulthurst, described as West Indian, featuring in the role of Othello at Sydney's Haymarket Theatre in late April 1867. Though allegedly his first time in the role, he carried it off successfully and it would become his signature piece thereafter. When the Haymarket Theatre closed down for remodeling, Coulthurst went on the road with a Melbourne-based company featuring a range of popular burlesque dramas, including *The Irish Emigrant*, Byron's *Little Don Giovanni* and *Uncle Tom's Cabin*. Coulthurst played Uncle Tom as well as Othello, billed as "The West Indian Roscius," a name generally associated with the great African American Shakespearean actor Ira Aldridge, after a famous Roman actor. The troupe played at Ballarat's Royal Theatre for a season that lasted from May 20 to mid–June 1867.[7]

Coulthurst then retired from the theatre to private business in Tasmania, but he would periodically give popular performances in Tasmania, including reprising his signature role of Othello. He performed—to acclaim from the *SA Register* on April 18, 1876—at White's Rooms, a popular entertainment venue in Adelaide. In 1880, when the R.B. Lewis Combined

Minstrel Company presented the drama *The Slave's Revenge* in Hobart (see Chapter 2), Coulthurst guest-starred in the role of the titular Avenger. He died in Tasmania on December 27, 1885, having played Othello for the last time just six months previously.

Ira Aldridge Junior

Around the time Coulthurst was finishing his Ballarat season, the *Argus* (June 19, 1867) was enthusiastically announcing the opening of an exciting dramatic event:

> We may also state that, on Saturday night, a young gentleman of education and talent, son of the well-known black tragedian Chevalier Ira Aldridge, will make his first appearance in the well-known old play "Mungo, or the Padlock," with which his father's name has been associated for something like half a century. There are few playgoers of any nation who have not seen Ira Aldridge, and curiosity, no doubt, will draw many to see his son.[8]

Mungo or The Padlock was a musical farce by Isaac Bickerstaffe, famous since its original production at Drury Lane Theatre in 1768 and later played with great success by Ira Aldridge senior.

The *Age* (June 19) also gushed: "Mr Aldridge is a young gentleman of acknowledged abilities, and has already won much distinction in the old world. He has performed in the presence of the principal European courts, and obtained such marks of favor as are seldom conferred upon members of the profession."

Alas, the son had not inherited the father's talent! The reactions to his debut included:

- Mr Aldridge was very tolerable, but is certainly very far removed from excellence; indeed, the admiration of the audience seemed chiefly excited not by the fact of his good acting, but by his ability to act at all. (*Argus* July 1, 1867)
- Mr Ira Aldridge played the part of Mungo, a negro servant. He is evidently a novice, and has much to learn before he can obtain a position. (*Age* July 1)
- Whatever merit [Aldridge] may have had, he has certainly transmitted none to his son, who on this his first appearance before a Victorian audience made the dullest, poorest, feeblest attempt at being funny I ever remember to have seen (*Australasian* July 6)

Mungo or the Padlock closed after a few performances, ending Ira Aldridge, Jr.'s career in the theatre.

Ira Daniel Aldridge, Jr., had arrived in Australia in February 1867, aged 19 and exiled by his father for an "innately bad disposition." After his failed dramatic career, he stayed in Australia. An early attempt to establish a private career as a teacher seemed promising but, having acquired a wife and children, he soon ran into financial difficulties. His public performances thereafter would be confined to the dock of various courts as he faced charges of uttering forged checks in the name of numerous respectable citizens. He was in and out of prison between 1871 and 1885 before fading from the public view, possibly having died in prison.[9]

Ethiopians, Minstrels and Serenaders

The next significant presence of genuine African American entertainers didn't occur until the late 1870s. This didn't mean that the Australasian world was unaware of African

Americans and their reputation as entertainers. The colonists' hunger for entertainment ensured that whatever could be found in the "home country" (England), or its North American offshoots, would sooner or later find its way down under. One of the most popular forms was the minstrel show.

How people who knew nothing of the real world of an enslaved race could be fascinated by a caricatured depiction of that race's life and culture is a story that requires some background explanation. A good general account of the phenomenon of minstrelsy can be found in Robert C. Toll's *Blacking Up.*[10] After the Naval War of 1812, Toll notes that

> many Americans expressed the need for native forms, symbols and institutions that would assert the nation's cultural distinctiveness as clearly and emphatically as the war had reaffirmed its political independence.... Almost inevitably, entertainment in America fragmented into "Highbrow" and "Lowbrow," elitist and popular. Out of this turmoil came unequivocally popular forms that were both products of and responses to the way common Americans transformed old cultural institutions to meet their new needs and desires. The minstrel show was the most important new form to grow out of this process.[11]

Over the course of its long history—the popular *Black and White Minstrel Show* ran on British TV until 1978—minstrelsy went through many transformations. Its defining characteristic, however, was the caricatured depiction of Negroes, with exaggerated facial features achieved by the application of burnt cork, known as "blackface." Along with this went a style of humor that showed black people as shuffling, simple-minded buffoons, prone to malapropisms but with a talent for music and dancing. Underlying this format lurked the dilemma that slavery posed for the American public. Minstrelsy softened the image of slavery by contrasting the Southern plantation Negro, happy-go-lucky, with simple needs (typically involving watermelons and chickens), and loyal to his owner, as opposed to the tricky free Northern Negro, arrogant, greedy but dumb. A romanticized view of the faithful plantation slave can be found in many of the charming ballads of composers like Stephen Foster.

Blackface white minstrels were performing in U.S. in the late 1820s, one of the most famous being Thomas D. Rice, described as "an Ethiopian delineator." He performed a dance he called "Jump Jim Crow," which he learned from watching a partially crippled black man. Exotic terms like "Ethiopian" and "Nubian" were euphemisms to suggest to Northern Americans, unfamiliar with Southern blacks, that they were seeing authentic African material. Although the music and dance of minstrelsy drew on a wide repertoire from the European tradition, including Irish step dancing and English clog dancing, the white performers were also aware of the powerful legacy of syncopated music that the slave population had inherited from Africa. In a foreshadowing of what would many years later emerge as jazz music, performers regularly drew on Southern blacks as a source of ideas for the fast, exciting music that pleased audiences.

Minstrelsy swept America in the 1840s, even being presented in the White House.[12] By the 1850s the minstrel show had developed the format that was to remain broadly unchanged for the rest of its existence. This involved a three-part structure. In the first part the whole troupe formed a semi-circle, with two end men, Brother Tambo (tambourine) and Brother Bones (rhythm clacker) at the sides. In the center was the Interlocutor, a pompous Master of Ceremonies, who was sometimes the butt of the end men's humor but usually came off better. His role was to subtly keep things moving and control the progress of the loose, partly improvised material. This would include sentimental ballads by a handsome male lead, interspersed with raucous humor from the end men. Part two, known as the olio, was essentially a variety show, with a range of entertaining acts that could include acrobats, ventriloquists, magicians, jugglers, and song-and-dance acts. The third part was a finale involving a one-act skit, typically (though not always) set on a plantation, with Negro low comedy, jokes, and finishing with a climactic rousing close-out involving the entire cast, the Walk-around.

It didn't take long for white minstrelsy to appear in Australia. As early as January 1838 the Hobart *Colonial Times* carried an advertisement announcing that "the far-famed song of JIM CROW, who came from ole Kentucky a long time ago" would be performed at the Theatre Royal as part of a benefit for a cash-strapped theatrical producer. In January 1849 the *Colonial Times* again announced a benefit performance at the Royal Victoria Theatre at which "the celebrated Ethiopian Minstrels will sing a number of their popular melodies." During the 1850s several white minstrel troupes from England and the United States toured in Australia, including the goldfields. It also became popular for local amateur minstrel troupes to form in Australian towns and cities and play on the local stage.[13]

In the homeland of the minstrel show things began to change after the American Civil War and the emancipation of the slaves. African Americans had previously found occasional, individual roles in minstrel troupes, and Tom Fletcher, in his seminal book *100 Years of the Negro in Show Business*, credits John Luca's touring family troupe, active in the 1840s and 1850s, with contributing to the development of the first part of the traditional minstrel format.[14] During and after the Civil War, African Americans started to break into the minstrel world in a big way. In a huge stroke of irony, they found that success with audiences required them to maintain the minstrel tradition of blackface performance and the stereotyping of their own culture and character. As the great George Walker (of Williams and Walker fame) commented, "Black-faced white comedians used to make themselves look as ridiculous as they could while portraying a 'darky' character. In their 'make-up' they always had tremendously big red lips, and their costumes were frightfully exaggerated. The one fatal result of this to the colored performers was that they imitated the white performers in their make-up as 'darkies.' Nothing seemed more absurd than to see a colored man making himself ridiculous in order to portray himself."[15]

Prominent author on black entertainment history Henry T. Sampson saw a more positive aspect:

> Minstrelsy created by white men in blackface, who purported to give a true delineation of slave amusements on the Southern plantations, provided a natural vehicle by which Blacks could gain access to American show business. Who else could give a more natural and authentic portrayal of slaves' lives than former slaves—real Negroes, the genuine article![16]

At any rate, genuine black minstrels did bring to the performance their natural heritage of syncopated music and dance. Much of what we know today as tap, or jazz, dance was first performed in minstrel shows. Even before minstrelsy developed fully, in the 1840s, the black dancer William Henry Lane, known as "Master Juba," was recognized as something special. It was almost certainly Lane that Charles Dickens described in his *American Notes* as follows:

> Single shuffle, double shuffle, cut and cross cut; snapping his fingers, rolling his eyes, turning in his knees, presenting the backs of his legs in front, spinning about on his toes and heels like nothing but the man's fingers on the tambourine; dancing with two left legs; two right legs, two wooden legs, two wire legs, two spring legs—all sorts of legs and no legs.[17]

The African American dance known as the Virginia Essence, associated with minstrel Billy Kersands, was the basis of the later tap dance fundamentals, the Buck and Wing, and Soft

Shoe, forerunners of "tap" as we know it today.[18] Nevertheless, despite their legitimate claim to having originated much of the content of minstrelsy, it proved difficult for black troupes to compete at home with the entrenched white professional troupes. As a result, black troupes turned to overseas opportunities, including the South Pacific and Australasia, starting in 1876.[19]

2

African American Minstrels Arrive: Dueling Georgians

Although it took a long time for genuine African American minstrel troupes to reach Australia, it finally happened with a vengeance when two rival troupes traversed the country in competition with each other. The first to appear in 1876, at the Sydney School of Arts on Boxing Day, was billed as "Corbyn's Original Georgia Minstrels." It was described as "a company comprised of REAL COLOURED MEN from the slave states of America." The program followed the standard American three-part minstrel format, Part 1 with comic songs and ballads, and two each of the Mr. Bones and Mr. Tambo personas; Part 2, the olio, featuring a variety of music and dance items (including "Plantation Juba," an obvious reference to the already mentioned Master Juba) and a "Comic Negro Sketch"; and Part 3 finishing the show with a depiction of slave life in the South, titled "Travelling Back to Georgia," including a final "Plantation Walk Around." The Walk Around was the origin of the dance that would later be known as the Cakewalk.

The Georgia Minstrels' manager, Sheridan Corbyn, was a white, English-born, Australian theatrical agent, whose father had been a noted London agent. The reference to "Original Georgia Minstrels" was an attempt to preempt the claims of another troupe, Charles B. Hick's Georgia Minstrels. The Hicks troupe had originally planned to arrive first, the delay being explained as "in consequence of their GREAT SUCCESS in San Francisco [at Maguire's Opera House]" though just as likely to be due to Hicks' machinations to gain control of the troupe from its white promoters.

The rivalry was foreshadowed in an advertisement placed in the *SMH*, on December 12, 1876, on behalf of the Hicks troupe, proclaiming:

THEATRICAL TRICKERY: FUTILE EFFORTS OF AN AUSTRALIAN AGENT TO SECURE THE GEORGIA MINSTRELS' ENGAGEMENT OF A FRAUD TROUPE TO IMPOSE UPON THE COLONISTS.

It accused Corbyn of "one of the most reprehensible pieces of sharp practices," in taking advantage of the delay in the Hicks' troupe arrival, to "engage all the coloured men in San Francisco who had any musical capacity at all, and [succeeding] in getting 10 whom he thinks will make a minstrel company good enough for Australia. It is said that none of them have ever yet appeared on any stage and have had no experience whatever in singing or acting." An advertisement by Hicks in the NZ *Herald*, on December 4, 1876, described the Corbyn troupe as a "Company of Non-professionals, BOOT-BLACKS, WAITERS, PORTERS, &c, USING OUR TITLE."

On January 27, 1877, the *Queenslander* carried an item about "rival Georgians," including in part:

> There is a negro war raging on this continent. From a manifesto of one of the negro chiefs, or chiefs of negroes, published in Sydney, and forwarded to us, we learn the names of the belligerent parties, and the nature of the conflicting claims. The important question is, which are the real Georgian Minstrels? The Schleswig Holstein problem was nothing [compared] to this. You see there are not only Georgians and Georgians, but there are the Georgia Minstrels, and the Callender's Georgia Minstrels, and the Original Georgia Minstrels, and a second Original Georgia Minstrels, and Corbyn's Original Georgia Minstrels! The present dispute is between the two last, each of which claims to be both Original and Georgian.

Despite a cynical and rather racist tone to the whole article, the summation is pretty much correct. While the trail is somewhat murky, Hicks undoubtedly had the better historical claim to the "Original Georgia" tag. Active in black minstrelsy since the end of the Civil War, Charles B. (Barney) Hicks helped start, and was business manager for, the first Georgia Minstrels, started in 1865 by two men called Brooker and Clayton. Hicks soon left the Brooker and Clayton Georgia Minstrels to play in a variety of troupes, including in England with the mixed black and white Sam Hague's Slave Troupe in 1870. On his return to America in 1871 he formed his own new Georgia Minstrels. Finding it hard to compete with the large white minstrel shows, Hicks sold his to N.D. Roberts in 1872, remaining as manager. Roberts soon sold it to white entrepreneur Charles Callender. Callender enlarged the troupe and kept Hicks as business manager, while calling it Callender's Georgia Minstrels.

In 1875, Hicks broke away and again formed a new troupe of Georgia Minstrels, touring successfully in the U.S. in competition with the Callender troupe. Financial difficulties forced Hicks once again to yield control of his troupe, this time to the white entrepreneurs Maguire and Haverley, who planned to send them on a world tour. Hicks later outsmarted (cheated?) his sponsors by persuading the troupe to come under his own management when they sailed for Australasia from San Francisco in 1877, appropriately on the steamer *Australia*.

Corbyn's Georgia Minstrels arrived via Auckland on the *City of Sydney* and opened at the Sydney School of Arts theatre on Boxing Day 1876. The eight members of the troupe were: G.H. Carter (bones); R. Moore (bones); F. Hewitt (musical director); C.H. Lewis (interlocutor); T. Jackson (singer); Horace Copeland (tambo); R.B. Lewis (tambo); R.W. Perkins (singer). Despite the disparaging remarks in the quoted advertisement, Horace Copeland, at least, had already enjoyed a long and successful career in minstrelsy.

The Sydney season was followed by a tour through country NSW towns (Goulburn, Wagga Wagga, Albury), and Vic (Kilmore, Bendigo, and Echuca), finishing up in Melbourne. Their review in the *Goulburn Herald and Chronicle* of March 14, 1877 was somewhat mixed:

> This company consisting of eight real coloured singers arrived in Goulburn on Monday afternoon per train and performed at the Mechanics' Institute. ... A good many of the curious assembled at the railway-station to see the sable gentlemen alight. Five of the number may be classed as absolute negroes. During the hour's singing and joking on the chairs, with which the entertainment opens, none of the company play instruments except the pianist (a coloured gentleman), who is aided by a violinist—the only instruments, with the exception of the indispensable tambourine, bones, and banjo, used during the performance. In this department when required as accompaniments the Corbyn Minstrels are weak, and this rather than assisting or improving the singing tends materially to spoil it. The jokes are on the whole new and funny, and the singing very good. ... The clog-dance by Mr Copeland was well executed. The latter portion of the programme was devoted to plantation

scenes and comicalities, some of them simple in the extreme. ... The main attraction then in the company is their negro melodies and dancing, which may be classed as fairly passable on the whole; the rest of the performance is inferior.

Despite this lukewarm endorsement, the Corbyn troupe was received rather enthusiastically at most venues. Their Melbourne season, which opened on June 4 at the Academy of Music

Charles B. Hicks' Original Georgia Minstrels. Photographer R.H. Bartlett, Auckland New Zealand, ca. 1877. Hicks is at center; see numeric key to match other identities. Courtesy State Library of Victoria.

Bijou Theatre, was integrated with a performance of Dion Boucicault's popular play *The Octoroon*, which dealt with the fate of a beautiful slave girl.

While the Corbyn troupe was still touring regional Vic, the Hicks Georgias arrived in New Zealand on April 20, 1877, some six months after the Corbyn troupe.[1]

They toured New Zealand successfully, visiting Auckland, Canterbury, Wellington, Dunedin, and other regional centers. On their Auckland opening the *NZ Herald* wrote:

> The Georgia Minstrels on their opening night in Auckland were greeted last night at the Theatre Royal with a house which might well be designated overflowing, from the fact that not only was every seat filled and every passage thronged, but numbers who had not taken the precaution to be early had to depart from the doors, unable to gain admission.

The members who finally arrived in Australia via Hobart on the SS *Albion* on July 30, 1877 were: David A. Bowman (singer); Taylor Brown (tambo); C.A. Crusoe (bones); Hosea Easton (banjo virtuoso); Thomas Ellis (musician); George Harris (musician); F. Hewitt (musician); C.B. Hicks (interlocutor); A.D. Jackson (musician); Sam Keenan (comedian); David Kennedy (manager); J. Lewis (singer); J.R. (Johnny) Matlock (singer, comedian); Jimmy Mills (bones, dancer); Johnny Morton (singer, dancer); Billy Saunders (comedian, female impersonator); Joseph G. Thomas (musician); Billy Wilson (tambo, comedian).

Their opening tour at Hobart's Theatre Royal on July 30 had a full house, attracted in part by the company's band giving a street concert in advance. The *Mercury* commented:

> Suffice it to say that the singing was good; that the jokes were original which is saying a good deal; that the four corner men were admirable in their display of tambourine and bone-playing; that there was plenty of genuine humour, and that at times the audience was convulsed with laughter.... The dancing of the company is equal to anything of the kind we ever saw. The acrobatic Song and Dance, The Rivals, by Messrs Keenan and Morton, is not only quite novel here, but it is a wonderful performance, and elicited roars of laughter from all parts of the house.... The entertainment concluded with a plantation festival of a much better kind than we have hitherto been accustomed to.

The Hicks troupe was larger, more talented, and in the Australian context, more significant than the Corbyn troupe. Several members of the Hicks ensemble would settle permanently in Australia and become important players in the local minstrelsy and variety scene. These included Sam Keenan, J.R. (Johnny) Matlock, and Hosea Easton.

By the time the Hicks' Georgians opened their Melbourne season on August 13, trouble was brewing in the ranks of the rival Corbyn's Georgians in that same city, a rebellion against Corbyn's management. The *Age* of August 28 reported: "In consequence of certain unexplained differences between the management and the company, there was no performance last night of Corbyn's Minstrels at the Princess Theatre. At eight o'clock a large audience assembled, and their money was returned." This was followed by a report in the August 31 *Herald*, which stated: "The Georgia Minstrels, who wore recently under the management of Mr Corbyn, have decided to re-open the Princess Theatre on tomorrow evening. They have associated with them an excellent ballet and variety company, and the entertainment ought to prove an enjoyable one."

The re-formed company was under the management of R.B. Lewis. By October 1878 Sheridan Corbyn was reported running a theatrical management agency in San Francisco. Despite the ex-Corbyn troupe's problems, both were competing directly in Melbourne, Hicks at the St. Georges Hall; Lewis Georgians at the Princess Theatre. The latter seemed to be acknowledging an underdog status, their advertisement in the September 6 *Herald* seeking to entice audiences with "TEN POUNDS OF GIFTS GIVEN AWAY."

For the next two years the rival troupes traversed the country, visiting provincial centers in New South Wales, Victoria, Queensland, Tasmania, and South Australia. Australian audiences seem to have had an insatiable appetite for their type of entertainment, partly perhaps due to the exotic value of seeing black people but certainly also a simple enjoyment of the fast-paced action and comedy. Both troupes loudly and frequently declared their unique claim to be the one and only true "original" Georgia Minstrels and denounced any other claimants as impostors. Both had considerable success with productions of *Uncle Tom's Cabin*, based on Harriet Beecher Stowe's famous (1852) anti-slavery novel. Audiences were fascinated at the idea of the plantation scenes being played by real-life "slaves." Sydney audiences were offered two versions of *Uncle Tom's Cabin* involving the rival Georgians in October 1878. The female roles, Topsy and Eva, were played by local white actresses.

It was soon New Zealand's turn to be offered dueling Uncle Toms. In January 1879, the Lewis Georgians arrived. Rather than presenting as the Georgia Minstrels, the troupe was now being billed as "Lewis's Georgia Jubilee Singers." They staged a production of *Uncle Tom* with much fanfare, the combined production company being known as "The Uncle Tom's Cabin Company." R.B. Lewis was Uncle Tom, and Topsy was played by a well-known English-born Australian actress by the name of Fanny Wiseman. She had already played the role opposite Hosea Easton in Melbourne with the Hicks' Georgians and would go on to make a lifetime specialty of it. Her singing and dancing routine for Topsy's song, "Oh golly I'se so wicked," was received with great enthusiasm. The Lewis company played major and regional New Zealand venues, occasionally alternating *The Octoroon* with *Uncle Tom*, until early April when they embarked for Hobart and, later, mainland Australia.

Hicks' Georgians Back in New Zealand

The Hicks' Georgians also returned to New Zealand in January 1879, initially minus Hosea Easton. He was allowed to follow later after a Melbourne court appearance in which he undertook to pay 15 shillings a week to his Australian wife during his absence from the colony. In Auckland, they presented their usual minstrel variety show, but were also reported as rehearsing their version of *Uncle Tom*, with Hosea Easton in the title role. The female and white roles were supplied by a local drama company. It was a symptom of the enduring appeal of Stowe's novel, especially when performed by "real" slaves, that despite the recent availability of the rival version, this one also played to full houses.

The two companies, while meandering around the country, soon found themselves again in direct competition, in Wellington in early March 1879. This was also when New Zealand had recently experienced the Kaitangata mine disaster, in which the lives of 34 miners were lost in an underground explosion. The contribution of the two troupes in staging benefits for the disaster relief fund was gratefully noted by the Wellington *Press*: "Our Kaitangata fund is assuming very respectable dimensions. I have no doubt the total for Wellington City will be about £1,000. The Uncle Tom's Cabin Company and the Georgia Minstrels have, with the characteristic generosity of their profession, each given a benefit for the fund."

While the Lewis Georgians relied mainly on their *Uncle Tom* presentations, alternating occasionally with *The Octoroon*, the Hicks troupe had considerable success with their conventional minstrelsy offering. Star turns included Keenan and Morton's clog dance or sand jig, Crusoe's humorous stump speech on astronomy, Easton's banjo solos, Matlock's singing, and Wilson's high energy humor.[2] When the Hicks tour finished at Invercargill in mid–April, they split into two groups. Those who arrived back in Australia on the S.S. *Ringarooma* were Chas. B. Hicks, F.D. Wade, J.W. Mills, J.R. Matlock, O.T. Jackson, Frank Hewitt, Billy Sanders, D.A. Bowman, T. Ellis, Sam Keenan, J. Morton, and T. Brown. Hosea Easton, Billy Wilson, and Charles Crusoe had opted to stay on in New Zealand.

There was no mention of any reason for the split, though as Easton seems to have acquired another wife in New Zealand, possible marital difficulties might have influenced his decision. Initially the New Zealand stayers merely referred to themselves as "formerly of the Georgia Minstrels," and billed their act as "The Blackbirds." Within a short while they too were claiming to be "The Original Georgia Minstrels," probably at least the fifth or sixth company to do so. To create a company large enough to fill a bill, they had in fact merged with some white minstrels, including an American basso, J.W. Marshall. They continued performing around NZ, as the "Georgia and Chicago Minstrels," then as part of R.W. Cary's "American Troubadours," until, by late 1880, it was just Easton and Wilson performing as added attractions with various white minstrel troupes.

Hicks Back in Australia

Meanwhile Hicks, having returned to Australia with his depleted troupe, carried on with his Georgia Minstrels for a while, described as "eight genuine darkies and some white auxiliaries." By early September he was listed in advertisements as part of the management team of the Lewis Uncle Tom company, and by September 9 the Lewis and Hicks Original Georgia Jubilee Singers were opening a "farewell season" at Sydney's Victoria Theatre. Thus, the dueling finished peacefully, with Copeland and Perkins of the original Corbyn Georgians now part of the Lewis and Hicks' Georgians, while a banjo solo by George Carter, originally a Corbyn, suggests he had taken over the instrumental role of Hosea Easton.

By the start of 1880, the new united Lewis-Hicks team had worked their way south and west, starting a successful season presenting *Uncle Tom* at the Adelaide Academy of Music. They remained there throughout January until mid–February, occasionally alternating with *The Octoroon*. This was followed by a tour of northern centers in South Australia until mid–March 1880, including Burra, Jamestown, Gladstone, Port Pirie, Laura, Melrose, and finishing with six nights at Port Augusta. They then swung through Bendigo, en route to Melbourne, with their "entirely New Drama, entitled The SLAVE'S REVENGE, and introducing Lewis and Hicks' Jubilee Singers in their great PLANTATION NEGRO FESTIVAL."

In Melbourne the company was reported preparing, in conjunction with a "full dramatic company, over 60 persons," for a melodrama entitled *Pomp, or Before the War*. Unlike the grim picture of slavery presented in *Uncle Tom's Cabin*, it was a tale of affectionate slaves concerned by the financial misfortunes of their kindly owners. It opened at the People's Theatre on May 8, but the media was lukewarm in its reception, one critic commenting that "as a literary production, it cannot be pronounced a success."[3] The May 10, 1880, *Argus* somewhat caustically summarized it as follows:

> The piece has no plot worthy of the name, but consists of one or two exciting scenes, such as the firing of a steamboat and the upsetting of a train, strung together by a few brief interviews between some abnormally good and preternaturally bad people, the whole being well sprinkled with plantation breakdowns and jubilee singing…. The mechanical effects of the sensation scenes are in need of improvement. It is unsatisfactory to see a locomotive fall over on its side then draw back to gather

strength, and clear a rock with a kangaroo-like bound, even under the exceptional circumstances which the engine in question had to contend with.

It is perhaps unsurprising, with this kind or reaction, that the show didn't prosper. In late May the *Newcastle Morning Chronicle*, carried a report under the heading "Uncle Tom up a Tree," stating that "Messrs Lewis, Hicks, and Hobbs, Georgia Minstrels and theatrical managers, of Melbourne, are insolvent; liabilities, £570; assets, nominal." The financial setback was enough for Hicks, who returned to U.S. via the RMS *City of Sydney* on May 22. The *New York Clipper* of June 26, 1880 reported that Charles B. Hicks, manager of the Georgia Minstrels, and Horace Copeland, comedian, had arrived in San Francisco from Australia and left for Chicago. According to Richard Waterhouse, Hicks departed "leaving his partners to settle creditors."[4] This was not the last Australia would see of Hicks and Copeland.

Georgia Minstrels Minus Hicks

With Hicks gone, the combined "Original Georgia Minstrels" troupe continued initially under R.B. Lewis. Lewis was advertised as the recipient of a benefit performance on June 12, prior to departing on a trip to the U.S. He returned to open with the troupe at Sydney's Queen's Theatre on July 31, followed by a visit to Tasmania, Launceston, and Hobart in September, during which they were briefly joined by Hackett Coulthurst starring in *The Slave's Revenge* (See Chapter 1). In the latter part of 1880 they took an extended lease on Melbourne's Apollo Theatre and, as a result, achieved some brief notoriety. On November 11, 1880, the notorious (heroic to some) bushranger Ned Kelly was executed at Old Melbourne Gaol. The next day the *Argus* noted:

> A disgraceful scene took place on Thursday night at the Apollo-hall, where Kate Kelly and her brother James Kelly were exhibited by some speculators. They occupied arm-chairs upon the stage, and conversed with those present. The charge for admission was one shilling, and several hundreds of persons paid for admission. The movement is said to be a private speculation, the hall having been let to the person showing the relatives of the executed bushranger by the Georgia Minstrels, whose lease has not yet expired. The Kellys told some persons that their object was to raise money to enable them to leave the country. Arrangements have been made for showing the horses on which Ned and Kate Kelly distinguished themselves. A good deal of money has been taken already.

The minstrels were urged to reclaim their lease, while the November 16, 1889 *Maitland Mercury* reported a that "a female who played a prominent part in the Kelly agitation has eloped with one of the darkies of the Georgia Minstrels. Rumour has not yet been confirmed, but caused some sensation."

During February 1881, R.B. Lewis and some of the ex-Georgians, including Sam Keenan and J.R. (Johnny) Matlock, formed a new troupe known as the Mastodon Minstrels, or the Coloured Mastodon Minstrels. It was a large troupe, as many as 60 being claimed, though not all of these were black. The term Mastodon was a generic term applied to very large troupes that were eclipsing traditional minstrel shows in the U.S., particularly that of J.S. Haverley, a former sponsor of Hicks. Lewis's adoption of the term had been preceded in Australia by the highly successful white American troupe known as Kelly and Leon's Mastodon Minstrels, which actually did include one African American, an acrobatic dwarf known as Japanese Tommy.

The Lewis Mastodons opened for a long season at the Sydney Opera House in April 1881. One of its successful specialties was to spoof popular shows, e.g., *H.M.S. Pin-a-4* for

H.M.S. Pinafore. They closed to go on the road at the end of May, with a tour of regional centers in NSW (Newcastle, Goulburn, Cooma, Young, Wagga Wagga, Forbes, and Mudgee), Vic (Echuca, Bendigo) and SA (Adelaide, Narracoorte, Mt. Gambier). While the reviews continued to be positive, low attendance was noted in several places. The August 27, 1881 *Australian Town and Country Journal* remarked of the Forbes (NSW) engagement: "Though the singing, &c, was very fair, a very scant audience rewarded their efforts to please. The fact is that there have been too many companies here of late."

The Gilbert and Sullivan spoofs were popular, Johnny Matlock's voice was praised highly, and G.H. Carter's virtuoso banjo playing was a good substitute for Hosea Easton. A very popular item, described by the November 2, 1881 Mount Gambier *Border Watch*, was the "Grand Statue Clogging Tournament" by Messrs. Morton, Young, Gilmore, Moody, and Delhorey, who interspersed their dancing with posing in various effective ways, imitating in rapid succession the well-known classic sculptures, "Tying the Sandal," "The Weight-throwers," "The Dying Gladiator," "The Brothers' Quarrel," "The Peace-maker," "The Roman Wrestlers," and "Ajax defying the Lightning."

Successful though the presentation may have been from an entertainment point of view, finances caught up with the troupe in Mt. Gambier, as reported in the November 5, 1881 *Border Watch*:

> Messrs Lewis and Woolfe, the managing men of the Mastodon Minstrels, made a sudden and unexpected departure from Mount Gambier on Wednesday evening. While the performance was going on they were advised that warrants had arrived from Adelaide for the collection of monies left unpaid there. They asked the agents of their creditors to wait till the entertainment was over, when they would settle up. Meantime they engaged a conveyance and ere the performance was over were en route for the Border, and were no more seen…. The main body of the troupe left Port MacDonnell per the Penola steamer on Thursday.

Lewis Mastodons in New Zealand Again

Lewis's Mastodons resurfaced briefly in Tasmania during December but by the end of the month they were in New Zealand, minus Keenan. Initially they were competing with Hosea Easton and Billy Wilson's "Original" Georgia Minstrels. By early January they were advertised as "strengthened by the assistance of Hosea Easton and Billy Wilson," so unity prevailed again. As before, they were enthusiastically received in New Zealand. Their itinerary included Christchurch, Wellington (twice), Napier, Auckland, Thames, Dunedin (twice), Oamaru, Timaru, Palmerston, Otago, and Invercargill.

They presented the usual fare, *Uncle Tom's Cabin*, *Dred or the Slaves Revenge*, the clog-dancing statues and again, the spectacular farce *Pomp, or Before and After the War*. The melodramatic effect of this piece again elicited a variety of critical reactions including, from the *Otago Daily Times*:

> We should certainly describe Pomp as an extraordinary production, probably the most extraordinary that has ever been seen in Dunedin…. It is nevertheless puzzling to determine whether or not the piece should be criticised as a legitimate drama. As a literary production our regard for Mr M'Closky's feelings cannot prevent us stigmatising Pomp as utter rubbish. The story is one containing either many plots or none at all, and, on reflection, the latter statement appears nearest the truth. But if there is no plot, there are death-grapples, and a great deal can be done with a properly managed death-grapple if it is introduced often enough. There are, over and above this, assassinations, incantations, a duel, a steamboat explosion, tears, curses, and enough villainy to make a hangman weep.

The presentation of *Uncle Tom's Cabin* in Napier gave rise to an incident of violence that was reported in the Hawkes Bay *Herald* on March 18, 1881. A member of the audience threw an apple at the stage and was ejected with some force by the stage director. The rest of the tour appears to have been free of incidents, and the troupe departed from Bluff Harbour on June 23, 1882, aboard the SS *Rotomahana*, bound for Melbourne. They were accompanied this time by Hosea Easton, but not without some real life drama for him, a re-run of his problems leaving Australia in 1879 over payments to his then wife. The *Otago Daily Times* of June 8 reported:

> Hosea Easton, a member of the Mastodon Minstrel Troupe, was yesterday brought before the R. M. on a charge of having deserted his wife, Elizabeth Easton, in Christchurch, leaving her without means of support. The accused denied the charge, stating that although he knew the party he was not married to her. His Worship said that on the sworn information he had no alternative but to remand the accused to Christchurch. Later in the day Easton reappeared in Court submitting a telegram received from the complainant, who offered to withdraw from the proceedings if he paid £10, or if the Magistrate made an order for the payment of that sum by instalments. The accused now paid the £10, upon which Mr Carew discharged him from custody.

Australia Again

Back in Melbourne, at St. Georges Hall, the Mastodons initially presented their traditional minstrelsy fare but soon switched back to drama, *Uncle Tom's Cabin* and *The Octoroon*. The Melbourne season lasted six weeks, with good houses, before moving to Bendigo for a week. From Bendigo they made their way via Geelong, Wagga Wagga and Goulburn, to open a Sydney season at the newly-named Academy of Music on September 23. A novelty item during this period was a baseball game between the Mastodons and a local team, the Union Base Ball Club, which was won by the latter, 13 runs to eight in six innings.

The next target was Queensland, via Newcastle, and Wagga Wagga again. They opened the Brisbane season of two weeks at the Theatre Royal on Boxing Day, to a crowded house that enjoyed the show "as much as the traditional pantomime." The drama critic for the January 6, 1883 *Queensland Figaro* was less kind, "Their fooling is of the flimsiest, and is nightly endured only in the hope that it will sometime come to an end. It is very true that they have been well patronised; but it must be borne in mind that they have rejoiced in a holiday season with an entire absence of competition." *Figaro's* critic relented slightly for the following Maryborough engagement noting that "their latest effort here,'Pin-A-4 in Black' was a decided improvement upon their previous performances; and it's to be hoped they'll remember that fact when they return to Brisbane about next March."

Further engagements followed in Rockhampton, Toowoomba, Charters Towers, and finally Townsville. The Townsville visit gave rise to one anomalous incident. The *Queensland Figaro* (March 3 and 17, 1883) reported gleefully:

> This is rather a good idea from the North. The Mastodon Minstrels, all of them gentlemen of' colour, have offered to give a benefit in Townsville, for—What do you think? Why, the Anti-coloured Labour League…. The Mastodon Minstrels have been giving a benefit up at Townville in aid of the Anti-Coolie League. Billy Wilson, 'the boss niggar,' promised that he would determinedly oppose the introduction of coloured labour into Queensland.

The initial report was accompanied by a cartoon showing the demure damsel Queensland seeking the help of the staunch white colonist to resist the invading hordes.

QUEENSLAND: No, no, we don't want any visitors of that kind here! COLONIST: Certainly not, miss; and what's more we won't have 'em either!" *Queensland Figaro* (Brisbane), 3 March 1883. Courtesy *Trove*, National Library of Australia.

The background to this story was the bitter battle being fought in Queensland over the use of cheap "coolie" labor on the sugar cane fields. It was opposed by the squatters, farmers who occupied tracts of Crown land in order to graze livestock. The importation of Pacific islanders into indentured labor, either by trickery or outright kidnapping—known as "Blackbirding"—had been practiced in Australia since the 1860s. While the opposition to cheap black labor undoubtedly had racial as well as economic undertones, foreshadowing the later White Australia policy, it was also motivated by genuine dislike of the exploitation of the workers. *Figaro* may have found it amusing or surprising that the colored minstrels would line up with the anti-coolie movement, but the African Americans would have had strong views of their own on the use of cheap, near slave, black labor.

After Townsville, the Mastodons departed for the Orient in March 1883. The December 15, 1883 *Otago Witness* reported that they had split into two troupes in Calcutta. It would be some years before the next significant wave of African American entertainers would arrive.

Australian Attitudes to African Americans

This seems a good point at which to assess the reaction of Australasian audiences to the black minstrel invasion. That they were generally accepted with enthusiasm as entertainers, by audiences and critics alike, is proven by the packed houses and mostly favorable newspaper reviews. Audiences seem generally to have been respectful, though occasional reports of noisy galleries hint at some doubtful behavior. This was probably no worse than African American performers would later expect on their home turf from the infamous "sharpshooters" at Harlem's Lafayette Theatre in the 1920s.

There was an obvious audience fascination with matters of color. The *Bendigo Advertiser* noted: "In colour they embrace all shades, from the scarcely distinguishable pale-brown to the coal black darky of unmistakable origin." The light-skinned Hicks himself had to print a denial that he was white, telling an NZ journalist that he was an octoroon.[5] A columnist in the June 28, 1877 *North Otago Times* referred to Hicks's troupe as ranging from:

> The coal black, full-blooded negro down to the copper-coloured quadroon. Of course, this is the principal novelty, or feature, for hitherto the towns of this colony have only been visited by minstrels who are transformed into 'darkies' by a liberal application of that most useful requisite for hiding blushes—burnt cork. To see a 'show' of true bred 'niggers' with all the accompanying peculiarities of 'Dixey's Land' is in itself a decided novelty.

The media made frequent use of terms nowadays considered offensive, "nigger," "darky," "coon," and the uncapitalized "negro."[6] There seems mostly to have been little malice in much of this, by comparison with the venom it would have carried in the Southern U.S. However, Hicks made a spirited response to a New Zealander who, commenting on their request for permission to use fireworks to celebrate American Independence Day, described the troupe as "a lot of travelling niggers to whom the celebration of American Independence was of no consequence." In a dignified rejoinder published in the July 4, 1877 *Otago Daily Times*, Hicks noted:

> We are utter strangers in this country, and have as yet had scarcely time to understand the manners of the people, but in our country any public official using such expressions … would be held up to public scorn as a person to whose nature common decency was unknown. Who can better appreciate the blessings of freedom than those who have been bought, sold, and held in bondage, as members of our company have been. If the person referred to had been better informed as to the loyalty existing among the 'niggers' in America who are not 'travelling,' especially since the Emancipation Proclamation, he would have better understood our request. We shall at any time be glad to enlarge his knowledge and also try to instruct him as to the courtesy usually extended to strangers.

In fact, during their travels the minstrels engaged in a high degree of popular community involvement, especially in regional centers. The Hicks troupe's skilled orchestra gave frequent, well-attended public concerts. During 1876 to 1878 there was a disastrous famine in India that raised much sympathy in Australia. The Georgia Minstrels participated in many aid concerts and fund-raising sporting events for that cause, including a footrace in which the Corbyn troupe ran in costume. Other events included baseball and cricket games, a rowing event, and an Adelaide Hospital benefit. The level of harmonious acceptance this implies contrasts with the rabid racism that would greet Sonny Clay's troupe in the 1920s.

The fact that the traveling companies of the 1870s and 1880s were well versed in Southern U.S. segregationist traditions may have made them more circumspect in their interaction with the white population, especially women, than Sonny Clay's later jazz musicians would have been. Nevertheless, that 30 or so fit young men would not have sought some female company during their long sojourn in Australia and New Zealand seems improbable. We know some of the long stayers married into the local population. The *SMH* of July 25,

1878 noted: "One of-the blackest of the Georgia Minstrels is about to be married to an exceedingly pretty Melbourne girl, who declares she is passionately devoted to him. Shakespeare knew what he was about when he made Desdemona in love with Othello." Such a report in 1928 would have caused questions in parliament, with former prime minister Billy Hughes foaming at the mouth, so why not in 1878, 50 years earlier?

Part of the answer probably lies in the different spirit of the times. In the earlier period racism certainly existed in Australia but was mainly directed at the Chinese "invasion" of the gold fields from the 1850s, leading to events like the Lambing Flats (Young, NSW) massacre in 1861. In Northern Queensland it was also directed against the practice of "blackbirding," the kidnapping or tricking of Islander people into servitude in the cane fields. This led to a union campaign for "European Labour only" in the 1870s and 1880s, whose results are still visible on some items of wooden manufacture. This can be considered to have contributed to the origin of the infamous "White Australia Policy," which was not made official until the passage of the "Immigration Restriction Act" in 1901. It was then promoted strongly by Prime Ministers Deakin and Barton, helping to create the atmosphere of hysteria that would lead to Billy Hughes's later outrageous behavior against respectable black entertainers.

Richard Waterhouse suggests that the black minstrels were attracted to Australia because any prejudice they might have encountered was trivial compared to the legal and deeply entrenched segregation laws, and associated violence, they routinely experienced at home. He also notes that "Afro-Americans occupied a special place in our society. As early as 1834 a judge in a Sydney court ruled that blacks were equal in the eyes of the law when he insisted that a Negro could not be objected against as a juror on grounds of colour.... The Australian Workers Union excluded 'coloureds' from its membership but exempted American Negroes from this discriminatory policy."[7]

Performer Profiles: Hosea Easton

Hosea Easton was born in Hartford, Connecticut, in 1854. By age 20 he had established himself as a professional banjo player in the world of black minstrelsy. He was recruited for C.B. Hicks Original Georgia Minstrels in 1874, touring Canada and the U.S. with them before the troupe left for Australasia, arriving in New Zealand in July 1877. Despite his minstrel background, Easton played a classical style banjo and was occasionally billed as "the world's greatest banjoist," and "The Banjo King." He had perfected a novel style known as "talking banjo" that appealed to audiences. He was also versatile, a neces-

Hosea Easton, at the home of William and Lydia Williams (banjo players), Carlyle Street, Napier, ca. 1882. Courtesy Alexander Turnbull Library, Wellington, New Zealand, records 22311733.

sity in minstrel troupes, being a talented singer, dancer and comedian, who frequently acted in amusing short farces.

In Melbourne in 1878, Easton became the first black man to play the lead in *Uncle Tom's Cabin*, an honor widely believed to have belonged to Sam Lucas back in America.[8] After the Georgia Minstrels finished their original tour in 1881, Easton stayed on to become a familiar figure in Australian and New Zealand theatrical circles, including the Tivoli circuit. He played engagements well outside the stereotyped minstrel role, though he rejoined the Hicks-Sawyer Minstrels in 1889.

Easton was noted for his generosity in giving lessons for three months to famous Australian banjo player Bessie Campbell. His professionalism is well illustrated by a letter written back to his U.S. banjo maker, Samuel S. Stewart, in 1886:

> My banjos, eight in number, arrived here three weeks ago perfectly safe and sound, and I have thoroughly tested every one of them. I find to my satisfaction that there is nothing in the shape of banjos in Australia to approach them. You deserve the name, 'King Banjo Maker,' and as you stated in your letter, the two large banjos are the finest ever seen in the colonies.... I have been playing one of the large ones with a full orchestra, and the banjo was heard above the orchestra outside the theatre doors.[9]

Easton was married twice to Australian women. The first marriage, to Matilda, ended when she sued him for non-support as he was leaving for New Zealand in January 1879. A common-law marriage to Elizabeth ended similarly, when he left New Zealand for Australia in July 1882. His final marriage, to Isabella, owner of a Sydney oyster salon, was more stable, though not without its dramas, including an incident which today would be seen as an example of racial profiling. In October 1893, while the couple was returning from his Tivoli engagement, Easton became engaged in a conversation with a theatrical agent, while his wife and a servant girl waited for him. Patrolling police accused Isabella of looking for men. When Easton questioned what was happening, the policeman told them to go home, telling her as she went "Take your blackfellow home with you." When Easton took the policeman's number, the two police arrested them both. They were charged with "behaving in a riotous manner." Despite numerous witnesses supporting their account of the events, they were fined 40 shillings. Easton outlived Isabella, who according to the July 8, 1899 *Critic* (Adelaide) had "ruled him with a bar of iron."

Though in regular demand on the Tivoli circuit, Easton experienced occasional financial difficulties. In 1888, the *Argus* carried a report under a list of insolvencies: "Hosea Easton, of Melbourne, comedian. Causes of insolvency: Losses sustained on theatrical ventures, and want of sufficient employment. Liabilities, £151 assets £8."

Easton spent most of 1896 and 1897 in WA, with his own Original Jubilee Minstrels, presenting *Uncle Tom's Cabin* and *The Octoroon*. Back in Sydney in March 1899, the *SMH* advertised a benefit to be held for him, as he was suffering from "a painful injury to his tongue." This was probably due to the cancer that would see him hospitalized in June at Alfred Hospital, Camperdown. Although advertised on June 22 to appear in a new Tivoli program, he died the following day. His funeral was arranged by Tivoli manager Harry Rickards. Hosea Easton was buried at Waverley Cemetery on June 25, escorted to the grave by the McAdoo Minstrels Parade Band, and followed by the members of the Tivoli company and the Georgia Minstrel company. A sad footnote followed a year later in the August 9, 1900 *Evening News*: "Tomorrow, August 10, at 11 a.m. A. G. Jenkins has been instructed by the Curator of Intestate Estates, to sell in the estate of HOSEA EASTON, a 'Very Fine BANJO (by S. S. Stewart, in case), First-class Violin (in case).'"

Performer Profiles: Sam Keenan

Sam Keenan was born in New York in 1855. By age 19 he was already established in the world of black minstrelsy. He played in a duel act with Johnny Morton, as comedians, acrobats, and dancers in the renowned Callender's Jubilee Minstrels. By 1876 the pair had joined C.B. Hicks's reformed Georgia Minstrels. They would eventually travel with Hicks to Australia, where Keenan would settle for the rest of his life.

Keenan was highly versatile, with an outstanding talent for comedy. The June 26, 1885 *Evening News* commented: "Sam Keenan has but to look and the audience are 'gone,' he opens his mouth and they roar, he speaks and they are convulsed." He was also an early exponent of the style of dancing that would come to be known as "acrobatic."[10] The combination of humor and exciting dancing made Keenan a favorite with Australian audiences. The July 31, 1877 Hobart *Mercury* noted:

> The acrobatic Song and Dance, "The Rivals," by Messrs Keenan and Morton … elicited roars of laughter from all parts of the house: Both men are excellent acrobats and dancers, and in connection with a song they succeeded in displaying their abilities in these lines in such a way that he would be a bold man who would attempt to imitate them, the probability being that he would break some bones in a very few moments.

Keenan stayed with the Hicks Georgias and R.B. Lewis's successor troupes until 1881, occasionally advertising professional dancing lessons, including "Golden Shoe, Sand Jig, Irish Jig." While in Adelaide with the Hicks and Lewis Jubilee Singers, he met and married Marion Emiline Collier, actress, with whom he had three children, sons George (1880), and Ernest (1882), and daughter Bessie (1884, died in infancy). In 1882 he joined a large American white minstrel troupe, Batchelders Christy Minstrels. This included another popular African American ex-Georgian, Alf Moynham, who was his partner at various times over a number of years. Together they joined the newly formed Hiscock's Federal Minstrels in 1884. It was a mark of the status Keenan had achieved with the Australian public that when the music publisher Palings put out their annual collection of the year's popular hits for Christmas 1885, it included "Bubbling Brook, an amusing song and chorus, effectively rendered by Mr. Sam Keenan, of the Federal Minstrels."

Keenan stayed with the Hiscock troupe until 1889, apart from a brief sojourn in 1887, playing Sydney's Alhambra Music Hall in a mixed black and white minstrel show that included former Georgian associates Hosea Easton, Johnny Matlock, and Moynham. He was back at the Alhambra in April 1889, where he stayed until late 1890 and then moved to Melbourne, playing the Gaiety Theatre there. He continued to be based in Melbourne until 1892, where his wife also performed on stage (including in Charles Dickens's *Bleak House*) under her professional name of Minnie Collier. Touring with various troupes in SA and WA during much of 1892–1893, Keenan returned to an enthusiastic reception in Sydney in August 1893 after a four-year absence. He was soon away again in Queensland, playing in several companies' productions of *Uncle Tom's Cabin* and *The Octoroon*.

Sam Keenan was to spend the remaining time of his life in Queensland, his last reported performance being on January 7, 1895 at the Gaiety Theatre in the Christmas pantomime *Dick Whittington*, on which the January 7 *Courier* reported, "Sam Keenan contributed a grotesque plantation dance, and in response to a vigorous demand gave a Highland fling, which was equally ludicrous." He died of tuberculosis, aged only 40 years, on April 2, 1895 in Brisbane Hospital, and was buried in Toowong Cemetery. The funeral was attended by a large crowd of theatrical associates who had contributed to the costs. These included 19-year-old Florrie Forde, a future star in English Music Hall, famed for introducing such quintessentially British songs as "Pack up Your Troubles in Your Old Kit Bag" and "Down at the Old Bull and Bush." Sam Keenan is still remembered today for his brilliantly popular career, and by a number of Australian descendants. His wife, Marion, died in 1931, aged 66.

3

The Fisk Jubilee Singers

In the 10 years since Corbyn's Georgians had launched the black minstrel invasion, Australians had plenty of time to come to terms with and learn to love their African American entertainers. However, the new African American phenomenon that descended on them in 1886, though of the same dark complexion, was of a very different nature. No more the gross caricatures and blackface buffoonery, the Fisk Jubilee Singers were deadly serious in their presentation of that great product of African American culture, the Sorrow Songs, or Negro Spirituals, that had nurtured the souls of slaves through generations of bondage.

After the Civil War, in 1866 Fisk School (soon to be Fisk University) was founded to offer first-class education to newly freed African Americans. By 1871 the school was heavily in debt, inspiring some of its students to take action to help.

> Fisk's world-famous Jubilee Singers originated as a group of traveling students who set out from Nashville, taking the entire contents of the University treasury with them for travel expenses, praying that through their music they could somehow raise money enough to keep open the doors of their debt-ridden school.[1]

They struggled at first, but before long their performances so electrified audiences that they traveled throughout the United States and Europe, moving to tears audiences that included Ulysses S. Grant, William Gladstone, Mark Twain, Johann Strauss, and Queen Victoria. Queen Victoria, impressed by their performance, was reported as declaring, "These young people sang so beautifully, surely they must come from the music city." This is credited in many sources as the origin of the title "Music City" for Nashville, nowadays home of the predominantly white American Country and Western music (the Grand Ole Opry).[2]

The original Fisk Jubilee Singers toured the UK and Europe with great success, raising $30,000 for the university. The touring routine was very demanding and the group disbanded in 1878 after three tours. The original founder and manager, Fisk treasurer and music director George Leonard White, a white Northern missionary and Union veteran of the Civil War, became too ill to continue touring. Frederick J. Loudin, a bass singer who had been part of the third tour from 1875 to 1878, took over as his successor and reformed the troupe in 1879. Thus a new, genuine Fisk group of 11 singers was formed, including seven who had previously been members. This was the genesis of the troupe that eventually came to Australia in 1886.

By then they were no longer formally affiliated with the university, though maintaining links with it. The new troupe was an independent commercial venture, with Loudin as its entrepreneur. He undertook whatever financial risks were involved, negotiating agreed

The Fisk Jubilee Singers, ca. 1882. Those also with the 1886 Australian troupe include Patti Malone (*first from left*), Mattie Lawrence (*third from left*) and F. J. Loudin (*center, arm resting on piano*). Wikimedia Commons.

salaries with the members. In view of issues that arose later in Australia, it is worth noting that Loudin originally wanted to retain the Fisk University connection but Fisk University president Erastus Milo Cravath demurred, merely giving his blessing in the form of a statement saying that this was "the genuine company of Jubilee Singers though not singing for the university." Loudin responded, "Some children go forth from the family and marry into other families, and yet they are children still…. Although we have ceased to work for Fisk University, we are one with you and you are one with us."[3]

The make-up of the 1886 Australian arrivals included Frederick J. Loudin (basso, leader, and spokesman), Mattie L. Lawrence (soprano), Patti J. Malone (soprano), Maggie Carnes (soprano), Belle F. Gibbons (soprano), Georgie A. Gibbons (contralto), Maggie E. Wilson (contralto), D.M. (Orpheus) McAdoo (basso), John T. Lane (tenor), R.B. Williams (tenor).

Not surprisingly, this list differs from the reformed group of 1879. Four of them were carryovers. Loudin and Carnes had been members of the Fisk's third tour (1875 to 1878) and Malone had joined them in Germany in 1877. Lawrence had been part of the 1879 troupe.

The public's interest in the Singers included a significant degree of fascination with their slavery background, the advance publicity declaring the majority of them "emancipated slaves." Most of the original Fisk Singers had experienced slavery at close quarters but their Australasian replacements were at a greater remove from that "peculiar institution." Probably closest was Maggie Carnes, aged 30 at the time of emancipation.

Her life in slavery had been [brief]. She was born in Shelby County, Tennessee, in 1854. When she was a baby, her owner announced he was going to exchange her for a pair of horses, whereupon her mother ran to a well and threatened to leap into it with Maggie until her master relented. Within three years of Maggie's birth, her entire family had been liberated.[4]

Of the rest, Patti Malone, Belle Gibbons, Orpheus McAdoo, John T. Lane, and R.B. Williams had been emancipated at fairly early ages.

Frederick Loudin was a proud, ambitious man, with "a voice the likes of which no one would hear again until the emergence of Roland Hayes and Paul Robeson."[5] Though never a slave himself, he had experienced severe prejudice in his early life. He stated, "My grandparents on my father's side were [slaves]. They were taken away from Africa to one of the Northern States, New England, while slavery was still an institution there. They were emancipated when emancipation became law." He was an eloquent spokesman for the troupe, conscious that having taken over from a white manager he needed to prove his abilities as a leader. While humorous and entertaining in his presentations, he did not hesitate to raise issues of racial equality and the status of his people, or present his viewpoint forcefully.[6]

Generally, the Fisk Singers presented as an ensemble, with little emphasis on individual roles, but Loudin and Mattie Lawrence were frequently featured with audience-pleasing specialties. Loudin even referred to her as his "leading lady," and she was listed on the program as "Assistant" to Loudin as "Musical Director." Mattie Lawrence was the daughter of a former student of the Oberlin Conservatory, today the oldest continuously operating Conservatory of Music in the United States. She had been a big success on the tours of England and Ireland but her availability for the Australasian tour had been in doubt due to health problems. Loudin had no formal agreement with her before departure and she did not finally decide to come until a week or so before starting. She was to prove a major drawing card. After a Prahran Town Hall concert, the June 26, 1866 *St Kilda Telegraph* reporter enthused:

> Another captivating member is Miss Mattie Lawrence. She has a lovely face when in repose, but when her bird-like voice carols forth those beautiful songs that face becomes a perfect picture. Her eyes seem to light up with the enthusiasm of her theme, and her lithe body sways gently to and fro in the rapt ecstasy of a devotee placing her song-offering upon the shrine.

In addition to the singers, Miss Leota F. Henson, Loudin's niece, was included as an organist and accompanist.

Leota's letters home give an interesting perspective on the reactions of visitors to Australasia in those early times. In Australia it was the flora and fauna that attracted her attention.

Leota Henson, accompanist for the Fisk Jubilee Singers in Australia and New Zealand. Courtesy Nina Gamble Kennedy.

There is a tree there that sheds its bark instead of its leaves, and a cherry tree that has the stone on the outside.... Among the animals, the Kangaroo is the most unusual. It stands about 8 ft. in height, and its hind legs and the tail are big and very strong, and it hops along 15 to 20 feet at a time. Its front feet are quite short and its back ones are covered with fur and there is a big pouch on its belly where its young is carried. Another unusual arrival is the Duck Billed Platypus. It is about the size of a cat and has a bill like a duck, thick fur on its back, and a flat tail. Its front feet are webbed, and hind feet have claws, and it is said to have internal ears.

In New Zealand she noted: "We found the [Maori people] very interesting. In looks they are much like our American Indians. Their mode of salutation is quite unusual. When they meet they clasp your hand and draw their faces close together and rub noses."[7]

Even though, being an *a cappella* group, the Fisk Singers did not rely heavily on instrumentation. Henson was nevertheless a significant figure in the public eye. Apart from her obvious competence, much attention was directed to the fact that she had studied for two years in Germany, at the prestigious Leipzig Conservatory, founded originally by composer Felix Mendelssohn. This was a challenge to the commonly held view of the times that African Americans were "natural" musicians, whose talent was best left untutored or unspoiled by formal education.

The notion of African Americans being untutored natural musicians may have helped audiences new to the Jubilee Singers to accept the unfamiliar cadences and rhythms of their music. However, it disguised the fact that this was not a primitive musical curiosity but a music with its own rules and conventions, different from the European classical tradition. The songs grew out of the transplanted African religious "Ring Shout" or "Ring Dance," which the slaves carried over with them into Christianity, adapting Christian hymns and psalms to fit their traditional model. The songs were of two main kinds: Sorrow Songs (spirituals), and Jubilees. The Sorrow Songs speak of the past and present trials and tribulations suffered by the slaves and their savior; examples are "Nobody Knows the Trouble I've Seen," and "Sometimes I Feel Like a Motherless Child." Jubilees express the joyful expectation of a better life in the future (e.g., "In the Great Gittin' Up Morning," "When the Saints Go Marching in.") Along with the slave's field and work songs, the spirituals and Jubilees would eventually feed into the Blues and Gospel traditions that evolved into jazz and a whole new world of American music.

Opening Weeks

The Fisk troupe left England in April 1886 on a 44-day voyage to Melbourne, arriving there on May 4. Their arrival was well publicized. They were accompanied by an advance agent or publicity manager, Edward Price. His role was to travel ahead, negotiating accommodation, theatrical bookings and logistics, arranging advertising publicity, and generally smoothing the path for the troupe's later arrival. Loudin had originally met Edward Price when touring in Ireland and had engaged him at £10 a month, in addition to board and lodging and traveling expenses.

Unlike the black minstrel troupes, the Fisk Singers were embraced enthusiastically by polite society from the outset. Their most ardent patrons were the Victorian governor, Sir Henry Brougham Loch, and his wife, Lady Elizabeth Loch. They hosted the singers socially and attended most of their Melbourne concerts. The opening public concert on June 7 was part of a three week booking at the Melbourne Town Hall.

Before that initial public appearance, they gave a private recital to "their Australian friends" at the Grand Hotel on May 31. It was a preview of the tried and true repertoire they would feature in their public appearances, including "Steal Away to Jesus," "We Shall Walk Through the Valley in Peace," "Swing Low, Sweet Chariot," and "I'm Rolling Through an Unfriendly World."

Their repertoire also included a selection of secular songs, either of European origin, or composed specially for them. One such, described as a glee song and "a vocal galop," composed by their original leader, G.L. White, was called "Jingle Bells" (not the well-known Christmas song) and proved very popular, including being greatly enjoyed by Queen Victoria.[8] The June 1 *Argus* noted: "The performance of this was dramatic and the effect of the happy manner in which it was rendered was such as to set going a contagion of merriment right throughout the room." The enthusiasm at the Grand Hotel recital was echoed at the official opening performance. The Town Hall saw a packed house in the presence of the governor and his wife. The June 8 *Argus* reported:

TOWN-HALL, MELBOURNE.

1871. — 1886.

FIFTEENTH SUCCESSFUL CONCERT SEASON.

First Visit to Australia
Of
THE FISK JUBILEE SINGERS,
From Nashville, Tennessee, U.S.A.,
Who have arranged to give a series of their unique and inimitable Concerts of
SLAVE SONGS or "SPIRITUELS"
In the
Town-hall, Melbourne
(Their first appearance in the colonies),
Commencing
MONDAY, JUNE 7, 1886.

These singers number 11 coloured persons, all the direct descendants of slaves, the majority emancipated slaves. Their melodies were composed and sung in the days of captivity. They have been honoured with special requests to sing in the presence of—

Her Most Gracious Majesty Queen Victoria.
The Emperor and Empress of Germany.
The Empress of Russia.
The King and Queen of the Netherlands.
The King and Queen of Saxony.
The Prince and Princess of Wales.
The Crown Prince and Princess of Germany, &c.

Full particulars will be duly announced.
Town-hall, Melbourne, May 21, 1886.

Advertisement for the first appearance of the Fisk Jubilee Singers in Australia, at Melbourne Town Hall, 7 June 1886 (Melbourne *Argus*, 22 May 1886). Courtesy *Trove*, National Library of Australia.

> In all their selections, the mood in which they were conceived—despairing, sorrowful, hopeful, or joyous—found ready response in the sympathies of the audience. The simple and natural fervour of the singers, their well-practiced musical declamation, their just accentuation at all points of the rhythms which are so familiar to their manner and so unaccustomed to our ears, their fine voices, and their perfect control of tonal light and shade, were quite exemplary.

Reports of the initial and later concerts focused heavily on the heroism of the little band of ex-slaves in their dedication to raising funds for their alma mater. This would lead to later claims that Loudin, in his introductory remarks, had failed to make it clear that they were now operating on their own, under his management. Loudin stoutly denied this, and when questioned several years later about the early reports—"You were reported by three newspapers and none of them contained this explanation. How do you account for that?"— he philosophically responded, "Reporters do not always report fully."[9]

In fact he had been widely reported in later times as emphasizing their independent role, even saying jocosely on one occasion that they were now working for the poor, namely the Fisk Singers themselves. As early as June 30, 1886, the *SMH* noted, referring to Marsh's book *The Story of the Jubilee Singers*, that after the three fundraising tours had raised $30,000 for Fisk University, "They organized on their own account."[10]

The Fisk Singers played three weeks at the Town Hall, while also making appearances at several other Melbourne venues, including Prahran Town Hall. Some of their appearances were at local churches, where a commentator in the July 24, 1886 *Argus* considered they were at their best, "They are very impressive in the Town Hall, but they can be seen at their best only in a suburban church." There had also been some muted criticism of the idea of religious material being performed in commercial venues, but overall the reaction from all sides was favorable. The "Melbourne Letter" in the June 26, 1886 *Sydney Globe* enthused:

> The Fisk Jubilee Singers have literally taken the place by storm. Wherever they have appeared the hall has been thronged. And I don't wonder at it, for the melodies they sing have a peculiarly taking effect. While singing their concerted music it is by no means difficult to imagine one's self "way back in old Virginny" attending a negro camp meeting, in the centre of one of the grand old forests, with the white tents of the sojourners, and the wagons drawn up in the foreground, while a darkey, with powerful lungs, is expounding the scriptures in true negroic style. The singers are an emphatic success.

The performers themselves didn't escape public attention, including the usual fascination with skin color.

> Some of the younger women are almost white, though they have the distinctly negro type of features. They may be seen any day walking about the streets of Melbourne, dressed in the height of fashion. One of them, Miss Mattie Lawrence, a charming girl and a sweet singer, has been winning the hearts of some of Melbourne's susceptible youths, who are not proof against her dark loveliness.[11]

The final concert in the Melbourne Town Hall season was staged on August 9. The troupe then embarked on a tour that would see them in Australia and New Zealand until late 1889. It is fair to note that throughout their travels in the region the Singers gave frequent free, or reduced price, performances for children, schools, charities, asylums, prisons, and church groups.

Musical Repertoire and Critical Reaction

The popular success of the Fisk Singers, initially in Melbourne, and later while touring the rest of Australia and New Zealand, is unquestionable. There was also universal agreement that their talents were of a very high technical and professional efficiency. Nevertheless, the reaction to their music included a mixture of puzzlement, amusement, and serious musical fascination.[12] For the general public, the unfamiliar nature of the rhythmic emphases and pronunciations, and the dramatic intonations of the performers, sometimes came over as odd, or even humorous. This may be partly due to the fact that some of the same spirituals had been previously parodied by minstrels. The January 20, 1887 NZ *Wanganui Herald* noted: "Sometimes the audience are quite unable to resist a laugh at the un-hymnlike words, or the ludicrous turns in the melody. (We are compelled to use the word 'ludicrous' because we can think of no other that nearly expresses the effect)." An example was the reaction to Loudin's performance of "I am Rolling Through an Unfriendly World" by the August 9, 1888 *Mount Alexander Mail*: "The voice of Mr Loudin was heard on the word rolling in sustained rumbling tones that had a comical effect." Serious attempts to capture the nature of the unfamiliar style, included the following comments from the September 25, 1886 *SMH*:

> The rhythm is always good, though at times complicated and often distinctly original. Three-part measure, or triple time is rarely found; more than half the melodies follow the national Scottish music, in the fact that in the scale the fourth and seventh tones are omitted.

And again from the November 13, 1886 *Queenslander*:

> Their part singing is the most perfect I have ever heard. It would be utterly useless to attempt a description of their unique music. As explained by the musical director, it was never "composed" in the ordinary acceptation of that term, but has sprung into life ready made from the white heat of religious fervour during some camp meeting, and is the simple ecstatic utterances of wholly untutored minds. The rhythm is complicated and strikingly original, and it is further noticeable that most of the melodies are written on what the late Rev. Mr M'Gavin called the 'Caledonian Scale,' that is with the fourth and seventh tones omitted. The harmony is simply perfect, and I have never in my experience heard expression so beautifully observed.

One of the most comprehensive reviews, praised by Loudin himself, appeared in the June 5, 1886 *Melbourne Daily Telegraph*, suggesting, "It will astonish many readers to learn what is really the closest analogue to this jubilee music. Not Christy minstrel songs or modern ballads, but the most ancient Gregorian music of the liturgy of the Romish Church."[13]

The main repertoire of the Jubilee Singers was the 128 "Jubilee Songs" published in *The Story of the Jubilee Singers, With Their Songs* by J.B.T. Marsh. This small book was sold at every performance, a good money spinner for the troupe. By the time they left Australasia these songs were being widely performed by local choral troupes. The songs contained therein were generally described as traditional, arising out of the slave experience in an informal way. "Steal Away" is today occasionally attributed to Stephen Foster but has also been credited, along with "Swing Low," to Wallace Willis, an African American "Choctaw freedman" in the Choctaw Indian Territory.[14] Nina Gamble Kennedy, whose father Matthew Kennedy was musical director of the Fisk Jubilee Singers for 23 years from 1957, advised the author that "Wallace Willis heard the song on various plantations, but versions of it were being sung all over the South long before he heard it."[15]

As already noted, the repertoire included a number of secular and popular pieces. Abbott and Seroff (21–22) suggest that the Singers came under pressure early on in their sojourn to include more secular pieces, special features for audience amusement or entertainment, and a concession to the difficulties local audiences had with the unusual material. This also served the purpose of illustrating that the singers had mastered the techniques of classical and European song, not just their "primitive" Jubilees. The secular pieces were typically either ballads like Mattie Lawrence's renditions of Balfe's "I Know a Maiden," and "The Flower Girl," or humorous pieces like Loudin's "The Laziest Man in All the Town" and "The Laughing Song." This latter was immensely popular, and regularly demanded by audiences wherever Loudin appeared.

4

Further Adventures
of the Jubilee Singers

After Melbourne, the next reported appearance of the Fisk Singers was at the Bendigo Masonic Hall on August 19, 1886, the August 26 *Argus* declaring, "The attendance was the largest and most fashionable yet seen in the hall. In fact, standing room could not be found, several hundred persons were refused admission at the doors." A favorable start to their touring activities! It would be tedious to describe in detail the full itinerary of the Fisk troupe over the following three plus years, until their eventual departure from Australasia in October 1889. Approximately a year of the total time was spent on two New Zealand tours. Much of their time in both countries saw them making short, often one-night, stands in a formidable range of regional towns and centers.[1] When traveling between major cities, there was a (perhaps convenient) pattern of stopovers in towns and communities along the way, generally to an enthusiastic reception. An overview of their movements can be seen in the list below:

- Melbourne — May 1886–August 1886
- Vic and NSW regional — August 1886–September 1886
- Sydney — October 1886–November 1886
- NZ — November 1886–May 1887
- Adelaide and SA regional — June 1887–July 1887
- Brisbane and Queensland regional — July 1887–August 1887
- NSW regional — September 1887
- Melbourne and Vic regional — October 1887–January 1888
- Tas, Hobart, Launceston and regional — January 1888–March 1888
- Sydney and regional NSW — April 1888–June 1888
- Vic regional — July 1888
- Adelaide and SA regional — August 1888–October 1888
- NZ — November 1888–April 1889
- Vic and NSW regional — May 1889
- Brisbane and Queensland regional — June 1889–August 1889
- NSW regional — September 1889–October 1889
- Melbourne final week — October 1889

That so much time was spent in Australia and New Zealand may have reflected a reluctance to return to the racially charged atmosphere of the U.S. but it probably also meant that the troupe felt at home in the region. Quoted in the November 25, 1886 Auckland *Evening Star*, Loudin gave a clue to their attitude and experience, saying:

> Australia, in fact, was a complete surprise. The prevailing idea in America with respect to those colonies is that they resemble—so far as the conditions of life are concerned—the newer recently

"Swing Low, Sweet Chariot": Jubilee Songs, No. 2, from *The Story of the Jubilee Singers* by J.B.T. Marsh (London: Hodder and Stoughton, 1887).

settled parts of our own country. We compare them with the goldfield townships of the early days of California, with our frontier settlements, regarding them as places where life is rough, most unceremonious, and where one must put up with a good deal of 'roughing.' This is what we expected to find but, to our astonishment, it was just as if we had been transported to a part of Great Britain itself, the only difference being that things here are seen under more favourable aspects than there.

And again from an interview with the October 18, 1887 *Courier*:

The cordiality and warmth of feeling of the people we have met with in Australia and New Zealand have surprised me. At Melbourne we were received with open arms, at Sydney we were welcomed, in Brisbane we were feted, and we have many pleasant recollections of our visit to Adelaide. So far away from home as we are, these receptions relieve the monotony of our lives, and, I can assure you, are very acceptable.

In a different context he commented that the colonies appeared to be prosperous and he could charge more for admissions and book sales than in England.

Back on the road in late August 1886, while in Echuca (Vic) en route to their Sydney opening, the singers visited the Aboriginal Maloga Mission. The Maloga Mission was founded as a private venture in 1870 by an English missionary couple, Daniel Matthews and his wife Janet, who were appalled by the treatment of Aborigines. Though run on strict religious principles, it was a benevolent environment that fostered the education and ability of its residents.[2] The residents of the mission were active participants in the life of their community, as evidenced by their involvement in the annual meeting of the Aborigines' Protection Association of NSW reported by *SMH* on March 12, 1886. The Fisk Singers gave a concert for the local people that was received with great enthusiasm. Speaking of it in the August 30, 1886 *Argus*, Loudin was quoted as saying:

> I shall never forget the effect of our singing there. The Aborigines were at first very shy of us, but when they heard us sing they went into a state I can only describe as one of almost ecstatic delight. The music of the plantations stirred their souls as no other music could have done, and they seemed to recognise us as brethren from a far distant tribe. They followed our carriages for miles along the road, and waved adieus from fences, trees, and rising grounds in a way which showed that were we ever able to return there we would be welcomed with a welcome white men seldom receive.

There was an echo of this event nearly a year later when the *Cootamundra Herald* reported in March 1887, "Four aborigines from the Maloga station, at Echuca, held a service here in the Assembly Hall on Sunday afternoon last. There was a very fair congregation…. They sang part of a hymn, and in their simple style tried to sing the 'Jubilee' after the manner of the Fisk Jubilee Singers."

Amusements.

A BORIGINAL MISSION SINGERS.

Royal Hall, Footscray.

SERVICE of SONG

Will be given on

WEDNESDAY, JANUARY 5, 1887

By the
Blacks from the Maloga Mission
Station, Murray River.

Proceeds in aid of the Aborigines' Protection Association.

Commence at 8.   Chairman, Rev. H. F. Scott

ADMISSION · ONE SHILLING.

DANIEL MATTHEWS, Superintendent.

Advertisement from the *Independent* (Footscray, Victoria) 1 January 1887, for a concert by the Maloga Aboriginal Mission Singers, 5 January 1887, at Royal Hall, Footscray. Courtesy *Trove*, National Library of Australia.

The residents of Maloga were already schooled in the singing of traditional Protestant hymns of the Wesleyan, and Moody and Sankey, variety. Nancy Cato, in her book *Mister Maloga*, mentions their repertoire as including the "haunting Negro spirituals of the Jubilee Singers," specifically mentioning "Steal Away."[3] It seems likely the Fisk exposure inspired them in a new direction, becoming regular public performers of choral music as evidenced by this advertisement from *The Independent* (Footscray):

This performance tradition was still alive in the 1930s, when from their new base in the Cummeragunja Mission, the Yorta Yorta people presented minstrel and vaudeville type entertainment under the leadership of James Little Senior. He was the father of later famous Aboriginal country singer Jimmy Little, composer of "Yorta Yorta Man."[4] Cummeragunja was also the home of the Indigenous girl singers *The Sapphires*, subject of a recently popular film of that name. The film's song ""Ngarra Burra Ferra," featuring the voice of current Australian Aboriginal pop idol Jessica Mauboy, was a translation into the Yorta Yorta language of the Jubilee song "Turn Back Pharaoh's Army."[5]

The willingness of the Fisk troupe to engage with the Indigenous inhabitants contrasted with earlier minstrel performers and some later ones, who preferred to distance themselves from the Aborigines, perhaps in fear of losing their relatively privileged status and acceptance as sophisticated Americans.

The Jubilee Singers arrived for their Sydney season in early October. As in Melbourne they were welcomed by local society and religious groups, the governor, Lord Carrington, declaring his patronage. However, Sydney saw the first negative reaction, when local hotels refused them accommodation on race grounds. The October 5, 1886 *Riverina Herald* reported:

> Our readers may scarcely credit the following statement, but we vouch for its accuracy. The cultured and talented and world renowned Fisk Jubilee Singers, who have been cordially received by almost all the crowned heads of Europe, and who have the cordial commendations of Queen Victoria and the proudest nobles of England, have, metaphorically, had the doors of the leading hotels in Sydney slammed in their faces, because of the color of their skin.... We could laugh if it were not for the humiliation of knowing that it will go forth to England and Europe that Sydney publicans have been able to offer such insult to persons of culture and refinement, and yet these very people have breakfasted by special invitation at Carlton House Terrace, with the Prime Minister of England and members of the British Cabinet, and ladies of the nobility.

The problem was resolved when room was eventually found at the hotel where manager Edward Price had made his advance stay, but a sour taste lingered, and there were several critical press comments. Despite the contretemps, the Sydney season proved a resounding success for the Singers. The promised Vice-Regal patronage occurred on October 15, the audience including "His Excellency the Governor and Lady Carrington, attended by two aides-de-Camp. A suite of furniture for the use of the Vice-Regal party was supplied by Messrs Campbell Bros of George Street, and a magnificent bouquet of flowers from Messrs Tresseder and Co., was presented to Lady Carrington."

The main Sydney season ended on October 23. A popular change to their repertoire on one evening was the inclusion of song 101 from their published *Jubilee Songs*, "John Brown's Body." "The singing of this was prefaced by a few remarks from Mr Loudin as to the circumstances which gave rise to the song, and it is easy to understand that what 'The Marseillaise' is to the Frenchman, 'John Brown' is to the oppressed bondsman"[6] The Singers continued to perform at suburban centers around the city, and engage in social activities, until November 18, when they departed for New Zealand on the SS *Manapouri*.

First New Zealand Tour

The SS *Manapouri* docked in Auckland on November 23, 1886. The Fisk Singers opened a two-week season at the Auckland City Hall three days later. Their reception in the Land of the Long White Cloud was every bit as enthusiastic as in Australia. The traditional opening items, "Steal Away" and "The Lord's Prayer" were described by the November 27, 1886 *NZ Herald* as "riveting the attention of the hearers, who listened with an almost entranced silence to the alternate piano and forte passages, in which the musicians so highly excel, and at the end applauded in a most enthusiastic manner." The *Auckland Star* noted: "They appeared before the audience last night in the plain and unconscious dress which has been characteristic of them from the beginning." Elsewhere, the *Star* noted as a sign of the lifting of the recent depression that "last night the Fisk Jubilee Singers had a house in the City Hall which represented at least £100."

Perhaps signaling a recurrence of the ill health that made her original membership of the troupe doubtful, Mattie Lawrence was reported as indisposed for several nights at Auckland. Though she soon returned, it may have been a sign of insurance against future problems that the final Auckland concert saw Maggie Wilson give her debut solo performance of the tour. After Auckland there was two months of whirlwind touring on one-, two-, and three-day dates at approximately 16 regional towns around the North Island. They were enthusiastically welcomed at each location, despite some low-key grumbling about ticket prices. During two nights at Wanganui, Maggie Wilson was again featured in her own right. She alternated with Mattie Lawrence between the two concerts, with different songs of her own, "Cleansing Fires" and "Keep Me in Thy Memory." Her performance earned strong approval: "Miss Wilson, has a sweet contralto voice of pleasing timbre…. In common with the other members of the company [she] enunciates the words of her song most clearly." Perhaps the competition was good for Mattie as some days later the January 27, 1887 *Taranaki Herald* reported on the opening night of a four-day stopover at New Plymouth, "Miss Mattie L. Lawrence quite took the house by storm, and was most vociferously recalled."

After the hectic touring, a short season at Wellington's New Opera House probably came as a welcome relief from traveling. The day after the final Wellington concert, in a fashion reminiscent of their visit to the Maloga Aboriginal Mission in Australia, the Singers were entertained at Greymouth by the local Maori community, as reported by the *Hawera & Normanby Star* on February 24, 1887:

> The Papawai Native Volunteers entertained the Fisk Jubilee Singers and a number of the residents of Greytown and neighborhood, in all numbering about 300, at a dinner held in their large meeting house at Papawai. The occasion was the distribution of prizes and the anniversary of the Company. The tables were spread with all the delicacies of the season, and after full justice had been done to them the natives gave a haka for the benefit of the Jubilees, who, in return, sang several of their choice selections, which so pleased the natives that they presented each member with either a handsome mat or a piece of greenstone [New Zealand Nephrite Jade].

Sometime later, Loudin commented:

> I was delighted with the effect of our music. I could see that my theory was confirmed that missionaries to the heathen could make more progress if they made more use of music and singing. The hearts of the people were touched. They came again and again, and when we asked them the reason, they indicated that they recognised a kinship. Said a Maori, 'How many in your tribe?' 'Seven million in our tribe,' I answered, and as they looked incredulous I explained that we were all one tribe in America. They but imperfectly understood this, but they were quite clear that Maoris were 'same,' pointing to our faces.

Wellington was followed by a short concert series in the local region, including Masterton, Blenheim, and Nelson. There was an emotional tone to the final Nelson concert on March 9, 1887, when Frederick Loudin announced from the stage the newly received news of the death of the Fisk Singers' early patron, Henry Ward Beecher. Beecher was an American Congregationalist clergyman, social reformer, and speaker, known for his support of the abolition of slavery. He was also the brother of Harriet Beecher Stowe, author of *Uncle Tom's Cabin*. Beecher had played a crucial role in the Singers' early success by introducing them enthusiastically to his congregation, telling them, "Folks can't live on air. Though they sing like nightingales, they need more to eat than nightingales do." Original Fisk singer Maggie Porter remembered, "That was our start. Every church wanted the Jubilee Singers to sing for them…. From that time on we had success."[7]

After Nelson the troupe departed by sea "for the South," essentially the lower half of the South Island, starting with a week in Christchurch. They received "a most flattering welcome, from a very large audience, which included a number of clergymen and others who are seldom seen at entertainments." The trip continued along the populous East Coast, arriving in early May for a lengthy two weeks at Dunedin, and finally finishing with a four-night stay at Invercargill. They then departed for Melbourne on the SS *Mararoa* on May 28, 1887.

Back in Australia

Arriving back in Melbourne on June 2, the Singers were soon off to a season in SA. The company had been augmented by the arrival from the U.S. of two new members, Addie M. Johnson and Rosa Nalle, both sopranos. Rosa Nalle appears to have dropped out early on, not being mentioned in any reports after Brisbane in July 1887. By 1891 she was certainly back in Washington, D.C., active in local choral circles as noted by the June 12, 1891 *Washington Bee*. Addie Johnson, however, was a significant addition, probably being groomed as a backup for the still occasionally ailing leading lady, Mattie Lawrence.

The SA season started in Adelaide at the YMCA Hall on June 21, an auspicious day. For much of 1887 the colonies had been agog with excitement over the forthcoming Golden Jubilee of Queen Victoria. There had been endless engagements and functions to raise money for the Jubilee Celebrations, with discussions and plans for how to celebrate it. In England, June 20 and 21 were designated official Jubilee holidays. In Adelaide, the press thought it necessary to explain that the Jubilee Singers had not been specially named for the day, but in commemoration of the emancipation of the slaves in America. In London, Queen (and Empress) Victoria marked the fiftieth anniversary of her accession with a banquet to which 50 foreign kings and princes were invited, along with the governing heads of Britain's overseas colonies and dominions.

Meanwhile, in Adelaide, for the Fisk Singers featuring in their opening performance before an immense audience, the hall was tastefully decorated with flags, those at the back of the platform being the queen's own Royal Standard and the stars and stripes, joined by the Union Jack. In order to fall in with the general festivities of the day, the first number was "God Save the Queen."

The SA season ended in mid–July after a series of regional concerts in Port Adelaide and Glenelg, the "indisposition of Miss Lawrence" being again noted. The troupe then wound its way through parts of NSW before embarking at Sydney on the *City of Melbourne* bound for Brisbane. The Brisbane and Queensland season opened on Monday July 25 at the Gaiety Theatre, to the now traditional support of polite society. The state parliament adjourned early so members could attend, along with a large number of clergy including a bishop. A short while later, the ladies of the company were given a cordial welcome to Government House by Lady Musgrave, who was herself American born. Addie Johnson's encore solo was hailed by the August 6, 1887 *Courier*:

> Miss Johnson, who possesses a light soprano voice, clear in the upper register, was encored for a graceful rendering of a pretty song, "When the Robins Nest again," and in response she sang the well-known solo "O, How Delightful." … Miss Wilson's rich but powerful contralto took the audience by surprise. It is within the truth to state that Miss Wilson's voice is equal to any contralto yet heard on the Brisbane concert platform.

The Queensland season was intended to include some northern regions of the state but, due to a period of severe flooding and storms, it was confined to visits to Ipswich and Toowoomba after the final Brisbane concert on August 23, 1887. This was followed by a highly successful trek through northern NSW (Armadale, Newcastle, Maitland) before arriving to open a new Melbourne season on October 6, 1887. As usual, they were back in the social gaze, a gossip columnist noting, "Lady Loch's garden party on 28 October was a brilliant social success.... Everyone was there, from the Premier to the Fisk Jubilee Singers."[8]

The troupe continued playing around Melbourne and its suburbs until early December 1887, and then after a whirlwind tour of Vic towns they set off for their first visit to Tasmania, though not without a price. While helping load luggage at one of the regional centers, Loudin suffered a severe injury to his back that would plague him for some time, and occasionally even inhibit performances, before eventually being fixed by surgery in Tas.

The Fisk Singers arrived in Tas on the SS *Te Anau* on January 26, 1888, straight into a short season in Hobart. The opening concert at Hobart's Town Hall had the usual vice-regal support: "Lady Hamilton and suite were present, as also the Premier." Lady Hamilton was the wife of the Tasmanian governor, Sir Robert George Hamilton. His illustrious career in public administration and diplomacy had come to halt when he supported the cause of Home Rule in Ireland, the governorship of Tasmania being a "safe" appointment far from home. Despite his recent injury, Loudin performed to a very enthusiastic response, as did Mattie Lawrence, though later she shared honors with Addie Johnson.

The Hobart engagement finished on Friday, February 3, and was followed by a season covering southern centers around Hobart (Glenorchy, New Norfolk, Campbelltown, Oatlands) before heading north to Launceston and other northern locations. The northern circuit, lasting about a month, involved three visits to Launceston, interspersed with short forays to other localities, Beaconsfield, Deloraine, Longford, Latrobe, Westbury, and Perth. It was during this time that Loudin's injury sidelined him for a substantial period, being at one stage "confined to his room at the Blenheim Hotel" (Longford), and missing performances from February 22 to March 2, 1888. During his absence, R.B. Williams was deputized as troupe leader and master of ceremonies. It was while the troupe was in Tas that Williams met Katherine Josephine Burke, an Australian resident white Irish-Catholic, who later became his wife.

Despite Loudin's absence, the local concerts were highly successful, it being reported at Oddfellows Hall, Latrobe:

> The solos by Miss Lawrence fairly sent the audience into ecstasies; at the end of the programme on the last evening, demands were made for her appearance, and voices from all parts of the hall were heard requesting a repetition of 'Who Will Buy My Roses Red?' which she rendered so sweetly on the previous evening, but, unfortunately, Miss Lawrence was too much overdone to be able to comply with the request.

For the one-week engagement starting March 13, 1888, at Launceston's Academy of Music, the troupe was fully reunited. "Mr Loudin, although not yet recovered from his recent indisposition, took part in several of the concerted items, his magnificent voice being welcomed and appreciated." The Tasmanian visit finished with a four-concert season back in Hobart. Most of the troupe sailed for Sydney on the SS *Flora*, departing March 26 and arriving on the 29th. They were joined later by the Loudins, and R.B. Williams, who arrived via Melbourne on April 5.

The Singers resumed their mainland activities in Sydney with a four-week season at the New Opera House. Mattie Lawrence was noted as being in good voice, her rendering of "Dear Heart" being described as the most popular of the secular pieces. Loudin was "quite recovered from his late severe indisposition, and sings every evening." The New Opera House season was followed by a week at the YMCA Hall on Pitt Street, then seven weeks until June 29, in suburban Sydney and nearby regional towns. Some important changes occurred during that time. By May 30, a Kiama concert seems to have marked Mattie Lawrence's final performance with the troupe. A few days later Addie Johnson was the lead soprano at Bathurst. The July 14, 1888 *North Melbourne Advertiser* shortly thereafter advised its readers that Miss Mattie L. Lawrence

> left Melbourne this week in the *Alameda* for London, via America, to enter the company of those who regard single blessedness as not the happiest state of life here. Miss Lawrence by her genial happy manner endeared herself to a very large circle of friends, who, whilst wishing her every happiness and prosperity in her future, expressed deep regret at parting with her. Miss Lawrence was no doubt one of the attractions of the Fisk Singers, her wonderful vocalization being a feature in the entertainments. Miss Lawrence's singing was characterized by a deep devotion which made its influence powerfully felt for good.

While Mattie Lawrence undoubtedly had made a big impact during her time in Australia and New Zealand, Addie Johnson was proving a sound replacement. The *Nepean Times* enthused about her Penrith appearance: "Her songs were a delightful interlude between the choruses. Her voice is exceedingly flute-like and flexible, and the final notes of her songs were clear and high, and it was certainly a matter of regret to all when her songs were concluded." The restructured troupe spent July and August in regional Vic towns, and September and October in Adelaide and region, in what were described as "farewell visits" to SA. Addie Johnson continued to gain praise for her solo singing, the final Mt. Gambier concert eliciting the following comment from the October 31, 1888 *Border Watch*: "In a song she sang 'The Song That Touched my Heart' she reached C in alt. with the greatest ease and clearness," but also, "Nor have we heard a better contralto than the rich and powerful voice of Miss Georgie Gibbons, which was proved capable of reaching a depth close to that attained by M. Loudin."

Following the SA farewell visits, the troupe took a well-earned rest, staying at the Oriental Coffee Palace, North Melbourne, in anticipation of a return to New Zealand. The NZ press widely reported in mid–November that their advance agent had arrived in the country on the SS *Mararoa*. The usual Edward Price had now been replaced by a new agent, Mr. Lauchlan G. Sharpe. Price's parting with the Fisk Singers appears initially to have been more or less amicable, but later events would shed a different light on it. The Fisk Singers left Melbourne via SS *Wairarapa*, bound for New Zealand, on November 20.

Second New Zealand Tour

The second New Zealand tour reversed the itinerary of the previous one, starting at the lower end of the South Island, at Dunedin on December 3. The public reaction was equally enthusiastic to that of the first visit. There was regret at the absence of Mattie Lawrence but also praise for Addie Johnson in her soprano solo work, and for Georgie Gibbons in her duet with the ever-popular Loudin. However, by mid–December, when they had barely begun working their way up the island, managerial matters arose to complicate Loudin's life.

Back in Australia, a Mr. Pegg, trading as Pegg, Chapman, and Co., had launched a legal claim against defendants Edward Price and F.J. Loudin, for a sum of £106, due from a September 1887 contract to print 100,000 copies of the Fisk Jubilee programs. The negotiations had been carried out by Price. The plaintiff claimed that Price had later changed the original conditions. Under Price's proposed new terms, Pegg was to pay his own printing costs, by collecting and retaining moneys for advertisements in the programs, and any surplus after paying the amount due to him should be divided equally between him, Price, and Loudin. On Price's new terms, a sum of £10 (which the defendants paid into the court) was all that would be due to Pegg, rather than the £106 he expected under the original terms. Pegg denied that the original agreement had been rescinded, and insisted on its being carried out. Mr. Justice Williams decided in favor of the Pegg and gave judgment for him for the amount claimed, with costs. It was noted that the defendant Price had ceased for some months to have any connection with the Jubilee Singers. Pending the final outcome of the case against Price, Loudin (reported as being in New Zealand but due to return to Australia in a few weeks) agreed to pay into the court sufficient money to cover the judgment and any associated costs.[9]

The court procedure was an irritant for Loudin during his NZ tour, but it had deeper ramifications, as the same Mr. Justice Williams would surface again in the not-too-distant future. By mid–February 1889, the troupe had reached the North Island, opening at the Wellington New Opera House for six nights. There followed five nights at the Theatre Royal, Napier, and nine nights at City Hall, Auckland. However, at Cambridge by late March, the *Waikato Times* was bewailing Loudin's departure back to Australia to deal with legal problems.

> The public were aware that Miss Lawrence would not be present, but they expected Mr Loudin and were greatly disappointed as they wanted to hear his celebrated laughing song again. His rich bass voice was also greatly missed in the choruses, for although Mr McAdoo has a fine voice, it is not nearly as deep as Mr Loudin's and consequently not so telling.

Loudin had departed a day or two earlier, on the SS *Manapouri*, ready to deal with his newest legal dilemma, a more serious one than the printing episode. While he confronted the new challenge in Melbourne, the rest of the troupe soldiered on for another three weeks, with continued public acclaim. The *Wanganui Herald* commented: "Mr McAdoo, however, fills his place very well," and "Miss Gibbons (the lady in black, as she is termed by those who are not aware of her name) is also one of the mainstays of the company. Miss Wilson, however, is the one of all others who takes the lion's share of the work, having taken up Miss Lawrence's role to a great extent." They finally departed from Wellington on the SS *Mararoa* on April 23, arriving in Melbourne on May 2, 1889.

Australia, the Final Round-Up

The cause that brought Loudin back to Australia ahead of schedule was a legal action taken against him by former advance agent Edward Price. Price alleged that he was entitled to either £2,400 salary, or £2,500 commission as a percentage of takings, for services rendered during his time with the Jubilee Singers. Loudin's defense was that Price had been paid everything he was due under the agreement made originally in England, by which he was engaged at £13 a month, to be increased at Loudin's will. His salary was increased at different times, until by the time he left the company owing to ill-health in 1888, it stood at £25 per month. Evidence was also provided that in August and October 1888 Price wrote to Loudin, thanking him for his kindness to himself and his wife and child, and expressing satisfaction at the manner in which he had been treated in regard to money matters.

Loudin's legal representative was Isaac Isaacs Q. C. the same Isaacs who would later (1931) become Australia's first home-born (and Jewish) Governor General. He was then at an early stage of his illustrious legal and political career. It was unfortunate for Loudin that the case was being heard by the same Justice Williams who had presided over the earlier printing action, and had formed a low opinion of Price, and perhaps also of the then absent Loudin. Doubly unfortunate was that Justice Williams showed a strong distaste for people he labeled "goody goodies," meaning the many religious and ecclesiastical people who supported the Singers. While peremptorily dismissing Price's claim as groundless, in his summation for the jury he reinforced the negative light in which Price's barrister, Mr. Purves QC, had sought to portray Loudin, as a money-grubbing schemer masquerading as a champion of Fisk University. He also caustically ridiculed the Singers' links to slavery, on the grounds that they were too young to have experienced the horrors of that institution.

The suggestion that Loudin had not been up-front with his supporters about the commercial nature of the troupe's activities and his own role in them, was based on Purves's comment that the initial Melbourne press reports had not mentioned it. However, with current access to media records it can be shown that Loudin persistently advised his audiences of this throughout the Australian and New Zealand tours. Loudin responded to the aggressive questioning of the QC in a dignified manner, frankly offering details of his financial affairs and business practices, occasionally with a touch of humor. There was general amusement in the court when the following exchange occurred:

> PURVES QC: Were not your agent's expenses very heavy?
> LOUDIN: Are you speaking of transportation charges?
> PURVES QC: We don't use that word here any oftener than we can help.[10]

Loudin's modest deportment in the witness box earned him sympathy, while the judge's evident bias was also noted:

> The case of Price v Loudin, the business managers of the Fisk Jubilee Singers, afforded some merriment in the Court, and some satisfaction, too, at the clever way the defendant answered Mr Purves, Q. C. It demonstrated also the lucrative market Mr Loudin found for his talented and sable songsters. It also afforded striking evidence of the bad taste of' Mr Justice Williams in his summing up, and of Mr Queen's counsel Purves, in his forensic remarks…. The learned Mr Justice Williams too, forgetting the dignity of his office … reiterated the silly twaddle about "goody-goody," and referred to infantile slaves as "little kids." It would have been much better if the learned gentleman had confined himself to the law of the case, and allowed such silly figures of speech to abide at the bar, and not disfigure the bench.

However, there was also some damage from the public airing of the Fisk Singers' internal management affairs. The *Maitland Mercury* reiterated much of the negative material espoused by the judge in a report stating:

> The Caucasian has been cunningly despoiled of shekels by a smart American with negro blood in his veins. His laughing song was always provocative of the highest merriment, but it turns out that he, of all concerned in the business of singing or listening, had the chief right to laugh.

It focused on the fact that Loudin personally benefited from the venture's profits, giving little credence to the positive information that had emerged on this topic. This had made it clear that:

- Loudin, as entrepreneur, had shouldered significant losses during the tour of England and Ireland, while paying all salaries in full from his own pocket.
- On the basis of the profitability of the Australasian venture, he had consistently raised singers' salaries (e.g., Mattie Lawrence was receiving £18 or £20 a month in the United Kingdom, and up to £33 in Australia).

Perhaps the best confirmation of this positive side is that none of the singers ever expressed any dissatisfaction with their terms and conditions, which allowed them to pursue their professional careers without worrying about administrative matters.[11]

Whatever view the public might have taken of the courtroom revelations, it did little to dampen their ardor for the Singers' performances. Their return destination in Australia was Brisbane and Queensland but in usual fashion, having arrived in Melbourne on the SS *Mararoa* on May 2, they made their leisurely way there via Vic (Gippsland, Bairnsdale, Traralgon, and Warragul) and NSW (Wagga Wagga, Yass, Moss Vale, and Goulburn). They opened at the Centennial Hall in Brisbane on June 5, to the usual enthusiastic response. It was advertised as their farewell visit to Queensland.

While they were en route a major catastrophe happened back in the U.S. This was the Johnstown Flood (or Great Flood of 1889) on May 31, 1889. It was the result of the catastrophic failure of a dam 14 miles (23 km) upstream of the town of Johnstown, Pennsylvania, made worse by several days of extremely heavy rainfall. The dam's failure unleashed a torrent of 20 million tons of water from the reservoir known as Lake Conemaugh. The flood killed 2,209 people and cost the U.S. $17 million of damage (the equivalent of about $425 million in modern dollars).[12] This tragedy had a major effect around the world, including Australia. The Singers devoted the proceeds of their concert on Monday June 8 to the relief fund for the flood. Speaking at the event, Loudin said he had been engaged in charitable work before, but never on such a sad occasion as this, unless it was when, as a boy, he gave some little assistance at the time of the great Irish famine. He then announced amid loud applause that the total receipts of the entertainment amounted to £78 10s, the whole of which would be available for the sufferers of the disaster. The Singers also performed some numbers to support another fundraising lecture for the cause.

When the Brisbane season finished on June 17, the plan to tour northern centers, which had been abandoned due to wild weather on the previous visit, was revived. The first beneficiary was Rockhampton, followed by Townsville, Cairns, and Charters Towers, all showing equal enthusiasm. On the return route the singers gave a concert at sea, reported by the August 16, 1899 *Courier*: "A very pleasant evening was spent on board the SS *Warrego* on the 12th instant between Townsville and Bowen, when a concert was given in aid of the National Shipwreck Relief Society Widows and Orphans Fund by the Fisk Jubilee Singers, aided by various members of the ship's company and passengers."

There was a last chance for Brisbane to catch the singers as they passed through the region with concerts at Warwick and Sandgate, and then it was back to Sydney via regional NSW towns. The Sydney season was advertised as a farewell. The opening night had a modest but enthusiastic audience and numbers picked up considerably for later evenings, with the finale on Friday, September 27. A brief run through Orange and Bathurst (where there were complaints that Loudin skipped the concert to visit the scenic Jenolan Caves), then saw them launch the Melbourne—and final—farewell, at their original venue, the Town Hall. The audiences were again reported as good and enthusiastic. The final concert occurred on October 19.

The Fisk Singers embarked for India on the Orient Lines SS *Orizaba*, sailing from Melbourne on October 25, 1889, having spent almost three and a half years in Australasia. On departure, it was reported of Loudin that "he leaves Australia with regret, and is well satisfied with his experience here." The passenger list showed the traveling members as Mr. and Mrs. Frederick J. Loudin, Miss Georgie Gibbons, Miss Addie M. Johnson, Miss Patti J. Malone, Miss Maggie A. Carnes, Miss Leota F. Henson, Miss Maggie E. Wilson, and Mr. J.T. Lane. Missing from the list, having stayed on in Australia, were Belle Gibbons, Orpheus McAdoo, and R.B. Williams.

McAdoo and Gibbons were to become significant players on the local scene over the next few years. R.B. Williams, who had made a reputation for himself as a lay preacher in many towns, and was a qualified lawyer, had been reported several times as planning to settle in either Rockhampton, or New Zealand, to establish a law practice.

There was a kind of epilogue, while the *Orizaba* was still in Australian waters, that would have pleased Loudin. It was reported that "this morning Edward Price, manager for Mr Charles Santley [a famous English baritone], was charged on warrant at the Water Police Court with stealing £156, the property of Mr Santley. A remand was granted for seven days, bail being allowed the accused in £206 and two sureties of £100 each." In the end, though the Magistrate condemned his behavior, Price escaped on a technicality, as there was a difficulty establishing conclusive proof that the money was Santley's.

Farewell the Fisk Jubilee Singers

Though Loudin's Fisk Singers were gone they had made an impact that would not soon be forgotten. Years down the track, later troupes would use the name in Australasia to cash in on their fame, with ever-decreasing claims to authenticity until eventually they were a sad parody of the real thing. For those who want to follow the full story, it is told in Appendix 3. It should, however, be acknowledged that back in the U.S. the genuine Fisk tradition has been maintained in an unbroken lineage to this day.

Mattie Lawrence was fondly remembered for some time after her departure. In 1890 she married Henry J. Thrift, owner of a large grocery business in Croydon, Surrey, England. Their home was a haven for visiting African Americans, sometimes referred there by Loudin.[13] They had two daughters, Gladys (born 1891) and Amy (Born 1893). Sadly, Henry died in 1905, aged merely 46, and was followed by Mattie, in 1907, aged 44.

Frederick Loudin continued to lead Jubilee troupes for many years, while also being a successful businessman at home, the majority stockholder in the F.J. Loudin Shoe Manufacturing Company. He and his wife adopted and educated a young man who became a distinguished Chicago physician and married Loudin's niece, accompanist Leota Henson. Loudin died in 1904, a wealthy man, and left his library to Fisk University.[14]

R.B. Williams (full name Robert Bradford Williams) was a BA graduate of Yale University. His later career is a fairy tale deserving a comprehensive profile. He was reported in the July 27, 1889 *Queenslander* as having been admitted to practice as a barrister, the paper noting that his background would make him knowledgeable about "crime on the High Cs." Having married an Australian woman, Katherine Josephine Burke, he settled in Wellington, NZ, in 1890. While establishing a successful career as a lawyer there, he continued to perform as a singer and choirmaster, with considerable popularity and success throughout the 1890s and well into the 20th century. He became a member of the

local council for the borough of
Onslow, a suburb of Wellington,
and was elected mayor in 1902, a
position he held until he stepped
down in 1907.

The *Wellington Evening Post*
(March 16, 1908) noted: "At the
Town Hall on Thursday next a
complimentary concert will be
tendered by the [choral society]
to Mr. R. B. Williams, who is
leaving the Dominion early next
month on a holiday trip home.
Mr. Williams is a popular member of the society." The legal community also paid tribute on the
occasion, reported by the *Dominion* on April 3, 1908: "Members
of the legal profession mustered
in goodly number at the Empire

Robert Bradford (R.B.) Williams in legal garb. From the col-
lection of Jane Paul, courtesy Gábor Tóth, Local and New
Zealand History Specialist, Wellington City Libraries, New
Zealand.

Hotel yesterday afternoon to express their esteem for Mr. R.B. Williams, and to drink a
parting glass with him prior to his departure on a trip to America."

Williams's U.S. visit included a 10-minute interview with President Theodore Roosevelt. The October 30, 1908 *NZ Herald* reporting that President Roosevelt expressed interest
in learning more about the way in which [New Zealand] had dealt with the Maori race.
Back in New Zealand, Williams suffered a setback in his attempts to win a seat in the
national parliament, though polling respectably in one election as an official opposition
candidate. He remained actively involved with the Wellington hospital board, animal protection and freemason roles, as well as his choral activities, until his death in 1942.[15]

5

Charles B. Hicks Returns

After the departure of the Lewis Mastodon Minstrels in March 1883 there was a five-year gap before genuine African American minstrel shows would appear in Australia and New Zealand again, though for some of that time the Fisk Jubilee Singers would maintain an African American presence. For those whose tastes leaned towards the broader humor and buffoonery of the minstrel format, there continued to be a regular diet of white black-face minstrelsy via many troupes, from professional American (e.g., Kelly & Leon Minstrels) and Australian white troupes, to local amateurs in towns all across the country, like the Mount Gambier Christy Minstrels.

Some professional minstrel troupes were happy to recruit the resident African Americans such as Hosea Easton, Sam Keenan, Alf Moynham, Johnny Gilmore, J.R. Matlock, and A.D. Jackson. The demands of the minstrel format required all of these to be versatile in comedy, singing, dancing, and dramatic acting. Easton was noted for his virtuoso skills on the banjo; Keenan and Moynham were highly skilled acrobatic dancers. Matlock had an outstanding baritone voice, and Gilmore's comedic singing was popular. Mostly they worked in Australia, though Johnny Gilmore did a stint of several months in NZ in 1886, with an American troupe known as Cogill's American Minstrels.

Charles B. Hicks Again

A little more than eight years after his hasty departure from Australia in 1880, Charles Barney (C.B.) Hicks was back in Sydney. He arrived via New Zealand on the RMS *Zealandia* on August 22, 1888, with his new minstrel troupe.[1] Reporting the troupe's departure from San Francisco on July 26, the August 11 *New York Clipper* seemed more interested in the fact that they were numerous enough to field two baseball teams to compete with locals they hoped to meet in Australasia, Hicks himself being captain and shortstop of the number-one team. African Americans even then were passionate about the national game, though it would be almost another 60 years before Jackie Robinson became the first African American to play Major League Baseball, in 1945.[2]

The newly arrived troupe had 22 members, the most noteworthy of whom were: Hicks (manager, interlocutor); the Connor Brothers, George, John, and Eddie (acrobats); Horace Copeland (end man, comedian, dancer); Wallace King (tenor); Charles Pope (end man, comedian); Irving Sayles (end man, comedian); William "Billy" Speed (musician, drum major, stage manager); and Little Dixie (mascot, musician, drummer).[3]

The only one, apart from Hicks, who had been in Australia previously was Horace

Copeland. He came originally as part of Corbyn's Georgia Minstrels but eventually ended up with Hicks, returning with him to America in 1880. Little Dixie was a homeless boy, adopted by the troupe, as explained by the November 5, 1896 *Otago Witness*: "When playing in one of their [U.S.] cities, he came to them and asked if they wanted a mascot (a regular institution in United States minstrel shows), and as they were about setting out for foreign parts they took him. He knew no name, so they dubbed him Little Dixie." The most significant names from an Australia/New Zealand long-term perspective were Irving Sayles and Charles Pope. They would become much-loved figures on the stage in both countries.

While this original membership would continue to be the backbone of the troupe, replacements and additions occurred along the way, including resident former minstrels such as Hosea Easton and Johnny Matlock. Hicks' Minstrels generally conformed to the traditional minstrelsy format, with occasional forays into drama like *Uncle Tom's Cabin*, and short, humorous farces with titles like *Striker's Revenge, Is Marriage a Failure?* or *The Blackville Duel*, with a mixture of humorous songs and more serious Jubilee songs.

Apart from the obvious humor factor, the success of the Hicks-Sawyer troupe was boosted by two important strengths. First, they were rated highly by critics for their vocal talent. Praise was particularly high for Wallace King (tenor) singing "When Mother Puts the Little Ones to Sleep," and Will Johnson (bass), with "One Hundred Fathoms Deep," a "marvel in its extent of range, power and purity." This was all the more important in that they were facing audiences already entranced by the Fisk Jubilee Singers, then still actively touring. Several critics compared their part-singing favorably to that of the Fisks.

The second factor that worked well for the Hicks troupe was their excellent brass band, used effectively to drum up support on arrival in a new town. Led by the drum major Billy Speed, with Little Dixie a sentimental favorite, the brass band would stage a dramatic march through the town center, attracting large crowds, especially children, as in Hay (NSW) described by the July 5, 1889 *Riverina Grazier*:

> The rat-tat-tat of a drum heard at the outskirts of the town about train time last night announced that the troupe had arrived. A few minutes later a great blare of trumpets and the sound of a moving multitude afforded additional proof of the fact, and half a minute later, followed by half the boys in the town, a band of colored gentlemen, many in all the glory of long hats and long mustachios, entered the town proper, marching gaily along between two lines of spectators to the strains of good music supplied by the company's band.

The people of the Vic country town of Bairnsdale had a chance to make a direct comparison between the Hicks' Minstrels and the Fisk Singers, when both performed there over four adjacent nights in May.

The respectful tone for the Fisk Singers engagement makes an interesting juxtaposition with the stereotyped description of the Hicks troupe, including the offensive "N" word. While the performers themselves never used that word, they would have understood that its use in Australia did not have the venomous connotations it carried in the U.S. Their material may to some extent have condoned its usage, because the humor pandered to the stereotyped image, the repertoire carrying titles such as "Father of a Little Black Coon" (a very popular item, it must be said, described by Hicks as getting "three and four encores nightly"), and "The Coon That Lived Next Door."

In fairness, it should also be said that, despite the use of stereotyped "coon" material, author Richard Waterhouse credits Hicks with more positive innovations. "In the United States Hicks had sought to break from the repertoire traditionally imposed on the black minstrels. The use of 'coon' material represented an alteration of one kind; and the use of humor with non-black themes, and which was not even told in dialect, was another."[4]

A popular feature on the dancing front was the Black Zouaves's drill dancing, a kind of military burlesque, similar to the March of the Wooden Soldiers that was later popular in the *Blackbirds* shows in the 1920s. The acrobatic performances of the three Connors Brothers were a source of amazement to audiences, the June 1, 1889 *Cumberland Argus* reviewer of a Parramatta performance rhapsodizing: "Certainly the piece de resistance of the evening was the extraordinary performance of the Connor Brothers in their acrobatic scenes. Their exercises and contortions were simply wonderful, and seldom has a house been filled with such a complete artillery of applause as was accorded this very clever trio."

The humorous byplay of the end men and the interlocutor was the glue that held a minstrelsy show together, even if clichéd and well worn. "Their staging is decidedly good, their comic business amusingly grotesque, and their jokes—if not exactly of the freshest flavor—have at any rate a characteristic humor which has its own distinctive stamp, and which is very enjoyable." Sayles and Pope were the most widely praised in this regard, e.g., "Charles Pope's specialty, 'De Trumpet in the Cornfield Blows,' is remarkable for its quaintness, and his dance is unique. Irving Sayles has a fortune in his mouth, the [lips] of which he uses like pieces of flannel."[5] As with Billy Wilson in an earlier troupe, Sayles's ability to create a yawning cavern with his mouth was hugely amusing to audiences, causing one reviewer to comment that his "smile resembles the entrance to a coal pit."

THEY ARE COMING.

THEY ARE COMING!!!

The World Renowned

HICKS SAYERS

MINSTRELS.

REAL NIGGERS.

THE MINSTRELS will appear in Bairnsdale, at the THEATRE ROYAL, on

Friday and Saturday,

May 10 and 11.

SEE FUTURE ADVERTISEMENT.

THE

FISK JUBILEE SINGERS

Will give Two

Farewell Concerts

In

PAYNE'S THEATRE ROYAL

BAIRNSDALE,

on

Wednesday & Thursday,

May 8th and 9th,

FOR TWO NIGHTS ONLY

Adjacent concert advertisements in the country town of Bairnsdale (Victoria) for the Fisk Jubilee Singers and Hicks-Sayers Minstrels in the same week (*Bairnsdale Advertiser*, 7 May 1889). Courtesy *Trove*, National Library of Australia.

Another factor that allowed the troupe to engage with local communities was their already mentioned passion for baseball. It may seem surprising today that in the 1880s there were baseball clubs in Australia and New Zealand, perhaps established by homesick Americans. In several cases the presence of the Hicks teams was the catalyst for forming a local club. Well-publicized matches were held in Wellington (NZ), Melbourne, Broken Hill, and Adelaide. In a message to the *New York Clipper* on June 22, 1889, Hicks claimed, "There are now about forty clubs in Australia."

Hicks launched his new tour in Sydney, with a grandiose proclamation in the September 1, 1889 *SMH*: "To the LAUGHTER-LOVING MILLIONS of the Human Race in the AUSTRALIAN COLONIES: My aim has always been to offer to the public pure, healthy, and refined entertainment." This was quintessential Hicks, the entrepreneurial manager, at his most exuberant. Though a capable performer on the minstrelsy stage, it was always his ambition to be a promoter/producer on a grand scale. This was difficult for a penniless black man in a world dominated in the U.S. by well-cashed-up white moguls like Haverley and Callender. However, the Antipodes offered a different range of opportunities, which he eagerly seized. Nevertheless, though Hicks was the leader, the theatrical engagements were usually advertised as presented by F.E. Hiscocks, a well-known Australian white minstrelsy entrepreneur.

Starting at the Sydney Opera House on September 1 and running to packed houses until October 5, the pattern of the Hicks Minstrels' new grand tour was similar to that of earlier troupes—lengthy seasons in the major cities, linked by a connect-the-dots series of short or one-night stands in regional towns. The regional towns had a better chance of inclusion if they happened to be on the railroad. A case in point was the NSW town of Molong, connected to Sydney by rail in 1886, while its neighbor Parkes was not connected until 1893, so Parkes missed out on a visit. Being a shipping port also helped, especially in New Zealand.

Sydney was followed by an equally successful season at Her Majesty's Opera House in Brisbane. In this instance they traveled by sea via SS *Leura*. For the Brisbane season, a figure of 30 performers was proudly proclaimed in the local press, with a full roll call of names, not including Hicks who seemed to be scaling back some of his interlocutor role in favor of Harry Thomas. The new names included Hosea Easton and Billy Saunders (sometimes spelled Sanders), both of whom had been part of the earlier Hicks "Original" Georgia Minstrels in 1877. Easton had been an Australian resident since then, while Saunders's whereabouts in the intervening years are unclear. He was originally billed as a "comedian and female impersonator."

The Brisbane engagement took up most of October. There was one jarring note, widely reported in the press, including the *Freeman's Journal* of October 27, 1888: "On Monday night C. H. Holmes, lessee of the Brisbane Opera House, pointed a pistol, which he imagined was unloaded, at the head of J. S. Smith, manager of the Hicks' Minstrels. Holmes pulled the trigger and a bullet passed through Smith's hat, slightly grazing the top of his head." By November the troupe had made the jump across the Tasman Sea, to the North Island of New Zealand, appearing for nine nights at the Theatre Royal, Wellington. Now advertised with 35 performers, they were grandiosely billed as:

> "A Colossal Company of Coloured Artists, As Black as the Crack of Doom,
> and the BLAZING KOH-I-NOORS OF FUN.
> The Brilliant Black Diamonds of MINSTRELSY
> Picked from the American Cotton Fields
> The Most Complete and EXPENSIVE COMPANY That Ever Crossed the Equator"

The Wellington visit finished up with what the Wellington *Evening Post* of November 17, 1889 described as "the first baseball match ever played in New Zealand … when a team representing the Hicks-Sawyer Minstrel Company defeated the newly-formed Wellington Baseball Club by 41 runs, scoring 51 against 10." From there they did a mini-tour of the North Island, via Napier and Gisborne, ending at Abbott's Opera House, Auckland, for nine performances. A short sea trip took them to the South Island, where they performed at Dunedin's Theatre Royal through the Christmas period into January. There followed brief visits to Gore and Invercargill before the company returned to Australia, landing in Hobart on January 15, 1889.

Once again advertised as 30 performers, they played a week each to full houses in

Hobart and Launceston, the *Launceston Examiner* noting: "Crowded audiences were the rule at the Academy of Music since the opening date of the [Hicks] Minstrels." Their next stop was Melbourne, opening at Her Majesty's Opera House on February 2 for a three-week engagement. The most noted feature of the engagement was a fire that broke out during one of the performances, reported by *NMH* on February 23, 1889: "Mr. Hicks, the manager, who was acting as interlocutor, rose from his seat, and advancing to the front, reassured the people by informing them that there was not the slightest danger, and the curtain was at once lowered."

Baseball also featured again, reported in the February 28, 1889 *Australian Town and Country Journal* between

> the newly formed Victoria Baseball Club and a team selected from the Hicks-Sawyer colored minstrel troupe. At the beginning of the game the local men were well in front, scoring 12 runs to the 3 made by their antagonists. Bad fielding threw away this initial advantage, and the burnt-cork men won a close game by 2 runs only.

Following the Melbourne season, the troupe embarked on a lengthy provincial tour including the townships of Bendigo, Ballarat, Geelong, then Adelaide (SA), Broken Hill (NSW), Williamston, Warragul, Bairnsdale, Gippsland, Morwell, (all Vic), Wagga Wagga, Goulburn, Parramatta, and Newcastle (all NSW). Most of these were for one or a few nights, but with longer stays in large centers like Adelaide (four weeks), Bendigo, Ballarat, and Newcastle. Mostly they played to packed houses with no unpleasant incidents, but some dramatic moments occurred, as described by the Melbourne *Table Talk* on March 8, 1889.

> At the Ballarat Academy of Music, when they were playing the farce, "Is Marriage a Failure?" one of the performers came from the auditorium and commenced to gag somebody on the stage, in the business of the farce. A constable rushed up and proceeded to take him prisoner as a disturber of the peace. The man resisted the policeman, and the audience became so alarmed at the uproar that they shouted "Fire" and confusion at once set in. Luckily enough, however, another performer came down to explain matters, rescue his comrade, and request the audience to be seated, as there was no danger.

The four-week season in Adelaide again enabled close involvement with the local baseball community. Home in the U.S. the *New York Clipper* of June 22, 1889, proudly noted that the Adelaide baseball club presented minstrel Irving Sayles with a three-and-a-half carat diamond ring, for pitching a game and winning for them. The minstrels' presence was also the catalyst for the formation of a combined league of already existing SA clubs.

After further touring in SA, Vic, and NSW, the Hicks troupe was in Newcastle (NSW) at the Victoria Theatre in early June. Around that time a rift of some kind occurred, with Hicks facing a mutiny by a group of his erstwhile followers. The troupe that made its way, along with Hicks himself, through the NSW country towns Bathurst, Molong, Wellington, Dubbo, Cootamundra, Hay, Narrandera, and ending at Echuca (Vic) on July 11, included Wallace King, Harry Thomas, W.H. Downs, Will Johnson, William Speed, the three Connor Brothers, trombonist Frank Duprey, and Little Dixie.

Meanwhile, a group designating itself the "American Colored Minstrels" cropped up in regional Vic, with the personnel: Irving Sayles, Hosea Easton, Chas Washington, Horace Copeland, John H. Taylor, Dick Johnson (brother of Will), and Billy Saunders. Billy Speed would soon switch sides to join the American Colored Minstrels group.

After finishing their regional round at Echuca, Hicks took his reduced troupe to Sydney, where he joined with a white minstrel troupe, led by American-born F.M. (Frank)

Clark. Their joint show opened at the Victoria Hall, Sydney, in late July 1889, Hicks's part being billed as "Chas B Hicks Coloured Minstrels." The combined show ran until August 16, when the public was advised this would be "the last chance you will have of seeing this great combination." With the close of the engagement, Hicks himself vanishes from the scene for a time. The remnants of his troupe formed the Alhambra Sextette, featuring the vocal quartet of Wallace King, W.H. Downs, Will Johnson, and Harry Thomas, supported by Sam Keenan and Jack Evans as dancers and comedians. They performed regularly at the Alhambra Music Hall in Sydney with reasonable success until mid–1890. The Alhambra was a leading venue for minstrelsy, black and white, for many years.

Meanwhile, the breakaway American Colored Minstrels clearly assumed the mantle of the leading troupe, featuring the brass band parades under Drum Major Billy Speed, and the Black Zouave dervish dancers. "Under the management of Hosea Easton," they played a number of Vic and NSW regional centers, including Colac, Portland, Horsham, Bendigo, Geelong, Euroa, Benalla (all Vic), and Goulburn, Wollongong (NSW) before starting a lengthy season in early November at Sydney's Haymarket Music Hall, until January 15, 1890.[6]

The Haymarket engagement put them in direct competition with the remnants of Hicks's troupe, the Alhambra Sextette, still playing at the Alhambra Music Hall, minus Hicks. The final performance at the Haymarket was billed as a benefit performance for Irving Sayles and Billy Speed. It included another white female performer, with "fair complexion and flaxen hair," Eva Germaine, a contortionist, described variously as "The only Lady Contortionist in the World," "The Greatest Wonder of the Age," "India Rubber Lady," and "Greatest Living Female Human Serpent." The inclusion of a white female element, in a way that could not have been done in the U.S., was obviously seen as beneficial. Eva Germaine would remain with the troupe for a year before resuming a vaudeville career in Australia.

The advertisement for the final performance proclaimed that the troupe was about to embark on a tour of New Zealand. This planned tour would see the return of C.B. Hicks as business manager of the American Colored Minstrels. The troupe that opened at Abbott's Opera House in Auckland on January 23, 1890 was advertised as 25 strong. The members, apart from Eva Germaine, were more or less the original Hicks troupe reunited, plus some local extras, but missing those who had joined the Alhambra Sextette. The most notable other absentees were Charles Pope and Hosea Easton. Along the way a canine mascot had been acquired, dubbed Little Jumbo, and described by Hicks as "the ugliest cur that ever walked, but faithful."

The tour followed the familiar pattern of playing many centers, big and small. Though visiting fewer than the previous one, it was still a grueling three months. They visited the North Island centers of Auckland (two weeks), Napier, Wellington, Wanganui, and Feilding. The audience response was enthusiastic and reviews generous, even fulsome. The *Wellington Evening Post*, of February 18, 1890, singling out Eva Germaine, is a good example:

> The American Coloured Minstrels, under the guidance of that veteran manager of negro entertainments, Mr Hicks, commenced their present season at the Theatre Royal last evening before a large, and, judging from the applause and hearty laughter evoked, a most delighted audience.... The contortionist act by Miss Eva Germaine was really a wonderful performance. This young lady apparently does not possess any spinal column, as she bends herself almost double, glides through small iron rings as subtly as an anaconda, and generally places herself with perfect ease in positions which one would deem to be almost impossible in a human being. The Connor Brothers are also remark-

ably good acrobats, and a like remark applies to the song and dance men, Sayles, Washington, Copeland, and Johnson.

The South Island part of the route started at the top of the island, at Nelson, followed by Christchurch (two weeks), then Ashburton, Timaru, Oamaru, and finishing in Dunedin, where the SS *Wairarapa* took them to Tas, arriving in Hobart on April 23, 1890. The troupe played a week each at Hobart's Theatre Royal and Launceston's Academy of Music. The Hobart visit was a social success for Hicks, meeting up with two former comrades. Walter Hates, formerly of Haverly's Minstrels, and now leader of the local garrison band of 40 pieces, entertained the troupe. Another professional associate, now a local detective, showed them around the notorious old convict prison, with its 36 inhuman solitary confinement cells, and took them for a drive up Mt. Wellington.[7]

However, the visit was tinged with sadness, Hicks reporting the death of their canine mascot, Jumbo. "After traveling over the entire route with us, Jumbo succumbed to La Grippe. He made his last appearance in *The Coming Man*.... We all felt sad to lose him, though only a dog." *The Coming Man* was well known since 1875, an "Ethiopian farce," popular with minstrel troupes. The cast called for "a good sized Black and Tan Dog." How well Jumbo matched this description is unknown.

Arriving in Melbourne on the SS *Flinders* from Launceston, the troupe was soon on the road to Sydney, stopping en route at Geelong (two nights) and Bendigo (six nights). They opened an engagement at the Sydney Opera House on May 31, 1890, announced as for six nights. After the opening six nights the format changed, offering a new presentation of *Uncle Tom's Cabin*, shared with a local dramatic group. The newly returned Hosea Easton was in his familiar Uncle Tom role. The new format, with the combined white and black troupe, ran until June 28. Following short engagements in Parramatta and Wollongong, they played several weeks at Newcastle's Victoria Theatre, where *The Octoroon* alternated with *Uncle Tom's Cabin*.

This trend continued when the SS *Eurimbla* ferried the combined minstrel and drama group to Brisbane. There, at the Theatre Royal on August 4, they opened "the First Appearance in Brisbane of CHAS. B. HICKS'S DRAMATIC AND MINSTREL COMBINATION. Dion Boucicault's Great Spectacular Drama, THE OCTOROON, will be produced for the first time for many years upon a scale of magnificence never before attempted in Brisbane."

Throughout the month they presented a changing program, including *Uncle Tom*, *The Octoroon*, the sensational drama *Across the Continent* with its "great telegraph scene on the Union Pacific Railway," and finally the popular English tearjerker melodrama *East Lynne*. A brief run at the Gaiety Theatre was followed by a three-week tour of North Queensland, mainly at Rockhampton, where their visit coincided with the Rockhampton Carnival week. It also included trips to Maryborough and Mt. Morgan. At Rockhampton, the *Morning Bulletin* reported: "The Hicks Minstrels at the Theatre Royal have been drawing phenomenal houses, and excellent business is anticipated during the ensuing week."

Back in Brisbane, the Hicks Minstrels returned to the Gaiety Theatre, initially with conventional minstrel fare, but then teamed again with a white drama group, the Murray Slade Burlesque Company. They continued through the Christmas pantomime season, presenting a large cast in *Cinderella*.

By January 5, 1891, however, the Murray Slade company announced in the press that due to the death of the lessee of the Gaiety Theatre, J.J. Liddy, they would be joining the cast of the rival pantomime, *The Forty Thieves*, at the New Theatre Royal. In a rival advert, Hicks as manager of the Gaiety denounced the unprofessional conduct of Slade and company, in withdrawing without notice despite his having guaranteed to maintain their contract until January 16, 1891.

Now with effective control of the Gaiety, and listed as Lessee/Manager, Hicks had his American Coloured Minstrels (including a returned Eva Germaine) back performing by January 7. Though reviewed favorably, it was a much-reduced version of his earlier troupe, depending heavily on white supporting acts. The core African American element was Hosea Easton, Horace Copeland, and Billy Speed. A farce, *The Thieving Forty*, an obvious sideswipe at the rival *Forty Thieves*, was well received. The January 8, 1891 *Courier* reported that after the opening performance, "Mr Hicks was presented by the company, stage hands, and doorkeepers, with a massive gold locket, bearing the inscription: Presented to Chas J Hicks by the boys, as a token of their respect, esteem, and friendship. Gaiety Theatre, Brisbane." Perhaps they sensed that Hicks was looking further afield for his future. The following Saturday performance was announced as "Positively Last Night. A Grand Farewell."

After a brief foray on the road to Warwick and Ipswich, Hicks was soon back in Brisbane, where the Opera House announced the opening on January 24 of "The Largest Enterprise on Earth. The Biggest, Best, and Costliest Company the world has ever known," involving:

GEO HERBERT'S GRAND TRANSATLANTIC COMBINATION
IN CONJUNCTION WITH
CHAS. B. HICKS'S FAMOUS COLOURED MINSTRELS

This was followed by an invitation to "twenty young ladies" to apply to C.B. Hicks for "Opera House Season: Grand Chorus and March." Hicks's ambitious show may have collapsed under its own weight, as by January 29 it was advertised playing its last night but two. By February 9, 1891, Hicks' Coloured Minstrels were back at the Gaiety Theatre, sharing a combined bill with Wirth's Wild West Show, which was also playing by day at the nearby Breakfast Creek Grounds. The combined format was:

- 8:00 p.m. Grand First Part, Minstrels.
- 9:00 p.m. Grand Second Part, Variety Olio.
- 9:35 p.m. Grand Third Part, Simply Wild West

Unlike the earlier dramatic troupe combinations, this was more than just a convenient alliance. Hicks had now found his ideal niche, and would move away from African American minstrelsy into the world of circus and Wild West shows. Instead of former slaves, the Wirth Brothers show promised "Red and Dusky Warriors, Genuine American Indians. All the Greatest Tribes Represented. GENUINE SIOUX INDIANS." The Gaiety continued to feature the Wild West component, in parallel with the full showground presentation at Breakfast Creek, until late February 1891, when they all traveled north to Rockhampton. Hicks Minstrels seem to have soon become merely an appendage to the larger show and dropped off somewhere along the way.

However, by now Hicks had found his mission for the rest of his life. He advised the *New York Clipper* on August 1, 1891, that he had "joined Harmston & Sons Circus & Wild West for a tour of Java and India as general manager, sailing from here [Cooktown] in the British India mail steamer 11 May. I have sold all interests in Australian shows." Thus ended the career of Charles Barney Hicks as an African American minstrel. His association with Australia was not quite over, as he would return briefly in his capacity as circus manager. He would make only rare visits to his homeland in the U.S. Hicks died, still on the road with the circus, in Surabaya, Java, in 1902.

6

Orpheus McAdoo
and the Return of the Fisks

With the departure of C.B. Hicks in mid–1891 the remainder of his troupe gradually dispersed. No African American wanted to play an entrepreneurial role in organizing a unified company from the leftover remnants of the various minstrel troupes that had arrived since 1877. This wasn't for lack of available talent; the roll call of stayers would have been enough to create a Mastodon-style company, including (alphabetically): the Connor Brothers, Horace Copeland, Little Dixie, W.H. Downs, Hosea Easton, Jack Evans, Johnny Gilmore, Dick Johnson, Will Johnson, Sam Keenan, Wallace King, J.R. Matlock, Alf Moynham, Charles Pope, Billy Saunders, Billy Speed, John H. Taylor, and Harry Thomas. Abbott and Seroff (*Out of Sight* 161) suggest that these were "stranded" in Australia when their troupes broke up, but it's equally likely that many of them preferred Australia to "Jim Crow" America.

The popularity of minstrelsy had not abated, and there were numerous white troupes, under producers like F.E. Hiscock and Frank Clark, happy to pick up talented black performers. The Alhambra Theatre in Sydney featured minstrelsy programs for many years. Throughout 1891 all of the names above could be found at various times and places, with such troupes as Frank M. Clark's Folly Company, Donegan's Minstrel Burlesque and Comedy Company, Frank Musgrove's Gaiety, Variety and Comedy Company, Harold Ashton's Federal Minstrels, Cogill Brothers Minstrels and similar, as well as at the Alhambra. Sayles and Pope, and Keenan and Moynham, were usually teamed as "end men." Keenan and Easton would occasionally reprise their roles in *Uncle Tom's Cabin* or *The Octoroon*. Wallace King was a very popular tenor. However, being an independent act was a precarious business, as evidenced by Easton's financial problems described earlier. Some fared better than others, Sayles and Pope enjoying a long career as favorites at Sydney's Tivoli Theatre.

The first sign of the next wave of African American entertainers came in the form of an advertisement in the October 17, 1891 *SMH* foreshadowing "The return of the Jubilee Singers.... SUPERIOR to any COLOURED Company ever organised."

The announced "Proprietor and General Manager" Orpheus Myron McAdoo (or M'Adoo as he was sometimes called) had been Frederick Loudin's backup in the earlier Australian visit. When the Australian visit ended, McAdoo had returned to the U.S. with the intention of forming his own company. He recruited former associate Belle F. Gibbons of the Fisk Singers and a number of other capable performers to create his "Virginia Concert Company and Jubilee Singers."[1] The use of Virginia in the name was a reference to McAdoo's early affiliation with the Hampton Institute, whose distinctive slave spirituals McAdoo used, as well as the Fisk collection.

During his first stay in Australia McAdoo had formed a friendship with the governor of Victoria, Lord Loch, and his wife. By 1890 Lord Loch had become governor of Cape Colony in South Africa. When McAdoo's company encountered difficulties during a tour of the United Kingdom he was happy to take up Lord Loch's suggestion of a South African tour. This was a great success, lasting 18 months.[2] While in South Africa, the strongly featured singer, Mattie Allen, had become Mrs. Orpheus McAdoo. According to a story told to *Christian World* by McAdoo, their initial marriage plan was blocked because, despite their status as "honorary whites," they were told that "Black folks don't marry here." Moves to seek a parliamentary exception were rendered unnecessary when an Irish Church of England clergyman said "My Church is the friend of all who are in trouble. Come, and I'll put up the banns, and marry you as well and legally as if you had a license."[3]

The news of the McAdoo visit was greeted with enthusiasm in Australia and New Zealand. McAdoo himself made it clear from the outset that this was a new independent company, telling the *Hobart Mercury*, "His company appears before the public on their own merits, and on their performances they desire to be judged. They do not ask for public sympathy and assistance on behalf of the Fisk or any other university, as they are on their own business just as any other travelling concert company." He was, no doubt, mindful of the criticism Frederick Loudin had encountered over the Fisk connection. Nevertheless, the presence of the well-remembered McAdoo and Belle Gibbons of the earlier Fisks caused a strong association in the public mind, the media frequently referring to them as "the Fisk Singers." Later on, McAdoo would abandon his early cautious approach, forthrightly and somewhat dubiously exploiting the Fisk legacy.

Most members of the troupe arrived in Hobart via the RMS *Kalkoura* on February 17, 1892. McAdoo himself had already arrived along with his wife, Mattie Allen, and his brother Fletcher McAdoo, who was the troupe's advance business manager. From their arrival in February 1892 until final departure on May 31, 1895, the troupe would spend a total of three years and four months in Australia and New Zealand.

Their typical itinerary pattern involved short seasons in major cities, using them as hubs for extensive touring through regional and provincial centers, and even small outlying communities. No place seems to have been too small for a one-night stand, with larger towns getting two or three days. Some of the places they visited can scarcely now be found on a map, being communities that sprang up around gold or other mining activities. The pace at which the schedules were conducted may explain why the warm contact that had occurred between the earlier Fisk Singers and the Maori and Aboriginal communities was not repeated. The only reference to Maoris and the Jubilee Singers was a story widely reported in the NZ press, including the November 10, 1892 *Taranaki Herald*, of an English migrant fresh from the Old Country, with very hazy notions as to things colonial, who found himself sharing his dinner table at the Grand Hotel in Dunedin with the Jubilee Singers:

> He seemed favourably impressed by them, and next day startled his acquaintances by remarking that he had no idea the Maori were so civilized, and that he thought those that he had met at the Grand on the previous evening must certainly have been chieftains and chieftainesses. He was somewhat surprised, however, that none of them were tattooed.

It would be tedious to follow the Jubilee Singers travels in detail, so lists of the locations visited are provided for reference purposes—over 130 locations, many of them two, three, or more times.[4] From the outset they were warmly welcomed, and patronized by polite

McAdoo's Fisk Jubilee Singers, early 1892. The original personnel, including Orpheus McAdoo (*back row, second from left*); Mattie Allen McAdoo (*back row, third from left*); Richard H. Collins (*back row, fourth from left*); Moses Hamilton Hodges (*front, first from left*), Belle Gibbons (*front, second from left*); and Eugene McAdoo (*front, end*). Photographer Talma Studios, Melbourne. Courtesy National Library of Australia (nla.obj-138067377).

society, including the governors-general of states visited. This was assisted by the fact that, at many venues, their events were promoted by the local YMCA. They seem to have encountered little racial prejudice, though in one instance, where accommodation had been engaged for them in advance by the YMCA, the landlady refused them admission to the dining room and was fined £100 by the local court.[5] They generally attracted full to overflowing houses, especially in the major centers. However, they were unfortunate that the early 1890s was a period of severe recession in Australia. Much foreign capital had been withdrawn because of disappointing returns on investments, causing low attendance at some regional centers.[6]

Their first Australian concert was at Hobart's Temperance Hall on February 23, 1892, in the presence of the Governor Sir Robert Hamilton and Lady Hamilton, for a one-week season. The makeup of the troupe was: Orpheus Myron McAdoo (bass); Mattie Allen (lady tenor); Belle F. Gibbons (soprano); Kate Slade (light soprano); Madame J. Stewart Ball (mezzo soprano); Julia Wormley (elocutionist); Moses Hamilton Hodges (baritone); Eugene McAdoo (bass, Orpheus's brother, sometimes known as Julius); Richard H. Collins (tenor); Lucy Moten (accompanist, piano, harmonium).

The Australian debut showed that McAdoo was not going to be constrained by the Jubilee tradition. The *Mercury*, of February 24, 1892, noted that the first section consisted of "secular selections, commencing with a medley of 'Popular airs'—a sort of hotchpotch of national songs of every English-speaking country under the sun, humorously strung together, and affording ample scope for good part singing." The second half offered enough

Jubilee material, supported by Lucy Moten's harmonium, to please the purists. This included well-loved items like "Steal Away" and the "Lord's Prayer" but also the lively "The Gospel Train is Coming":

> It's nearing now the station,
> Oh, children, don't be vain,
> But come and get your tickets
> And get aboard the train[7]

The general critical reaction was that, though the troupe was smaller in numbers than the earlier Fisks, they were superior in several respects, including part singing. While it was universally agreed that the vocal talent of the singers was technically outstanding, there was also a fascination with the uniquely African American characteristics of the music, as described by the *Argus* on April 4, 1892:

> The pleasing harmonies, the variations in light and shade, the frequent repetitions of the same words with continual change of tone and expression, the bodies swaying to the rhythm, and the faces of the singers lighting up or clouding in sympathy with the theme, form the peculiar charm of these melodies.

And by the *Oamaru Mail*, October 20, 1892:

> Most of the creepy effects are produced by the use of a weird crescendo and diminuendo superadded to a muted falsetto chorus. Of course, the music is responsible to a great extent—wild minor chants and almost discordant intervals being largely employed.

The inclusion of an elocutionist, Julia Wormley, in what was essentially a singing group, might seem odd but her dramatic recitations proved highly successful.[8] Her most popular piece was "Trouble in the Amen Corner," combining humor and pathos in the story of an elderly chorister, cruelly rejected by his community, who finds his niche in the Heavenly Choir.[9] The tenor voice of Mattie Allen was a source of wonderment: "The great novelty of the evening was the tenor solo by a lady, Mrs. O. M. McAdoo. She has a powerful voice of good tenor tone." Belle Gibbons was enthusiastically welcomed back. Apart from solo singing, the male quartet of McAdoo, his brother Eugene, Hamilton Hodges, and Richard Collins were popular in part singing.

After Hobart, the Virginia Jubilee Singers did a mini-tour of Tasmanian regional towns with a week at Launceston's Academy of Music. In Launceston they made a joint appearance with English composer W.H. Jude, who was also then on a tour of Australia and New Zealand. Somewhat obscure today, William Herbert Jude (1851–1922) was a well-known composer of operettas, hymns, and popular ballads into the early 20th century.[10] The unusual combination was well received and some of Jude's compositions remained as part of the troupe's repertoire later.

After Tasmania, the Jubilee Singers opened at Melbourne's Athenaeum Hall on April 15, playing there and around Vic regional centers (Geelong, Ballarat, Echuca, Bendigo, and Benalla). The Bendigo visit saw a changeover in personnel. The original member Kate Slade shared the stage with her replacement, Laura Carr, also a "light soprano." Miss Carr had arrived by sea from San Francisco in March 1892, so was obviously a planned replacement. She proved a popular addition, though seems to have excited as much interest by her color as by her excellent voice.

> Miss Carr is the most typical specimen of the negro race in the gathering; but this fact is forgotten when she is singing. She possesses a voice of remarkable purity and sweetness, and her individual

effort was one of the best features of the performance, and [she] is as black as the negro race ever gets to be, but when she sings "When the Swallows Come Again," you forget her color.[11]

The swallow song became her popular signature piece throughout the tour.

After brief stopovers in NSW regional towns (Wagga Wagga, Cootamundra, and Goulburn), a Sydney season opened at the Centenary Hall on June 11. The final Sydney concert coincided with America's National Day, the Fourth of July, the anniversary of the declaration of American independence. For the occasion, the concert that night was under the patronage of Mr. Alexander Cameron (U.S. Consul), with a large attendance of American citizens. To celebrate the day, baseball once again came into focus, with a match arranged between "Australia" and the "U.S." This brought together the McAdoo troupe and the resident African American stayers from the Alhambra Theatre.

> Our good American friends, who are members of Mr McAdoo's Concert Company, better known as the Jubilee Singers, with the assistance of those prominent ball players, the Connor Bros., Messrs Sayles, Pope, Johnson and Downes, will form the American contingent, and the Australian battlers will be chosen from the players representing various city clubs.... Five innings were played, the Australians eventually winning by 5 runs.[12]

Following a trek through regional NSW, the singers opened at Brisbane's Centennial Hall on August 29. This was the first time McAdoo was reported singing the song "One Hundred Fathoms Deep," so favored by bassos, especially Loudin. The Brisbane season was a short six days, followed by a brief Queensland regional tour (Maryborough, Ipswich, Warwick), then back to Sydney, and stopping briefly in Hobart en route to New Zealand.

New Zealand greeted the new arrivals as warmly as their forerunners, packed houses being the norm. The tour opened with a week in Dunedin on October 10, before they worked their way up the South Island, to arrive in the North Island at Wellington on November 16. This was followed by a rambling tour of North Island venues, winding up at Wellington with a five-night season at the Opera House, finishing on December 12.

During the South Island tour the November 10 *Wairarapa Daily Times* had reported: "Two new lady vocalists have just arrived at Auckland by the last Frisco mail to join the Jubilee Singers." The two were elocutionist Enola Saunders and contralto Emma Ingram. They were quickly fitted into the program, making their first appearance at Blenheim on November 11. Miss Saunders was popular, but why a second elocutionist was deemed necessary is puzzling. It may have been related to this later story: "Miss Julia Wormley, the accomplished elocutionist of the Jubilee Singers, is engaged to Mr Eugene McAdoo [brother to Orpheus] one of the bass singers of the troupe."[13] Somewhere along the way Miss Wormley did marry Eugene McAdoo, so the foreshadowed romance had probably fueled concerns that she would be unavailable for performance duties. In fact, she long outstayed the presence of Miss Saunders in the troupe.[14]

The reason for the recruitment of Miss Ingram was clearer, the departure of veteran member Belle Gibbons. She had finished her engagement on completion of the final Wellington season in early December. This was by no means the last of Belle Gibbons, as she would rejoin the troupe later in their tour, and would continue to play a significant role in the region well into the 20th century.

The Wellington season gave an opportunity for some members to renew acquaintance with a former comrade. "An interesting sight of the season of the Jubilee Singers in Wellington was the appearance of Mr R B Williams in the dress circle every evening," the *Otago Witness* reported on December 22, 1892. "It was a treat to watch the effect of the singing upon the old member of the Fisk Jubilee Singers. His expressive features betrayed intense pleasure."

After Wellington they worked their way back down the South Island, to finish at Invercargill on January 9, 1893, cutting their planned two nights there to one in order to catch the SS *Wairarapa* to Tas. The total trip lasted four months, including whirlwind visits to 32 centers, three times to Wellington, and twice each to regional hubs like Christchurch, Hastings, Napier, and Dunedin. Most of these were one-night stands, typified by the inland run from Napier to Wellington over a 12-day period in November–December.

The McAdoo troupe arrived back in Hobart in early February 1893 and "by general desire" took a month's rest before their next performance. There was a good reason for the break. Mattie Allen McAdoo had finished performing with the troupe in New Zealand early in December and left New Zealand on December 12, traveling alone on the SS *Talune* to Hobart. A day before Orpheus and his troupe departed from Invercargill on the SS *Wairarapa*, she gave birth in Hobart to a son, Myron Holder Ward McAdoo, registered on February 9, 1893. Orpheus later advised the *Cleveland Gazette* that "Master Myron McAdoo and mother are quite well, thank you, and at home every afternoon from 4:30 to 6 o'clock."[15]

After their break, the troupe opened to a warm welcome at Hobart's Temperance Hall on March 6, 1893. However, their tour of northern Tas centers drew poor audiences due to the recession, making them pleased to be back in Sydney's Centenary Hall by Good Friday, where, recession or not, they could still count on a good audience. The Hall was home to the Central Methodist Mission, a church to which several members of the troupe were affiliated, and where the recently born McAdoo son was christened at a Sunday service on April 16.

The completion of the Sydney season brought some changes to the troupe's membership. It's usual in a long tour to see occasional departures and arrivals. In the case of the Jubilee Singers keeping track of this is complicated by the fact that only some members were featured solo performers, the others being either part of the male quartet, or contributors to the choral part singing. The troupe that departed from Sydney for regional NSW towns was without elocutionist Enola Saunders. Eugene McAdoo was also missing from adverts, apparently replaced by one M Eugene (the name similarity appears to be a coincidence). Eugene McAdoo's departure was confirmed, after a performance at Wagga Wagga in May, when he made a formal farewell and thanks to the audience. After the departure from Sydney, and for the rest of their time in Australia (two years), the troupe's engagements were always described as "farewell performances."

May 1893 also saw both Orpheus McAdoo and Julia Wormley miss performances in several towns in NSW due to illness (a "throat affliction," in McAdoo's case). This may have reflected the physical stress of the punishing itinerary but could also have been a harbinger of problems to come. While McAdoo continued to be reported as indisposed for further engagements, he embarked at the end of May on the RMS *Miowera* from Sydney to Vancouver, to spend three months attending the Chicago World's Fair.

The depleted troupe suffered further setbacks in June, when the severe floods of 1893 disrupted plans for visits to northern NSW and Queensland. After re-grouping for a while in Sydney they resumed in late June at Newcastle, but those performances were the last for both Julia Wormley and accompanist Lucy Moten. In view of Eugene (Julius) McAdoo's recent farewell, it's likely he and Julia Wormley departed to pursue married life together. There was a further break in performances until August, probably due to the floods, before they resumed again in Queensland.

Having lost a substantial amount of talent, the advertising now heavily promoted Mattie Allen, the "Lady Tenor" as the star of the show. She proved well able for the task, gaining strong audience responses. They worked their way up through Queensland to Townsville but were probably relieved when, in early September, Orpheus returned on the *Miowera*, bringing reinforcements in the form of singer Elsie Laws. He also brought to Australia the recent (1892) top U.S. hit song, "After the Ball." It would prove a big success for his wife. Music publisher Paling made it the banner feature of their Christmas Annual, "AS SUNG BY MISS MATTIE ALLEN."

With Orpheus firmly back in control, they continued their extended farewell tour, via Brisbane, northern NSW, Melbourne, and regional Vic, arriving in Adelaide to open on Christmas Day. By this time they were forthrightly advertising as the "Fisk Jubilee Singers," boldly claiming the royal and international successes of the original troupe, as having been "honoured with special requests to sing in the presence of Her Most Gracious Majesty Queen Victoria, the Emperor and Empress of Germany" and other monarchs and elites. In his introductory remarks Orpheus would describe this early history, the May 29 *Bunbury Southern Times* repeating his claim, "Mr McAdoo himself was a member of that company which travelled for over 8 years and sang before most of the Crowned Heads of Europe, including Her Majesty the Queen." This was a rather dubious claim by McAdoo, who had joined the Loudin troupe in England in 1885, at which time it had not performed before the Queen or visited continental Europe.

The Adelaide season was followed by a whirlwind tour of 29 SA towns, and a sea voyage to Albany in WA. While changes in personnel had been coped with effectively, the defection of accompanist Lucy Moten seems to have weighed heavily. The *Adelaide Advertiser* (March 23, 1894) mentioned that during the Adelaide engagement the singers had been "assisted by Mr Pybus, the city organist." For a while in July 1894 Emma Ingram had taken on the accompanist role but she seems also to have left the troupe shortly after. Back in Adelaide again, after their WA farewell tour, the *South Australian Register* offered:

A RARE OPPORTUNITY.—The FISK JUBILEE SINGERS require the services of a young lady (one of dark complexion preferred) of good family to fill position of ACCOMPANIST both on piano and organ; tour Australasia, probably India, China, and Japan. Apply Monday, between 11 and 1 o'clock, to Mrs. O. M. McAdoo, Imperial Hotel, King William Street.

This appeal apparently produced a result, a report mentioning: "A lady organist ably assisted the performance," and the *National Advocate* on February 20, 1895, later identified her as "Miss Tizley, a young lady from Adelaide, [who] played the accompaniments with great skill and taste." Whether she was of suitably "dark complexion" we are not told. By now the farewell performances were being described as "[positively the] last appearance prior to visiting India, China, Japan, and England." There was a ferment of activity, with comings and goings, as the troupe wended its way through SA, Vic and NSW from July 1894 until May 1895, while preparing for their next big overseas adventure. Baritone Moses Hamilton Hodges left to establish himself as an independent singer affiliated with the Methodist community at Centenary Hall. His departure was more than offset by the return of Belle Gibbons who, in addition to her singing role, also took on the dramatic recitations previously associated with Julia Wormley. Another significant addition was Miss Marshall Webb, "a rich, sympathetic, and cultured contralto voice." Both were popular additions for the Sydney Christmas concert at Centenary Hall.

More changes were foreshadowed when Mrs. (Mattie Allan) McAdoo sailed from Sydney for San Francisco on the RMS *Mariposa*, according to the Adelaide *Advertiser* of January 24, 1895, to "organize another troupe to tour the Australian colonies." The new recruits were not actually for Australia but to boost the numbers in readiness for the planned move overseas. The result was the addition of three new arrivals from America in May, "Mrs Edwards, a soprano, who reaches with ease the high E flat; Messrs Thompson (tenor) and Walley (bass)." They had arrived in time to perform at the Newcastle farewell; "[Mrs Edwards] possesses a soprano organ of power and sweetness, fully cultivated and under control." The Sydney suburb of Richmond appears to have been the last to see the singers before they departed for Capetown on the SS *Arawa* on May 31, 1895. Those reported to be on board included Orpheus McAdoo, W. Thompson, Richard H. Collins, Mrs. Edwards, Belle Gibbons, Laura Carr, and Miss Marshall Webb. They would presumably be joined in South Africa by Mrs. Mattie (Allan) McAdoo, who at that time was still making preparations in the U.S. This was not to be the last Australia would see of McAdoo's Jubilee Singers.

7

The Tivoli Era Starts

In 1893 an event occurred that would have far-reaching significance for theatrical performers in Australia and New Zealand. Harry Rickards, an English born entrepreneur with extensive experience in the English music hall scene, founded his "New Tivoli Minstrel and Grand Specialty Company" at the Opera House in Sydney. This would soon lead to the emergence of centrally controlled theatrical circuits instead of the ad hoc arrangements that had previously characterized the bookings of visiting troupes and acts.[1]

Rickards would go on to extend his Sydney Tivoli base to a chain covering all the major Australian cities. Other rival circuits would soon emerge in both Australia and New Zealand. The main Australian circuits were Rickards's Tivoli (later controlled by Hugh D. McIntosh after Rickards's death in 1911) and, from 1906 to 1912, James Brennan's Sydney National Amphitheatre and Melbourne's Gaiety Theatre. In New Zealand there were the Fullers' theatres (owned initially by John Fuller, and later his sons, Benjamin and John Jr.) and the Dix's theatres. By 1912 the Fullers had absorbed both Dix in New Zealand and James Brennan in Australia, trading for some years as the Brennan-Fuller vaudeville circuit. There were other smaller local circuits, most notably Harry Clay's Sydney city/suburban circuit, with other NSW off-shoots, but the Tivoli and Fullers were the big players. Sydney's Tivoli became the home of a new Australian form of variety theatre that combined the American minstrel and English music hall genres, in a fashion that paralleled the simultaneous emergence of vaudeville in America.[2]

The emergence of centrally controlled theatrical circuits made a huge difference for visiting acts. Before then, the independent troupes had followed idiosyncratic patterns, with promoters like Hicks, McAdoo, and Loudin carrying the financial responsibilities themselves. An advance road manager would negotiate forward venues and accommodation on an ad-hoc basis. Under the new regime, visiting entertainers had their routes determined by either Brennan-Fuller or the rival Tivoli circuits. Acts were pumped through a process that resembled a sausage machine. The typical pattern involved a tour of major Australian cities, followed by a short tour of NZ cities, and a repeat Australian tour before making way for a new round of acts.

This did not mean that regional areas missed out entirely. Once he acquired ownership of the Tivoli chain, Hugh McIntosh set about enlarging its reach. By mid–1915 his circuit included Tivoli theatres in Sydney, Melbourne, Adelaide. Perth, Brisbane, Fremantle, Kalgoorlie, and Adelaide, plus subsidiary theatres in Newcastle, Bendigo, Ballarat, Brunswick, Fitzroy, and others.[3] Brennan-Fuller had a similar network in Australia and New Zealand.

The insatiable demand of this vaudeville empire for high-class acts was backed up by

THE TIVOLI THEATRE (Grand Opera House), SYDNEY, N.S.W.

Rickard's Tivoli Theatre, Sydney, as in 1917 featuring Ada Reeve and Hector Napier. Courtesy Nicholas Charlesworth publisher, *Variety at Night Is Good for You*, J.O. Blake, compiled and illustrated by Nicholas Charlesworth, Badger Press.

a network of talent scouts in Europe and the United States. They would check out promising acts, cabling information back about their quality, and the likely cost to bring them to Australia. For the Tivoli circuit these judgments were collected in a system of index cards, many of which are still held at the Australian National Film & Sound Archive (NFSA) in Canberra. Here are some samples from the London talent scout, Tom Holt (father of later Australian Prime Minister Harold Holt):

> Florence Mills is one of the cleverest women on the stage. Coloured, sings, dances, acts and talks, and looks as good as it is possible for a dark woman to look. Wonderful troupe with her and her dancing is a revelation. Any one of her ballets could do a specialty dancing act. Troupe in its entirety would be beyond us for Australia as they get very good money, but I am on the look out to pull a couple of good dancing teams which would make a great act. [Written after he saw the 1920s show *Blackbirds*].

And less enthusiastically, "Sissle and Blake: Two negroes at present playing Piccadilly cabaret. Played in *Shuffle Along* in America. Though excellent performers, do not suit English audiences…. Valued them at £60 but would not send out unless absolutely stuck." Many leading African American acts were checked out in this way, including the great Bill "Bojangles" Robinson, and some would find their way down under over the ensuing years.[4]

As the next invasion of African American entertainers was poised to arrive, two new trends were changing the course of black entertainment and the wider world of popular culture. These were ragtime music, and the entertainment genre known as vaudeville. Though minstrelsy would continue to flourish for many years, the format and content of stage entertainment changed fundamentally with these new developments, particularly for black entertainers.

Ragtime

Like its close relative jazz, ragtime didn't spring into being fully formed at one point in time but was a natural development out of many things that had been going on for years in the world of black syncopated music and dance.[5] Notable of these from the world of minstrelsy were the Cakewalk and the stereotypical "Coon song." Other influences contributed to the development of ragtime, such as brass band music in the style of John Philip Sousa. Given the complexity of its origins, ragtime eludes a simple definition. Contemporary ragtime expert Terry Waldo describes it thus:

> Syncopation is the continuous superimposition of an irregular rhythm overtop of a regular one. In the piano rags a regular pulse is maintained by the left hand alternating a low bass note with a chord in the midrange. This produces a heavy accent on the first and third beats of the measure. Pitted against this regular meter is a constant series of rhythmic displacements in the right hand.[6]

A ragtime craze swept the world from the 1890s onwards. Pianist, composer, and ragtime pioneer Scott Joplin was a big hit at the 1893 Chicago World's Fair. In 1899, the publication of his "Maple Leaf Rag" earned him the soubriquet "King of Ragtime." Large numbers of songs appeared with the word "rag" or "ragtime" in the title, many of which were not truly ragtime (Irving Berlin's "Alexander's Ragtime Band" is an example). On the other hand, there were many others, including some of the "coon" songs that had significant ragtime elements.

Vaudeville

Vaudeville had its origins in 15th century France, and the term was already familiar in Australia by the 1820s, in association with English "variety," which featured a quick-fire succession of different acts.[7] Similar developments had occurred in the U.S. from around that time.

Vaudeville became a major feature of American entertainment when B.F. Keith established his Bijou Theatre in Boston in 1886. Keith went on, in partnership with E.F. Albee, to establish a string of theatres in major U.S. cities, featuring "continuous vaudeville."[8] Known as the Keith circuit, it was largely confined to white acts, with a few notable exceptions, one being the great tap dancer Bill "Bojangles" Robinson. However, there soon sprang up rival circuits such as those of John

Tivoli Theatre program cover. Author's collection.

Considine and Alexander Pantages, which were happy to feature talented black acts. There were also circuits that were black-owned or specialized in black acts.[9]

Vaudeville had much in common with minstrelsy, particularly the olio part, which was essentially a string of variety acts. However, vaudeville was not tied to the stereotypical portrayal of blacks as shiftless, lazy, or devious. Stereotypes would continue for many years, and black entertainers were still expected to perform in blackface. However, when the great Bert Williams portrayed his lugubrious "Nobody" character, he was a universal human figure, like Chaplin's tramp, or Marcel Marceau's Bip. Audiences laughed with him, not at him, and the dominant paradigm was gradually subverted by a new generation of black performers. The opportunities available to them through vaudeville were demonstrated in Australia by Irving Sayles and Charles Pope's success at Sydney's Tivoli.

The Resident African Americans: 1895–1898

In the early years of the new circuits, the departure of McAdoo's Jubilee Singers created a temporary gap in the seemingly endless parade of African American troupes in Australasia. The initial African American beneficiaries, before the new circuits began actively recruiting from overseas, were the individual residents left over from the earlier larger groups. By now time was beginning to take its toll with some of them. Sam Keenan had died in early 1895. Alf Moynham died in Jakarta in 1893 while touring with a circus. There was considerable emotion in New Zealand over the death of Little Dixie, who had made a popular career for himself in the Land of the Long White Cloud. Feeling ill while performing at Napier, he refused a doctor and was found dead in the morning, diagnosed with peritonitis and a ruptured artery. The *Marlborough Express* (November 4, 1896) reported:

> No more impressive scene has been witnessed in the Napier cemetery than the interment of poor "Little Dixie." He was only an African negro, a kettle drum player, but although far from his mother's home his friends gave him a funeral such as they might have tendered to one occupying the highest position amongst them.

The ever-popular Hosea Easton continued playing at venues around Sydney including the Tivoli, and in Brisbane, occasionally reprising his Uncle Tom specialty, until August 1896. (His later career is covered in his Chapter 2 profile.) Horace Copeland, one of the earliest arrivals with Corbyn's Georgians, suffered a stroke at Albany (WA) in early 1897. The *West Australian* (June 19, 1897) reported him being found wandering in the streets, and later removed to the Fremantle Lunatic Asylum. He survived but was stranded in WA. Later, back in America, he wrote a bitter letter to the *Freeman*, dated May 19, 1900, condemning those entertainers he believed had failed to help him, and praising those who had. The villains of the piece were C.B. Hicks, Charles Pope, Irving Sayles, Billy Speed, and Wallace King, while the heroes were Orpheus and Mrs. McAdoo, McAdoo's orchestra leader Henderson Smith, and the members of McAdoo's later company. Wallace King (*Freeman*, August 11, 1900) vigorously defended himself, describing things he had done to help Copeland, and criticizing him as an ingrate who had caused mischief with the original Hicks troupe.

Others who were active during this period included J.R. (Johnny) Matlock and Wallace King. The Connor Brothers (acrobats) settled permanently in New Zealand. The two most noteworthy stayovers in Australia from the Hicks 1888 arrivals were Irving Sayles and Charles Pope. Fortuitously for them (and Wallace King), the newly founded Tivoli was to provide a theatrical home for them and numerous other African American performers, for many years to come. As end men in the olio they were among the Tivoli's most popular acts.

In addition to his Tivoli successes, Sayles found a new outlet for his talents in foot racing. Between 1895 and 1898, Sayles ran many highly publicized challenge foot races over 100 yards for high stakes, winning all except handicap events, where he was usually the final starter. The *Australian Town and Country Journal* (August 17, 1895) described one of his triumphs:

> At the Sydney Carrington Grounds on August 9 a match for £25 a-side over 100 yards took place between Irving Sayles, the well-known comedian at the Tivoli Theatre, and Franks, a Victorian. Sayles was favorite at 2 to 1 on, while 6 to 4 against Franks was on offer. The Victorian gained nearly two yards at the start, but Sayles ran in a most determined fashion and, drawing level with his opponent ten yards from the [tape], won by a bare foot in 10.5 secs. It was a magnificent race from start to finish.

While Sayles's athletic activities were a sideshow to his main profession, they were also a forerunner of the significance African American sports figures would soon acquire on the Australian scene.

8

The Return of Orpheus McAdoo
and a Rival

After their departure from Australia in mid–1895, McAdoo and his Jubilee Singers had repeated their earlier success for several years in South Africa.[1] However, in 1898, with storm clouds gathering for the second Boer War, and with disputes in his troupe over pay, McAdoo conceived the ambitious idea of returning to Australia with a large troupe of top-of-the-line black acts featuring the new vaudeville style of entertainment, while continuing to run his Jubilee Singers in parallel. He had already dabbled in this direction in South Africa by expanding the regular Jubilee Singers line-up with two variety acts: Joe Jalvan, an outstanding juggler; and Jerry Mills, a versatile veteran entertainer who would later be stage manager for the famous Black Patti Troubadours.

McAdoo's new plan involved a two-pronged approach. Phase one was to get the augmented Jubilee Singers to Australia and establish them on the usual circuits in Australia and New Zealand, while he recruited and organized his new vaudeville line-up overseas. This first phase started in July 1898, when McAdoo, with wife and child, arrived in Hobart from Capetown on the RMS *Ruahine*, and traveled on to Melbourne. There they joined up with the rest of the Jubilee troupe who had separately arrived in Melbourne via the White Star steamer *Australasian*. The Jubilee Singers opened a short season at the Athenaeum Hall, Melbourne, on July 21, 1898. The line-up, six of whom had been part of the earlier (1892) troupe, included: Orpheus McAdoo, basso (performing except when engaged on other business matters); Mattie Allen (Mrs. McAdoo) the "Lady Tenor"; Susie Anderson, dramatic soprano (styled "The Black Melba"); Jennie Robinson (Mrs. Hamilton Hodges), soprano, specializing in classical music; Belle Gibbons, soprano, monologist (and Fisk Singers veteran); Marshall Webb, contralto; Moses Hamilton Hodges, baritone; Richard Collins, tenor; William Nott, tenor; Eugene McAdoo, basso (and sometimes backup for brother Orpheus); Jerry Mills, comedian, acrobat, female impersonator; Joe Jalvan, juggler extraordinaire; and Professor C.A. White, accompanist, piano, organ (Gold medalist of Boston Conservatory of Music).

The new approach, with its vaudeville component, proved popular with audiences, as noted by the *West Australian* on August 30, 1898:

> Since the company was here rather more than three years ago, it has witnessed many changes, and a marked alteration has taken place in its performance. Formerly the jubilee songs and choruses, with solos and part songs by members of the company, formed the entire programme. Now the jubilee songs form the first part of the programme, and with the encores it is a very liberal first part, whilst the second part is made up entirely of secular music, and the performances of a clever contortionist and one of the best jugglers ever seen in this colony.

70

Photo. by Talma.

THE CAKE WALKERS—M'ADOO'S GEORGIA MINSTREL COMPANY.

McAdoo's Cakewalkers, 1899. Probable personnel include Jackson and Mabel Hearde, John and Maud Brewer, Dave and Edith Barton, Charles Walker and Ida May, Henry "Hen" Wise and Katie Milton, Grace Turner and George Henry. From the *Sydney Mail and New South Wales Advertiser* 15 July 1899 (page 153). Photograph by Talma Studios (Melbourne). Courtesy *Trove*, National Library of Australia.

The secular music referred to in the second half reflected the very large repertoire of the company, who enjoyed being able to vary their presentation. A popular item was Sir Arthur Sullivan's "The Lost Chord." Jennie Robinson (Mrs. Hamilton Hodges), regularly performed operatic airs from Balfe's *The Bohemian Girl* and Verdi's *Il Trovatore*. Other popular items included "The Blue Danube" and "Morning is Breaking." On the vaudeville side, Jalvan's juggling was enthusiastically received.

The Melbourne season lasted until the end of August 1899, when the troupe sailed around the coast to Perth and Fremantle, then into the western gold fields (Kalgoorlie, Coolgardie, etc.), finishing in the southwest (Albany, Bunbury) before reaching SA in early November. Their leisurely progress en route to an opening at Sydney's Palace Theatre, on December 17, 1899, was severely disrupted by two unfortunate events. First, Fred Dawson, the company's advance agent, fractured his skull by falling down stairs at Stuart's Hotel, Ballarat. He was reported in a critical state but would eventually make a good recovery after two-week hospital stay. At the same time McAdoo himself was hospitalized in Melbourne, needing an operation for peritonitis that put him out of action for several weeks, leaving the redoubtable Mrs. McAdoo to manage the troupe through their Sydney opening.

The Sydney season ran successfully until late January 1900, followed by a short tour of Sydney suburban centers. A recovered McAdoo rejoined the troupe briefly in early January, but remained in Sydney preparing to head off to America in search of his new large vaudeville team. The main Jubilee troupe embarked for New Zealand, arriving at Auckland on February 12, 1899, via the SS *Mokoia*. The *NZ Observer*, on February 25, 1899, was impressed by the female members' style of dress.

The original Jubilee Singers had been noted for their sober mien and conservative dress style. Not so their latest successors; the ladies of the company dress with great taste, Madame McAdoo's dresses being especially lovely. The lady possesses a tall, elegant and graceful figure, which shows off her beautiful dresses perfectly. On Monday evening, she appeared in a beautiful dress of black silk embroidered net over white silk, the foot of the skirt finished with tiny frills, which sparkled with either sequins or jet. The bodice was made high, with long transparent sleeves of net. A touch of bright crimson on the bodice was added with excellent effect.

Similar details were provided for the other ladies of the troupe.

In mid–March 1899, McAdoo traveled to San Francisco on the SS *Alameda*. The *Freeman* had already carried the following advertisement:

McAdoo made a big impression on his courtesy visit to the *Freeman* office, as reported on April 1, 1899:

> Mr McAdoo has seen the better part of the world. He is prosperous, and an Australian by adoption. He was a classmate of Booker T. Washington. In his accent he is decidedly English. He dresses well in the style of the English upper class—high [silk] hat, band of black approaching the top, Prince Albert coat unusually long, from the waist down. He wears the everlasting, stout looking, patent leather shoes. He wears a few diamonds within the bounds of propriety.

McAdoo's advertisement ran continuously in the *Freeman* for the next two months, with occasional reports of his recruiting successes. One of his major coups was recruiting band leader Professor Henderson Smith and his orchestra, variously described as a military, brass, or concert band. In the fashion of the time, he was referred to as "The Black Sousa."

IMPORTANT ANNOUNCEMENT

MR. ORPHEUS M. McADOO,
(Sole Lessee Palace Theatre. Sidney, Australia)
WILL ARRIVE IN
Indianapolis from Australia
(About Middle of March)
SEEKING
Musical, Minstrel and Vaudeville attractions.

Tour:—Australia, New Zealand, Japan, China and India. Engagements from 6 to 12 months. Good salaries and return fares.

Only Colored Artists Engaged. None but Best Need Apply. Also Sopranos, contraltos, tenors and bassos required for Jubilee Singers and Concert company.

The Palace Theatre, Sidney, is the handsomest and most complete vaudeville house in the world.

Address all communications

Orpheus M. McAdoo,

Care THE FREEMAN, Indianapolis Ind.

McAdoo's recruitment advertisement in the *Indianapolis Freeman*, 4 March 1899.

Smith was a veteran of black minstrelsy, having at one time or another owned Henderson Smith's Creole Company, and McCabe and Young's Minstrels. He was for a while band leader of the white-owned Mahara's Colored Minstrels, a role in which his immediate successor was the great W.C. Handy ("Father of the Blues"). Smith had followed that by being band leader for the highly successful *Darkest America*, a show with a huge black cast that toured America for several years. An advertisement in the *New York Clipper* (November 20, 1897) for *Darkest America* described Henderson Smith as "America's Leading Colored Bandmaster."

On May 17, 1899, McAdoo and his entourage, including the full Henderson Smith orchestra, left the U.S. on the SS *Moana*, arriving at Sydney via Hawaii and Samoa, on June 6. Although they were generally reported in the media as having arrived in Australia, Sydney was then the capital of the British colony of NSW, there not yet being a nation state called Australia. However, on June 28, the citizens of NSW voted by referendum to surrender the colony's sovereignty to enable a planned federation. By the end of July the other five Australian colonies followed suit, and the path was then clear for Queen Victoria to issue a royal proclamation of the new Commonwealth of Australia, with effect from January 1, 1901.

McAdoo's new Georgia Minstrels and American Cakewalkers opened at the Palace Theatre on June 17, 1899. The lineup he had secured on his U.S. trip was of high quality, including: Ed Tolliver (monologist, also tuba player with orchestra); Jackson and Mabel Hearde (character sketch artists and dancers); John Pramplin (juggler, gun manipulator); Flora Batson (soprano and baritone); Maud and John Brewer (Buck and Wing dancers, John also alto Sax with orchestra); William Ferry (Ferry the Human Frog, contortionist); Willis Gauze (male soprano, female impersonator); Hen Wise (comedian, impersonator); Katie Milton (singing and dancing soubrette); Gerard Miller (bass baritone and interlocutor); Dave and Edith Barton (character sketches); Grace Turner (singer, dancer); Leon P. Rooks (tenor); George Henry (Buck and Wing dancer); Charles W. Walker (basso, comedian) and his wife, Ida May (dancer); Turner Jones (tenor, also bass drum, orchestra); Frank Poole (tenor, and snare drums, orchestra). In addition there was the Henderson Smith orchestra of about 14, including some already listed above.[2]

All of the cast listed were well respected names in African American vaudeville. The one most remembered today is Flora Batson. Known as the "Double voiced Queen of Song" for her phenomenal range, she was described by Sylvester Russell (dean of black stage critics) as "the greatest female ballad singer of her race and time, once the rival of Black Patti (Sissieretta Jones) on the concert stage, and the most popular singer among the people of her own race ever known."[3] In April 1896, she had performed at Carnegie Hall along with the other two leading African American female concert singers, Marie Selika and Black Patti.

Probably the cast member who made the biggest impact in Australasia at the time, and over many further years, was William Ferry (The Human Frog). His rubber-boned displays evoked responses of amazement. The *Courier* (May 20, 1922) reported that after

Photo. by Talma.   MR. O. M. M'ADOO AND HIS GEORGIA MINSTREL COMPANY.

The full ensemble of McAdoo's Georgia Minstrel and Alabama Cakewalkers troupe, McAdoo himself is seated at center and wearing top hat. From the *Sydney Mail and New South Wales Advertiser* 15 July 1899 (page 153). Photographer Talma Studios (Melbourne). Courtesy *Trove*, National Library of Australia.

a performance in Fiji, the local chieftain told Ferry, "God takes your bones out at night, and gives them back to you in the morning."

The adoption of the term "Cakewalk" in the troupe's title was a calculated ploy to cash in on the then current craze for the dance of that name in New York. The dance's history stretched back to plantation days, when enslaved African Americans dressed up and parodied the high-flown ways of their white mistresses and masters, while "walkin' for dat cake," the cake being the prize awarded to the best couple.[4] It had been known through the minstrelsy "walk-around" for many years but had become fashionable in New York social circles by 1899. The unquestioned "Queen of the Cakewalk" was the beautiful, brilliantly talented Aida (Ada) Overton Walker. Starting out as a teenager with Black Patti's Troubadours, Aida soon joined the team of Bert Williams and George Walker, marrying Walker in June 1899. Their stylish Cakewalk was the sensation of New York in several Williams and Walker shows, including *The Octoroons* and *In Dahomey*, which was later performed at Buckingham Palace. Aida was also in demand to teach the Cakewalk to elite white society matrons in New York.[5] Even before the show opened, the Sydney media was building up a keen anticipation for the Cakewalk, including *Truth* (June 11, 1899):

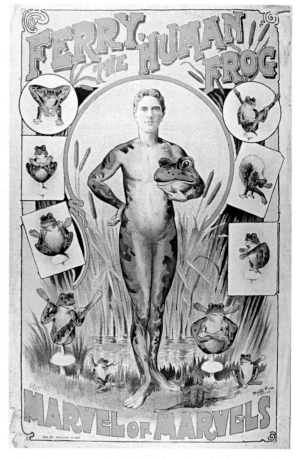

Poster of Ferry the Human Frog, ca. 1901, at the time of Ferry's February appearance in Dunedin. Creator Caxton, lithographer Dunedin, New Zealand. Collection of Toitū Otago Settlers Museum, Dunedin, New Zealand.

> Something distinctly novel is promised for us next Saturday evening, when Mr. O. M. McAdoo will introduce his Georgia Minstrels.... No doubt the great attraction will be the "Coons" Cake Walk.... This extraordinary dance attracted general attention in London two years ago, and is all the vogue in New York and Chicago, where Society has adopted it as the closing dance of the evening, in place of the Sir Roger de Coverley.

It referred later (June 25) to "the indescribable Cake Walk.... *Truth* will not attempt to describe it, but advises everyone to see it."

Apart from the cakewalk, the program included a comic song titled "Dora Dean," a lady who would have been well known to the cast for her cakewalking skills, among others. (She will feature later in this book.) On a sad note, around this time McAdoo's Parade Band escorted the body of Hosea Easton to Waverley Cemetery. Despite that gloomy note, there

The Mc'Adoo Minstrels In Their Cake-Walking Entertainment at St. George's Hall. The *Australasian,* **19 August 1899.**

was every reason McAdoo should view his situation with optimism, given that he now had two troupes successfully touring the antipodes, the Georgia Minstrels in Australia, and the Jubilee Singers in New Zealand. Nevertheless, there were dark clouds on the horizon. While he had been pursuing his recruitment campaign in the U.S. with much fanfare, another had been pursuing a similar agenda in secrecy.

M.B. Curtis Arrives

McAdoo's rival was one M.B. (Maurice Bertram) Curtis, a white actor turned promoter. He was born Mauritz Strelinger in Bohemia, then part of the Austro-Hungarian empire, around 1850. His parents took him from England to America at an early age. He became an actor, adopting M.B. Curtis as his stage name, and achieved some fame with a play *Sam'l of Posen* in which he portrayed a comic Jewish salesman. His success enabled him to make a large amount of money in real estate but his career took a downward turn when he was charged with killing a policeman while in a drunken state. After four notorious trials he was eventually acquitted in 1893, but his fortune had vanished and his career was languishing.[6]

Around the late 1890s he re-invented himself as a manager and promoter, having discovered a talented magician, Oscar Eliason, a Mormon from Salt Lake City, whom he dubbed Dante the Great. After a short season in Hawaii, he presented Dante along with

Dante's attractive wife and professional assistant, Mlle. Edmunda, for a successful season of several months in New Zealand, followed by a lengthy run at the Palace Theatre in Sydney.

While they were still in New Zealand, the *Wanganui Herald*, on February 3, 1899, reported a split between Curtis and the Dantes. There followed accusations of dishonesty and fraud against Curtis by Dante, with Curtis seeking a legal injunction to stop Dante performing without him. The case dragged on for several months and was eventually settled out of court, leaving Dante free to follow a successful season in Australia, and Curtis looking for a new attraction to promote.

It was during this time that Curtis came up with the idea of a rival venture to McAdoo's already advertised vaudeville scheme. In a boastful interview with *Truth* on July 23, 1899, Curtis claimed that the original idea was his, and that he had generously offered McAdoo a 50 percent share of the venture but, while he was in New Zealand with Dante, McAdoo had treacherously "jumped right under my waistcoat. I was naturally rattled at the would-be coup d'état of this colored gentleman. I gave my wife a power of attorney, transferred my banking account to her, put £5000 in circular notes right here in this pocket, and in five hours was on board the *Aorangi*, en route for Vancouver."

While it's possible the two men could have met and discussed showbiz matters of mutual interest, it's highly improbable that a seasoned, successful, promoter like McAdoo would have agreed to play second fiddle to a less experienced white manager, particularly one of Curtis's dubious record. In a letter written on arrival in Sydney (June 10), Henderson Smith had told the *Freeman* on July 29, 1899: "We have learned that a man named Curtis has gone to America after another colored show and my advice to performers there is not to come here at present, as the country is too small for 3 colored companies. Besides this man Curtis' reputation here is not the best."

Henderson Smith's warning was already too late. Curtis's "All Star Afro-American Minstrels" sailed from Vancouver on the RMS *Miowera* on June 1, 1899, nine days before McAdoo arrived back in Australia from his recruiting trip to the U.S. The Curtis troupe was scheduled to arrive in Sydney on June 26, 1899. While McAdoo had recruited a stellar line-up on his trip, Curtis had taken matters a notch higher, recruiting some of the crème de la crème—virtual royalty—of African American entertainment.

The Curtis performing group, opening at the Criterion Theatre on July 1, was declared as the "Largest and Best Aggregation of Coloured Talent ever engaged under one management" (probably a true statement for Australia). It included (with advertised hyperbolic descriptions): Ernest Hogan (The Unbleached American); Miss Madah A. Hyer (The Bronze Patti); Billy McClain (The Black Buffalo); Black Dante (The original Dante the Great); Marion Blake (The Greatest Female Baritone Living): Robert Logan (America's Eminent Basso); Little Siren (The Creole Contortion Danseuse); Tom Logan (character Artist, Hebrew, Irish, Dutch, Chinese, Aged Darkey and Dago Characters); Miss Laura Moss (Boston's Favorite Soprano); The Kentucky Four (Katie Carter, Muriel Ringgold, Master Blutch, Master Levers); The Criterion Quartette (George Jones, William Jones, Irving Jones, Amon Davis); Lawrence Chenault (dramatic lyric tenor and female impersonator); Lewis H. Saulsbury (tenor robusto); Miss Vincent Bradley (character artist); C.F. Alexander (musical director); Miss Luella Price (The Dainty Soubrette); Miss Carrie Carter (comedienne); and including Major N. (Nathaniel) Clark Smith's Kansas Pickaninny Band (see endnote for the full extended company of almost 50 names).[7]

Before considering the status of the most illustrious of these performers, it may help to put into perspective the overall status and quality of the two troupes via a comparison of their standing in current black entertainment literature. For this purpose the well-known reference books of Bernard L. Peterson Jr., have been used, scoring both troupes on their number of primary entries (those with their own individual entry in the main directory), and secondary entries (those included in an appendix of significant figures not included in the main directory). For the Curtis troupe the score is five primary entries and two secondaries (three, if one counts Curtis's own entry which describes him as "notorious for non-payment of salaries"). For the McAdoo troupe the score is one primary and seven secondaries. Both scores certainly attest to the high quality of both troupes but clearly favor the Curtis troupe, no doubt due to the extravagant financial inducements Curtis had promised.[8] So, what can one say of those who rank as virtual royalty of black entertainment?

Ernest Hogan

Certainly, the first must be Ernest Hogan, a man of immense influence in the late nineties and early 20th century. Born Ernest Reuben Crowders, Bowling Green, Kentucky, in 1865, he adopted the name Ernest Hogan after a Doctor Hogan, whose traveling medicine show gave him his early start in show business. The soubriquet "The Unbleached American" reflected Hogan's boast that he didn't have a drop of white blood in his ancestry. He was credited with subtly changing the role of the end man in minstrelsy from buffoonery to a more rounded character. At the time of his Australian visit some of his greatest achievements were still in the future, but he had already established a strong claim to fame.

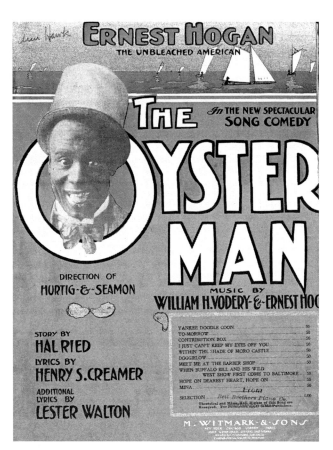

To a considerable extent, Hogan's fame was based on his 1896 song composition "All Coons Look Alike to Me." Before considering the wider context of the much despised "coon song" genre, it's worth noting that this song, along with his 1895 composition "La Pas Ma La," earned Hogan a large degree of historic credit for popularizing the new Ragtime music. He was one of the first to use the words "Ragtime" and "Rag" in his publications. The song was popular with leading

Cover of music album for Ernest Hogan's 1907 hit show "The Oyster Man." Author's collection.

white performers like May Irwin, earning Hogan a lot of money, and starting a "coon song" craze.

Late in his life Hogan expressed regret for writing the song. Examination of the lyrics shows that they are not as offensive as the title suggests—it expresses a young maiden's view that beside her new lover, everyone else looks alike. Furthermore, Hogan was far from unique in black entertainment circles in adopting the offensive "coon" word. As early as 1889, famous black minstrel Billy Kersands's 1880 song "Mary's Gone with a Coon" was being performed by white minstrel troupes in Australia. The great Bert Williams and George Walker started out in show business billed as "The Two Real Coons," and the team of Bob Cole and Billy Johnson wrote a successful show called *A Trip to Coontown*.

In an interview with the *Sunday Times* on July 9, 1899, Hogan claimed that the song title arose from an incident when, as an innocent bystander, he was mistakenly arrested for being part of a fracas. According to this story, on being rebuked for the wrongful arrest, the Irish policeman defended himself in the words of the title. However, it's likely the expression had been around long before that. Hogan had also told Tom Fletcher that he pinched the song from a piano player in the Chicago red-light district whose girlfriend had kicked him out, telling him, "All pimps look alike to me."[9]

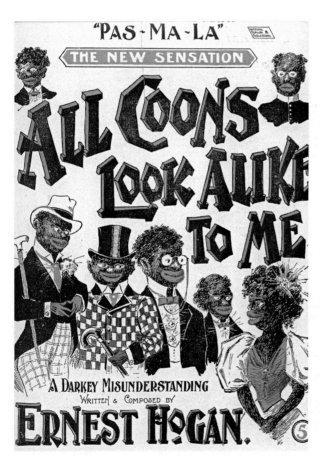

Cover of sheet music for Ernest Hogan 1896 composition "All Coons Look Alike to Me." Author's collection.

Though the term "coon" had been used widely by black performers in shows and song titles, the particularly dehumanizing connotations of the title certainly increased its offensiveness to black people. Nevertheless, it was heavily promoted in the advertisements for Curtis's troupe in Australia and was very popular with audiences. This was in large part due to Hogan's brilliant performance.

Apart from his association with the infamous, though successful, song, Ernest Hogan had several other achievements to his credit before he arrived in Australia. Following early success in a variety of minstrel shows, he spent two years (1897–1898) as a featured performer with the Black Patti Troubadours. In 1898, he starred as a comedian and dancer in the first black musical sketch on Broadway, Will Marion Cook's *Clorindy, or the Origin of the Cakewalk*.[10] Hogan's Cakewalk, with Belle Davis, was a highlight of the show. After Australia, Hogan would become one of the leading figures of black musical theatre, with notable Broadway successes like

Rufus Rastus (1905) and *The Oyster Man* (1907), before his early death in 1910, aged only 45.

Billy McClain

Next to Hogan in status must be Billy McClain ("The Black Buffalo"), born in Indianapolis in 1866.[11] Described as an "important organizer of black talent ... with the additional gift of persuading moneyed men to back his ideas,"[12] he had a long history of promoting large black shows, including *South Before the War* (1893), and the biggest of all, *Black America* (1895).[13] ("Conceived, produced and staged by Billy McClain, under the management of Nate Salisbury, best known previously as the producer of the Buffalo Bill Cody *Wild West Show*.") After *Black America*, McClain, like Hogan, joined the Black Patti Troubadours. His wife, Cordelia, partnered him in most of his ventures, though she didn't join him in Australia until later.

Madah Hyers

(Anna) Madah Hyers was one of the biggest success stories of black music in the 19th century, although by the time of her arrival in Australia she was coasting, late in her career. Born around 1855 in Sacramento, California, she had an early classical training as a soprano under the supervision of her tenor father, Sam Hyers. Along with her younger sister Emma (Louise), contralto, she made her concert debut in April 1867 to great acclaim. The Hyers Sisters became the first of many black prima donnas,[14] and the first African American women to gain success on the American stage.

Under their father's management, they formed The Hyers Sisters Concert Company. They presented musical, dramatic, and variety shows from 1876 to 1896, generally promoting the black cause. It was "the first black repertory company and the only one for more than a decade. Until the 1890s, it offered the sole avenue to a stage career for those musicians and actors who wished to bypass the minstrel circuit, if only temporarily."[15] One of those who had gained a start with the sisters' company was tenor Wallace King, an Australian resident by the time Madah arrived. By 1897 the sisters had closed their own company and joined a large minstrel and variety troupe, Isham's Octoroons, one of the first such troupes to feature African American women. By 1898 Emma had dropped out (and died shortly thereafter), leaving Madah on her own, and soon to join the Curtis troupe en route to Australia.

Rest of the Curtis Troupe

While those three were the highest profile performers, all of Curtis's troupe were top flight stars in their own right. Not content with having such top of the bill stars, Curtis sought to outbid the McAdoo troupe on every front. If McAdoo had a contortionist (Ferry the Human Frog), Curtis would have one (the diminutive Siren Nevarro)[16]; if McAdoo had a female impersonator (Willis Gauze), Curtis would have one (Lawrence Chenault)[17]; If McAdoo had a female baritone (Flora Batson), then Curtis would have "the greatest female baritone living," (Marion Blake); if McAdoo had Henderson Smith's orchestra, then Curtis would have Major N. Clark Smith's Kansas Pickaninny Band, a high-profile catch. Major Clark Smith had been director of music at Western University, Kansas City, and also a composer of note. The members of the band were musical pupils of the university, aged typically between 16 and 20 years, specially selected to visit Australia and New Zealand. Several members of the Australia band went on to become part of the wider jazz or entertainment scene in later years, including Harry Hull (tuba and bass with Mamie Smith, Johnny Dunn, and other big names), and Harry St .Clair, who was president of the Musicians Protective Union, Local No. 627, known as "the Cradle of Kansas City Jazz."

Contortionist Siren Nevarro later had prominent roles on Broadway in the Williams and Walker show *Mr. Lode of Koal* (1909) and Cole and Johnson's *The Shoo-Fly Regiment* (1907), for which she also did choreography and costume design.

Perhaps the most curious of Curtis's recruitments was the leading black magician, William Carl, known as "Black Carl," whose illustrious career had also included playing

with Williams and Walker. In an obviously spiteful retaliation for the acrimonious New Zealand split with the Great Dante, Curtis billed Black Carl as "the original Great Dante." Promoting another magician would have been in contravention of the legal settlement between Curtis and Dante, which had specified, according to the *Otago Witness* on April 13, 1899: "The plaintiff [Curtis] to be at liberty to engage in other theatrical performances, provided they do not enter into competition with the defendant [Dante]." The true Dante (Oscar Eliason) was still playing the Australian circuits, though sadly he would die in November 1899, as a result of a shooting accident in Dubbo, NSW, aged just 28. Black Carl continued to use the Dante soubriquet after his return to the U.S.

The arrival of the Curtis troupe set the scene for a fierce competition between it and McAdoo's two troupes, and incidentally an opportunity for Australasian audiences to enjoy some of the greatest African American talent, with over a hundred high profile performers, touring extensively over a period of eight months (July 1899–February 1900).

Siren Nevarro (dancer, contortionist, choreographer and costume designer) in *The New York Age*, 14 January 1909.

9

McAdoo and Curtis:
The Battle Begins

McAdoo and his troupe had a mere two weeks to enjoy the success of their Sydney opening at the Palace Theatre before the barnstorming Curtis outfit opened at the Criterion on July 1, 1899. Curtis's Afro-Americans opened to "a densely packed house,"[1] and a prediction that "judging by its initial reception, the combination should have a very prosperous season." With such a feast of talent they were assured of a good reaction. Referring to them as "the much boomed American Minstrel Company and troupe of cake-walkers," the *Sunday Times* reviewer praised Hogan in fulsome terms:

> In the first part the turn of Mr Ernest Hogan … completely eclipsed all others. Mr Hogan possesses an extremely pleasant voice for a comedian, while his 'business' stamped him as an artist of the very front rank…. Next in order of merit to Mr Hogan was Mr Billy McClain, who was also thoroughly amusing. Between them they were almost solely responsible for the success of this portion of the entertainment.

The reviewer went on to praise the Buck and Wing dancing of the Kentucky Four: "Their turn was indeed a revelation, and fairly brought down the house"; Madah Hyers, an emphatic hit, "proved herself the-possessor of a voice of remarkable range in a couple of operatic selections"; "Siren Nevarro, a Lilliputian contortion danseuse, did some wonderfully clever work"; "The Black Dante did some astonishingly clever feats of sleight-of-hand." Finally, "a rag-time opera, *Negro Love Story* in one act, with Mr Ernest Hogan appearing as Rastus Hotbones, an interloper, and Billy McClain as Chauncey M Dispute (who thinks he is a bosom friend of Albert Prince of Whales), created endless amusement."

The same issue of the *Sunday Times* also carried a favorable review of the McAdoo troupe, who were still at the Palace. However, for McAdoo, the writing was on the wall. Any doubts he had, at least as far as Sydney was concerned, would have been dispelled by the cut-throat competitiveness of Curtis. For example, when McAdoo changed his matinee day from Wednesday to Tuesday, Curtis made the same switch.[2] McAdoo soon took his troupe out of town, via regional centers starting with Goulburn, to Melbourne and further west. This left a clear field in Sydney for the Curtis troupe. However, after initial strong support and continuing good notices, their audiences also began to drop off, perhaps confirming Henderson Smith's prediction that the market was too small for so many black troupes. The high salaries Curtis had used to lure his big stars were probably also a factor, reducing his commercial viability.

In an attempt to revive his flagging business fortunes, Curtis closed the minstrel show, and along with his troupe, formed an alliance with the promoter of a drama about the notorious Kelly Gang, which had been running successfully at the Opera House.[3] The joint venture played at the Criterion Theatre, with the Afro-American Minstrels somewhat incongruously blended in "depicting aboriginal life in Australia." The venture was short-lived, and rumors of dissension within the minstrel camp soon began to appear. Like a Greek chorus commenting on the drama, Henderson Smith of the McAdoo troupe, in a regular series of letters to the *Freeman*, told a tale of betrayal by Curtis and despair for the Afro-American Minstrels. This included Curtis threatening members of his troupe with a revolver, and leaving them stranded, with McAdoo and his troupe raising £225 to rescue them from penury.[4]

As Henderson Smith was traveling in Vic and points west with McAdoo at the time, his information must have come from gossip. An article in the Sydney *Bulletin* declared: "The Curtis Afro-American Company … is today stranded in Sydney, without money to pay current expenses, without the means to return to America, and with no prospects except bad ones. There are sixteen boys, ten ladies and nineteen men in the company."[5] It laid the blame squarely at Curtis's feet. However, the reality was not quite so bad, as Smith acknowledged apologetically to Hogan in the *Freeman*'s columns much later. Clearly there had been serious ill feelings but Curtis had managed to patch things up. In a letter to the *Evening News* on August 12, acknowledging the many people who had helped and supported them in their difficulties, Ernest Hogan and Tom Logan wrote:

> Notwithstanding that our engagement has not been a financial success altogether, the cordial reception we have met with has more than counter-balanced this. We are also pleased to state that the citizens of your city admire ability and do not recognize caste. Our stay, though brief, has been exceptionally pleasant, and it is with considerable regret that we are leaving our many kind friends in Sydney. We are leaving today by the steamer *Waihora* for Auckland where we hope we will meet with the same hearty welcome that we did in Sydney.

The absence of Curtis's name, and the presence of those of McAdoo and the American Consul, lend credence to part of Henderson Smith's reports. Nevertheless, it was an almost complete company, including Curtis himself, that departed for New Zealand on the *Waihora*, arriving in Auckland on August 15 after a stormy voyage. In the fallout from the dissension, Billy McClain reported to the *Freeman* (September 23, 1899) that he had left Curtis and "opened with the Orpheus McAdoo Georgia Minstrels, at a larger salary than ever before."

Curtis in New Zealand

The Auckland opening was well received, some roughness in presentation being excused on the grounds that "the members of the company had a very uncomfortable time during the passage of the *Waihora* from Sydney, and had not recovered.… The feature of the evening was the appearance of Madame Hyers (the Black Melba), who possesses a well-trained soprano … she scored a decided success." Hogan's comedy was highly praised, the overall conclusion being that "the company's season should be a highly successful one." Siren Nevarro got her share of praise from the NZ *Herald* on August 16, 1899: "Little Siren, a Creole Lilliputian contortionist, contributed a very clever act, twisting and turning about like an eel. This little performer was loudly and deservedly applauded."

After the auspicious Auckland opening, the next engagement at New Plymouth, on the West Coast of the North Island, saw signs that the dissensions of Sydney were unresolved. Originally advertised as involving the full troupe, the actual performance was a considerably truncated version. Expressing disappointment, the August 23 *Taranaki Herald* reported:

> When the Company was first announced the general impression was that the same combination that performed in Sydney and Auckland would appear here, and knowing the favourable impression created in those cities, it was only natural the public should anticipate its arrival with feelings of pleasure. Those feelings underwent a change on Tuesday night. Instead of an entertainment by a company of first-class artists the halo of real merit only floated round two or three, the remaining members being very lesser lights. The Company, which originally consisted of between 40 and 50 members, has been divided up. This explains the absence of several prominent members, notably Mr E Hogan, who, we understand, is about to tour with the second portion of the company on the East Coast.

Whatever turmoil had caused the New Plymouth fiasco, all was apparently serene again a few days later at Wanganui, when the full troupe performed to an enthusiastic full house at the Drill Hall Theatre. Things continued tranquilly through successful seasons at Wellington and Dunedin, though the *Tuapeka Times* (September 30, 1899) suggested the Dunedin season was truncated due to poor audiences. After brief stopovers at Oamaru, Timaru, and Ashburton, the next substantial season was due to start at Christchurch (Theatre Royal, Lyttelton) on October 2. On the appointed night a sign was posted at the theatre entrance saying, "In consequence of illness of some of the performers, the opening performance is postponed." Rather belying the tale of illness was the NZ *Press* (October 3, 1899) report that "the brass band attached to Mr M B Curtis's Afro-American Minstrel Company, created quite a sensation. The streets were lined with people, and the procession was escorted and followed by a large number of cyclists and pedestrians."

The true facts behind the non-appearance were revealed by the October 5 NZ *Star*, reporting that the company's members had taken legal action against Curtis for arrears of salary in Christchurch, just as he was about to leave for Wellington by the SS *Rotomahana*. Judgment was awarded against Curtis. As the scenery and theatrical effects had been seized by the court and held against Curtis's debts, the company had to bid for them at auction. Hogan duly purchased the scenery and the troupe now became "Ernest Hogan's Afro-American Minstrels." They resumed successful touring and whatever managerial talent (or lack thereof) Curtis had contributed was clearly matched by Black Carl (Dante) as the new manager.

The departing Curtis told the *Wanganui Chronicle* (October 4, 1899) that he intended "to make New Zealand his headquarters in future, and purposes visiting America and England once a year in search of novelties." Curtis did reappear briefly in New Zealand during 1903 and 1905, as manager of touring American drama troupes. His time there included several court appearances for non-payment of bills. Later, until his death in the early 1920s, he continued to present his comedy *Sam'l of Posen* in America, which earned him a niche in theatre history, credited with being "the first time that a Jewish actor played a Jewish character in a stage play intended for Jewish audiences and clearly dates the beginning of the Jewish-American comic performance tradition in the English language to the 1880s."[6]

From Christchurch the born-again Hogan troupe toured a number of South Island centers (Blenheim, Nelson, Greymouth), featuring *Uncle Tom's Cabin* with a young NZ girl, Gertie Osborne, as Eva. They returned to the North Island and gradually worked their way up to Auckland, where they embarked on the SS *Waihora* on December 18, arriving in Sydney on December 22, 1899.

Hogan Back in Australia

Hogan and company didn't stay long in Sydney, perhaps with memories of their previous difficulties there. Within five days of arrival they opened for a season at the Victoria Theatre in Newcastle. The Australia they had returned to was one caught up in a fever of Empire patriotism, triggered by the Second Boer War, which ran from October 1899 until May 1902, between the United Kingdom on one hand, and the South African Republic and Orange Free State on the other. In just about every community around the country the local mayor sponsored a branch of the Patriotic Fund, set up to raise money to be sent back to the United Kingdom for the war effort. A popular form of fundraising involved the singing at public events of a poem by Rudyard Kipling, set to music by Sir Arthur Sullivan (of Gilbert and Sullivan fame), "The Absent-Minded Beggar." This included the following jingoistic sentiments:

> When you've shouted "Rule Britannia,"
> when you've sung "God Save the Queen,"
> When you've finished killing Kruger with your mouth,
> Will you kindly drop a shilling in my little tambourine?
> For a gentleman in khaki ordered South?
> He's an absent-minded beggar, and his weaknesses are great—
> But we and Paul must take him as we find him.[7]

Each verse finished with the chorus: "Pass the hat for your credit's sake, and pay—pay—pay!" At this point the audience would enthusiastically shower money on the stage to be gathered up for the Fund. Hogan's Negro Minstrels embraced the practice with gusto, tenor Lewis Saulsbury dramatically delivering "The Absent-Minded Beggar" at every performance. Audiences responded generously, and the local media duly listed the money raised for the appeal, with the Minstrels usually high on the list. The January 3 *NMH* reported that Hogan had received a message of thanks from the mayor of Newcastle for the company's services at a benefit concert.

This pattern would be repeated throughout the company's remaining dates. The Newcastle engagement closed on a mutually congratulatory note reported in *NMH* on January 8, 1900:

> Towards the close of the performance on Saturday night, Mr Dante, the manager, on behalf of Mr Hogan and the company, thanked the citizens for the kind reception they had given them, and for the hearty patronage bestowed upon their performances. They came as strangers to the city, but they had not been treated as such; they had been successful far beyond their expectations, and the company desired to express their cordial thanks for the kindness they had received, from the Mayor downwards.

After Newcastle, the company opened a two-week season at the Royal Theatre, Brisbane, where Hogan's "Genuine Negro Minstrels and Original Alabama Cakewalkers" shared their opening night in direct competition with McAdoo's "Genuine Georgia Minstrels and Original Alabama Cakewalkers" at the Brisbane Opera House. McAdoo had also embraced the Patriotic Fund concept, even to the extent of advertising tenor Richard Collins as "The Absent-Minded Beggar." Unlike the Curtis era, both sides warmly greeted their competition, inviting each other to matinee performances, the *Brisbane Telegraph* reporting on January 20, 1900: "There was an enthusiastic audience at the Theatre Royal yesterday afternoon, when a special professional matinee was given. The members of the McAdoo Company were the guests of the Hogan Company. All the performers received handsome bouquets of flowers from the members of the McAdoo Company."

The Brisbane meeting was the first time the Hogan troupe was reunited with former member Billy McClain. McClain was now partnered with his talented wife, Cordelia, who had arrived in Australia by the steamer *Alameda* on Christmas Eve and joined the McAdoo troupe. The final night of the Hogan season saw further positive sentiment, reported by the *Courier* on January 20, 1900, when a surprised Carl Dante was presented by the company with a watch inscribed "To Mr Dante, our beloved friend and manager" in appreciation of the way he had managed their fortunes through the difficult period.

Their congratulatory statement made it clear that the company's priority was for a return to America at an early opportunity. Despite the positive tone, and brave face in some public statements expressing appreciation of their treatment by the Australian public, a warning from Tom Logan, senior member and stage manager, published in the columns of the *Freeman* on February 20, 1900, showed a negative side to the troupe's experience down under. "[Tom Logan advises] all colored performers, that if they know on which side their bread is buttered they will stay away from Australia as far as possible … 99% of those now here are wishing to God they'd never left the United States." In view of the lengthy, and apparently happy, residence of the two McAdoo troupes, one might question how far Logan could fairly blame Australia, rather than the turpitude of one M.B. Curtis, for the company's misfortunes.

Following the Brisbane engagement, the Hogan troupe played brief engagements at local towns (Ipswich, Toowoomba, and Warwick in Queensland, Tenterfield, Muswellbrook, Singleton, and Maitland in NSW) en route to a return season at Newcastle. At Newcastle they presented the Cole and Johnson musical drama *A Trip to Coontown*, a farce comedy in three acts, considered to be the first black musical-comedy, one of the earliest shows to break away from the minstrel tradition, and "the spark that fully ignited the development of black theatricals."[8] Miss Vincent Bradley had actually been part of the original Cole and Johnson company for that show on Broadway in 1898, as had Hen Wise of McAdoo's Georgia Minstrels. The production was described as having "delighted a fairly large house…. The piece is practically without a plot, but the music, specialties, and snatches of sparkling humour introduced during its action made an entertainment the novelty and variety of which were keenly appreciated."

The Newcastle engagement was essentially the troupe's swan song for Australia. They played one last date for two nights in Goulburn (February 22 and 23, 1900), en route to their departure from Sydney. The Goulburn visit came close to preventing the planned departure. On the previous day, one of the Pickaninny Band members, Frank Sandford, was "charged with stealing a gold ring of the value of £3, the property of Florrie Paulett, at Goulburn, on 23 February." Sandford's defense was that he had been fooling around with the waitress and her ring, with no intention of keeping it, but had discovered that his train left five hours earlier than he had been told. Not knowing her name, he had no way of returning the ring at the time, and had handed it over as soon as he was challenged. Miss Paulett stated that she had no desire for anyone to be prosecuted over the ring, but just wanted it back.

After evidence of good character was given on Sandford's behalf by Tom Logan, the court discharged him without conviction. With that crisis over, the troupe left Sydney on February 27 via the RMS *Warrimoo*, en route for the U.S. via Honolulu.

Hogan still had his greatest triumphs to come before his early death in 1909: *Rufus, Rastus* (1905–1907) and *The Oyster Man* (1907–1908).

10

McAdoo Reigns Again

With the final departure of the remnants of the original Curtis—later called Hogan—company, it's time to once again pick up the threads of the McAdoo troupes. First the Jubilee Singers, who were last seen in New Zealand, opening at Auckland in February 1899. This was the beginning of an eight-month tour, under the tight control of Madame McAdoo, taking them to all major centers and a vast number of regional towns. At every one they were greeted with capacity houses and enthusiastic notices. The following review from the Wellington *Evening Post* of March 21 is a typical example:

> The Singers had a hearty welcome on their reappearance in Wellington at the Opera House last evening. The programme differs in its arrangement from that of the past. The Singers are moving with the times. The camp and plantation melodies are still the particular feature of the entertainment, but for variety's sake and possibly because they have discovered that it pleases a wider public there is now more of the secular element, and in the second part juggling and acrobatism is introduced. The entertainment as a whole is very pleasing…. All the singers were recalled, in some instances twice. The acrobat of the company, Mr Jerry Mills, is a sort of loose-jointed humorist, who flings himself about in a most perplexing manner, and can kick half way into the flies. The juggler, Jalvan, is an Eastern artist, whose particular forte is balancing, and he gives a diverting quarter of an hour's exhibition of these feats.

The only disturbance to their tranquil progress came from occasional departures from the ranks. Soon after the March opening, (Moses) Hamilton Hodges left the troupe. In a fashion reminiscent of an earlier Fisk Jubilee Singer, R.B. Williams, he had decided that Auckland was a good place to settle. Unlike Williams, who traded music for the law, Hodges continued his musical vocation, setting up a voice training school. Jennie Robinson, soprano classical specialist of the troupe, who was also Mrs. Hamilton Hodges, did not initially leave with him. She stayed on until July 1899 before rejoining him as part of a duo musical team. Even then, she would later join a jubilee troupe for a time in 1903, and again in 1910. The Hamilton Hodges would be major figures of musical and concert life in New Zealand for many years to come, and were popular in social circles.[1] Mrs. Hodges died on a visit to her homeland in 1920 and Hamilton Hodges returned there in 1924, dying in Boston in 1930.[2]

While Mrs. McAdoo managed the troupe in their New Zealand travels, her husband, Orpheus McAdoo himself, passed through New Zealand, en route to Australia from America, with his newly recruited vaudeville company. This was reported in several papers as bringing reinforcements of eight performers to the Jubilee Singers. The reality was less dramatic: there was just one addition. Henderson Smith, in one of his *Freeman* letters, this one dated July 29, 1899, reported their arrival in Auckland; "Mrs O M McAdoo met her husband here and spent the day with him. Miss Ganey went with Mrs McAdoo to strengthen the Jubilee company." The July 24 *Marlborough Express* later reported: "Miss Ellen Gage, a well-known Wellington contralto vocalist, is now touring the South Island as a member of the Fisk Jubilee Singers."

The Jubilee Singers wound up their New Zealand tour in Dunedin on August 3, traveling south by train with a final appearance in Invercargill on August 4, before embarking for Tasmania. The dramatic July events in Sydney, described in the previous chapter, which had created dissension within the Curtis troupe, had bypassed them. The Curtis troupe arrived in New Zealand in the same week that the Jubilee Singers left there, while the other McAdoo (vaudeville) troupe were traveling west in Australia.

The McAdoo Jubilee Singers arrived in Hobart on August 5 to open at the Temperance Hall on August 14. The reviewer for the *Clipper* (September 2, 1899) couldn't resist a tongue-in-cheek, somewhat sexist, comment on the audience.

> Many hundreds of those who crowded the Albert Hall last week to hear the Jubilee Singers were much gratified to notice that the Examiner had the temerity to attack the theatre hat plague and knock some of the glycerin out of it. It is only on the long, flat floor space of the Albert Hall that the female headgear can be seen at its best. The ladies (especially the sweet seventeens) seem to vie with one another in sporting the biggest hats. Some of them are fearfully and wonderfully made. They were in rich profusion last week, from the big Gainsborough with the wobbly feathers, built on the Eiffel Tower principle, to the ponderous large built brute with bulwarks as broad as a Mexican sombrero.

A new initiative in the Singers program, starting with the Hobart season, was an Edison Kinetoscope film of *The Passion Play of Oberammergau* (1898), which McAdoo had brought on his return from America with the vaudeville minstrel troupe. The *Horsham Times* (September 8, 1899) described one of the many dramatic scenes from it: "The thieves are seen on two crosses, in the centre is the cross of our Lord Jesus Christ lying on the ground. The Saviour is placed and fastened to the cross, and so realistic is the scene, that one can almost see the nails pierce the flesh as they are driven into his hands."

The introduction of the Passion Play was part of a move back towards a more traditional jubilee focus. Joe Jalvan, "King of Jugglers," had already left around mid–May 1899, along with his wife, contralto Marshall Webb, though they would continue playing local theatrical engagements. Within a short time acrobat Jerry Mills also left, joining McAdoo's vaudeville troupe. The renewed traditional Jubilee emphasis still saw some popular secular material featured, like Sullivan's "Lost Chord" and operatic material like *The Bohemian Girl* and *Il Trovatore*, as well as the ever-popular, patriotic "Absent Minded Beggar."

As always with lengthy tours, attrition had wrought other changes with the troupe's personnel. McAdoo himself was busy managing the Georgia Minstrels and rarely performed. Those remaining from the original roster were: Mrs. McAdoo (Mattie Allen), the "Lady Tenor," Susie Anderson, dramatic soprano (styled the Black Melba); Belle Gibbons, soprano, monologist; Richard Collins, tenor; William Nott, tenor; Eugene McAdoo, bass; Professor C.A. White, accompanist, piano, organ.

Replacements coming on board at various times included: Robert Allen, baritone, brother of Mattie Allen, and Lula Allen, contralto, her sister; Sadie Ganey, soprano; Dazalia Underwood, soprano ("The American Nightingale"); Mary Mitchell, soprano; and John Ransom, tenor. The new recruits seem to have played subsidiary roles, except family member Robert Allen, and Dazalia Underwood who was a featured soloist. Sadie Ganey was part of a popular quartet with Mrs. McAdoo, Susie Anderson, and Belle Gibbons.

After a short tour of Tasmania, the Jubilee Singers were soon back on the mainland. They made a series of whirlwind tours through regional Vic (September), SA (October),

WA and the goldfields (November–December), and were back to Melbourne and regional Vic by the start of 1900. The New Year also saw McAdoo's Georgia Minstrels in Tasmania. It was a good time to be out of Sydney for both troupes, as January 1900 saw the outbreak of an epidemic of Bubonic Plague in the city. Health authorities had been aware for some years that plague, already active in places like Hong Kong and New Caledonia, could be spread from shipping arrivals. When plague did reach Australia in 1900, the response was one of panic and dread, fueled by the knowledge of the history and ravenous potential of the disease. Between 1900 and 1910, government health archives record 1,371 cases and 535 deaths across Australia. Sydney was hit hardest but the disease also spread to North Queensland while more sporadic cases were documented in Melbourne, Adelaide, and Fremantle.[3] During the Jubilee Singers season in North Queensland the Cairns *Morning Post* (June 1, 1900) carried immediately above the announcement of their appearance, an advertisement of the need to "disinfect every building in Cairns … to kill rats who are the real Plague carriers … with Crude Carbolic Acid."

By April 1900, McAdoo's Jubilee Singers were back again in Tasmania, and his Georgia Minstrels were in (the presumably now safe) Sydney, with a highly successful season at the Palace Theatre. Elated with the success of his ventures, McAdoo told the *Melbourne Punch* (April 26, 1900) that although "Sydney and the country are 'upside down' owing to the plague," his company was playing to very good business, so he would delay a planned visit to inland towns of NSW for a few weeks yet.

Unfortunately, McAdoo's good fortunes were not destined to last. He would soon face a challenge greater than Curtis or similar could have presented, and as grave as the plague itself. He had apparently recovered good health from the illness that afflicted him in late 1898. However, in May 1900 while his troupe was still performing at the Palace, he fell ill and was persuaded to take to his bed for a few days. Gradually growing worse, he left his hotel and went into a private hospital in Moore Park, Sydney. Mrs. McAdoo left the Jubilee Singers in Tasmania under the management of Eugene McAdoo, to be by her husband's side, her last performance there being in mid–April.

Gradually, McAdoo's condition worsened, the *Referee* (July 18, 1900) stating that for "five weeks he was so low that no one was allowed to see him—not even his wife or little son." When it became obvious that there was no hope, this restriction was lifted. He died on July 17, aged only 42 years.[4] He was buried in the Church of England portion of Waverley Cemetery, where an impressive monument marks his grave. While many generous tributes were paid to him in the media, perhaps the sincerest was that by Willis Gauze, printed in the *Freeman* on October 6, 1900.

Toowoomba, Queensland, Jul. 23, '00.

Stage Editor of The Freeman:—"I wish to inform you of our beloved manager's, Mr. M. McAdoo, death, and we mourn for him as manager and gentleman—for a better man never lived—and his treatment of us was so very nice that we say, may his soul rest in peace. The minstrel company he brought out was the cause of his death. I never traveled with such people before. You need not believe any base reports you hear about our deceased manager for they are untrue. I, myself, was never treated better in all my life by a manager. The company that Mr. McAdoo brought over here was not all a very clever set, and he treated them too good, now they are trying to villify him in lowest terms, but God is just, and Mrs. McAdoo is a fine lady. I have been transferred to the Jubilee company, and I feel as if I was in another world. I like them so much, and I have improved already. I will not return home for six months yet. We are on our way to New Zealand. Regards to friends.
Yours truly,
WILLIS F. GAUZE."
No. 338 George street, Sydney, N. S. W., Australia.

Letter from Willis Gauze, written 23 July 1900, advising the *Indianapolis Freeman* (6 October 1900) of Orpheus McAdoo's death in Australia.

Post McAdoo: End of an Era

Orpheus Myron McAdoo's passing ended an era in African American entertainment in Australasia. He was the last of the ambitious entrepreneurs, like Frederick J. Loudin, C.B. Hicks, and the infamous M.B. Curtis, who brought large troupes to the region for extended touring. African American minstrelsy and vaudeville acts would continue to arrive but no longer for such extended periods, and concentrating mainly on the major cities. No longer would small towns and regional centers enjoy the exotic sight of black minstrel bands parading through their streets and parks. The one exception to this was the Jubilee tradition, which had struck deep roots, and would continue for many more years to come, albeit with dubious authenticity in some cases. Rather than let the sporadic re-emergence of black Jubilee troupes continually interrupt this narrative, it's convenient to cover their later story in a separate combined section [for which see Appendix 3: The Later Fisk Jubilee Singers].[5]

With their leader and manager out of action and clearly doomed, the Georgia Minstrels and Alabama Cakewalkers, who had arrived with such fanfare in mid–1899, saw the proverbial writing on the wall. Having embarked on the previously postponed tour of regional NSW from May 9, they closed in the small country NSW town of Moss Vale on June 30, and departed on the SS *Alameda* on July 4, 10 days before McAdoo's passing. The passenger list included most of the original members who had not already left. After Mrs. McAdoo's departure from Tasmania to care for her husband, the Jubilee Singers had moved to Queensland and were touring regional centers there when the news of McAdoo's death reached them. Their Toowoomba engagement was disrupted, as family members Eugene McAdoo, and Mrs. McAdoo's brother Robert Allen, and sister Lula Allen traveled to Sydney to attend the funeral. Shortly thereafter, the troupe returned to complete the emotional Toowoomba engagement. They regrouped under the management of R.H. Collins, in joint proprietorship with Eugene McAdoo, and played a series of engagements in and around Sydney and down the NSW coast (Wollongong, Kiama, Nowra). They departed for New Zealand via the SS *Mararoa* on September 21, 1900, the company including Eugene McAdoo, R.H. Collins, Robert Allen, Lula Allen, Belle Gibbons, Dazalia Underwood, and Professor C.A. White. William Nott, usually a tenor performer, traveled separately and was also functioning as advance representative for the troupe. Willis Gauze (female impersonator) joined the Jubilee Singers, featured as a "male soprano."

Ill and distraught after nursing her husband through his lingering death, Mrs. McAdoo took no further part in performance down under. However, she retained connection with the Jubilee Singers for several months, joining them in New Zealand, where she was listed as lessee of the theatres they played.[6] She finally severed connection with the troupe in Dunedin. She sailed for Boston via England, with her son, Myron Holder McAdoo, departing Sydney on his eight birthday, February 9, 1901, via the P & O steamer *China*. In later years she performed again with her sister, Lula Allen, and brother, Robert Allen. Mrs. Mattie Allen McAdoo died in 1936, aged approximately 68 years.[7]

Aftermath and Stayers

We have already seen how the emergence of vaudeville circuits in Australia and New Zealand in the early 1890s made a huge difference for visiting acts. The departure of the rival McAdoo and Hogan minstrels left some flotsam and jetsam for which the vaudeville circuits offered excellent opportunities. Apart from the Jubilee Singers, who were still on tour, those staying on included Billy and Cordelia McClain; William Ferry (The Human Frog); Charles Walker and his partner, Ida May (cakewalk dancers); Joe Jalvan (juggler) with his wife, Marshall Webb. Susie Anderson, originally of the Jubilee Singers, had also decided to stay and switch to variety. Harry Rickards, always pleased to recruit talented black artists for the Tivoli, didn't pass up the opportunity to harvest this rich crop of talent. For most of their remaining time, many of the stayers would feature on his Tivoli circuit, in Sydney, Melbourne, Adelaide, Perth and other regional centers, as well as time spent by some on the affiliated NZ Dix circuit.[8]

Billy and Cordelia McClain

The McClains had already switched to the Tivoli by the time it became obvious that Orpheus McAdoo was not going to recover. They made their debut there on May 12, 1900. The *Freeman* (June 16, 1900) reported them "at present filling a six-month engagement with Harry Rickards's vaudeville company. At the end of the engagement they will return to America. Mr McClain writes that he intends to bring Peter Felix, the Australian heavyweight pugilist, over with him."

By July the McClains had been joined at the Tivoli by Charles W. Walker and partner Ida May (cakewalkers), as well as the long-established Wallace King. By September Ferry the Human Frog had also joined them. The McClains, Walker and May, and Ferry the Frog continued performing under the Rickards banner, at the Tivoli in Sydney, the Bijou in Melbourne, and the New Tivoli in Adelaide up to late 1901, when the McClains departed for New Zealand. Their New Zealand season opened on November 6 at the Alhambra Theatre on the Dix circuit in Dunedin. It was not destined to be a long one. The December 4 *Otago Witness* reported:

> Mr Billy McClain and Madame Cordelia … departed [the Alhambra] theatre suddenly, never to return. Trouble arose on Friday night when Mr Dix's local manager asked Mr McClain to occupy a seat on the corner in the Alhambra first part. Mr McClain refused, said he was not engaged as an end-man, but as a specialty turn for the second part … on being threatened with the loss of four nights' salary, [McClain] consented to break his rule until matters might be satisfactorily arranged. Saturday arrived…. Throughout the whole evening he worked exceedingly hard…. Mr McClain received his full week's salary. The same day [he] removed his boxes from the Alhambra. Monday evening, no appearance of Mr McClain or Madame Cordelia. Next day they were gone, having departed for the north by the Mararoa.

A short while later, the *New York Clipper* reported, "BILLY MCCLAIN AND MADAME CORDELIA opened at the Orpheum, Honolulu last month, having just come from Australia. Their success was most emphatic, newspaper comment on their work being glowing in its praise." Billy McClain had a long and prosperous career as a performer, composer, show business and boxing promoter, even, as he told Tom Fletcher, qualifying as an osteopath.[9] He died accidentally in a fire while sleeping in a trailer in 1950, aged 84.

William Ferry (the Human Frog)

Having shared the Tivoli circuit in Sydney, Melbourne, and Adelaide with several of his erstwhile McAdoo vaudeville companions until late 1900, the Frog had "hopped the ditch" to New Zealand in January 1901, ahead of the McClains. His debut in Auckland delighted the critic for the January 22 *Auckland Star*:

> The stage was artistically arranged, so as to present the appearance of the frog's favourite abode, a leafy dell with a stagnant pool. After a bird in the boughs of the tree above had twittered sweetly, the harsh croak of the frog was heard and Ferry, got up in excellent style, hopped lightly before the footlights. Froggy then went through some marvellous acrobatic feats, which appeared to defy the usual rules of anatomy as to the way the joints of ordinary individuals work.

Ferry continued touring New Zealand successfully until November 1901. He was sharing the Alhambra bill with the McClains when they did their vanishing act. It may have been this that precipitated his departure to Hobart. Back in Australia he toured Tasmanian regional centers on the Tivoli circuit until March 1902. He then toured regional NSW and Vic centers at small theatres under his own billing during March to mid–June. On May 2, 1902, the Benalla *North Eastern Ensign* reported he was running a Wild West show, with a cousin of Ned Kelly (T. Lloyd) as a rough-rider. By mid–June he had run out of options and advertised his act as being "open for engagement after 14 June."

By October 1902 Ferry was again touring small centers with a variety of troupes, including Fitzgerald Brothers Circus and Menagerie, and later with a small-time white American vaudeville troupe, the American Globetrotters. While playing a few more months in small NSW towns, the *Queanbeyan Age* (February 11, 1903) noted sympathetically: "Ferry, wherever he goes deserves success, and no doubt would do much better were he with a bigger company and not ruthlessly squandering his time travelling through small towns." By early April the Sydney *Sunday Times* reported, under the headline "THE FROG JUMPS," that Ferry had left for a tour of China, Japan, and India. Although his illustrious Australasian sojourn had ended "not with a bang but a whimper," or perhaps a croak, it was not the last the region would see of the Human Frog. He was back in 1920, successfully touring Australia and New Zealand, and again in 1945, eliciting positive reviews but also amazement at the very idea of a 78-year-old contortionist.[10]

Joe Jalvan and Marshall Webb

After leaving the Jubilee Singers and New Zealand, Jalvan advertised the services of the pair in the Australian media in July 1899. They played local engagements around Melbourne, and for a brief period during October–November 1899, they toured regional Vic towns, Warragul, Traralgon, Maffra, and Sale as part of troupe known as "Chillie and Jalvan's Jubilee Entertainers and Cakewalkers." The troupe was described by the *Warragul Guardian* (October 13, 1899) as "an arrangement in black and white, some members being of fair complexion." Apart from the Jalvans themselves, the only member identifiable as African American was Bertha Miller, billed as "Black Melba." She is the same Bertha Miller (also known as Bertha Haynes-Miller) who shows up, again as Black Melba, with the later Fisk Singers troupe in 1910. During her time with that troupe it was mentioned by the *Age*, on March 19, 1917, that although she was clearly black she had been born in Melbourne.

The Chillie and Jalvan troupe did not last long. Their final November date at the Mechanics Institute in Sunbury, though declared an artistic success by the local media, was unfortunately a financial disaster. Jalvan and Marshall Webb were soon back again playing concert engagements for local clubs and societies around Melbourne until about September

1900. By April 1900 Marshall Webb was being billed simply as Madame Jalvan, assisting her husband. Things looked up when they joined the Tivoli circuit, at Rickards's Melbourne Bijou Theatre, in October 1900. Although Jalvan's African American ancestry was well authenticated, publicity handouts often described him as oriental, Egyptian, or even Japanese. The new Tivoli season wholeheartedly embraced this approach, billing him as an "Oriental wonder worker, trick juggler and conjurer," assisted by "Stri Webb, Tokey Jarra," the name by which Marshall Webb would be known for most of the rest of her time in Australia, presumably to foster the oriental illusion. They continued playing the Melbourne, Sydney, and Adelaide Tivoli circuits, sharing or alternating with the McClains, Walker and May, and Wallace King, until April 1901. By 1903 the Jalvans were reported in a successful act in London. They were still working together in England in 1905; and Jalvan was still performing in 1929.[11]

Susie Anderson (The Black Melba)

Susie Anderson had arrived in mid–1898 with McAdoo's Jubilee Singers, billed as the Black, or sometimes Bronze, Melba. Following McAdoo's death, she made her debut at the Sydney Tivoli on November 17, 1900, on the same bill as Ferry the Frog, in "positively" his last week in Sydney. Christmas 1900 saw Susie on the bill at Rickards's Melbourne Bijou Theatre along with Charles Pope and Irving Sayles. By mid–January 1901 all three were at the Adelaide Tivoli, replacing the McClains, and Walker and May. By February they had been joined by Jalvan and Wallace King, on a bill that was almost 50 percent African American. By March, Susie Anderson was the last of these remaining, but was reunited with Charles Walker and Ida May in April, until she left Adelaide in early May for a trip home to America. Susie Anderson was back with the Jubilee Singers in Christchurch at the Theatre Royal on August 16, 1901. She played the NZ circuit with them until early October, after which they toured Tas until mid–December, followed by a tour of regional Vic.

She was reported in the *Newsletter* (May 3, 1902) as having "lately obtained a verdict for £60, salary due, in a suit against the McAdoo Jubilee Singers management." She sailed on the liner *Sierra* for San Francisco on May 13, 1902. In July, the New York *Clipper* reported her back in her home town of Springfield, Illinois.

Charles Walker and Ida May

Charles (C.W.) Walker and his wife, Ida May, had arrived with McAdoo's Georgia Minstrels at the start in June 1899 on the SS *Moana*. They were billed together as "America's Gold Medal Champion Cakewalkers."[12] In the aftermath of McAdoo's death, they joined the Tivoli circuit, appearing on the same bill as the McClains and Ferry the Frog in late July 1900. They continued to play the Tivoli circuit, in Sydney, Melbourne (Bijou Theatre and New Opera House) and Adelaide (New Tivoli) until March 1902. Apart from the Cakewalk, they were variously billed as coon singers, comedians. and—along with Billy and Cordelia McClain—as the Four American Minstrels, "who not only contribute their individual turn but conclude the part with a cakewalk."

In a typical Tivoli pattern, the *Southern Argus* (January 17, 1901) reported:

The Adelaide season of Messrs W McClain, Charles W Walker, Madame Cordelia, and Miss Ida May will terminate on Thursday evening, and on Saturday evening Messrs Pope and Sayles, the popular favorites, will make their reappearance at the Tivoli. They are sure to meet with a most enthusiastic welcome. Saturday will also witness the first appearance at the Tivoli of Miss Susie Anderson, professionally known as the "Black Melba."

Miss Ida May and Mr. Charles Walker. The Clever Cakewalking Double at the Tivoli Theatre. *Quiz* (Adelaide), 3 July 1901, page 15. Courtesy *Trove*, National Library of Australia.

In August 1901, Walker and May were on the same Tivoli bill as the legendary British Music Hall star Marie Lloyd, famous for classic tunes like "My Old Man Said Follow the Van." March 1902 saw them on the opening bill for Harry Rickards's take-over of Brisbane's Theatre Royal. They remained there until they departed on the *Westralia* for New Zealand on April 26.

Charles Walker and Ida May, billed as "America's champion gold medal cakewalkers and specialty artists," were the only African Americans on the bill. The tour included Napier, Hastings, Auckland, New Plymouth, Wanganui, Palmerston North, Masterton, Wellington, and Christchurch, finishing in Dunedin on July 2. Having proved highly popular at all NZ venues, the package moved on to Tas, to open at Hobart's Theatre Royal on July 10, 1902, and later in Launceston.

After returning to Sydney and the Tivoli during August and September, Walker and May spent four months in Perth and regional WA, until February 1903. Back in Melbourne, they played the Opera House until July 3, 1903, sharing the bill at one stage with an "eccentric American juggler," one W.C. Fields. On conclusion of the Opera House engagement they departed for England, the last of that round of stayovers to depart.

There was a sad irony to their successful sojourn in Australia. By the time they left, Charles had gone totally blind through atrophy of the optic nerve. Despite the immense handicap this must have been for a dancer, he managed to continue his stage career. For 18 months in England he successfully concealed his handicap from theatre managers. Using aural information from the position of the orchestra instruments, and whispered comments from his wife, he was able to dance, sing, and tell jokes. The pair was still performing successfully in England in 1908.

11

Eva Taylor (Irene Gibbons)
and Josephine Gassman

Following the gradual fade-out of the performers leftover from the McAdoo-Curtis troupe, the next arrival was very much in the new vaudeville trend. The July 20, 1901, *Evening News* reported that the American All-Star Vaudeville company would make its first appearance about the beginning of August at the Sydney Palace Theatre. The lessee and manager of the Palace was American-born J.C. Williamson, Australia's leading theatre manager and founder of Australia's largest theatrical empire.[1] The predominantly white all-star bill included "Josephine Gassman and her Louisiana Pickaninnies."[2] The *SMH* reported the arrival on the liner *Sierra* of "Miss Josephine Gassman, maid and 2 picaninnies." The picaninnies, colloquially referred to as "picks," were a female, Irene Gibbons, and a male, Bill Bailey. Irene is better known today by her professional name of later years, Eva Taylor, the great jazz singer and wife of jazz pianist, composer and publisher Clarence Williams.

The term "picks" needs some explanation. Earlier reference to Major Clark Smith's Pickaninny Band was a generic reference to the fact that the band's members were young black musicians, aged around 16 to 20 years. The newly arrived "pickaninnies" or "picks" were part of a tradition associated mainly with prominent white female performers, who gave their act extra zip by including young black kids. Tom Fletcher, who lived through the era, wrote:

> In the early days, women in show business, both white and colored, would often put young colored children into their specialty acts. This was when ragtime coon songs and cake-walking were the rage.... The billing was generally "Miss (whoever it was) and Her Picaninnies." The kids didn't just supply the atmosphere but were clever performers. The activity gave them a chance both to get rid of their extra energy and to further their ambitions as well as be a help to their parents. The youngsters were well cared for, being kept well-dressed both in the theater and outside.[3]

Some of the famous white stars who used "picks" included Sophie Tucker, Nora Bayes, Blossom Seeley, and Bonita (Pauline Hall). Black performers who used picks included Belle Davis and Mabel Whitman. Probably the earliest to adopt the practice was the white French-born performer Mayme Remington in 1893. The troupe of picks she put together for the mixed black-white show, *The South Before the War*, included the famous Bill "Bojangles" Robinson and other notables. Another who got early experience as a pick was the great Florence Mills, as part of "Bonita and her Picks."[4]

Josephine Gassman was using picks as early as 1897. She had originally trained as an opera singer but, as related by Eva Taylor, had "ruined her voice by attempting to sing too soon after an operation." Describing how she came to be recruited by Gassman for her act,

Eva said, "My father had died when I was aged fifteen months and my mother had a hard time providing for us, so when Miss Josephine asked if I could join her act my mother let me go."[5]

Gassman must have recognized some latent talent in Irene, even at that early age. Born January 22, 1895, by the time she came to Australia, Irene (Eva Taylor) was five and a half years old. Her fellow pick, Bill, was the younger of the two, aged four. Describing the experience of traveling as a performer in racist America, Eva recalled:

> Whenever possible we used to stay with a family rather than book at a hotel … some of those families were very nice and we used to look forward very much to seeing them … but others weren't so nice. At the end of the season Miss Josephine used to take us to see our mothers—she never allowed them to visit us—I suppose she worried in case we got upset.[6]

Josephine Gassman was born in San Francisco around 1877. She played child parts in the theatre until she was about 15 years of age, including in *Hans the Boatman* around 1889, a play that had already been popular in Australia.[7] After that she played soubrette parts with several companies touring the Pacific Coast. She received lessons in singing from May Yohé, a singer popular in America and England in musical-comedy and operetta.

Though Josephine Gassman was white, she performed as a "coon shouter" in blackface make-up. This led many of her Australasian audience, including theatre reviewers, to believe she was black. As the New Zealand *Otago Witness* (May 20, 1902) put it:

MISS JOSEPHINE GASSMAN AND HER PICANINNIES.

Miss Josephine Gassman and her "picaninnies." Irene (Eva) at front kneeling. Published in *The Australasian*, 30 November 1901. Courtesy Trove, National Library of Australia.

> Not generally known that Miss Josephine Gassman, the talented coon warbler of the present World's Entertainers Company … is a white woman. The popular belief is that Miss Gassman, by reason of her copper-coloured skin, is a quadroon, an octoroon, or a 'roon' of some description and this belief is further given effect to by the appearance of her two little Louisiana picaninnies, Bill and Irene.

The deception was due to a special preparation of brown greasepaint, applied so artistically and delicately that its presence was difficult to detect even standing close beside her. In the latter part of her Australian tour she had become more open about her color, the January 25, 1902, *Australian Town & Country Journal* noting, "Miss Josephine Gassman has relinquished the use of the wonderful staining preparation, and now shows her own fair, clear skin on face, neck, and arms," though apparently not in New Zealand.

The American All Star Vaudeville company, generally billed as "The World's Entertainers," opened their season at the Palace on August 10, 1901. Next day, the tabloid *Truth* commented:

The Palace Theatre has certainly never seen so large and so enthusiastic an audience as that which welcomed The World's Entertainers last night…. A clever, bright, well-dressed variety entertainment without a single dull moment was presented. Every item was excellent, but since Truth can't reprint the whole programme, it gives pride of place to Henry Lee with his impersonations and Miss Josephine Gassman with her picaninnies. These latter brought down the house with laughter and wild cheering.

The success of the company at large, and Josephine Gassman and her Picaninnies in particular, was reflected throughout the Palace season. Sydney audiences took the little kids to their heart, thoroughly enjoying their spontaneous antics. It must be said, however, that the act reflected the stereotypical "coon" antics that typified minstrelsy humor at the time, parodying African Americans, including clichés like chickens, watermelons, and google-eyes:

The two little black coons, who made their entrance on the stage struggling with a white rooster of apparently robust proclivities, convulsed the house for some minutes. The diminutive pair did some 'tumbling' on their own account, and the 'goo-goo' eyes made by Irene were responsible for fresh outbursts of laughter.[8]

Audiences responded enthusiastically to the spontaneous antics of the kids. Such apparent spontaneity was expected of picks, but in this case, given the youth of the pair, it was probably genuine. The racism reflected in Australian audiences' enjoyment of such stereotypical material was generally of a more benign variety than would have been true in America. The August 27 *Evening News* ventured behind the scenes at the Palace:

THE PICANINNIES.

Down a winding stair that suffers from so many severe twists that it is like walking round a large corkscrew which comes to a point suddenly and lands you on your feet with a sudden jerk in Miss Gassman's dressing-room. Irene, the biggest pickaninny, had retired into strict seclusion on the floor, and rolled her eyes and hugged her knees as she sat in front of a big glass, with the air of a young colored lady who knows her worth. Not so Bill, who wore white muslin skirts and a smart hat. Bill was standing on a chair, trying the effect of a pink rose colored bangle on his small black arm.

The Palace season ended on October 30 after a season of eight weeks. The troupe then went on extended tour. While the acts comprising the whole variety show varied over the rest of the time in Australia, Josephine Gassman and her Picks continued to be a major feature on the traveling bill, drawing large audiences everywhere. They played two weeks in Adelaide's Theatre Royal during November, six weeks in Melbourne at the Bijou Theatre over December 1901 to February 1902, and another week in Sydney in March 1902. Then, after visiting regional centers in Goulburn and Wagga Wagga (NSW), Geelong and

Josephine Gassman's "picaninnies," Irene and Bill. *Punch* (Melbourne), 19 December 1901. Courtesy *Trove*, National Library of Australia.

Albury (Vic), they spent March–April in Brisbane and regional Queensland (Charters Towers, Mackay, Toowoomba). They finished their Australian trip at Newcastle's Victoria Theatre in early May, before departing to New Zealand on the SS *Waihora*.

Josephine and Picks in New Zealand 1902

The World's Entertainers troupe opened in New Zealand's Dunedin Princess Theatre on May 10, 1902. The reaction was as enthusiastic as it had been in Australia, the May 14 *Otago Times* commenting: "The World's Entertainers made so good an impression on Monday evening, their opening night, that it was not surprising to see a crowded audience at the theatre last evening on the occasion of the company's second performance. Without doubt the Entertainers form the strongest combination that has ever visited the city."

There was generous praise for Josephine Gassman's singing ("a plump and comely coon singer with a strong contralto voice"), but it was the picks' supporting performance that again elicited audience response, the June 17 *NZ Herald* noting: "Her little picaninnies 'come on' just at the right moment to knock her sentimental songs into shrieks of laughter. For instance, when Josephine, at the footlights, is melodiously informing you they're in their beauty sleep, watched over by the angels, a scene shifts and displays them fighting in bed."

After a week in Dunedin the troupe went on tour, visiting Timaru, Christchurch, Wellington (one week), Hastings, Masterton, Feilding, Wanganui, and New Plymouth. They finished with a week at the Opera House, Auckland, from July 1 to 8, after which it was reported, "The World's Entertainers N.Z. touring company was disbanded in Auckland at the conclusion of the Maoriland season. The majority of them returned to America, Miss Josephine Gassman amongst the number."

Josephine and Her Picks Return in 1914

Twelve years after their original successful tour, Josephine and her now more mature picks returned to the scene of their earlier triumphs. It seems logical to follow the troupe's later adventures here rather than in strict chronological sequence. In the intervening years, after their earlier visit, they continued to tour widely. Apart from U.S. circuits their itinerary included London, Paris, Magdeburg, Frankfurt, Hanover, and Berlin. Eva Taylor recalled:

> In the States we used to play a season, usually working from New York down to California and then back through most of the Southern states. We had an [East Indian] lady who came along to teach us and take care of us … and you know there were some towns in the South where they wouldn't even let Negroes in, so whenever we were walking down the street and we passed someone we used to talk a lot of mumbo-jumbo so they would think we were Indians.[9]

The first indication of their return came in the form of advertisements for a new show at the National Amphitheatre, starting on March 5, 1914. The National Amphitheatre was the Sydney home of the Brennan-Fuller vaudeville circuit, and was situated close to the rival Tivoli. The artists for the show had arrived on the RMS *Ventura* from San Francisco on Monday, March 2.

This time Josephine was advertised as having "four picaninnies," including her original pair, Irene and Bill. That they were still with her is something of an anomaly. "The tenure of work as a pick, because of age and size requirements, was limited. After a job as a pick with a famous star, a youngster had the difficult adjustment to make when they grew too large and were no longer 'cute' enough for the job."[10] Assuming the four must all be new, the *Newsletter* (March 14, 1914) commented: "Her picaninnies are seemingly a new tribe, but picaninnies cannot be pickled like eggs, and retained for future use through a decade of time."

Josephine resolved the problem by having the younger picks (both female, the elder named Mabel Brown and the youngest Kathleen) in the traditional cute role, with Irene and Bill offering a more sophisticated element. Josephine described them as "trained on the imperial Russian dancing system, in addition to the coon business." The *Courier*, on April 6, 1914, described their act:

> Opening with a song by Miss Gassman, the performance was continued by each member of the company in turn.[11] A young coloured lady [Irene], garbed in a man's evening dress, sang sweetly, and this was followed by a dance by another pickaninny [Mabel]. A boy [Bill], perhaps 15 years of age, next made his appearance, dressed as a fashionable lady, and his manner of singing, together with his assumed facial expression and method of moving his eyes, had the spectators in roars of laughter…. Still the audience clamoured for more, and it was then that the fifth artist—a child of about four years of age [Little Kathleen, also known as "Only Me"]—made an appearance. The little one came forward, and sang a love song. The humour of it so appealed to the audience that they applauded continuously for several minutes.

Another reviewer said of the "old" picks, "Now they are capable comedians spontaneously making their fun, dancing neatly, and agilely, and wearing their evening or fantastic dress with the assurance of old professionals." And, continuing on: "Then the picaninny Irene whose voice is singularly clear and sweet, chants a little love song to the infinite pleasure of her hearers."[12] Shades of the future great jazz singer! Whereas the Gassman Picks had been the only African Americans on the 1901 bill, the new Amphitheatre bill included one "William Sumner, The Black Caruso, America's Foremost Negro Tenor."

Sumner is a mystery man. While this clearly identifies him as African American, and it's unlikely he would have a key role on the Fuller circuit without significant credentials, no previous trace of him can be found before he came to Australasia in 1914.[13] After the opening season with Josephine Gassman, he played independently over the Brennan-Fuller circuit, in New Zealand during April/May, then in Adelaide, WA, Melbourne, and Sydney up to the end of 1914. He was back in New Zealand by March 1915. He probably settled there for an extended period as he was listed on Brennan-Fuller bills in 1917 and in 1920, performing in one instance with Hamilton Hodges.

For Josephine and her Picks, the opening Sydney

Little Kathleen, the smallest picaninny, featured on poster for "Only Me," *Brunswick and Coburg Leader* (Victoria), 24 July 1914. Courtesy *Trove*, National Library of Australia.

season lasted four weeks. This was followed by three weeks at the Empire Theatre in Brisbane, eliciting the following summary from the April 13 *Telegraph*: "There is the sweet and tender singing of the two girls, the inimitable facial contortion work of the boy Bill Bailey, the all-round dancing (both graceful and eccentric) of these three children, and then the highly successful efforts of 'the infant' [Little Kathleen]."

This was the forerunner of a hop across the Tasman Sea to New Zealand, opening at the Auckland Opera House on May 4. The New Zealand trip spanned from early May to mid-June, taking in Auckland, Wellington, Christchurch, and Dunedin. The audience reaction was as enthusiastic as in Australia, summed up by the *NZ Herald* (May 5, 1914) review of the Auckland opening: "Miss Gassman's imitations of a negro woman singing ragtime were, to say the least of them, novel, and met with a great reception, but the comic singing and extremely clever eccentric dancing of the picaninnies took the large audience by storm."

The reviewer in Wellington was impressed by the opulence of the costumes worn by the members, noting that they were created by leading Paris fashion couturier Redfern and Worth.[14] Whether the picks appreciated the style they were decked out in is unknown, but Irene had a distinct memory, many years later, of the food: "Travel in Australia in those days was very hard and I didn't like it at all. We also visited Tasmania and New Zealand, where I remember the hotels were particularly bad and they seemed to live on potatoes and greens which were cooked to be absolutely tasteless."[15]

The return from New Zealand gave Melbourne its first chance of seeing the new Gassman act. They opened in late June at the Bijou Theatre, which would have been familiar to them from the last visit but was now a Brennan-Fuller vaudeville house instead of on the Tivoli circuit. As in Wellington, the finery of the picks' costumes excited interest from the fashion enthusiasts, the July 11 *Table Talk* noting: "The one which suggests the latest modistic ideas is the red velvet worn by the coon Billy when he impersonates a fashionable dame. It is carried out in rather crude coloring, red and gold, but the line is the latest correct thing, for it is a copy of a Paris model, and has the full pannier drapery about the hips."

After two weeks in Melbourne the show moved to Bendigo (Vic) for a week, and then to the Empire Theatre at suburban Brunswick on July 25, where it was promised, "Every child attending the matinee will receive a photo of little Baby Kathleen." During this booking Australia joined the Great War, on July 28, 1914, initiating a wave of patriotic sentiment.

Following some engagements around Melbourne suburbs, the King's Theatre, Adelaide, was next on their itinerary, opening on August 27. Already patriotism was making itself felt, as the media reported the Germans threatening to overrun Paris. A patriotic concert was held at Adelaide's Theatre Royal on September 4, with Josephine and her Picks included in the "galaxy of theatrical talent."

The same story applied in Perth, where they opened at the Melrose Theatre on September 26. Even before their show had opened the Perth *Daily News* (September 25, 1914) reported that "the Brennan-Fuller artists now appearing at the Melrose Theatre, including Miss Josephine Gassman and her Picaninnies, held a street parade and collection in aid of the Patriotic Fund."

After two successful weeks in Perth, Josephine and the Picks reappeared back east for a season in Newcastle, followed by Sydney and Melbourne until late December, when they embarked on a new venture: a Christmas pantomime at the Adelphi Theatre in Sydney. The lavishly produced pantomime was *Babes in the Wood* and the advertisements announced that the part of Principal Girl, Maid Marian, would be filled by the internationally sensational Daisy Jerome.

When Daisy Jerome landed in Adelaide in 1913 she was dripping with jewels and carried a scent of the scandalous. The American born, but English raised, comedienne was a small woman with a wiry frame topped with a carroty mop of red hair. She had a sparkling and wicked sense of humour and a vibrant manner…. The contrast between her delicate ladylike frame and the raucous vulgarity of her comic songs shocked audiences.[16]

Probably the best-known song associated with Daisy Jerome today is the James Monaco, William Jerome (no relative) "Row, Row, Row" (with its well-known chorus "And then he'd row, row, row, Way up the river he would row, row, row").

Early advertising for the pantomime billed Irene Gibbons, under her own name, singing "The Curse of an Aching Heart." However, nearly 50 years later, it was sharing a bill with Daisy Jerome that took pride of place in Irene's (Eva's) memories of Australia.[17] The reviewer for the December 24, 1914, *SMH* enthused over Daisy Jerome's "magnetic personality, and almost uncanny charm," while commenting also, "Another success was that of Josephine Gassman and her pickaninnies, with their wonderful coon-dancing." Inevitably, the patriotic note was sounded: "The entertainment closed brilliantly with 'The March of the Allies,' in which groups of girls descended a grand staircase in uniform to the national anthem of the various nations concerned."

The vaudeville performance, masquerading as pantomime, was mainly a vehicle for Daisy Jerome. Josephine and her Picks were really an add-on but as the plot-line was very flimsy it didn't matter. The Sydney season ended in early February but it was to be their meal ticket for the next three months as they toured with Daisy, through Newcastle, Brisbane, and regional Queensland (Maryborough, Rockhampton, Toowoomba) before opening a New Zealand season at Ashburton on March 25, 1915. Despite Christmas being long gone, the pantomime rolled on through NZ centers until they closed in Auckland on 15 May.[18] As in Australia, the background of war was evident, with the plight of Belgium foremost, as noted by NZ *Press* on April 16, 1915: "The Willoughby Pantomime Company have things well in hand for today's demonstration and procession in aid of the Belgium Fund…. The lorries, which have been lent by Brightlings, are to be decorated with Belgian colours and flags."

The advertised entertainment included Little Kathleen, now billed as the "Wonder Child," singing "Tipperary." Further evidence of the war influence came with the report that the ship on which the troupe sailed back to Australia, the SS *Maheno*, had been commandeered on arrival at Sydney to become New Zealand's official hospital ship, "primarily intended for the conveyance of wounded New Zealanders from the front to the base hospitals."[19]

With the pantomime season gone, Josephine Gassman and Picks were back at the Sydney National Amphitheatre on May 30, still with Daisy Jerome, on a new conventional vaudeville bill. During June and July, they were in Brisbane, Rockhampton, and Charters Towers, where the July 15 *Northern Miner* reported:

On Thursday night every person attending will receive a beautiful souvenir of Miss Josephine Gassman and her Picaninnies. This souvenir is most elaborate and is really worth having, being in the form of a Paris panel photograph of the whole troupe, artistically engraved in gold with the name and date of the Olympia, Charters Towers, on the cover.

In August they were back at the familiar Melbourne Bijou (including a carnival for wounded soldiers), followed by Ballarat, and then Adelaide in September. Again, patriotic activities featured in Adelaide, with a French Flag Day concert. One wonders if Josephine noticed that *Hans the Boatman*, in which she got her juvenile start, was playing at Port Adelaide Town Hall.

The finale to their venture came when, still with Daisy Jerome, they traveled to Tasmania, opening in Hobart on September 25. The Hobart *Mercury*, describing it as "one of the most powerful vaudeville combinations that has ever visited Tasmania," also commented that one of the highlights was Little Kathleen's impersonation of Daisy Jerome. After a final season at Launceston, leaving Daisy to finish the Tasmanian season, the "Gassman Family" (so listed) departed on the SS *Loongana*, back to the mainland, en route home to the U.S. They traveled to San Francisco on the SS *Sonoma*, departing Sydney on October 23. Josephine and her husband traveled under their married names, Mr. and Mrs. Sullivan, Bill Bailey under his own name, while the three female picks were all listed under Gibbons, with Katherine, "Little Me" as "Baby Gibbons."

Shortly afterwards, the November 6 *West Australian* reported that "Miss Josephine Gassman, who has been managing the picaninny act, which has been appearing in Australia, has decided to retire from vaudeville at the conclusion of her present contract." Despite this, Josephine, under the name "Phina and her Picks," continued performing back in the U.S., appearing regularly at the Palace Theatre and still active in 1923. As late as February 1920, she still had the same four Picks, "Irene Gibbons, Mabel Brown, Bill Bailey and Little Kathleen" (*Duluth Herald*, February 21, 1920).

Irene's (Eva's) Later Career

Around 1921, Irene Gibbons became too old for pick work and adopted the name Eva Taylor. The name was a combination of the surname of a New York Irish family who had been good to her, and her sister's name. She met pianist/composer/publisher Clarence Williams and they were married in New York on November 8, 1921.[20] Sometime in 1922 her skills as a dancer and singer gained her a place in the successful all-black show *Shuffle Along*, where she got to perform with her idol, the show's sensational star Florence Mills. Around August/September, Eva started the prolific recording career that would make her a jazz legend, initially with the historic Black Swan label, and later the OKeh label. Her 1923 recording, with Louis Armstrong and Sydney Bechet, of the Florence Mills theme song "I'm a Little Blackbird Looking for a Bluebird" became an iconic jazz record. She continued performing into her eighties until she died in 1977.[21]

12

This Sporting Life:
Major Taylor

The intense interest the African American visitors had in sport has already been seen, whether their own baseball, or trying out the unfamiliar Australian cricket, or Irving Sayles's successes at sprint running (pedestrianism, as the media of the day called it). There was also Billy McClain's interest in promoting boxing. The bare-knuckle pugilistic career of Black Perry has been covered (Chapter 1), and African American boxers would soon emerge as a major focus of interest in the Australasian sporting world. In 1903, however, a different form of athleticism brought African American sporting prowess to the attention of the local public, namely cycling. An African American, Marshall W. "Major" Taylor, dubbed "The fastest bicycle rider in the world" grabbed the imaginations of sporting Australians in 1903 and 1904.[1]

In the opening years of the 20th century just about everyone owned and used a bike. Around the world, big professional sport as we know it today did not exist—no tennis, golf or motor racing. Cycling was far and away the largest professional sport worldwide. Within a decade, the motor car and the motorcycle would surpass it but they were still in their infancy in 1903. Australian crowds flocked in huge numbers—30,000 plus—to venues like the Sydney Cricket Ground, to watch cycle races on dedicated cycling tracks, with sophisticated lighting systems for night viewing. The sport was managed in Sydney by the NSW League of Wheelmen.

As always, when big money and gambling interests are involved, there were murky sides to the administration of cycling in Australia. In the thick of it was a flamboyant personality, Hugh D. McIntosh, who will loom large in further episodes of our tale.[2] Hugh Donald McIntosh was born September 10, 1876, in a massive storm that battered Sydney. His father, a policeman, died when Hugh was four years old. The youngster was making his own way in the world by the time he was nine, at a variety of odd jobs. Along the way he dabbled in boxing (trained by the famous Larry Foley), cycling and theatrics, with only modest success in each. His experiences soon convinced him that it was more profitable to be on the promoting rather than the practicing side.

McIntosh was a natural born entrepreneur, with immense self-confidence, earning him the nickname "Huge Deal." In parallel with his quintessentially Australian catering business—selling meat pies at public venues—he pursued an executive role in the cycling world. His first role was as council member, then assistant secretary, and by 1903 general secretary of the League of Wheelmen, giving him effective control of the Sydney-centered League. He was the right man for the job. At the time a combination of discontent from regional groups over Sydney dominance, and disillusionment among followers over the dubious tactics of competitors colluding to share prize funds, was causing declining public support.

McIntosh's solution was to inject a surprise element that would stimulate interest—import the black American World Champion sprint cyclist Major Taylor! Suddenly the cycling public was agog with excitement. The cycling news, always prominent in the Sports section of the media, now appeared in the News section, with daily reports of when, and if, Taylor would arrive.

Marshall Walter Taylor was born in Indianapolis on November 26, 1878. Showing early talent at cycling, he was sponsored by a local bicycle store. His publicity stunts for the store, wearing military-style uniform, earned him the nickname "Major," which stayed with him. Major Taylor was the world champion in sprint cycling at the time of his visit to Australia, having won the World Professional one-mile Championship in Montreal in 1899, and also set world record times for distance. He had been the three-time professional cycling champion of the U.S. The most remarkable thing about his achievements was that he was the lone black competitor in his field. Although his career had been supported by generous white sponsors and mentors, and he was highly popular with the crowds for his sportsmanship, he had faced nasty spoiling tactics by racist white rivals. These included dubious practices like "pocketing" (i.e., boxing a competitor in so he couldn't make a break from the group) and even physical violence.

By the time McIntosh's representatives approached Taylor for a possible Australian visit he was deeply disillusioned by the vicious opposition he could expect to continue facing in the U.S. He believed this would deny him any fair chance to win the national championship again. Apart from being away from the racist U.S., Australia was attractive for several reasons. Being in the Southern Hemisphere, it allowed him to compete in both the European and Australian Summer seasons. Another carrot was the chance to compete in the recently announced international Sydney Thousand, the world's richest cycle race. Finally, unlike Europe and America, it was not common practice in Australia to run races on Sundays, which had cost Taylor a lot of prize money due to his strict Sabbath Day observance that was part of his Christian principles. He signed up to compete in the summer season of 1903, on attractive terms that guaranteed him £1,500 for 16 appearances, plus whatever prize money he could win.

In November 1902, Taylor and his wife, Daisy, embarked on the SS *Ventura* from San Francisco, effectively a belated honeymoon trip. They arrived in Sydney on December 22. En route he had been alarmed by reports that the White Australia policy, recently in effect, might subject him and Daisy to the same humiliations they had experienced at home.[3] His fears were soon dispelled when the ship was welcomed into a thronged Sydney Harbour by enthusiastic Taylor fans waving U.S.

Portrait of Major Taylor from the frontispiece of his autobiography *The Fastest Bicycle Rider in the World.*

flags. The effect was further confirmed when the pair was afforded a mayoral civic reception.

1903: Sydney

From the outset Major Taylor made a good impression on cycling fans and the general public. He was admired for his open, friendly manner, and willingness to train with his Australian rivals and share tips with them. The January 3, 1903, *Newsletter* commented: "There are some very pleasant impressions going about Sydney re Major Taylor, who seems to be a kindly-hearted all-round intelligent fellow that everyone truly likes…. His manners are most gracious, simple, and dignified, and make one realise the title, 'A gentleman of colour' forcibly."

There was some surprise at his stature, being of only moderate height, but superbly conditioned from years of specialist training. His teetotalism, non-smoking policy, and his advocacy of a clean Christian lifestyle endeared him to many but earned him a "wowser" tag in some quarters, notably the racier parts of the media like *Truth* and *The Bulletin*.[4] His general popularity discouraged these from open racism in their comments but *Truth*, on January 18, 1903, betrayed its true colors in its caricature depiction.

Despite suffering severe seasickness on the voyage, Taylor quickly got into training to offset the effects of several months layoff since the European season. Large crowds turned up to watch his training sessions and were surprised at his dedication. A feature of the Australian cycling scene that would present problems for Taylor was the Australian preference for Handicap events rather than the Scratch races favored in U.S. and Europe. In Taylor's view, handicap races were for second- and third-class riders who couldn't face direct competition, and they could create big problems for back markers like him.

Taylor's Australian venture started on January 3, 1903, at the Sydney Cricket Ground, day one of a three-day series popularly named the "Major Taylor Carnival." Coincidentally, the *SMH* announcement of his appearance was juxtaposed with an ad for the latest Fisk Jubilee Singers.

Taylor's most serious contender was the Australian

Top: Major Taylor, the champion track cyclist of America, from his autobiography. *Bottom:* Caricature of Major Taylor from *Truth,* 11 January 1903. Courtesy *Trove* National Library of Australia.

MA-JAW TAYLOR.

champion Don Walker. The two men were on good terms from the outset, even training together. While excited at seeing a world champion, the Australian fans were hoping to see their local champ hold his own against the invader. The main event on day one was the Quarter Mile International Championship. The fans got their money's worth. Just when it looked like Bob Lewis, former Australian mile record holder, was going to win the race, Taylor executed the dramatic "jump" for which he was famous, shooting past the post to wild cheering.

> When the time comes for him to move he fairly shakes up his wheel, lifts it along through the air, as it were, and jumps past his competitors. Taylor applied so much power that he sometimes lost momentary traction with his rear wheel. The net effect, as Lewis commented afterward, was that "suddenly something flashed past me. Then I gave up thinking I could win."[5]

Don Walker sneaked past the dumbfounded Lewis into second place. Walker had other successes on the program, including a Five Mile handicap, in which a game but not yet fully fit Taylor finished a close fourth. Nevertheless, Taylor had done enough to convince the spectators of his world-class status.

Over the following nights of the carnival, Taylor continued to notch up impressive wins. There was, however, a minor sensation on January 17, when W. McDonald, from WA, eliminated him in a heat of the League Cup Mile Scratch race, with Walker eventually winning the final. This led to a hint of a possibility that the Australians might, after all, be good enough to beat Taylor. McIntosh and the League exploited this hope by organizing a special event for the final night of the carnival, prompting the *SMH* (January 19, 1903) to write: "The question [as to] whether Major Taylor can defeat the best Australian sprinters is still rather undecided, and the League officials have decided to conduct a test scratch mile tournament on the concluding dates of the carnival—to-night and Wednesday night—which should definitely settle the question."

The format was an elimination bout to decide which Australian should compete with Walker for the privilege of challenging Major Taylor over three events of a mile each on the final night. Against expectations Arthur Gudgeon of NSW not only qualified to race Walker but beat him, thereby qualifying to challenge Taylor. Despite a brave effort by Gudgeon he was outclassed by Taylor, again demonstrating his phenomenal jump. Taylor had clearly demonstrated his superiority over the local talent. Summarizing his Sydney experience, he said, "I was deeply impressed with the treatment accorded me by the sport loving public of Sydney in my first month's racing there. Likewise, I was grateful for the fair treatment accorded me twice by the race track officials, the riders and the newspaper men of that metropolis."

1903: Melbourne

After Sydney it was Melbourne's turn to witness the Taylor phenomenon. He was welcomed with great enthusiasm but there was a temporary setback when he came down with influenza, which lasted two weeks. During his illness, apart from a few lackluster exhibition events, Taylor accepted one significant challenge. His presence in Melbourne coincided with that of Thaddeus Robl, the German world champion of motor-paced racing, a format popular in Europe and America, in which the competitors rode behind a car or motorcycle, taking advantage of the slipstream to achieve high speeds. The prospect of a contest between two overseas world champions was a big attraction for Melbourne cycling fans. The Melbourne Bicycling Club arranged an event at the Exhibition Oval on January 31, involving "Three events of One Mile and two of Two Miles. The winner of two events, best two of three, who takes a purse of 100 sovereigns." In scorching heat, in a format that didn't suit his style, the unwell Taylor was no match for Robl, losing all three races.

It wasn't until late February that Melbourne would finally get to see the real Major Taylor. Two events were organized—a "best of three" races against Don Walker for £100, and a similar event for £125 against the winner of a series of heats amongst leading Australians, for which George Morgan was the qualifier. In brilliant form, again demonstrating his amazing jump, Taylor won the Walker challenge in two races, and similarly disposed of Morgan. It had been agreed that should Taylor win in two straight races, there would be a special mile race later in the evening, pitting all of the major contestants against one another. Boxed in at the finishing stage, the crowd was convinced Taylor couldn't win, but again he showed his tactical skill by briefly dropping back, then shooting past with what the *Sydney Mail* (March 4, 1903) described as "one of the most marvellous sprints yet seen in Australia, for he came like a meteor, and beat Walne by 15 inches. Such a finish fairly staggered everyone present and it will be many years before the American's phenomenal ride is forgotten." The Melbournians were dumbfounded. After two weeks of illness and only a few days of training Taylor had beaten Don Walker and George Morgan in straight heat victories, and then defeated the best riders in the country in a special mile. One reporter concluded that Major Taylor was nothing less than "a super man on a bicycle. He left the city in a blaze of glory."[6]

The Sydney Thousand (1903)

Taylor returned to Sydney for the Sydney Thousand, the "biggest handicap ever run in the world," according to the *SMH*. The event was to be run over six nights in a two-week period. The field included New Zealanders, Englishmen, Italians, Irishmen, Canadians, and Danes. The 115 entries would be whittled down to 11 for the final. The winner would take home the phenomenal sum of £750. In the end, it turned out to be a major anti-climax, not just for Taylor but for the fans eager to see the world champion in action against a massive international field.

The problem stemmed from the Australian liking for handicap races instead of the Scratch racing preferred in Europe and the U.S. One of the features of the Australian system was the practice of groups of competitors agreeing ahead of time whose turn it was to be a winner, with winners sharing their prize with helpers. Taylor's code of sportsmanship forbade his entering into any such agreements. As the back marker, starting from scratch (or even behind it, in some races), this presented special problems.

With wind resistance a big factor, handicap races would frequently break up into two main bunches, the early starters in front being chased by the back markers. It was essential for the rear group to "stay in touch" if they were to have any chance of winning, but this depended on a fair sharing of the pace-making role amongst the group, to avoid individual exhaustion. If that didn't happen it was extremely difficult for the Scratch man to get to the front.

With the impressive amount of prize money at stake, not to mention large-scale associated gambling, it was predictable that skullduggery would eventuate in the Thousand.

Taylor got through the first qualifying heat. In the semi-final, the back markers "ran dead," leaving a fiercely competitive Taylor no real chance of catching the lead group. Horrified at the prospect of losing their star attraction, the officials declared it "no race" with a re-run the following Monday. Again, the back markers ran dead and Taylor made a desperate bid to catch the leaders without pacing, but was too exhausted to sprint at the finish. This time, the result was allowed to stand, and Taylor was out of the final. The furious public hooted the delinquent back markers for the rest of the meet. Taylor said that he could have bought his way into the final but was "out here to win races, not buy them." The *SMH* summarized the result: "MAJOR TAYLOR BEATEN. A SPLENDID EFFORT. PUBLIC DISAPPOINT-MENT."

The media generally viewed the outcome as a scandal, with suggestions that the delinquent back markers should be banned for life. There were also some comments that Taylor's single-minded determination to go it alone had contributed to his misfortune. The final was fought between a team led by the lone other American, Norman Hopper, and one headed by Don Walker. The result was an Australian record. Hopper later admitted he paid out £500 of the £750 first prize to his "team" members. In the aftermath, three riders were disqualified for three months "for not taking a proper share in the pace work in the semi-final heat of the Sydney Thousand Handicap."

After the Sydney events, Taylor had a successful visit to Adelaide, where "in 14 starts over three days he won 11 firsts and 3 seconds. He picked up £150 appearance money, £178 in stakes, and set new Australian quarter and half-mile records."[7] Before his departure for the European season he finished up with a triumph in an International five-mile championship race on April 13 in Melbourne. Despite the fiasco of the Thousand, it had been a highly successful season, and Taylor was upbeat in his assessment:

> My conquests on the tracks of Australia netted me a total of $10,735. I received a bonus of $7,500, and won $2,235 in prize money and received $2,500 additional for establishing new records.... My stay in Australia is one of my most pleasant recollections, especially in view of the fact that I entered the country with dire misgivings because of my color. While I experienced team-work and combinations in my racing tour of Australia, I am satisfied that the field was interested in bringing about my defeat simply because I was [the] champion, and not because of my color. With that color bugaboo dispensed with I got more pleasure out of my highly successful Australian tour than had hitherto been my lot in my entire racing career.[8]

1904 Season

If the 1903 season had been a euphoric one for Major Taylor, 1904 was totally different. He had shown that he was clearly head and shoulders above the local opposition and could only be beaten by shutting him out, a tactic unpopular with fans. For McIntosh and the League this meant waning public interest. In addition, after his earlier success, Taylor was holding out for more money. The solution—bring in Taylor's racist nemesis from the U.S., Floyd MacFarland, and his protégé, Iver Lawson, reputed to be the likely next world champion. MacFarland had organized nasty racial opposition to Taylor in the U.S. This was made all the more bitter by the fact that the pragmatic MacFarland, recognizing Taylor's ability despite his racial bias, had tried to co-opt him into his race-fixing schemes. McIntosh was not averse to playing the race card for publicity reasons, and the rivalry would be promoted as an American battle between white and black, appealing to "White Australia" prejudice.

En route to Australia, Taylor and his wife stopped in Christchurch, New Zealand, where some important local races were scheduled. Having been extremely seasick en route, he was far from fit. A combination of this and collusive interference saw him lose to the New Zealand champion, George Sutherland, in the main event. The press reported the interference but Taylor refused to use it as an excuse, saying only, "'I wish to say nothing to detract from Mr. Sutherland's victory, I take off my hat to him, and congratulate him on winning a fair, hard-run race. It was his day, and he deserves all the credit." A second event produced no better. It was Taylor's worst ever result and he apologized to the New Zealand public for his poor showing before traveling on to Australia.

By the time Taylor arrived in Sydney in late December 1903, MacFarland and Lawson were already well established, and dominating the Australian racing scene, along with several other American MacFarland "recruits." They were to prove a powerful cabal. Taylor claimed that they combined against him during the tour, pooling their winnings, and splitting them evenly at the end. To complicate matters further, MacFarland's persuasive patter convinced some local riders, even to some extent Don Walker, that Taylor, with his generous contractual money, local appearance fees, and the ability to win many prizes, was being selfish in not sharing with the locals. Despite his awareness of this, Taylor could not bend his principles, so had to go it alone. The resulting rivalry resulted in dramatic and dangerous racing, much to McIntosh's glee. For Taylor it meant a grueling series of races around all the major Australian cities, in which he would be subjected to racist opposition and vicious tactics aimed at blocking any winning chances. The very same things that had led him to abandon racing in America had followed him to Australia.

The Sydney series, starting on New Year's Day, set the tone for what was to follow.

> The four International Test races spaced throughout the month comprised an elite series and only 20 riders were selected. The first three races were over a half mile, four miles, and five miles, respectively. The finishers were awarded one point for first, two for second, and so on. Those with the lowest number of points would compete in the final one mile Test. The winner of that race would be crowned series champion and receive all the prize money.[9]

In the opening half-mile event MacFarland and Lawson boxed Taylor in and MacFarland forced him off the course. The crowd booed MacFarland and the stewards declared a "No race." With MacFarland and Lawson refusing the re-run, it produced a dead-heat between Walker and Taylor. MacFarland was suspended but later reinstated on appeal. The next two races, Four Mile and Five Mile, again saw Taylor blocked by the white Americans, allowing Lawson to win narrowly in both, with Taylor second. Going into the final, Taylor had not yet won a race in the series.

With MacFarland under suspension, the final was fought out between four qualifiers from preliminary heats, three Americans (Taylor, Lawson, and Downing) and one Australian, McDonald (NSW). Described by the *SMH* as "perhaps the best race ever witnessed on the Sydney course," it came down to a straight sprint between Taylor and Lawson. Neck and neck with 20 yards to go, Taylor produced his famous jump to win by half a length. Thus, to the chagrin of his rivals, Taylor scooped the pool, winning the International Series and the prize money.

The rest of Major Taylor's 1904 season, in Melbourne, Adelaide and other localities involved a similar litany of blocking tactics and physical harassment. Perhaps the most telling statistic is that at least nine riders were disqualified that year over their involvement in plans to stop Taylor. It would be tedious to follow the details of all the events involved, so three significant events will be examined.[10]

Battle of the Champions

In view of the fierceness of the rivalry between Taylor and his enemies, MacFarland and Lawson, and the public fascination with it, the League decided to run a series pitting them one-on-one against each other, billed as "The Battle of the Champions." In his book, Taylor claimed it was to decide the Championship of the World. The battle took place in Melbourne, the opening races being between Major Taylor and Iver Lawson on Monday night, February 8. There would be three heats, the first to win two receiving the £100 prize money. Despite the two riders being closely matched, Taylor's superb tactical skills saw him wrap it up without a need for the third.

MacFarland was not to be so easily disposed of. Their first match took place on February 13 in front of 20,000 fans. To wild crowd enthusiasm, the first one-mile race saw MacFarland hold off Taylor's finishing burst to win by half a length. The second mile race had to be re-run when MacFarland responded to Taylor's slow-riding tactical attempts to force him into the lead by simply hanging on to a post, to the crowd's amusement. The re-run was almost a repeat of the first race, the crowd being convinced MacFarland had again crossed the line just ahead of a supreme effort by Taylor. However, the steward's decision was that though MacFarland's head and neck had been just in front, the wheels were a dead heat, a decision unpopular with the crowd. Disgusted with what he considered a wrong decision, MacFarland stormed off, preventing a run-off race.

The final night was on the following Wednesday. It was billed as the last chance for Melbourne fans to view the champions. It would see Taylor take on both of his rivals individually on the same night. Peeved by MacFarland's no-show on the previous evening, and an obviously fake claim by him to be too ill to race, the committee advised him that if either rider failed to appear, the other would take the prize money. MacFarland showed up but this decision would come back to haunt the committee. The first stage of the evening was the Taylor-Lawson clash. Taylor won the first with ease.

The second race, a two-miler with early pacing by an Australian trio, settled down at the bell lap to a full-on neck-and-neck sprint, with both riders jostling and bumping each other to jockey for position. As they charged into the final straight, they collided. Taylor was thrown violently to the track, and the American Lawson swept on to win. Taylor lay motionless as a doctor rushed towards him. The crowd's mood changed radically and there was a storm of booing hurled at Lawson as he slowly wound down around the track.

Taylor's injuries were severe, with serious cuts and bruises that would take some time to heal. The stewards declared it a no-race. Meantime, MacFarland presented himself on the track, ready for his race with Taylor. When advised that Taylor was too injured to race, he pointed out that the committee's own rules entitled him to the prize money. Unimpressed, the officials declared the Championship series "indefinitely postponed," an ignominious end to the promotional venture.

In the aftermath, following lengthy hearings behind closed doors, the Victorian League declared Lawson guilty of deliberate foul play and suspended him for 12 months. On appeal, this was reduced to three months for unintentional dangerous behavior. That was the end of Lawson's Australian venture but left him free to compete in Europe and America.

Adelaide: "The Most Thrilling Episode of My Career"

The next scheduled phase of the cycling circuit was three days of racing in Adelaide, starting Saturday, February 20. With Lawson out, and Taylor injured, the only one of the American drawcards available was MacFarland, a disaster for the organizers. MacFarland was soon cleaning up the prize money in front of meager audiences. Taylor, recuperating in Melbourne, was receiving regular appeals from the Adelaide organizers to come to their meet if at all possible. Remembering the generous welcome he and Daisy had received in Adelaide the previous year, he decided against medical advice to attend for the International One Mile Championship on February 27, in a powerful field depleted only by the absence of Lawson. The day of the race was the first time Taylor had sat on a bicycle for 10 days. The loosening up process to get him going caused bleeding from a broken leg wound but enabled him to move freely.

The race was to prove a sensation and was also one of the rare occasions when Major Taylor was persuaded, however slightly, to compromise his rigid principles. One of the Australian riders, Bill MacDonald, was incensed over a plan he had heard MacFarland and his cohorts hatching. He offered his services in any way that Taylor wished. "MacDonald said he knew I could take care of myself when I was well and fit, but he said he could not remain idle when he heard them framing me up when I scarcely had a leg to stand on." In typical fashion Taylor thanked him for his support, but declined to form a partnership. Then, in a parting shot, Taylor said, "Now, if you *really* want to see me bring that bunch into camp, and if you would like to have a hand in it, I will give you your opportunity." MacDonald beamed as he said, "Certainly, I want to help you. What shall I do, you just say the word and it will be done." Taylor replied, "All I want you to do is to go to the last lap at top speed, and be sure to hold the black line (the pole) all the way regardless of what position I am in. Take no notice of me whatsoever. I will be on the lookout for you nevertheless. But above everything else, keep pedaling for all you are worth."[11]

MacDonald did exactly as promised. Taylor describes the sequel:

> Downing, who was pacing for MacFarland, was on MacDonald's wheel with MacFarland tacked on to his rear wheel. I quickly dashed to the front as MacDonald rushed ahead of me giving me his rear wheel just as I had figured. At this tense moment, just as we were turning into the back stretch, Downing rushed up and undertook to wrest the lead from MacDonald, and it was a battle royal down that back stretch. On reaching the last turn MacDonald had a slight advantage over Downing, and this placed me in a very bad pocket. Seeing my predicament, MacFarland made a terrific bolt for the tape. Simultaneously I shot through on the inside of MacDonald, inside the black line, on the pole snatching the lead by inches from MacFarland. We tore around the turn into the home stretch. I was gaining on MacFarland with every kick of the pedals down that long home stretch, but it was a savage battle right on up to the tape, which I reached about a length ahead of the surprised and raging MacFarland.[12]

A furious MacFarland tried to raise a protest that Taylor had been assisted but received scant sympathy. For Taylor it was "the most thrilling episode of my career."

The 1904 Sydney Thousand

The 1903 Sydney Thousand had seen Taylor frozen out by dubious tactics. Despite his injuries, he had shown at the Adelaide meeting that he was still a force to be reckoned with. It was also an open secret that he had been "helped" by MacDonald in Adelaide, raising the tantalizing possibility that he might be open to further collusion in the Thousand. The race was a one-mile handicap, with heats staggered over several nights, and the last day of the carnival, Wednesday, March 23, 1904, for the final. Taylor and MacFarland qualified comfortably off scratch in their separate heats, on March 12 and 14, respectively. Both showed good form in the subsidiary events, including a world record for MacFarland.

The final of the Sydney Thousand attracted an audience of 30,000 to the Cricket Ground. The field had been whittled down to 11 competitors, with Taylor and MacFarland off scratch and Downing, the other American off 10 yards. The front bunch were between 100 and 200 yards ahead, described as "extra-long starts" in the public advertisements. Australian Larry Corbett, off 120 yards, was an odds-on favorite to win. At the bell for the final lap three Australians, Corbett, Plunkett, and O'Brien were in the leading bunch, with Taylor, MacFarland, and Walker chasing 30 yards back, and the other five having dropped out. Walker and Taylor had done the lion's share of pacing for the back markers. In the final stages, MacFarland rejected several invitations from Taylor to take over. By the time Taylor made a last ditch effort to catch the leading trio it was too late. Corbett won by inches from O'Brien, with Plunkett third and Major Taylor fourth. The drama on the track was over but the real drama was only about to begin.

Immediately after the race O'Brien submitted a protest, alleging collusion between Corbett and Plunkett. The issue was subject to a lengthy, detailed enquiry by the NSW League. The issues considered went wider than just the O'Brien versus Corbett matter. There had been wide public discontent over the failure of MacFarland to take what was seen as a fair share of the pace making, thereby spoiling a possible dramatic finish. A telling comment from O'Brien was "Well, if MacFarland had done his share of the pacing, the winner would have come from the back men."

A week later the League announced its dramatic verdict. O'Brien's appeal was upheld, making him the winner of the £750. Seven of the 11 starters were suspended from cycle racing. The longest was MacFarland, for three years, next longest the "winner," Corbett, for two years. The effective result was that the only official finishers were O'Brien, Taylor, and Walker. Taylor eventually received his £100 for second place, though not until a further lengthy legal battle by Corbett was concluded a year hence. MacIntosh explained later that MacFarland had assured him he would ride hard but didn't do so. A side effect was that a foreshadowed one-on-one series of races between Taylor and MacFarland, originally proposed by Taylor, was canceled.

With the Sydney Thousand completed, Taylor's contractual obligations in Australia were fulfilled. But as Daisy was expecting their child, they decided to stay on for their big family event. Taylor made a few more appearances in Melbourne, Adelaide, and NSW country towns Wagga Wagga, Wyalong, and Narrandera. Their daughter, Rita Sydney Taylor (named after her birth city and always known as Sydney), was born on May 11, 1904, at 170 Windsor Street, Paddington.[13] The family returned to America, departing on the *Sierra* on June 6. *The Worker* (Wagga), of June 18, 1904, reported that they were leaving Australia with "a live wallaby, some cockatoos, parrots; and other Australian birds," as well as Australian champion Don Walker.

Taylor summed up his 1904 Australian visit thusly:

As I look back over my last season's work in Australia I was highly pleased with my accomplishments. Shortly after I arrived there and learned that several American riders had preceded me, I realized that they were in a combination to prevent my winning a race. Not satisfied with that underhanded procedure, they enlisted all of the Australian riders to help them put the program over, coupled with that all of the other riders had the advantage over me of having been in training for several months before I left the ship. As a result I was beaten several times before I reached my best sprinting form, but I quickly found myself and swept my way to a number of victories in spite of the powerful combinations against me.[14]

Epilogue

Despite his positive assessment, the strain of the Australian season was such that after his homecoming Taylor had a near-nervous breakdown, and it would be three years before he would again compete, in 1907. He resumed a successful career in Europe for several years until he retired in 1910, aged 32. He was wealthy at that stage but a succession of bad luck, bad investments, and ill health reduced him to poverty. He died, largely forgotten, in 1932. In later years his reputation has been revived, with several books, and a Major Taylor Association, to perpetuate his honor.[15] Taylor's nemesis Floyd MacFarland died in 1915 after a fracas at a New Jersey velodrome.

Major Taylor (*center*) with wife Daisy and daughter Sydney, ca. 1906. From his autobiography.

13

George Sorlie and Cassie Walmer

After the departure of Major Taylor, some long-term resident entertainers from earlier troupes were still active on the local scene, with some departures from their ranks through the Grim Reaper.

Wallace King died in February 1903. He had originally made his name in the U.S. with the Hyer Sisters Concert Company and arrived in Australia with the Hicks Minstrels in 1888, staying on when that troupe disbanded. He had been a favorite for many years on the Tivoli circuit. In early 1901, along with Pope and Sayles, he had gone to New Zealand with the Tivoli-affiliated P.R. Dix Company. There he toured successfully until May 1902, in Wellington, when it became clear on stage that he was a victim of dementia, struggling to remember the words of his most popular song, "Sally Horner," of which he was himself co-composer. A fund was raised by P.R. Dix to send him back to the U.S. where, after a stroke, he died in Oakland, California. He was described in a *Freeman* obituary as "the greatest colored tenor of his time."

Another death was that of J.R. (Johnny) Matlock, in June 1904, in Melbourne, aged 57. He had arrived even earlier than King, with the first Hicks troupe in 1877. He stayed on after the troupe disbanded, playing with various white minstrel troupes during the 1890s, sometimes under his own name, until ill health stopped him. His wife, Louisa, also a performer, continued running a vaudeville company under her own name, with assistance from her son Ernest, until her death at age 60 in 1917.

Will and Butch Jones, who had come with the Curtis troupe, were still actively performing in Australia, though both would be dead, of consumption, by 1910.

Irving Sayles and Charles Pope continued to be firm favorites at the Tivoli. From April 1901 until February 1902, they toured the affiliated P.R. Dix circuit in New Zealand, along with Wallace King on his ill-fated final engagement. After their return to the Tivoli they played SA venues from April 1902 with their own mostly white minstrel troupe, until Sayles rejoined the Tivoli in November, while Pope continued with Pope's Federal Minstrels. They were back together on the Tivoli circuit by March 1903.

In New Zealand, the Hamilton Hodges continued to be stalwarts of the local classical music scene, Mrs. Hodges occasionally joining Fisk Jubilee troupes, whose activities are covered in Appendix 3.

W.H. (Billy) Speed had played with several minstrel troupes in the late 1890s, until he settled in WA in early 1900. He teamed with his former original Hicks (1877) associate, A.D. Jackson, as his advance manager for a time, until Jackson went out on his own, possibly becoming involved with horse-racing, a sport in which he and Speed liked to dabble. Speed was apparently running a successful dramatic troupe, based in Perth and touring the goldfields and regional WA towns. However, in April 1903 it was reported that while bathing off the beach in the coastal town of Onslow he had gone missing, apparently taken by a shark. The June 13 *Daily News* (Perth) reported the police response to a request from Mrs. Speed, stating that they had:

> brought to the surface the trousers which Mr Speed had been wearing, but further dragging failed to disclose any additional trace of the object of the search. In one pocket of the trousers was a pocket-book containing telegrams, money, receipts, and sundry papers, and in the other was 9 shillings in silver, but the pocket had been torn almost to the bottom. There was the print of a good-sized shark's mouth on the waist of the garment, which was turned completely inside out.

The story had a twist ending when it was reported later in June that Speed had been found alive in Singapore, on his way to England. No full explanation of his escapade has been forthcoming (although it is possible he was running from gambling debts). It would seem that Mrs. Speed, herself a performer described as an "elocutionist in pathetic and dramatic recitals," was not in on the plot, assuming she is the same Mrs. W.H. Speed described by the *West Australian* (December 29, 1906) as having "proved herself an actress of much dramatic power" in the lead role of *Lady Audley's Secret*.

George Sorlie

A significant new face on the local African American scene before 1907 was one George Sorlie. Born of West Indian ancestry in Liverpool, England, in 1885, George Brown Sorlie was taken by his parents to Australia at an early age. They lived initially in Melbourne but after his father's death in 1894 he and his mother joined family members in Perth. An early talent for singing and entertaining helped George support the family. He first shows up in the media on the professional scene in February 1905, at the Palace Gardens in Perth, billed as an "American coon impersonator," exhibiting skill in a baton-spinning act. Later in the year he was in Footscray (Vic) with Mrs. Matlock's Variety and Vaudeville Company, and "took the house by storm, being encored no less than four times." George Sorlie would continue to be a fixture on the Australian entertainment scene for the next 40 years, not just for his own talents, but for the huge influence he would have on several generations of performers, through his traveling tent show and vaudeville troupe from the 1920s on. Among those whose careers he helped shape were film star Peter Finch, actor Ron Shand, and TV pioneer Bobby Le Brun. The great Shakespearean actor John Bell rated his youthful exposure to Sorlie's Christmas pantomimes as "the most anticipated event of the year till I was about ten."

Portrait of George Sorlie. Courtesy Gracie Le Brun.

Following the Matlock engagement, Sorlie was a regular feature on all the vaudeville circuits, Tivoli, Brennan-Fuller, Clay, and J.C. Bain. By 1914 he was the president of the Australian Vaudeville Artists' Association and involved in registering it as a bona fide union, against opposition from all the circuit managements except Bain, whose support Sorlie praised highly in a *Daily Telegraph* interview dated January 1, 1914.[1] In July of that year he teamed up with the ex–Kersands troupe comedian Billy C. Brown. Their partnership lasted two and a half successful years, including New Zealand for the second half of 1914, extensive tours of Australia with the Brennan-Fuller circuit in 1915, and a second New Zealand tour in early 1916. The NZ *Times* (March 1, 1916) commented: "Billy Brown and George Sorlie, coloured comedians, sang well and danced well, and their ragtime duet and dance, with Sorlie as a lady of colour, was vociferously encored." The partnership finished up with further touring on the Australian Brennan-Fuller circuit until the end of 1916.

Sorlie then continued on the Clay circuit, mainly around Sydney, until 1920. In that year a pivotal event occurred in his career, when he teamed with Philip Lytton, an actor turned producer/manager who was an early pioneer of tent shows in Australia from 1907. Lytton's shows were performed under large traveling marquees with stackable seating for the audiences, and he took them around the agricultural shows in country towns. In 1920, Lytton sold part of his operation, including a marquee, to Sorlie. Both men continued operating independently, Sorlie's shows initially being advertised under Lytton's banner. By 1923, however, Sorlie's tent shows were generally running under his own name. Audiences today would probably assume that the tent show was like a circus, with a performers' ring, but it actually featured a full traditional proscenium theatre, with separate dressing rooms for male and female performers, behind-the-scenes technical support facilities, and seating for an audience of up to 1,000.[2]

Sorlie's pattern followed a well-worn track, visiting country towns, large and small, during their annual agricultural show weeks. Large Queensland towns like Rockhampton might get two weeks, medium NSW towns like Wagga Wagga and Cootamundra a week, and smaller centers like Narromine and Gilgandra one or two nights.

> At the height of his career (1920–40) Sorlie was known as the 'King of the Road,' both as an actor and a producer of drama, pantomime, musical-comedy and vaudeville. His cheery smile and devotion to 'clean' entertainment earned him the respect of the theatrical world. Zebra-striped cars heralded a Sorlie show in many a country town. His most famous part was the lead in *Uncle Tom's Cabin*.[3]

Bobby Le Brun described Sorlie, with his beautiful singing voice and juggling and baton-twirling skills, as a "complete entertainer," *Uncle Tom* being his masterpiece.[4]

George Sorlie would continue to be a major figure in the world of Australian entertainment for many years up to his death in 1948 and even later, as his tent shows continued under the leadership of his widow, Grace. Several African Americans would feature in his productions along the way.

Cassie Walmer (1906)

Another performer who arrived in Australia around the time Sorlie was launching his professional career was Cassandra "Cassie" Walmer. She was one of the most successful results of Harry Rickards's forays into England seeking new talent for the Tivoli circuit. Born in London in 1888, of a U.S.–born African American father and a French mother, she was already on the English music hall stage as a baby in *Uncle Tom's Cabin* at age three, while her father played Uncle Tom.[5] By the time Rickards recruited her she already had a successful career in English music halls. Cassie arrived in Melbourne, accompanied by her mother, Stephanie, on the SS *Orient* on June 16, 1906, a few days before her 19th birthday. Her debut in Australia was delayed by a severe bout of typhoid, contracted en route at Colombo.

CASSIE WALMER.

Cassie Walmer portrait from postcard, ca. 1905. Courtesy of Mitch Mader.

Her opening at the Melbourne Opera House finally occurred on August 11, on a vaudeville bill headed by a popular juggler, Brinn, and including Irving Sayles. She was billed as a "contralto eccentrique," a buck dancer and a "coon impersonator." Despite her English birth, she was widely described in the Australian media as being American, a status she was legally entitled to in view of her father being a U.S. citizen.[6]

The August 16 issue of *Punch* noted: "Another new appearance on Saturday night was that of Miss Cassie Walmer, a very clever artist and mimic and said to be the world's champion buck-dancer. Her turn was a decidedly successful one, and met with great applause." She moved to the Sydney Tivoli on September 29, where a reviewer for the October 10 *Sydney Sportsman* caught her act:

> An easy first in the programme … Miss Walmer is an exceedingly clever artiste, and her engagement represents one of the very best Mr. Rickards has made. Her dressing is distinctly fresh and pretty; she has a deep, rich contralto voice, which has received all the training it needs, and as a buck-dancer she is undoubtedly what the programme represents her to be—one of the champions of the world.

For one born in cosmopolitan London and raised in a sophisticated mixed-race family, it is ironic that so many of her notices described her as a "coon impersonator," with coon songs like Harry von Tilzer's 1906 hit "Moving Day." Actually her repertoire leaned equally towards English music hall numbers like "Don't Tell the World Your Troubles," "Come Down, Joanna Brown, Come Down," or traditional Americana, like "You Never Miss the Water Till the Well Runs Dry." The "impersonator" tag related to more than so-called "coon" elements. One report commented: "Her imitations of the various styles of singers and actresses on the stage are very acceptable." This was based on her version of how various well-known stage personalities might have performed a "coon" song. Whatever the nature of her material, she proved extremely popular. By Christmas 1906 her songs were being widely advertised as available in sheet music format, such as the "Imperial Songster" collection, from outlets like Coles' Book Arcade.

One of the features of her act that impressed reviewers was the wide selection of elaborate frocks she wore. On a later visit the interviewer from the Adelaide *Critic* (April 16, 1913) quizzed her on the topic:

"I am told you design all your own frocks."
"Yes; I always make a sketch and write pink here and blue there, and silver to go along this part, etc., and send it over to a firm in Paris; then in a month's time I get [it], absolutely correct. Of course, they charge a great deal."
"What does a short frock of that description average?"
"From twenty to thirty pounds. Of course, it has to be made of the best silk, and then all the chiffon frills beneath. How much chiffon do you think it takes for one frock?"
"Fifty yards?"
"More than double that; it takes over a hundred; so you see you get a good deal for your money."

Cassie Walmer's originally planned 18-week stay would turn into 15 months. The Sydney season lasted nearly three months before she returned to the Melbourne Opera House for six weeks until late January 1907, and then back to Sydney again for a "farewell season" until mid–March. It was during this farewell season that she also attended a send-off for Jack Johnson at the end of his first Australian visit, when *Truth* espied Johnson joining a private party "with the Tivolian Cassie Walmer on his ebon wing."[7] This was followed by a Melbourne farewell season, then a week at Newcastle's Victoria Theatre, where billed as the "Dusky Princess" she was described as "the highest-salaried artiste on the Australian stage." It was also reported that "hundreds were turned away, never before has such enthusiasm been heard."[8]

The week at Newcastle was followed by three weeks at Brisbane's Theatre Royal, where even the frequently racist *Truth* (this one dated May 12) gushed over the "Dusky Princess."

A capital stage presence; a sweetly powerful voice; strong dramatic instinct, and a wonderful gift of easy, graceful dancing—the very poetry of motion—to say nothing of a magnificent wardrobe—all her frocks are Paris made—and a well-filled jewel box—she has received numerous testimonies of admiration from personages in very high places.

From the Brisbane Theatre Royal Cassie sent Harry Rickards a postcard, simply addressed "Tivoli Sydney," asking if he wanted her to perform her hit song "Moving Day" on her forthcoming New Zealand tour.

Cassie and the Rickards troupe set off for New Zealand at the end of May, opening at Dunedin's His Majesty's Theatre on June 4. With a touch of theatrical hyperbole, Harry Rickards was quoted in the June 12 *Timaru Herald* that the company was "the very best selected as well as the most expensive … that I

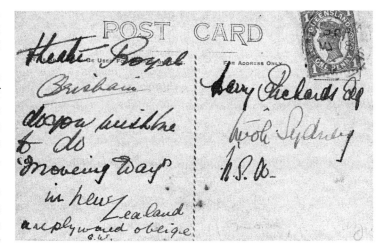

Postcard from Cassie Walmer to Harry Rickards, 1907. Courtesy of Mitch Mader.

have ever sent to New Zealand." The audience reaction lived up to the promise, the August 13 *Auckland Star* declaring Cassie "the representative of that type which is an unfailing adjunct of present day vaudeville—the rather masculine maiden who is ready for anything from a vigorous song with mountain calls [yodeling] in it to a cake-walk almost alarming in its vigour."

Harry Rickards had obviously responded in the affirmative to Cassie's postcard because the advertising for the show loudly trumpeted: "CASSIE WALMER, The Dusky Princess (Everybody's Favourite), in her Original Descriptive Scene 'Moving Day.'" The sheet music was also heavily promoted, along with "'My Bungalow in Borneo' (Miss Cassie Walmer's success)."

The July 8 *NZ Times* commented:

> Miss Cassie Walmer … is an artist to her fingertips. She impersonates various kinds of stage-persons, on and off the boards, sings descriptive songs and coon songs as they are sung and as they ought to be, and concludes with a remarkable sand-dance during one part of which she converts herself into a veritable human spinning-top, using only one leg for her support and pivot.

The New Zealand itinerary was the usual hectic schedule of one- and two-night stands in regional towns, interspersed with longer breaks in the major cities including, overall, Dunedin (one week), Timaru (two days), Christchurch (two weeks), Wellington (three weeks), Masterton (two nights), Dannevirke (one night), Hastings (one night), Palmerston North (two nights), Wanganui (two nights), New Plymouth (one night) and finally two weeks at Auckland, finishing on August 24. Cassie and her mother sailed from Sydney home to London on the RMS *India* on August 31, 1907, almost 15 months after their arrival in June 1906.

The Return of Cassie Walmer (1913)

It was again the Tivoli circuit that would bring Cassie Walmer back to Australia six years after her departure, but with one significant difference. Harry Rickards had died in 1911 and Hugh D. McIntosh was now in control, though still running the circuit under Rickards' name. Cassie had not been forgotten in the intervening years. Her recording of "Come Down, Joanna Brown, Come Down" was regularly advertised in the local media, and theatrical reports occasionally mentioned her whereabouts on the English circuits.[9] Another difference was that this time she was accompanied not by her mother but by her husband, Joseph Edward Louisson, whom she married in 1911. The sea trip out had been their first chance for a honeymoon. She explained that her mother had to stay home to look after the dogs she breeds, "the sweetest, tiniest little Poms."[10]

She opened her new Australian season at Rickards' Melbourne Opera House on February 8, 1913. The repertoire was, as before, a mixture of "coon songs" and music hall fare but with new material. On the "coon" side, there was "Pucker up Your Lips, Miss Lindy" by Albert von Tilzer, brother of Harry von Tilzer, composer of the previous visit's "Moving Day."

The music hall tradition was represented by "Anna Maria":

> I'm Anna Maria from the sweet stuff shop,
> Into my shop the boys all pop,
> Sweets they buy and they all have a try
> To spoon with Anna Maria[11]

There was one concession to Australian tastes. Since her previous visit Cassie had specialized in vocals, dropping dance from her act. In view of the local popularity of her one-legged dance she reintroduced it, a move that was well received. The local press (e.g., *Sunday Times*, March 30) carried teaser adds with the words: "How long can a chicken dance on one leg? See Cassie Walmer at the Tivoli."

The Melbourne opening proved she was as popular as ever, *Table Talk*, on February 13, enthusing:

> Miss Cassie Walmer received a very hearty welcome to the Opera House last Saturday, and at once got into the good graces of her audience, who appeared to thoroughly approve her songs. Her manner upon the stage is good, and she sings with that semi-confidential style which puts her at once en rapport with her hearers. She dresses in a particularly smart fashion and carries her clothes well, for she has a very pretty figure.... She had the extreme gratification of hearing the choruses of her songs taken up by the gallery at once, which is always proof positive that the turn goes.

Asked whether this time her tour would be "elastic" like the previous one, Cassie replied, "No, I am a far more important person now. I cannot exceed my eighteen weeks this time. I have every-night booked up to 1920 when I get back to London." Following three weeks in Melbourne, she opened at the Sydney Tivoli for the full month of March, *Truth* (March 2) noting: "Miss Cassie Walmer made her reappearance at the Tivoli last night, and met with a reception calculated to make her heart feel glad. Miss Walmer has lost none of her old dash and vivacity, and simply took the house by storm with her stunts."

Next port of call was Adelaide on April 7, for a three-week season at the newly reopening local Tivoli. Reporting on the opening, the local *Daily Herald* got its facts confused: "Although this lady has previously visited Australia she has not appeared in Adelaide [wrong!]. According to press reports she is an accomplished American comedienne and danseuse, interpreting the ragtime compositions with an abandon only found in American performers."

Despite the confusion, the April 19 Adelaide *Mail* reported she was well received: "Cassie Walmer has a fascinating personality, and it is not so much the songs she sings as the manner in which she sings them. 'Anna Maria' never fails to secure her unlimited applause."

By May 3, Cassie was back at the Melbourne Opera House for what was described as a "short farewell season," though it actually lasted four weeks before being followed by a one-week farewell at the Sydney Tivoli, finishing June 13, 1913. That was the last Australia would see of Cassie Walmer under that name, but she would reappear many years later under a new persona, of which more later.

14

Big, Bad Jack Johnson

Between the early story of Black Perry (see Chapter 1), and the arrival of Jack Johnson, there had been a lengthy history of African American boxers in Australasia. Details of their careers can be found at Appendix 1. If the quiet demeanor and soft-spoken personality of Major Taylor had endeared him to the Australian public, they were in for a shock with Jack Johnson. Long before Cassius Clay/Muhammad Ali's "I am the greatest," Jack Johnson knew he was "The Greatest" and was happy to tell the world so, especially white people.

John Arthur "Jack" Johnson was born in Galveston, Texas, on March 31, 1878. His parents, Henry and Tina Johnson, were former slaves. Jack was the first son and the third child of nine (only five of whom survived to adulthood). Growing up in Galveston, he didn't experience the racial prejudice that was the lot of most black people of the time. In Galveston, "Negroes and Caucasian people were poor and lived in the same neighborhood, ate the same food, suffered the same problems."[1] Jack recalled that he was a member on equal terms of a neighborhood gang of mixed race: "I ate with them, played with them and slept at their homes…. No one ever taught me that white men were superior to me."

An early fascination with sports included an attempt to emulate Major Taylor's cycling achievements, which ended in injury. At 17 he had his first taste of boxing, when he won $1.50 in an illegal prizefight. There followed a grueling apprenticeship, as a paid sparring partner for obscure boxers, and a participant in irregular boxing spectacles. By age 21 he had experienced some early professional successes. The era was one in which the heavyweight world was dominated by white champions like John L. Sullivan (1885–1892), James J. Corbett (1982–1897), Bob Fitzsimmons (1897–1899), and James J. Jeffries (1899–1905). These white champions were happy to fight black fighters on their way up but, once on the throne, they adamantly refused to give black boxers a chance at the title.

By 1903, Johnson was on his way up, with a long string of victories over anyone who would fight him, black or white. He had won the "world colored heavyweight championship," which he valued little. He desperately wanted a world title bout with Jeffries, and later with new champion Canadian Tommy Burns. Frustrated, in 1906 he decided to go to Australia, hoping a victory over the Australian champion, Bill Squires, would provide leverage for the elusive world title bout. His manager, Alec McLean, negotiated a deal with James Brennan, sports promoter, theatre and circuit owner, who had recently converted the athletic hall of the Sydney National Sporting Club into the National Amphitheatre. In early November 1906 the *Referee* reported the signing of a contract for return tickets for Johnson and his manager, with Brennan having tight control over Johnson's boxing activities in Australia.

The announcement of the imminent arrival of one of the world's top heavyweights aroused great excitement in Australian sporting circles. The two men arrived in Sydney on the SS *Sonoma* on January 25, 1907, met by a flotilla of launches loaded with fans eager for a glimpse of the famous boxer. James Brennan organized a reception for Johnson at the National Amphitheatre, with representatives of the sporting community, including boxing veteran Larry Foley. The Brisbane *Truth* (February 3) reported, "DE NEW COON COMES TO TOWN; a genial face, somewhat babyish-looking and of the type of the little coons who may be seen devouring water-melons in a well-known American picture." Johnson's amiable, open personality

Jack Johnson and his "golden smile," ca. 1910. Courtesy Library of Congress (Control Number: 2011649817).

made a good impression, but the burning issue was the status of plans for an Australian title bout between him and Bill Squires.

Squires had made frequent earlier references to his willingness to face Johnson. However, Squires was now under the management of Brennan's rival Melbourne promoter John Wren.[2] Wren's plan for Squires was to try to lure Jeffries out of retirement to fight him in America. Squires was already booked to leave for America on February 18, 1907. Wren declared his willingness to arrange a fight with Johnson, offering a stake of £1,000, but stipulated that the fight must take place quickly. Johnson had just spent a month at sea, and though he had trained on board, was more than 20 pounds (10 kilograms) above his fighting weight. There was no way he could get down to a reasonable weight and fitness in the time proposed. It was soon apparent that the Squires camp was not serious about a Johnson bout. Despite compromise proposals from the Johnson camp, the Wren offer was withdrawn and Squires departed for America. He never did get his bout with Jeffries, and suffered three losses by knockout in the U.S.

With the Squires bout off, the next-best option arranged was a 20-round match between Johnson and resident African American Peter Felix (See Appendix 1), to be held on February 19, 1907, billed as being for the colored heavyweight championship of the world. At 41, Felix was well past his prime but the bout was still anticipated with excitement. The event was anticlimactic, ending in under three minutes, the only blows of note being landed by a smiling Johnson. Following the Felix fiasco, Wren put up a purse of £500 for Johnson to fight Bill Lang, in Melbourne, on March 4. Lang would soon be the Australian champion in his own right, and was considered a worthy opponent. The fight would be held outdoors, at the Richmond racecourse under electric lights.

In the meantime, Johnson was earning some attention for his activities outside the ring. His training camp, and his exhibition sparring bouts at local theatres, were a popular tourist attraction for fight fans. His social activities also attracted interest. After one evening's drinking with his entourage at the Grand Pacific Hotel, Watson's Bay, Jack was approached next day at the theatre by the hotel's lady proprietor, seeking his assistance to find a gold pin missing from the hotel. He invited them to call later at his hotel, by which time the pin had been recovered from its pilferer. Jack invited the lady and her daughter Lillian (Lola) Toy, to watch him train, and later escorted them home. The two ladies were charmed by Jack's personality and physical beauty, especially Lola, who became a visitor to his camp.

Despite torrential rain on the night, 20,000 fans showed up to watch the Johnson-Lang fight. After an exciting preliminary bout, the sodden crowd—and Jack Johnson—waited impatiently and noisily for Lang to appear. Probably the best entertainment they got was Johnson's antics as he made his appearance, described by the *Freeman* on April 27:

> Johnson's entry into the ring was as theatrical as it was funny, and a gentle cachinnation that started to simmer round the edges of the platform spread out among the crowd, and developed into a roar of laughter, as an elongated figure, attired in a duchesse robe, made of chintz or cretonne, besprinkled with damask roses and lilac sprays, with fruits round the hem and a hood attachment similarly figured with flowers, stepped through the ropes. "We don't want to see Mrs Johnson," yelled a humorist. "Go away, woman, and send your husband; this is no place for ladies." The crowd entered into the spirit of the thing, and Johnson was chaffed unmercifully. Then from under the edge of the tricky hood a pair of rolling white encircled eyes made 'goo-goos' at the crowd, while his auriferous cavity bewitched all beholders in a smile that would have made Irving Sayles turn white with envy.... Finally, when he lifted his skirts and showed his sinewy black shins as he did an impatient double shuffle because his opponent was absent, the crowd fairly broke up, and encored him.

Once Lang appeared the fight was thoroughly one-sided, though not a fiasco on the Felix scale. Lang fought gamely, forcing the fight throughout, but was outclassed as Johnson toyed with him in the rain for nine rounds. In the ninth round Lang was down several times, and towards the close of it, the towel was thrown in from his corner. This ended Johnson's contractual obligations in Australia, with little benefit to show for his travels.

He stayed on for a brief tour of Vic regional towns, Ballarat, Bendigo, and Geelong, showing fight films and performing shadow boxing shows. Johnson and manager McLean returned to Sydney early in March.

Despite rumors of possible further fights, Johnson told the *Sunday Sun* on March 17 that he planned to return to the U.S., asking them to thank the Australian public for their kindness and support. "Please don't forget to thank Australians for the kind way they have treated me, and tell them that next to my own country I like Australia, better than any other place I have been in." In a later interview with the *Sun*, on March 24, Johnson added cryptically, "I may also say that I expect to get married shortly, and I'm liable to make this my home."

The March 13 *Referee* foreshadowed that the following day the Colored Progressive Association (CPA) would tender Jack Johnson a farewell, and make him a presentation. The CPA was "an organization comprised of about forty to fifty African American, Afro-Caribbean, and Aboriginal men who crossed paths as sailors and stevedores on Sydney's docks." One of those present at the event was Aboriginal activist Fred Maynard, who in later years would help to found the Australian Aboriginal Progressive Association, possibly inspired by the CPA.[3] Others present included Tivoli stars Cassie Walmer and Charles Pope, as well as Lola Toy, "escorted by her brother for appearance's sake."[4]

Johnson gave a display of ball punching, and there was music, dancing, and singing from 8 p.m. until midnight. *Truth* gave some caustic coverage of the event, describing it as a "coon corroboree," noting the presence of women both white and colored, and that "the sight of Mistah Johnsing picking his gold tooth with the wishbone of a baked turkey was too reminiscent of a Cannibal Island King and baked missionary."[5]

Johnson and his manager were planning to return to U.S. on the SS *Ventura* on Monday, March 18, the same boat carrying Bill Squires on his delayed U.S. trip, with a notion of lining up a Squires fight in the U.S. Though he got as far as boarding the ship with his baggage, dramatic events were to ensure Johnson's departure would not happen so soon. The day after the *Ventura* sailed, an *Australian Star* (March 19, 1907) headline proclaimed: "JACK JOHNSON ASSAULTS HIS MANAGER, WHO SUSTAINS A BROKEN NOSE. JOHNSON IS FINED FIVE POUNDS."

The evidence was that the previously friendly pair had quarreled over money that McLean claimed Johnson owed him. When he called Johnson a "big, black bastard," Johnson punched him. The magistrate took the view that "if a man calls another man those names he is likely to get something for it," and imposed a lenient £5 fine. However, there was still a matter of McLean's civil claim for £112 to prevent both men from leaving. They must have patched up their legal quarrel because on April 12 they sailed together for San Francisco on the SS *Sonoma*, "with the breach between them only partially healed" (*Referee*).

However, Johnson's departure from Australian shores did not mean he would drop out of the local headlines. Interviewed en route home, in Honolulu on April 30, he said, "I am going back there again to get married to Mrs Toy, an Australian lady whom I met while there."[6] Maybe it was the inaccurate "Mrs" that threw keen-nosed reporters off the scent, but it wasn't until Johnson was back in the U.S. that the *Referee* pursued the topic. It reproduced a California newspaper report in which, pressed about the marriage rumor, Johnson had said:

> Yes, It is true that I am to marry Miss Toy. She is a native of Sydney, and I expect to marry her in November. She will come from Sydney, Australia, and I expect that our wedding will take place in this country. I met her in Australia, and after, my courtship she consented to accept me. I am very happy.[7]

This set the cat among the pigeons in earnest. Stung by caustic comments on the street, and abusive private letters, an indignant Lola Toy initiated a libel suit against the *Referee*'s parent company, Sydney Sunday Times Ltd., for £2000. This ignited a social cause célèbre in Sydney that would reverberate well into 1908.

Lola Toy was just over 21 years old at the time of the court case. Her mother was the proprietor of the Grand Pacific Hotel, Watson's Bay, a popular Sydney seaside resort, a lively venue occasionally charged with licensing law breaches. Lola was an attractive, intelligent and talented young lady, who had for some years accompanied her brother Ernest, a celebrated violinist, as piano accompanist on his concert tours. The main problem in her life was her mother's marriage to a man only a few years older than Lola herself. Once established in the

ADELAIDE LILLIAN TOY.

Portrait of Adelaide Lillian (Lola) Toy at a court hearing, by the artist Dick Tait. *Truth* (Brisbane), 29 March 1908. Courtesy *Trove*, National Library of Australia.

tavern, he had proved to be an aggressive figure, mistreating his older wife. The animosity between him and Lola had resulted in a court hearing in which the stepfather accused her of stealing a gold chain. According to the April 30 *SMH*, the magistrate completely accepted her defense that the incident was a legitimate part of an attempt to defend her mother from violence, and the case was dismissed "without a stain on her character."

It's not surprising in these circumstances that Lola had seen the fortuitous meeting with Jack Johnson as an opportunity to spend time away from her detested stepfather. The proprietor of Johnson's base, the Joseph Banks Hotel in the suburb of Botany, was a friend of her family. The court proceedings in the libel case gave eager Sydney-siders much spicy material to enjoy over their morning toast, or in the court audience. The newspaper's defense team sought to portray a significant level of intimate contact between the pair, without stepping over the bounds of implying immoral conduct.

Witnesses, including various members of Johnson's training squad, gave evidence that Johnson and Miss Toy were frequently seen together, both publicly and in private, including in his room; that he referred to her as "Baby" and she called him Jack; that she brushed mosquitoes away from him, and described him as a "beautiful man." A policeman who attended the Grand Pacific testified that Miss Toy had described Johnson as a gentleman, and that she declared she had sent for Johnson to punch her stepfather, after he had criticized her for spending time with a black man. Much was made of the fact that in a group photo, Johnson appeared to have his hand on her shoulder. Asked about this, Miss Toy responded that she had not been aware of it. There was laughter in the court, when the defense solicitor commented, "But look at the hand, it must be a hundredweight."[8]

Backed by witnesses from the hotel management, Lola Toy's defense was to deny staunchly that there had been anything like the intimacy suggested. She spoke articulately, described as an "admirable witness," and at one stage fainted on leaving the witness box. It was apparent that the court's sympathies lay with "a respectable white girl" against a "professional 'black pugilist'" who wasn't even present in the court. The judge's summing up included, inter alia, that (1) nothing improper was imputed to Miss Toy by the defense, and (2) that it was not claimed that the defendant company had published the words complained of with malice. After two hours, the jury returned a verdict for Miss Toy of £500.[9] There was no further record of any contact between Jack Johnson and Lola Toy. She resumed her career as piano accompanist for her brother Ernest until he took up a position in the U.S. in 1916, after which she dropped from public view.[10]

The Return of Jack Johnson

Following Jack Johnson's return to the U.S. in April 1907, there was no expectation of a near-future visit by him to Australia, despite his suggestion that he might marry and settle there. Media speculation was rife during 1907 and 1908 about the possibility of a bout between Johnson and Tommy Burns, the Canadian-born, U.S. resident, heavyweight champion since 1906. However, following the precedent set by earlier white champions, Burns avoided title defenses with black challengers, especially Johnson, and spent much of his time out of the U.S. in Europe. Johnson and his manager doggedly chased him to Europe in early 1908 to seek a bout, but without success.

An event remote from the boxing scene would soon change the dynamics of the situation. In late 1907, a large armada of U.S. naval ships, known as the Great White Fleet (for its white-painted hulls), set out on a worldwide tour lasting into 1909. It was President Theodore Roosevelt's demonstration to the world that the U.S. was now a major naval power. The ships arrived in Sydney on August 20, 1908, to an enthusiastic welcome on the harbor.

There was one who viewed the prospect of 14,000 entertainment-hungry U.S. sailors landing in Sydney as a license to print money. "It seemed to me that someone ought to make a whole lot of money out of that visit. I saw no reason why it should not be Hugh D. McIntosh."[11] Since the end of the Major Taylor visit and the controversy that followed it, cycling had been in decline in Sydney and McIntosh was looking around for fresh opportunities. In anticipation of the fleet's arrival, he secured options on a host of entertainment venues for the period of the visit. He then came up with an inspiration for a guaranteed crowd puller. The American sailors would surely flock to see their own champion Tommy Burns fight an Australian!

Despite having lost twice to the world champion overseas, Bill Squires assured McIntosh he could beat Burns "under the Australian sun." Burns accepted a cabled offer of £4,000 for two fights, against Squires and Bill Lang. As a setting for the contest, McIntosh acquired a lease at a bargain price (with option to buy), on a large paddock at Rushcutters Bay, close to the city. With remarkable enterprise, in six weeks he had a stadium constructed that could seat 20,000. Though he never intended it as more than a temporary venue for the fleet's visit, by the time the Sydney Stadium closed in 1970 it had hosted world-class attractions like Bob Hope, Ella Fitzgerald, and Frank Sinatra.

The Burns-Squires fight, on August 24, attracted a capacity crowd to the stadium, variously estimated between 15,000 and 20,000, with an even larger number outside. Optimistically hoping for an Australian world championship win, the fans got their money's worth. Squires attacked from the outset and appeared to be winning on points. However, despite suffering from influenza, Burns was considered by the experts to be in control throughout, and he dispatched a worn-down Squires clinically in the 13th round. Ironically, though McIntosh's various other organized entertainments did extremely well financially from the fleet visit, only two drunken U.S. sailors were known to have turned up for the fight.

The Burns-Lang fight in Melbourne on September 3 was an even shorter one-sided win for Burns, with a sixth-round knockout. Nevertheless, McIntosh was now convinced that there was a lucrative following for professional boxing in Australia, provided big enough names could be enticed to appear. Once again playing the race card, as he had done with Major Taylor and his white rivals, the idea of a contest between black Jack Johnson and white Tommy Burns gripped McIntosh. Predictably, Burns rejected his idea, quoting a prohibitively high price of £6,000 ($30,000 in the then U.S. currency). When McIntosh called his bluff by accepting the offer, the reluctant Burns felt he had no option but to agree. Thus, McIntosh achieved what no promoter in U.S., or Johnson's own efforts, had been able to do. Australia was now to stage the long-awaited world-title bout between a white world champion and a black challenger. To get the fight he had long wanted, Johnson had little choice but to accept the much less generous £1,000 for his share, a matter that would rankle him.

After an initial venue suggestion of Melbourne city on the day of the Melbourne Cup horse race ("First Tuesday in November, the race that stops a nation") the date for the fight was finally settled for McIntosh's own Sydney Stadium on Boxing Day 1908. Johnson's trainer/manager was former Australian boxer Sam Fitzpatrick. Still in Europe, they set sail for Australia from Naples on the RMS *Ortona* in early October, accompanied by Jack's new white wife, Hattie McClay. They arrived by rail in Sydney from Melbourne, on October 29, and settled into Johnson's former base, Sir Joseph Banks Hotel, Botany.

Johnson was greeted by an enthusiastic crowd, and a formal welcome was held, attended by McIntosh and many prominent sportsmen, as well as fellow African American Irving Sayles. The welcome on his second Australian visit was cooler than on the previous occasion, perhaps with undertones of the Lola Toy issue. There was only one oblique reference to that in a provincial paper, the Bathurst *National Advocate* (November 14, 1908): "Mrs Jack Johnson does all the cooking for the big black. It was too bad of him to jilt the Australian millionairess!" At the time of the Johnson-Burns fight Miss Toy was conveniently touring New Zealand as piano accompanist for her brother Ernest.

The two boxers settled into training, Burns at a luxury resort in the Blue Mountains. There was the usual rhetorical back-and-forth that accompanies major boxing bouts, much being made of Burns's accusation that Johnson had a "yellow streak." Johnson patronizingly referred to Burns as "Little Tahmy," expressing a hope his health would remain good until the fight. In response to a message from Burns, "Tell that nigger I'll knock his black head off." Johnson replied, "Tell him if he beats me, I'll be the first to shake his hand."[12] An issue to be resolved was finding a referee acceptable to both sides. Several candidates were proposed but Johnson resolved the issue by telling McIntosh that if he (McIntosh) did not referee the bout himself, Johnson would refuse to fight. Burns had no objection, so the matter was settled.

McIntosh's build-up to the fight played up the racial element, one advertisement describing it as the first time the "Champion Representatives of the White and Black races have met for RACIAL and INDIVIDUAL supremacy."[13] He invited the ladies of the city, who were not permitted to attend fights, to afternoon teas hosted by Mrs. Burns at her husband's weekly exhibition training bouts at the stadium. He didn't do the same for the similar public events staged by Johnson and his wife at their headquarters. McIntosh's friend, famous Australian artist Norman Lindsay, who was better known for his depiction of nubile female nudes, produced a portrait of the boxers that emphasized the racial contrast, the hulking brute Johnson towering over his smaller opponent. It was published in *The Lone Hand* magazine, a supporter of the White Australia policy.

The other side of Jack Johnson, the man who destroyed Tommy Burns at Sydney Stadium in 1908. In the week before the fight, Johnson poses with his wife, a tiny admirer, and the bass viol, of which he was an accomplished player.

Jack Johnson and his wife Hattie McClay, with a young admirer, 1908. Courtesy collection of Ian Heads.

The *Referee*'s portrait was a more realistic portrayal.

Burns was the early favorite in betting but as news trickled in that big money was being placed on Johnson in America, the odds swung the other way, leaving Burns only a narrow favorite. Ticket sales opened four weeks ahead and advance bookings reached a world record. On the fight day, doors opened at 6 a.m. and 10,000 had been seated by 7:30 a.m., with the bout scheduled to start at 11 a.m. By the time capacity had been reached, another 40,000 were seeking admission, many trying to gain a vantage point by climbing on poles and walls.

As the moment arrived there were threatened last-minute hitches. Johnson, having already gouged an extra £500 from McIntosh, declared he would not fight unless more was forthcoming. Threatened by McIntosh with a revolver, he backed down and entered the ring to a mild welcome, which he cheerfully acknowledged. Burns received "five minutes of delirious cheering." He spurned Johnson's handshake offer. Spying some bandage wrapping on Burns's elbows, Johnson demanded they be removed. Advised by Larry Foley that, though they were technically illegal, they weren't worth making an issue of, he held his ground. Threatened by McIntosh that he would declare Burns the winner, Johnson replied, "You can do as you damned well like." The stand-off was only resolved when Burns volunteered to remove the bandages, and the fight was on.[14]

FIGHT FOR THE WORLD'S CHAMPIONSHIP

TOMMY BURNS AND JACK JOHNSON

Top: Pre-fight portrayal of Jack Johnson and Tommy Burns by artist Norman Lindsay. From the cover of *The Lone Hand* magazine, 1 December 1908. Courtesy National Library of Australia. *Bottom:* Fight for the World's Championship, Tommy Burns and Jack Johnson, in the ring at the stadium in Rushcutters Bay, NSW, Saturday, December 26, 1908. (From Supplement to *The Referee*, January 6, 1909.) Courtesy National Library of Australia.

For the thousands of fans eager for a white Anglo-Saxon victory, the result was a fiasco. Burns was on the canvas within seconds of the start. In a manner reminiscent of Muhammad Ali, Johnson invited Burns to hit him in his exposed stomach, taunting him as he did so. After 14 rounds, the police, on medical advice, stopped the fight to save a battered Burns. Novelist Jack London, who was there to report for a U.S. newspaper, declared: "There was no fight. No American massacre could compare to the hopeless slaughter that took place in the Sydney Stadium. The fight, if fight it must be called, was like that between a pygmy and a colossus."[15] The stunned crowd gave only a few straggling cheers for the victorious Johnson.

While McIntosh might not have got his preferred result, the event had been a financial killing for him, the gate being more than double that of the previous Australian record. Perhaps even more significant was that he had organized a high-quality film of the whole event, to which he now held lucrative world rights. The film had cost £1,500 to produce; MacIntosh estimated it grossed £37,000.

In the aftermath there was an avalanche of racist abuse of Johnson in the local media, fueled by the fear that his victory might encourage racial inter-marriage. There was support for the White Australia Policy (the 1901 Immigration Restriction Act), even from such a revered figure as poet Henry Lawson.[16]

Stung from his usual genial composure, Johnson hit back, knowing the low regard held for Aboriginal people by many in the white community. In an interview with the *SMH* (December 31, 1908), he mischievously remarked:

> I spend most of my spare time in the art galleries and the museum. My principal hobby is archaeology. When I visit your museum and see the numerous specimens of prehistoric man's art, your boomerangs of many varieties, your stone axes from various States and the many examples of Paleolithic and Neolithic man's skill, I simply envy you. We in America have our rude stone flint quartz implements, but they do not show anything like the same forethought or skill as yours. Your central Australian natives must have been men of genius to have turned out such artistic and ideal weapons.

In anticipation of a Burns victory, Harry Rickards had booked the now ex-champ for a tour on his Tivoli circuit, demonstrating training routines, ball-punching, shadow boxing, and sparring with local stars. Johnson, a natural showman, was happy to sign up with Rickards for a similar tour. Even though this was for less than Burns got, it still netted Johnson considerably more than he got from the fight. Faced with a hostile, booing audience on his first night, Johnson won them over, asking "Ladies and gentlemen, I came to Australia to win the world championship. I won it. Could I have done more?" There was a stunned silence, followed by a great cheer, and from that night Johnson was given an enthusiastic reception at every show.[17] The Tivoli tour took him to Sydney, Melbourne, Perth, Kalgoorlie, Adelaide, Ballarat, and Geelong.

Departing for home from Sydney on the Vancouver-bound SS *Makura* on February 15, 1909, Johnson gave a brief exhibition in Brisbane en route, and also made a pilgrimage to the Toowong grave of West Indian–born Australian heavyweight champion Peter Jackson (See Appendix 1). In his farewell message, reported in the February 15 *Evening News*, while noting some bias against him in Sydney, he thanked the Australian people for their kindness, noting, "On the whole I have been treated well and if a man can be unearthed to meet me, I have no hesitation in coming back to Australia to have the match decided here."

Jack Johnson never returned to Australia, despite later negotiations to bring him back (described below). He held the world title until May 1915, when he was defeated by the white Texan Jess Willard. Though many believe that Willard won the fight squarely against an aging Johnson, there were many who believed Johnson "threw" the fight to escape the trumped-up legal charges that racist American society pursued him under the notorious Mann Act, basically in retaliation for his consorting with white women.[18]

The Aftermath

Delighted with the success of his boxing ventures, and with money rolling in from the Burns-Johnson film, Hugh D. McIntosh continued his promotional activities, mainly overseas in London and Paris. When James J. Jeffries came back from retirement to wrest the title from Johnson, McIntosh attempted to get the much-anticipated fight for Australia but was outbid by a local American promoter. Nevertheless, he made a nice profit by betting on Johnson, who won convincingly. After several ventures in Europe, McIntosh returned to Australia in late 1911. One of his first promotions was between two of the leading African American heavyweight contenders, Sam Langford (the Boston Tar Baby) and Sam McVea, for the vacant Australian Heavyweight title. Langford is considered by many experts to be the greatest fighter never to win a world title. McIntosh had signed up both men for a series of bouts. The first, on Boxing Day 1911, was staged at the stadium, for the first time open to ladies, including a special ladies box. The result was a thrilling victory for McVea.

At the return bout, in May 1912, it was Langford's turn to take the title. Between December 1911 and June 1913, these two would beat the best that Australia could offer, and fight each other six times, Langford winning four, McVea one, and one draw. In June 1913, after a draw with Australian Colin Bell, Langford relinquished his title and returned to America, where both men would continue their rivalry until 1920. Their lifetime score was seven wins to Langford, six draws, and two wins to McVea.

McIntosh's plans had been to lure Jack Johnson back to Australia to fight the two men. The first match, with Langford was already being announced in the local media for Boxing Day 1912, with Johnson to receive £10,000. However, in America, scandal enveloped Johnson over his legal problems, exacerbated by the tragic suicide of his recent new white wife, Etta Terry Duryea Johnson. This was fanned to white heat by his subsequent liaison with another white woman, Lucille Cameron. Before Johnson could embark on his predicted October 25 voyage to Australia, Lucille's mother demanded, against Lucille's wishes, that the police rescue her daughter from Johnson's influence. The media line, repeated in headlines around the world, was that Johnson had "abducted a white girl." He was arrested under the Mann Act, amid massive public outcry against him. McIntosh was already becoming disillusioned by the large sums needed to finance world-class boxing matches. He declared in the *Evening News* of October 21, 1912, that he now considered "it was in the best interest of the manly sport that he should bar Johnson" from Australia.

From here on, McIntosh's interests turned towards the theatre. It wouldn't be until after World War I that African American boxers would appear again on the Australian scene. None of them, with the exception of the great Archie Moore, had anything like the world status of those already seen. A summary of their Australian activities and records can be found in Appendix 2.

15

The Lay of the Last Minstrel: Billy Kersands (1912)[1]

In the opening years of the 20th century, the era of the minstrel show was slowly fading in favor of vaudeville and variety. This received added impetus when Hugh D. McIntosh switched his energies to theatrical entertainments following the death of Harry Rickards in 1911. McIntosh then gained control of the Tivoli circuit. However, there was still one significant kick in the not quite moribund minstrel world in Australasia. It came in the form of no less a person than the man considered the all-time greatest of the black minstrels, Billy Kersands, now in the twilight of his long career.

Billy Kersands was born about 1842. He started in black minstrelsy in the 1860s, joining the earliest black troupe, organized by Charles B. Hicks in 1866. He became a leading star of top troupes like Callender's Original Georgia Minstrels and Haverly's Colored Minstrels, as well as his own Kersands Minstrels. He was hugely popular in southern U.S. among blacks and whites alike. Tom Fletcher said, "In the South, a minstrel show without Billy Kersands was like a circus without elephants."[2] His most notable characteristic, which formed the basis of his humorous style, was his cavernous mouth, in which he held objects like billiard balls, while dancing nimbly despite his bulk. "If God wanted to make my mouth any bigger," he quipped, "he would have to move my ears." Later black comedians who amazed audiences with their gaping mouths, e.g., Billy Wilson with Hicks Georgia Minstrels in 1877, were following a trail blazed by Kersands.

By the 1880s Kersands was the leading black minstrel, earning as much as many top white stars. In 1883, the April 7 *Launceston Examiner* commented on the U.S. scene: "Even the genuine darkies on the minstrel stage command pretty good salaries. Billy Kersands, the man with a wonderful mouth, who three years ago got only $15 a week, now receives $80 and has his own and his wife's travelling and hotel expenses paid."

Kersands' material was stereotypical of the era, playing a dimwitted black man. However, he was immensely versatile, with his act including acrobatics, singing, dancing, and playing musical instruments. Mel Watkins, historian of African American humor, commented that "[Kersands] was probably the first prominent black entertainer to confront a dilemma that would plague a succession of black show business people, especially comedians—the conflict between satirizing social images of blacks and contributing to whites' negative stereotypes of blacks in general."[3] Despite adhering to the stereotype portrayal, Kersands was also capable of gently subverting racist attitudes in a fashion similar to the great Bert Williams, as seen in some of his routines, including the following:

SAM: Do you think there are any coloured angels in heaven?

FRANK: It's a cinch. Who else would wash all dem angels' snowy robes, and clean dem golden streets, ah'd lak to know![4]

One of Kersands's most popular numbers was the song "Mary's Gone with a Coon."[5] Written around 1880, it was already a stock-in-trade item of Australian amateur minstrel troupes by 1883, as featured by the "Black Diamond Minstrels" of Goulburn, in a performance at the country town of Crookwell, reported by the May 19, 1883, Goulburn *Evening Penny Post*. Another Kersands song that created a stereotypical figure was "Old Aunt Jemima" (1875). "Aunt Jemima" became the iconic advertising face of a brand of pancake mix and syrup, personified in later years by singer Edith Wilson, until eventually swept away by the 1960 civil rights campaigns.

Kersands's association with negative stereotypes should not obscure his importance in more positive developments. His skill as a dancer made him an important figure in dance history. His dance specialty was known as "The Virginia Essence," or the "Essence of Old Virginia." Tom Fletcher

Sheet music cover for Billy Kersands' popular song "Mary's Gone With a Coon." Author's collection.

wrote, "He danced it to a slow, four-four rhythm, and for all of his two hundred pounds, was as light on his feet as a person half his size."[6] Jazz dance historians (including Marshall and Jean Stearns, Lynne Fauley Emery and Jacqui Malone) credit Kersands' Essence dance with an important role in the development of the Soft Shoe Shuffle, and Buck-and-Wing, forerunners of today's jazz and tap dance.

As early as 1886 the *Lorgnette* (Melbourne) reported the possibility that C.B. Hicks would bring Kersands to Australia. However, it didn't happen until 1912, and then it was New Zealand that got the first chance to see the legendary minstrel. The first indication of what was in store came in the form of an advertisement in the *New York Clipper* on January 20, 1912, seeking "Colored Minstrel Performers for Hugo's Greater American Minstrels Touring the World." Stipulations were for "best male talent in show business," preference for those "doubling brass and orchestra," promising "board and transportation back to [the] U.S. ... but 'Salary must be low.'" The itinerary was said to include "Australia, Philippines, India, China, Japan, Java, etc."

Billy Kersands in New Zealand

The Kersands troupe, also described as Hugo's American Minstrels, or Greater American Minstrels,[7] arrived in Auckland from Honolulu, on the SS *Marama*, on June 4, 1912.

They were variously advertised as 30 or 35 strong, including a brass band, and described as "the latest, the greatest, the most complete vaudeville organisation that has ever crossed the seas." Advance publicity hailed Kersands as "the only living colored comedian who has appeared before her late Gracious Majesty Queen Victoria." They opened at Auckland on June 10. Publicity activities included a Grand Parade through the streets at noon, and street concerts before the theatre opening. The parade band was 35-strong, reflecting the versatile ability of many performers to double up on instruments.

The opening night was completely sold out, with people turned away. A sufficiently long time had passed since the last black minstrels tour for the new troupe to be seen as a novelty, the *Auckland Star* (June 10, 1912) noting, "Everyone was recalled, and many of the dusky artists had to respond several times." There was some nostalgic complaint that the singing wasn't up to the standard of the Fisk Jubilee Singers, or McAdoo's Wallace King.

The troupe was almost entirely male (including Pearl Moppin, despite the confusing first name). The only females were Mrs. Kersands and the popular band singer Leah Clark, described as "the queen of ragtime." Her featured number was the 1911 hit song "Everybody's Doing It," written by 23-year-old Irving Berlin, for performance by 19-year-old Eddie Cantor. The "it" referred to the Turkey Trot, a dance craze soon to be eclipsed by the Foxtrot. Clark also scored a hit with the recently popular "When Ragtime Rosie Ragged the Rosary."[8]

The show lasted a lengthy three hours, though Kersands himself was only on for a fairly brief part of the action. Nevertheless he was well received, despite the questionable taste of some of the humor. Apart from the usual singing, monologues, and jokes, the variety acts included trick cycling, hoop rolling, and rapid cartooning. The Adelaide *Advertiser* (December 9, 1912) described the layout of the show:

> There was the conventional interlocutor in the centre and the circle in the foreground, and there were six end men. Some of the company were arrayed in white silk costumes—the centre man had a wig as well—others were in black, two wore violent check waistcoats, and two were in red, with blue facings. The chairs were draped in red, with a silver monogram ... there was none of the bones and tambourine work in which the old minstrel performers were so expert.

Kersands's own dancing has already been described, but there was another dance specialty that excited great interest, the Texas Tommy. This was a new dance that was sweeping the United States since its introduction in an all-black show, *Darktown Follies*.[9] Ethel Williams, the featured dancer of that show, described it to Marshall Stearns this way: "There were two basic steps—a kick and hop three times on each foot, and then add whatever you want, turning, pulling, sliding. Your partner had to keep you from falling—I've slid into the orchestra pit more than once." Another description noted: "Poise and gentleness of handling must regulate the seemingly fierce toss of his partner, first in the air, then toward the ground."[10] This is now recognized as the forerunner of the Lindy Hop jitterbugging style of social swing dancing that would become all the rage in the 1930s. The June 24 *Waikato Argus* commented: "Perhaps one of the most sensational numbers is the Texas Tommy.... The dance itself is one of those peculiar affairs which cannot be described but has to be seen to be appreciated."

The following are the cast members of the show who can be individually identified: Billy Kersands (leader), Mrs. Kersands (soprano), James Lacey (bandmaster), Attrus[s] Hughes (conductor, violinist), Billy C. Brown (eccentric comedian), Frank B. Poole (basso), W. Huntley Spencer (tenor), Charles Thurman (baritone), Will C. Washington (comedian), Alonzo Bosan (trombone), H. Qualli Clark (cornetist), Jeff Smith (cornetist), Ed Tolliver (monologist), Leah Clark (band singer), Pearl Moppin (hoop tricks, trombonist), Arthur Maxwell (trick cyclist), Brown and Hodges (singing cartoonists), Charles Marrs (tenor), Henry Morgan Prince (interlocutor, singer, dancer), Era Comedy Four (Spencer, Brown, Poole and Marrs), Verona Biggs (clarinet), Happy Young (drum major, baton juggling), Leonard Scott, Owen Granger, and Jay Elliott (soft shoe and buck-and-wing dancers).

Tolliver and Poole had both been members of McAdoo's Georgia Minstrels in 1899. H. Qualli Clark is known to jazz fans as the co-composer of the classic trad tune "Shake it and Break It." Attrus Hughes, like W.C. Handy, had been an orchestra leader for the prestigious Mahara's Colored Minstrels. Alonzo Bosan would go on to a long career on Broadway, up to 1955. Henry Morgan Prince had been a member of Freddie Keppard's famous Creole Jazz Band. He married a part-Maori pianist, Ollie Fitzsimmons, in New Zealand.[11]

The Auckland season lasted almost two weeks. It was followed by a tour of the north and south islands that saw Christchurch and Wellington get a week each, and lesser centers one or more days (e.g., Dunedin, three nights), including Hamilton, Eltham, Stratford, Hawera, Wanganui, Masterton, Palmerston, Ashburton, Timaru, Invercargill, Gore, Balclutha, Milton, Oamaru, Woodville, and finishing at Feilding on August 21. The troupe departed from Auckland for Sydney via the RMS *Marama* on August 28. Reports suggest their visit had been successful from the point of view of patronage. Whether it was financially lucrative enough to support such a large company was less clear.

Billy Kersands in Australia

The RMS *Marama* delivered the Kersands troupe to Sydney on August 31, though the media showed more interest in their fellow passengers, Captain Rose's "Wild West Company." En route to a Melbourne opening, the Kersands troupe made a whistle-stop tour of one-night stands in country towns, including Parramatta, Moss Vale, Goulburn, Cootamundra, Wagga Wagga, Albury, and Benalla. They opened a two-week engagement at the Melbourne Hippodrome on September 21, billed as Hugo Brothers Greater American Minstrels. *Table Talk* (September 26, 1912) commented:

> A crowd of over 2,000 people attended the opening performance and they enjoyed the big programme to the end. Billy Kersands is the bright star of the show. He is a comedian to the finger tips and his work is clever and original all the time. The play of his features adds to the humour of his acts and sends the audience in to fits of laughter. Kersands is a comedian to be seen as well as heard.

The Hippodrome was only available for two weeks, so the troupe had to fill in with some regional engagements before opening a further Melbourne season for four weeks at the Bijou Theatre. Their four-day visit to Bendigo was the most successful, not merely because of full houses each evening, but for an event that brought them much public kudos. On October 12, 1912 a major disaster at the Mount Lyell mine on the West Coast of Tas had cost 43 miners' lives, eliciting widespread sympathy around Australia for the dependents of the victims. The Kersands troupe offered to give a sacred concert in aid of the Bendigo mayor's relief fund. The theatre was packed, with hundreds unable to gain admittance. A sum of £72 was raised, more than $8,000 in today's terms.[12]

The four-week season at the Melbourne Bijou Theatre was generally reported as successful, without attracting major publicity. It was followed by another string of brief visits to regional towns—Ballarat and Horsham in Vic, Broken Hill (NSW) four nights, Gawler,

Petersburg, Yorke Peninsula, Wallaroo, Kadina and Port Pirie in SA—en route to a two-week engagement at Adelaide. While noting the audience's enthusiastic response, and that they insisted on Billy Kersands reappearing time and time again, the reviewer for the *Barrier Miner* (December 3, 1912) made an unfavorable comparison with the Hicks-Sawyers minstrels of 24 years previously: "The ragtime craze has taken the place of the soft shoe song and dance, and of the old negro plantation sketches, and it is by no means an improvement. There is plenty of noise with the 'rag-time' music which by no means can be called melodious or artistic." However, he still allowed, "The instrumentalists are artists and the beautiful melody and harmony produced by the combination of instruments was undoubtedly artistic."

The season at Adelaide's Theatre Royal lasted two weeks. The reviews were enthusiastic, the December 9 *Register* taking a more generous view of ragtime:

> What some people mistake for row is an ecstatic enthusiasm which gives to the performance exhilarating rhythm. Ragtime is a hurricane of melody, eccentric and animated, almost desperate in its exuberance. At first, the swift intensity of the music is half repellant, but an appreciation grows, and before the night is ended a generous enjoyment has conquered the early prejudice.

Although the Adelaide press reported strong attendances, the December 24 *Referee* reported the season as only "fairly successful." Perhaps this explains a *New York Clipper* (March 22, 1913) report that "the title and rights to the show were sold to one C.N. Coleman, an Australian amusement promoter," who proposed to continue touring one-night stands in the smaller towns not already played by the Kersands show on its tour.

After Adelaide, the troupe continued touring regional NSW, but Billy Kersands made his last appearance at Wollongong on January 18, 1913. He and his wife were back in San Francisco by February 20. The *Clipper* reported that, apart from the Kersands, only two members of the troupe, James Lacey and Verona Biggs, had exercised their right to a return fare, 28 having opted to continue touring. Kersands' reasons for leaving were canvassed in several conflicting reports. Uncertainty about the new management was mentioned: "I did not care to take chances with a manager we did not know," and also concern over "so many small towns to play to" with such a large troupe.[13] For Kersands, in his seventies, the many short stays in small towns might well have been stressful. In America, he resumed touring, but on June 29, 1916, as lead performer of the Dixie Minstrels, he died of a heart attack in his mid-seventies, having just completed the second of two shows. Thus ended the career of the man "considered to be the world's greatest and most widely known black minstrel."[14]

The Aftermath

While 28 members of the troupe were reported as staying on in Australia, the Era Comedy Four—Billy C. Brown (eccentric comedian), Frank B. Poole (basso), W. Huntley Spencer (tenor) and Charles Marrs (tenor)—had signed their own private deal with the Brennan-Fuller circuit, which saw them open as a featured act at the Sydney National Amphitheatre on January 25, 1913. They would continue to be a local presence for several years, with some personnel changes over time.

The remainder of the main troupe continued touring under the Hugo Brothers banner. From February until November 1913, they toured extensively in regional NSW and Queensland, with reasonable success, though a white American promoter who encountered them was quoted by the *New York Clipper* (July 26, 1913): "I met on my travels a colored minstrel show that came out here with Billy Kersands. They are doing well but the show of about twenty people is badly managed."

On July 19, the troupe started a four-week engagement with the Brennan-Fuller circuit at Sydney's National Amphitheatre, billed as a "grand ragtime review" of 25 performers. They were the first part of the show, the rest of the acts being white. They then moved on to Melbourne, initially Brennan-Fuller's Gaiety Theatre, and later, Melbourne's National Amphitheatre. Around this time, the management problems alluded to earlier seem to have proven true.

Following the Melbourne season, after much advance publicity and keen local anticipation, a season scheduled to start in Hobart, on September 6, never happened. When the troupe arrived at the Melbourne docks to find that they had been booked on third-class passages, they refused to embark. By the time a promise of first-class passage was offered two days later, it was too late; the company had scattered. As the Hobart *Mercury* (October 24, 1913) reported, the matter later became the subject of a legal action by the members for breach of contract and loss of earnings. Presumably, the case was settled out of court as there were no further reports.

By the first of October the troupe were regrouped and back on the road in Bendigo, albeit as only half a show, shared with moving pictures. The writing was clearly on the wall, and after a few more dates in regional Vic, they finally closed in Wagga Wagga on November 11. With the exception of Attruss Hughes, they sailed back to U.S. on the RMS *Ventura*, leaving Sydney on Monday, November 15. Hughes continued to lead a mixed black and white troupe billed as Hugo's New Minstrels around regional Vic, until he dropped out after a performance in Rutherglen in early 1914. In April, he played some local dates with Percy Foster's Vaudeville in Geelong. By early 1915 he was back in Oakland, California, as a member of Sid Le Protti's Crescent Orchestra, which played banquets and society affairs.[15]

Death of Irving Sayles

It's ironic that shortly after the last of the Kersands-Hugo troupe departed, the man who had most notably straddled the world of minstrelsy and vaudeville in Australia, Irving Sayles, dropped dead on a public street in Christchurch, New Zealand, of a massive heart attack on February 8, 1914. He had started a 16-week tour on the Brennan-Fuller circuit on December 3, 1913, with his Australian partner Les Walton. The February 8 Christchurch *Star* commented: "It is probable that no man connected with the theatrical pro-

Irving Sayles portrait from Tivoli postcard. The handwriting quotes a song title "I Must Love Somebody" from the popular 1900 musical *Florodora*. Author's collection.

fession was better or more popularly known to the people of Australasia than the late Irving Sayles."

Sayles had originally come to the region in 1888 with the Hicks-Sawyers Minstrels. Along with his end man partner, Charles Pope, he had opted to settle in Australia. In 1897, he married English-born Edith Carter. He became a firm favorite at Rickards' Tivoli. Quoting Percy Crawford that "Sayles was the life and soul of the Tivoli," Frank Van Straten comments: "Sayles played the Tivoli more or less continuously for twenty years, delighting audiences with numbers like 'There'll be a Hot Time in the Old Town Tonight.'"[16] He was only 42 when he died.

16

Throw the Switch to Vaudeville[1]

The Kersands troupe was not only the last black minstrel show to visit Australasia, but also the last large troupe to independently tour small regional centers, with the exception of some of the perennial Jubilee Singers. Local resident stayers continued performing at various vaudeville venues. By September 1914 Charles Pope had joined the Era Comedy Four on the Brennan-Fuller (and later Tivoli) circuit, replacing comedian Billy Brown, who had teamed with George Sorlie. Somewhere around October 1915 the Era Comedy Four split up. Pope would go on performing around various circuits well in to the 1920s. Huntley Spencer remained, and was associated with one of the later Fisk Jubilee troupes (see Appendix 3). Brown and Sorlie continued together on the Brennan-Fuller circuit until December 1916, when Sorlie went his own way. Brown continued playing on Brennan-Fuller, including New Zealand until late 1917, when he returned to America.[2]

New Arrivals

The war years made it easier for McIntosh to strike deals with white English acts who were happy to come to Australia. It probably made little difference to U.S. acts, and for African Americans the relatively privileged status they had occupied on the racial front in earlier years had faded with the increasingly strident White Australia policy making things more difficult. Lester Walton, dean of black theatrical journalists, in a *New York Age* article, April 11, 1911, warned African Americans about the hazards of being lured to Australia.

> In recent years many colored performers have been lured away from the United States by promoters glib of tongue and possessing the power to draw pretty verbal pictures that so appealed to the imagination of many colored artists that they were enticed to foreign shores only to find conditions entirely different than what they had been represented. It would, therefore, be well for those thinking of leaving with the minstrel company to investigate fully into the reliability of the person or persons sending the show to Australia.

For several years to come, new black arrivals would be individual acts recruited as part of a package put together by the local rival entrepreneurs. It's time to backtrack a few years chronologically to pick up on some who had featured strongly before the arrival of the Kersands troupe. The coverage of the later Fisk Singers activities after McAdoo's death is covered in Appendix 3, but there were inevitable crossovers between these and the wider theatrical and vaudeville traditions.

Clarence Tisdale

One such was the arrival of Clarence Tisdale in 1904, recruited by Fisks manager Richard Collins to boost the strength of his troupe. Born in Louisville, Kentucky, in 1878, Tisdale was a talented tenor, described as a "silver-voiced" second Wallace King. He arrived on the RMS *Manuka* on October 8, 1904, and stayed with the Fisk Singers until March 1907, when he was recruited for the Fuller circuit's next planned New Zealand tour. Tisdale would become a fixture on the Fuller circuit in both countries for three years and three months. During that time he would frequently share bills with other African American residents, including Sam Keenan, Irving Sayles, Blutch Jones, and George Sorlie.

Being a support for the latest top-line imported acts meant he was usually quite low on the billing, but the reviews throughout that time show that he was a firm favorite with audiences. His itinerary over the time included:

- 1907: Christchurch, Wellington, Dunedin, Wellington, Auckland, Brisbane, Sydney
- 1908: Sydney, Melbourne, Sydney, Melbourne
- 1909: Melbourne, Kalgoorlie, Perth, Adelaide, Melbourne, Brisbane, Sydney, Adelaide
- 1910: Adelaide, Perth, Adelaide, Melbourne, Sydney

After finishing on the Fuller circuit in August 1910, Tisdale reappears in U.S. later that year, playing in musical comedies with Chicago's Pekin Theatre Company. In 1912, he joined James Lightfoot's Right Quintette, with whom he made four recordings in 1915, two of which have survived. He continued performing with the Lightfoot group, and later until 1940 with his own Tisdale Trio.[3] He died on January 1, 1945.

Charles J. Johnson

As if Jack Johnson had not been enough of his clan to satisfy public demand, for several years after his departure the Johnson name would feature prominently on Australasian marquees. No fewer than three acts would include the name Johnson between 1909 and 1912. The first of these arrived just six months after Jack's departure. Under a report headed "Boastful Black Buck," the Perth *Sunday Times* (August 15, 1909) reported the arrival in Australia on the RMS *Otway*, of Jack Johnson's alleged cousin, Charles J. Johnson. The interviewer's bias is betrayed by his description of Johnson as a "Kolored Koon Komedian." The basis of Charles J.'s claim to being a cousin of Jack is unclear. Jack had an adopted brother named Charles, who is not the same person, so the relationship must be considered doubtful. The boastful tag was probably provoked by Johnson's staunch support for his recently present "cousin," and his confident (and soon to be proven true) prediction that Jack would easily defeat former world heavyweight champion James J. Jeffries.

By the time he arrived, Charles J. Johnson had already had a successful career in England, dating back to 1903. Before then, in the U.S., he had served an apprenticeship during the late 1890s in touring black shows like Col. Robinson's "Old Southern Life Company," where he was recruited initially as a "gun juggler," later billed as a "comedian."[4]

Johnson started at the Sydney Tivoli on August 21, billed as "The Black Diamond; cornerman and champion cakewalker of the world." His act included singing, dancing, and humorous patter. Whether his claim to the cakewalk title had any more basis than his claim to be Jack's cousin is unclear. His name does not feature in any of the canonical literature on jazz and black dance, all references therein being to Charles Johnson of Johnson and Dean, with whom he would later share an Australian stage. Nevertheless, audiences and reviewers were highly impressed with his whirlwind dancing. The August 22 *Sydney Sun* enthused:

> Charles J Johnson, a cousin of the gentleman who made such a dramatic Australian debut at the Stadium last Christmas, upheld his reputation as 'the world's champion cake-walker' last night. That is to say, he is the best cake-walker Tivoli critics have seen, and in the complicated art of side stepping and elaborate foot work, it is safe to say that he is a lot more graceful, if not quite so industrious and forceful, as his punching namesake.

While cakewalking is not typically a solo effort, Johnson's presentation compensated with an elaborate costume, described in the August 28 *Newsletter*: "Red spats, red ribbons flying at the wrists, flying red ribbons at the neck, and a red ribbon for a watch chain." By then, he was sharing the bill with Captain Winston's Performing Seals, but holding his own, as the *Sunday Sun* observed: "There are other good things in the Tivoli show. Charles J Johnson, the black diamond, who does the cake-walk in a way that really does take the cake, is just as good in his own way as is his cousin Jack in the fighting line."

Johnson finished in Sydney on October 15. He opened at Melbourne's Opera House the following day, and as in Sydney, it was his cakewalking that attracted the most attention. He was soon sharing the bill with the seals again, and they all moved on to Adelaide for the reopening of the local Tivoli on November 27. He finally parted company with the seals when he entered their traditional habitat, joining the SS *Orsova* bound for London on December 16, 1909. However, this was not the last of Charles J. Johnson in Australia.

Charles J. Johnson Returns (1912)

The "Black Diamond" arrived back in Sydney via the SS *Orontes* on January 4, 1912. He played the matinee at the Tivoli the following day. The January 7 *Sunday Times* remarked: "Charles J Johnson had the welcome of an old favorite at the Tivoli yesterday. Johnson has put some new twists and turns into his act since his first visit to Australia." He was sharing the bill, among others, with "GEORGE THE 1ST AND ROSIE, The Most Cultured Chimpanzee Living, and a Clever Dog."

After a six-week season, Johnson switched to the Adelaide Tivoli. Devotees of black entertainment might have felt confused by the surfeit of Johnsons, as Charles J. was sharing the bill there with Johnson and Dean, as well as the familiar Irving Sayles. Within two weeks Adelaide's rival Fuller's King Theatre would be featuring the team of Johnson and Wells, just returned from their New Zealand tour. Johnson and Dean departed for Brisbane at the end of February, leaving Charles J. as sole Johnsonian custodian for the Tivoli against Fuller. He moved to the Melbourne Opera House on March 30, where *Table Talk* (April 4, 1912) reported: "His dancing is of a distinctly high order; his [timing] is perfect, and the steps and movements differ from any that we have had here. His songs are given with good emphasis and point, but it is his dancing that is the special feature of the turn."

The Melbourne season finished late in May, and on May 25 Charles J. opened at Brisbane's Empire Theatre, the June 15 *Queenslander* noting: "That genial coloured gentleman,

Mr. Charles J Johnson, has sung and danced himself into the hearts of Empire patrons, and his familiar coon smile would provoke a responsive laugh from the most pronounced misanthrope. His champion coloured Cakewalk is the poetry of motion, and above all, his turn is stamped with refinement."

Charles J.'s Brisbane season lasted until June 28, during the last weeks of which he was competing with Johnson and Wells at the rival Fuller's Theatre Royal. He was announced as starting "a short farewell season" at Sydney's Tivoli on July 13. He finished there on July 24, appropriately on a bill that again included Irving Sayles. His departure coincided with extensive media coverage of Hugh D. McIntosh's plans to bring "cousin" Jack Johnson back to Australia, a scheme that was abandoned due to Jack's involvement in scandals and legal problems. Charles J. Johnson resumed his successful English career until at least May 1917, after which it seems likely he returned to the U. S.[5]

Johnson and Wells

It's symbolic of the keen competition between the Brennan-Fuller and the Tivoli circuits that in 1911 both should feature black singing and dancing acts called, respectively, "Johnson and Wells" and "Johnson and Dean." Johnson and Wells were the first to arrive.

Duke Johnson and Mae Wells arrived in Sydney via the RMS *Zealandia* on September 4, 1911, without their 10-year-old daughter Helena, who had previously traveled through Europe with them, and would be better known in her own right later under the name Helena Justa. They had been recruited by the Brennan-Fuller circuit on the basis of a highly successful vaudeville career spanning many years in the U.S. and Europe. They present something of an enigma as, despite their high profile in Europe, it is difficult to trace anything significant about their joint career in the usual sources of information about black entertainers. This is because they performed over the prestigious Orpheum and Proctor circuits, which featured only the most highly regarded black acts, such as Bill "Bojangles" Robinson. They therefore went largely unnoticed by the usual black entertainment media, which concentrated on the circuits that traditionally used black acts.

Duke Johnson and Mae Wells, "America's Foremost Colored Singers and Dancers," published in *The Critic* (Adelaide), 28 February 1912. Courtesy *Trove*, National Library of Australia.

Duke Johnson had served an early apprenticeship in minstrel shows, including with the Georgia Up To Date Minstrels, who had an association with P G Lowery's Orchestra, an early nursery of jazz musicians. Mae Wells had similarly made a reputation for herself during two seasons with Isham's Octoroons, a large minstrel type show that glorified black females. A New York *Clipper* advertisement declared the show had "30 Olive Hued Operatic Queens." Mae's portrait can be seen on a poster for "John W. Isham's Famous Octoroons" around 1898.[6] The couple had married in New York around 1900. In 1907, Johnson and Wells had played the London Coliseum and the London Hippodrome (six weeks) with their own show, the "Sunny South Company," before touring all the major cities of England, Ireland, and Scotland. They had also played the leading cities of Germany, Hungary, Austria, Belgium, and Holland.[7]

They opened their Australian season at Newcastle's King's Hall on September 9, and a week later were at the Brennan-Fuller home base, the National Amphitheatre in Sydney. Duke's eccentric dancing and Mae's singing were "an instantaneous success." According to the Adelaide *Register* (March 30, 1912), they had a repertory of 50 songs, their specialty routines being "A Coon Opera" and Johnson's "One-man Quadrille," which "must be heard and seen to be appreciated." Their Sydney season lasted a lengthy five weeks, followed by two weeks in Brisbane and another three weeks in Newcastle at the local Brennan-Fuller houses.

At this stage their Australian season was interrupted for a New Zealand tour lasting most of January–February 1912. They were part of a package put together by Brennan-Fuller that included as the bill topper an act known as Prince Charles, who was a most wonderful orangutan, as described by the *Southland Times* of December 26 and 27, 1911:

> Who cooks, eats, skates, cycles, motors and does other things so much after the manner of an accomplished man that we are told, one is sufficiently puzzled and interested to re-read The Origin of the Species…. The monkey seems to understand etiquette, and he was extremely polite at the lunch table. He dined becomingly, donned his spectacles, read the bill, summoned the waiter, paid him, and accepted the change, which he duly pocketed.

W. C. Fields, a recent visitor to Australia in 1903, is reputed to have said, "Never work with animals or children." Johnson and Wells might have shared that sentiment about Prince Charles but, despite the monkey business, their reception in New Zealand was every bit as positive as in Australia.

They opened the New Zealand season at Dunedin's His Majesty's Theatre on December 28 for six nights. Following a sea voyage and train trip, their simian competition was too ill to complete his act on the first night. However, it illustrates the hazards of long-distance touring that his human companions were not immune to the same problem. The journalist for the *Southland Times* (December 30, 1911), who interviewed Duke Johnson at the first-night interval, found the dancer sitting in a chair, completely exhausted. "He explained that he was quite unable to give a response to the recall, because though the dancing looks easy, and though he gives the impression he enjoys it, it is still very hard work."

For the rest of their itinerary they played a week in each of the major centers— Christchurch, Wellington, and Napier—finishing at Auckland. Along the way they played shorter one- or two-night stops at Oamaru, Masterton, Wanganui, Hastings, and Hamilton. Towards the end of their closing week, the Lorgnette column of the NZ *Observer*, on February 24, 1912, commented:

> Of course, Prince Charles is in the front as a draw to the curious, and this ape is certainly marvellously trained, and such a grotesque caricature of humanity that one is kept on the grin through the whole of his turn. His supper party act is one of the best. Prince Charles's manner, from the ordering of the wine to the smoking of the final cigarette, being inimitable…. The coloured comedians, Johnson and Wells, came here with an American reputation which Auckland audiences made haste to endorse. Their singing is delightful, and their dancing is as much so, particularly Johnson's eccentric dance.

Their Australian season resumed on March 2 at Adelaide's King's Theatre, where they followed on the heels of Johnson and Dean, who had just finished at the Adelaide Tivoli. The March 5 *Advertiser* noted of Johnson and Wells, "Their footwork is intricate, almost impossible to describe. Their catchy songs delighted the audience, and their popularity is assured." They stayed four weeks in Adelaide, followed by four weeks at the Melbourne's Amphitheatre. There was then a three-week tour of Northern Queensland (Rockhampton, Townsville, and Charters Towers) followed by a return visit to Brisbane for two weeks starting June 10. At Brisbane they were on the same bill as a young Roy Rene, later to find fame as Australia's favorite "Mo" McCackie. At the end of the run the June 28 *Brisbane Telegraph* reported that they "had a splendid send-off—Miss Mae being loaded with floral favours and bon-bons."

They returned for a final two-week farewell visit to the Sydney home of Brennan-Fuller, after which July 15 at Newcastle saw "Absolutely the Last Night in Australia of JOHNSON AND WELLS." The Honolulu *Star-Bulletin* (August 15, 1912) reported their having a successful season at Honolulu, en route home to visit their daughter in Chicago, after "a sensationally successful tour of Australia."

They continued performing for some years, including an act in 1919 with daughter Helena Justa, and Duke's brother Charlie. The brothers were still together in late 1921 but the family fades from performing after that. Helena had a successful career of her own, including a role in Lew Leslie's *Blackbirds of 1930*. In 1927, father Duke and daughter Helena both played in the show *Struttin' Sam from Alabam'* but by 1934 he was referred to as "the late Duke Johnson."

Johnson and Dean

> Say have you ever seen Miss Dora Dean?
> She is the finest girl you have ever seen.
> I'm a-goin' to try and make this girl my queen
> Next Sunday morning I'm goin' to marry Dora Dean.

This was the chorus of the song written by Bert Williams for an early Williams and Walker show, in tribute to the famed voluptuous beauty and personal charm of Dora Dean (Babbage). Top vaudeville stars, Dora and husband Charles Johnson were known as the "King and Queen of colored aristocracy." Spanning the era of the cakewalk and vaudeville, they epitomized style and class. "Way back in those first days," Johnson told the *Toledo Blade* on March 23, 1952: "We decided the one thing that would make our act different would be 'class.' None of that 'Uncle Tom' humor for us."

They were the first black dance team to play Broadway (1897), and the first dance team, black or white, to wear evening clothes on stage.[8] Charles wore a monocle, gloves and cane. Dora's lavish gowns were reported to cost more than a thousand dollars. A portrait of her wearing one, painted in Europe by a German artist, was unveiled in London at the coronation of King Edward VII in 1902.[9] Their bookings in Europe had included two months a year, for five years, in Berlin's Wintergarten, three summer months for three years in Budapest, and two months for three years in London's Palace Theatre. Apart from elegance and style, their dancing skills were hugely admired. Charles was an eccentric, or legomania (rubber legs), dancer. The Stearnses (*Jazz Dance*) considered the pair to be forerunners in the category they called the "Class acts" which later included such notables as (Honi) Coles and (Cholly) Atkins.

While Johnson and Dean were promoted in Europe as "coloured fashion plates," back home in the U.S. not everyone approved of their style, and racism greatly affected their reception. The New York *Morning Telegraph* (November 1, 1899) commented:

> Johnson and Dean are real negroes. For this reason they sing "coon" songs well and do ragtime in a fashion beyond their white imitators. Nevertheless they are real "coons" and this destroys much of the effectiveness their work. The negro is never a pleasing sight on the stage, and when he wears dress clothes much better in material and cut than those of his white fellows, and acts up to his dress with an impudence and self-assertion as offensive as it is foolish, he fails to entertain and simply bores. The negro makes a good waiter, is often a splendid barber and in the South, when properly looked after by the shotgun squads, becomes a good voter, but there is no wild cry from the country at large for him to come to the rescue of a stage in need of elevating. The negro can do all the elevating that is needed in the hotels and big office buildings.

Charles Johnson and Dora Dean. Courtesy of the Marshall Winslow Stearns Collection (MC 030), Institute of Jazz Studies, Rutgers University Libraries.

Johnson and Dean opened a five-month season on the Tivoli circuit at the Sydney Tivoli theatre on November 4, 1911. They were the last African American act booked personally by Harry Rickards before his death. The November 5 *Sunday Times* declared them a "sweeping success," while *Punch* thought they "swept the floor," declaring them the "Best coon turn the Tivoli management has ever put on." While there was lavish praise for Charles's dancing, much of the fascination centered on Dora's figure and her extravagant costumes. Some examples:

- The dusky Miss Dora wore two gorgeous train dresses, and then suggested the [lady with nothing on] when she strutted the stage in tights, and showed her fine figure (*Punch*, Sydney)
- Miss Dean has a superb figure, which the several very smart costumes in which she appears show off to the utmost advantage (*Table Talk*, Sydney)
- Miss Dean is possessed of a figure guaranteed to attract the bald heads of Adelaide (*Sport*, Adelaide)

Under the heading "Darkness and Beauty" the Adelaide *Observer* (February 24, 1912) gave the following detailed description:

Miss Dean appears in a splendid garment of earth coloured satin, with a long snakelike train, which shows off her figure beautifully; four sash-ends of burnished gold tissue, with touches of emerald, hang from the waist, one sleeve is of flesh-coloured lattice of silver, and the other does not exist. She wears a high-crowned hat with a quaintly turned brim, lined with black velvet, no blacker than her hair, and floating pale pink plumes crown the whole.

The itinerary of the duo on the Tivoli circuit included Sydney (Tivoli) four weeks; Melbourne (Rickards' Opera House) four weeks; Perth (Melrose Theatre) three weeks; Adelaide (Tivoli) two weeks; Brisbane (Empire Theatre) three weeks, and finishing with a two-week farewell season back at the Sydney Tivoli on April 5, 1912. In Brisbane they had shared the bill with the 20-year-old Gladys Moncrieff, later to be famed as Australia's "Our Glad." The May 18 *New York Clipper* reported that "heavy bookings in America and England compel them to return home at once." Johnson and Dean continued their joint career up to 1919, when they split to form separate acts. They reunited in the 1930s and had a revival of sorts before retiring to live comfortably until their deaths, Dora in 1949, Charles in 1953. He was still planning a solo comeback in 1952, as per the *Toledo Blade* interview.

Tim (Kingfish) Moore and Gerty Moore (1917)

After the departure of the various Johnsons, and the Kersands remnants, and Josephine Gassman with her Picks, there was a brief hiatus in new arrivals, perhaps attributable to the war. In 1917, there was a flurry of new activity on the Brennan-Fuller front. First to arrive, in February, were Tim and Gertie Moore, followed soon after by Jolly John Larkins in May. All of these were seasoned black vaudeville performers.

Harry Roscoe "Tim" Moore was born in Rock Island, Illinois, in 1888. His early career followed the classic trajectory of many black entertainers, including a stint with a traveling medicine show. Around 1903 or 1904, he was recruited by a white vaudeville performer, Cora Miskel, as one of her two picaninnies, billed as The Gold Dust Twins. This was a reference to a popular series of advertisements for washing powder products featuring two piccaninnies. There are reports that he

Top: Dora Dean portrait from the sheet music cover of "Don't You Think You'd Like to Fondle Me" by Hughie Cannon, ca. 1900. *Bottom:* Miss Dean (Johnson and Dean), *Table Talk* (Melbourne, Victoria) 21 December 1911. Courtesy *Trove,* National Library of Australia.

toured English music halls with Miskel.[10] Later he had brief careers as a boxer and in horse racing stables. One of his notable achievements was a one-man version of *Uncle Tom's Cabin*, in which he portrayed both Simon Legree and Uncle Tom, performing with half of his face made up with white chalk and the other with burnt cork.

By the time he arrived in Australia, in February 1917, Tim Moore had been running his own vaudeville troupe, Tim Moore's Georgia Sunflowers, and had married his second wife, Gertrude, in 1916. They would stay together until she died in 1934. Billed as "Chocolate in color with rare humor and nimble feet," they opened in Sydney at Fuller's National Amphitheatre on February 3, sharing the bill with a female trick cyclist, a ventriloquist, and a xylophone player. Despite some initial difficulty with the acoustics of the amphitheater, they were soon receiving favorable reviews, albeit reflecting rather stereotypical material.

Tim Moore as he appeared in the Broadway production of *Blackbirds of 1928*.

> One of the most attractive of the new items was that presented by Tim and Gertie Moore, who had an encouraging reception. They were styled 'America's so different coloured entertainers,' and they gave a pleasing display of eccentricities, strongly reminiscent of the old-time nigger minstrels, with the introduction of plantation melodies.

Tim was compared favorably as a humorist to Irving Sayles and Charles Pope.[11] With varying vaudeville bills, the pair followed an Australian itinerary on the Fuller circuit with Sydney (National Amphitheatre, three weeks); Melbourne (Bijou Theatre, four weeks, plus one week at Brunswick Empire); Adelaide (Majestic Theatre, two weeks); Perth (Melrose Theatre, and some split weeks at Fremantle's King's Theatre).

The Moores finished the WA dates on May 11 and opened at His Majesty's Theatre, Wellington (NZ) on May 28, where Billy C. Brown was also on the bill. They toured on the local Fuller circuit, again sharing a varying vaudeville bill that in Auckland included Japanese acrobats, female trapeze artists, a comedy juggler, a pair of Italian singers, and the previously familiar xylophone player. Their schedule was: Wellington (two weeks); Dunedin (three weeks); Wellington again (three weeks, with Billy C. Brown on the same bill), and Auckland again (two weeks).

They were generally well received everywhere, though their return visit to Auckland elicited a comment from *NZ Herald* (September 4, 1917): "The coloured comedians, Tim and Gertie Moore, made a reappearance and received an excellent reception. It is a pity they have not acquired any new 'patter' since their last appearance, as it tends to mar their items somewhat."

They finished in New Zealand on September 8, but their scheduled opening at Brisbane's Empire Theatre on September 22 was delayed by a day, due to their being unable to get through from New Zealand in time. The Brisbane engagement lasted three weeks until

October 19, when they moved to Newcastle for two weeks, sharing a bill with a show titled "Fuzzy Wuzzy," though not apparently with any intended reference to them. The remainder of their time, until November 28, was spent in sporadic appearances in Sydney, sometimes with split days, between the three Fuller theatres, National, Majestic, and Princess. They were next reported by the *Chicago Defender*, on February 2, 1918, as enjoying success in Honolulu, having arrived there on December 11 "via New Zealand, Samoa and the Fiji Islands."

Although their Australasian sojourn could be considered only moderately successful, Tim Moore's career prospered after his return to America. Initially he played in his own "Chicago Follies," which toured the black circuits in several versions into the 1920s. During the twenties he played in many touring musical-comedy shows, sometimes under his own direction. While most of these were only moderately successful, they contributed to his reputation as a leading black comic. His big Broadway break came in 1928, when white producer Lew Leslie selected him for a leading comedy role in the major hit show *Blackbirds of 1928*, alongside such stars as Bojangles Robinson, Aida Ward, and Adelaide Hall. He played in several less notable *Blackbirds* shows during the thirties and continued playing nightclubs, occasional films, and stage shows.

While Moore was living in quiet retirement in 1951, his friend Flournoy Miller recommended him for the part of George "the Kingfish" Stevens in the planned television adaptation of the long-running radio show *Amos 'n' Andy*. The original show was the creation of two blackface white comedians, Freeman Gosden and Charles Correll, borrowing heavily from the comedy style of Flournoy Miller and Aubrey Lyles in the 1921 show *Shuffle Along*. The radio show started in 1928 and ran with great popularity until 1960.

When the television series was planned in 1951, in an era of rising civil liberties consciousness, it was no longer acceptable to use white blackface characters so most of the cast was black. Even with black actors, there was considerable opposition on the grounds of stereotyping. Nevertheless, Tim Moore's portrayal of Kingfish on TV proved so popular that by the time the third series was planned in 1953, it featured Kingfish as the leading character. Opposition from the NAACP did eventually get the program withdrawn, though it ran in syndication for many years. Tim Moore died in 1958. Having lived through, and been part of, the stereotype era, he probably wondered what the fuss was about.

The Mysteries of Jolly John Larkins

On May 18, 1917, the *Melbourne Age* advertised at Fuller's Bijou Theatre, "A New Style [of] Singing, Dancing and Talking Comedian," Jolly John Larkins (also frequently spelled Larkin).[12] New he may have been to the Australian public but he had long been familiar to devotees of black vaudeville. He was born in 1882 in Norfolk, Virginia.[13] He had been active on the black vaudeville circuits since the 1890s. In addition to his performance skills, he was a writer, producer, and songwriter.

In 1903, Larkins wrote a show called *A Trip to the Jungles* as a vehicle for himself and his female partner Dora Patterson. In 1904, the show was renamed *A Trip to Africa* and Larkins collaborated on the music for it with two legendary figures of African American music, James Reese Europe and Will Vodery. James Reese Europe would go on to be the dominant society dance band leader of the New York social scene, pioneering the foxtrot dance, as their chosen orchestra for the sensational white dance team of Vernon and Irene

Castle.[14] Vodery and Reese Europe were early mentors for both Duke Ellington and George Gershwin. A record of Larkins's collaboration with Europe, sheet music for a song, is preserved in the Library of Congress.[15]

Between 1907 and 1911, *A Trip to Africa* was incorporated into the famous Black Patti (Sissieretta Jones) Troubadours, with Larkins as a stage manager and lead performer. A *New York Clipper* report (October 2, 1909) declared that "Jolly John Larkins, as Raz Jenkins, was said to be the funniest negro comedian ever seen on the Hot Springs stage, having to respond to innumerable encores."

Larkins crossed paths with James Reese Europe again in 1914. On April 8 of that year, the now-famous James Europe and his National Negro Orchestra staged a concert at the Manhattan Casino, featuring Vernon and Irene Castle, at which the stellar lineup of top black entertainers included Larkins. He was billed under the soubriquet that would also be applied to him in Australia, "The Rajah of Mirth."[16]

Larkins was brought to Australia, like Tim and Gertie Moore, by the ever hungry-for-talent Brennan-Fuller cir-

Jolly John Larkins on the sheet music cover for "A Royal Coon." Composed by James Reese Europe, lyrics by Jolly John Larkins, published by Will Rossiter, Chicago, 1907. Courtesy Library of Congress, Music Division.

cuit. Unlike the Moores and many others who came, did their stint, and left, Larkins was to prove a long stayer, eight years in all, traversing an ever more puzzling itinerary in Australia and New Zealand. Exploring the reasons behind this reveals a tale of romance and tragedy. Initially, Larkins followed the normal pattern, touring with ever varying vaudeville bills in Melbourne and Sydney from May to August 1917. From September he spent the remainder of the year touring New Zealand (Auckland, Dunedin, Christchurch, Wellington, and Auckland again) before reappearing in Adelaide for the Christmas season, then returning to Melbourne in late January 1918 until mid–February.

He received warm reviews at all venues. His presentation involved singing and dancing, interspersed with humorous anecdotes known as "patter." This was delivered in the continuous laughing style that had earned him the title "Jolly," one reviewer describing him as "a happy-style performer, who has laughed his way to the weight of 18 stone [or 252 pounds]." Much of the material was of the traditional minstrel-style repertoire always popular with Australian audiences, and greeted with the usual media insensitivity. An otherwise enthusiastic review in the Brisbane *Telegraph* (August 31, 1918) included "Jolly John Larkin, one of the festive coons in the minstrel first part at the Empire, cavorts round the stage like a cannibal after two serves of boiled missionary."

Throughout 1918 Larkins played in Sydney, Newcastle, Brisbane, Melbourne, and Adelaide. While most of this was on the Fuller circuit, much of his Sydney time was also spent on the lesser known Clay circuit.[17] The Clay circuit advertised itself as having "the cheapest shows in the world." Their theatres would share acts, often with split weeks, or even days. Newspaper advertising was limited, billposting being preferred, which made tracking Larkins's engagements more difficult than with the Fuller chain.

By 1917 Hugh McIntosh had switched the emphasis of his Tivoli circuit away from vaudeville to musical-comedy, so Fuller and Clay then had the field largely to themselves. Larkins was popular on the Clay circuit. As Clay relied mainly on local vaudeville talent, picking up a high-profile import like Larkin was a bonus. By early 1919 Larkins was back in Adelaide, and then from March to September repeating the New Zealand circuit. He saw out the rest of the year in Brisbane, except for part of November, when he made a brief foray northwards to Rockhampton, Charters Towers, and Townsville. Throughout 1920 he stayed busy at Australian venues, Adelaide, Newcastle, Sydney (six months on the Clay Sydney and suburban circuit), Melbourne, Adelaide, Sydney, Newcastle, Brisbane, and then off again to New Zealand in May 1921.

In the normal course of events Larkins might have been expected to finish his original Fuller circuit contract and resume his U.S. vaudeville career sometime in 1918. The unusual trajectory of his Australasian activities over the following years is attributable to the fact that he had formed a romantic liaison with a local lady, Rachel (Rae) Anderson, a costume designer. They had two daughters, Olga, born 1921, and Joan, born 1924. The need to protect the privacy of his irregular relationship in the face of the prevailing racial prejudice in Australia helps account for the lack of public information about Larkins's private life in a local media usually hungry for personal interviews.[18]

After several months at the usual major New Zealand venues (Wellington, Auckland, Dunedin, Christchurch), Larkins drops off the radar for a large part of 1922 and well into 1923, showing up only at smaller NZ regional centers, leading troupes under his own name, Jolly John Larkin's "Happy Folks," and "Royal Troubadours." For someone who had been used to being a top-line performer, this must have been a depressing step down, and financially much less lucrative than he was accustomed to. Letters written around this time to his partner suggest he was struggling financially. During June–July 1923 he was briefly back for his last Australian visit, playing Goulburn, and at the Sydney Stadium as support entertainment for a boxing program, suggesting he was running out of options in Australia.

He was soon back in New Zealand, again touring minor regional centers with his own troupe, Whangarei and Tauranga. By late 1924 the same troupe was being billed as *Lee Smith's Follies* or *New Follies*, with Larkins billed as "the world's greatest comedian." However, the troupe appears to have folded in late 1925, and with it Jolly John fades from the Australasian public scene. Before leaving New Zealand he offered to take Olga, the eldest of his daughters, to the U.S., but Rae opted to keep her. Joan, the younger, was put in foster care. His Australian family lost contact with Larkins after his departure.

Larkins's reappearance in the U.S. was confirmed by a report in *Variety*, on August 19, 1925, that he was now in New York. The *Pittsburgh Courier* (May 24, 1926) reported him playing *The Cotton Club Revue* at Harlem's Lafayette Theatre, and shortly after at the Harlem Cotton Club itself. By 1930 he had relocated to the West Coast, still playing vaudeville, in a revue called *Harlem Scandals* at south-side Los Angeles's famous Lincoln Theatre.

Larkins had left the U.S. at the height of the minstrelsy-ragtime era. By the time he returned, the new Jazz Age was in full swing, a world of Prohibition, speakeasies, and jazz clubs. His style of entertainment was old hat, so he reinvented himself in the new world of Hollywood and movies, initially in bit parts at low rates. However, in July 1931, the black *Pittsburgh Courier* proudly proclaimed: "John Larkin is new star in cinema firmament," adding "After three years of studious application John Larkin has arrived in filmland. No longer shall we conjecture who shall amongst us climb the dizzy heights of movie stardom."

Between 1930 and 1936 Larkins was one of the most in-demand African American actors. His IMDb listing of 46 credits, even though most were minor roles, puts him on a par for those years with such top African American names as Clarence Muse, Stepin Fetchit, Rex Ingram, and Mantan Moreland. Oddly, his movie career is largely ignored in the literature of black cinema, probably partly because of his early death, and the fact that his appearances were generally in Hollywood movies rather than the numerous B-grade black movies, by directors such as Oscar Micheaux, which have tended to attract historians' interest in recent years.

By 1936 Larkins was reported in poor health with heart disease, and his death, on March 18, 1936, was announced in the March 20 *Eagle*. The *Eagle* carried a funeral report on March 27, at which the attendance included many notable African American show business names, among them Billy McClain, Hattie McDaniel (soon to be of *Gone with the Wind* fame), Clarence Muse, and Bill "Bojangles" Robinson.

His death report listed the following achievements:

> Outstanding and noteworthy of films wherein his work won him praise were "Sporting Blood," an MGM studio film, "Alexander Hamilton" and "Dangerous Gentleman," "Diamond Jim Brady" and lately he had appeared in "Trail of the Lonesome Pine," "Green Pastures," and the last before his death, the Marion Davies-starred Warner Bros. film "Hearts Divided."

Larkins was survived by his wife of two years, Mary Prudence, but no American offspring. Eventually, with the help of Steve Goldstein, in 2011 Larkins's Australian granddaughter located and visited her ancestor's grave, helping bring closure to his then still living daughter Joan, who died in 2014. The *Eagle* (May 27, 1936) eulogy by fellow actor Clarence Muse on Larkins's death suggests he paid a high price for his lost family: "All of his woes and all of his cares were carried within and only when they were a little too much to hold he sought a loved one to tell his story. He was slow to confide in people. He moved about the world a little shy, sometimes almost afraid of fellow artists."

17

The Jazz Age
(1923–1925)

The first references to jazz music and jazz bands in the Australian media appeared in the second half of 1917, usually associated with being loud, discordant, and disreputable.[1] The first performance of jazz by a local band occurred in June 1918, when Ben Fuller of the Fuller circuit organized the formation of a jazz band with the help of a local resident American musician. Fuller wanted to be the first to present the "new American craze" and on June 21 advertised the appearance at his National Theatre of the Sydney-based American singer Belle Sylvia "and her jazz band."[2] Audiences responded enthusiastically and jazz had arrived. Many of the later African American arrivals would present themselves as jazz performers.

After the Fuller circuit had featured the Moores and Jolly John Larkins in 1917 there was a gap until 1923, with no significant African American acts arriving apart from the already well-known Ferry the Frog (see Chapter 10). That doesn't mean there was a lack of African American entertainment down under. Apart from the continuing presence of Larkins, many of the earlier long term stayers were still active. These included: various incarnations of the Fisk Jubilee Singers; Charlie Pope, who had switched from the Tivoli to the Fuller circuit in 1906 where he remained till 1918, continuing to perform in Australia until his death in 1928; and Will Sumner, who, having shared the bill with Josephine Gassman and her Picks in 1914, continued in New Zealand until 1924.

We have already noted the death in 1920 of Mrs. Hamilton Hodges (Jennie Robinson) of Fisk Singers fame. Mrs. Louisa (Johnny) Matlock died in 1917, having conducted vaudeville entertainments in the suburbs of Melbourne, in conjunction with her son, Ernest (Ernie) Matlock, for many years.

The Tivoli Returns

When the next African American performers arrived in 1923, it was the Tivoli circuit that brought them. In 1921, Hugh D. McIntosh had announced his retirement from theatrical management and production, and negotiated a lease of his Rickards theatres to Harry G. Musgrove, under the J.C. Williamson banner. By 1923, after some initial uncertainty about whether the Tivoli would become a first-run cinema circuit, it was again the home of live vaudeville under Harry's cousin Jack Musgrove, and was actively recruiting African American acts. The first of these was the Royal Southern Singers.

The Royal Southern Singers

The Royal Southern Singers arrived in Melbourne on the Orient Line's RMS *Ormonde* on February 12, 1923. They were a quartette comprising Robert Williams, Joseph C. Covington, Frank Arthur Dennie, and Crescent Clinton Rosemond. Advance publicity made much of the fact that they had appeared by Royal Command before King George and Queen Mary at Buckingham Palace in 1919. This was probably while they were members of Will Marion Cook's Southern Syncopated Orchestra (SSO), which had spent time in England and Europe in 1919 and 1920. The SSO was of major importance in the early history of jazz, and also notable because of the inclusion in its ranks of jazz legend Sydney Bechet.

The Southern Singers opened at Melbourne's Tivoli on February 24, described as "dressed immaculately in brown suits" and billed as presenting "Harmony, Humor, Syncopation." This was a fair description of their combination of traditional ballads and snappy jazz tunes, combining spirituals like "Roll on Jordan" with recent Tin Pan Alley hits like "The Sheik of Araby." Another item in the repertoire was their former associate Will Marion Cook's lively signature piece "Swing Along," described as "a remarkable song for its period. A lilting melody with lyrics encouraging black children to be proud of who they are."[3]

The Royal Southern Singers, from top: Robert Williams, Crescent Clinton Rosemond, Joseph C. Covington and Frank A. Dennie. From sheet music cover, author's collection.

Comparing the Singers with a recently heard Fisk Jubilee group, *Table Talk* (March 8, 1923) commented: "There is more syncopation and less of the spiritual element in the vaudeville offering," but also mentioned that Frank A. Dennie's sister Carrie had sung in Melbourne as a member of the Fisk Singers. One of the Southern Singers' popular items was a monologue written by dialect poet and novelist Paul Laurence Dunbar and performed by C.C. Rosemond, "an antebellum sermon, or characteristic monologue, giving an impression of an old negro preacher in the Southern States of America before the Civil War, in which he exhorts his downtrodden fellow slaves to preserve faith in their eventual deliverance." another humorous item was "When the Royal Southern Singers ... harmonised a cats' courtship yesterday at the Tivoli, everybody's hands went instinctively in search of the bedroom slipper. It was an extraordinary piece of realistic trick singing, with a blend of the humorous that caused roars of laughter."

The Singers closed their five-week Melbourne season on March 29, 1923, and opened at Sydney's Tivoli at Easter for another five weeks, the *Adelaide Mail* (May 5, 1923) noting:

> [They] have beautiful voices, which blend perfectly, but, apart from the artistry of their singing, every number, whether plantation ditty, old English melody, light jazz number, or negro spiritual, is invested with a human appeal that strikes home not only to the ear, but to the heart. Each member of the quartette has a beaming, sunny smile that puts the audience on good terms with itself and its entertainers.

Their next port of call was Adelaide, opening at the Prince of Wales Theatre on May 12 for two weeks, then returning to an enthusiastic reception for a repeat three-week Melbourne season. After a return week by public demand in Adelaide, they headed west to Perth, arriving via the RMS *Khyber* at Fremantle to open at Perth's Prince of Wales Theatre on June 30. Announcing the Perth season, the June 28 *Daily News* wrote:

> The Eastern States are loathe to let them depart; return seasons have been played at every theatre, but these wonderful singers are booked for our Prince of Wales Theatre for Saturday, and so Adelaide was compelled to say good-bye to them last Tuesday, when they left, on the RMS *Khyber*. A great send-off was accorded the Royal Southern Singers, for these colored gentlemen are popular wherever they go.

The *Sunday Times* described the audience reaction to their initial performance as "a flattering reception; remarkable in its spontaneity." Originally scheduled to finish on July 21, the Perth season was extended for a week, finishing July 26. They departed for England via the RMS *Mongolia* on July 27, without Frank A. Dennie, who maintained the stayover tradition by remaining in Adelaide, performing as a singer but also as a saxophone player, and advertising his services as a saxophone teacher.

Frank Dennie had married in Australia in 1924 and after a brief period performing and teaching locally, he moved with his wife to New Zealand. There he was a popular solo act, singing and playing saxophone and banjo until late 1927. Financial problems resulting from a lengthy illness of his wife, and poor audiences due to bad weather conditions in towns he was touring, resulted in his declaring bankruptcy, after which he seems to have dropped out of public sight. The October 26 *Auckland Star* reported his death on October 24, 1933, in Auckland. He was survived by his wife.

Of the members who returned to England, Crescent Clinton Rosemond had the most notable later career. Back in England, he teamed with former SSO associate John Payne, and Welsh-born African American Mabel Mercer as the Southern Trio, or the Royal Southern Three. They had a featured role in Lew Leslie's *Blackbirds of 1927*, in which Mabel Mercer later replaced the ailing star Florence Mills. Mabel went on to be a famed New York cabaret singer, whose style influenced Frank Sinatra. Returning to the U.S. in 1929, Rosemond forged a new career in movies, with 45 credits on IMDb. He died in March 1966, aged 83. His daughter Bertha (Rosemond) Hope is a notable jazz pianist today.

Scott and Whaley

The next Tivoli arrival was the team of Scott and Whaley, opening at the Melbourne Tivoli on September 23, 1924. Though Harry Scott and Eddie Whaley were unquestionably

African American, most of their working life was spent in England. They arrived in 1909 on an English tour intended to last eight weeks, making their London debut at the Empire Theatre, Leicester Square, in 1910. They became firm favorites with the English public and spent the rest of their lives based in England.[4] At the Tivoli they were billed as "The highest salaried Negro comedians in the world." The September 25 *Table Talk* observed: "When they went to London some few years ago, they were receiving thirty dollars between them, but their last contract in England, netted over three hundred pounds per week." Tivoli records at the NFSA also show their Australian salary as £300 weekly.[5] They were heading a large vaudeville bill that included Australian caricaturist Bert Levy, and later, the English comedienne Marie Kendall (grandmother of English film star Kay Kendall).

Their act consisted of singing and dancing, interspersed with a series of comedy sketches, e.g., "an absurd yet clever travesty of the expensive experiences of a simpleton who invokes the law to save him from an awkward situation."

A popular finale was a burlesque speech of thanks to the audience, in which "conventional phrases are used regardless of meaning." In a lengthy report in *Table Talk* (October 9, 1924), Scott commented on the emergence of jazz and the initial difficulty local musicians had with jazz inflections.

> Folks talk of coon and nigger melodies, but such terms are offensive to us. The [younger generation] call for something different, jazz or humorous songs.... We were the first to take jazz music to England, and when we gave it to the conductor he told us it was an insult to ask any decent musicians to play such stuff. I told him, "There is the music by an American composer. I am not asking you to do anything but play it as it is written," and they could not do it. They simply could not get the rhythm at all. Now they have jazz bands everywhere in England.

Scott and Whaley played a month each in Sydney and Melbourne, to great enthusiasm. The October 4 *Melbourne Weekly Times* commented: "Scott and Whaley, the negro comedians at the Tivoli, are the best performers of their class seen in Melbourne for many a day." The November 12 *Referee* agreed: "Scott and Whaley, the colored comedians, made a great hit at their first appearance, and they kept the audience fairly rippling with laughter.... They have such a variety of [comedy] that wit and humor flows from them every moment they are on the stage." Closing in Sydney on December 5, 1924, they made a short farewell appearance in Melbourne before departing for England on the Orient liner *Ormuz* on December 16. They remained based there, playing together until Scott died in 1947. Whaley retired

Scott and Whaley in their sketch "For the Defense." *Table Talk* (Melbourne) 9 October 1924. Courtesy *Trove*, **National Library of Australia.**

to run a hotel in Brighton, which was a popular holiday home for black entertainers, until his death in 1960.

The Dixie Jubilee Singers

On October 27, 1924, New Zealand welcomed a new troupe of Jubilee Singers, who arrived in Wellington on the SS *Maunganui*. Known as the Dixie Jubilee Singers, they were led by W.C. Buckner (basso and conductor).[6] Unlike the Royal Southern Singers, and the soon-to-arrive Versatile Three, who combined jazz-style syncopation with their harmony singing, the Dixies were very much in the older Jubilee tradition. Buckner claimed that his troupe were legitimate successors to an early contemporary of the original Fisks, the Donavin Tennesseans, variously known as the "Original" or "Famous" Tennesseans.

There had been numerous claims to the title "Tennessee Jubilee Singers" over many years, several of whom were closer to minstrelsy, but Donavin's troupe had a legitimate claim. They had been formed two years after the Fisk Singers, for a similar purpose, to raise money for the impoverished Central Tennessee College, also of Nashville and today known as Walden University. Like the Fisk Singers under Loudin, they later became a private commercial venture under the management of J.W. Donavin.[7]

Buckner claimed that he and his wife formed the Dixie Jubilee Singers as a successor troupe in 1901, when the Tennesseans disbanded. Whether there was a direct link is difficult to determine, but one member of Buckner's 1909 troupe, Belle Stone (contralto), had been a member of the Original Tennessee Jubilee Singers in 1895.[8] The Dixies adhered rather stringently to the Jubilee tradition, albeit with some mixture of secular or classical items. On January 3, 1908, the *Sturgis Weekly Record* (South Dakota) had reported: "The Columbia Tennesseeans have been out for a number of years. They have been carefully drilled by W.C. Buckner, who has spent a life time as director of coloured jubilee singers." In 1923, Buckner had joined a group known

Poster (ca. 1890s) of Ferguson's Dixie Jubilee Concert Company, the forerunner of Buckner's Dixie Jubilee Singers. Madame Neale Gertrude Buckner, center; W.C. Buckner top left. Courtesy Schubertiade Music & Arts.

as the Sunset Four Quartette, who recorded four tunes for Paramount Records in 1924, one of which, "Barnum's Steam Calliope," heavily featured Buckner's "explosive" basso voice. Later that year he left the Quartette to reform the Dixie Jubilee Singers for their New Zealand trip.

The troupe that arrived in Wellington included Buckner (basso, conductor), his wife Madame Neale Gertrude Buckner (soprano), Helen Smallwood (contralto), C. Osceola Como (tenor), Willis Gauze (baritone), and L.A. Morris (tenor). Early accompanist Al M'Gurder seems to have been a temporary replacement for Marcus D'Albert, who filled that role from late November onwards, including solo items. Willis Gauze is the same Willis Gauze who had arrived with McAdoo's Georgia Minstrels in 1899, featured as a "female impersonator" and "male soprano." In addition to his role as a tenor voice, Morris was also a lightning cartoonist, which added a humorous touch that was appreciated by audiences.

The Dixies repertoire included a solid selection straight from the original Fisk's songbook, including "Steal Away," "Roll, Jordan, Roll," "Swing Low, Sweet Chariot," "The Gospel Train is Coming," and "I'm Rolling Through an Unfriendly World." There was also some non-spiritual African American material, including recitations by Buckner of dialect poems by Paul Laurence Dunbar, and the popular James P. Johnson song "Old Fashioned Love" from the recently successful all-black musical *Runnin' Wild*. Other secular music included Stephen Foster songs such as "Old Black Joe," "Old Folks at Home," "My Old Kentucky Home," and African American James A. Bland's "Carry Me Back to Old Virginny." There were also some classical items.

They opened at the Wellington Tivoli Theatre on November 1, 1924, to an enthusiastic reception, described by the November 6 *Evening Post*:

> It seems difficult for those who have not heard the singers to realise that an audience can be entertained by vocal items alone for two hours, but such is the case, and the numbers are so varied and well rendered that interest is at a high pitch throughout the performance. All the members of the company are talented, but one or two are outstanding.

From the outset it was clear that the media considered the Dixie Jubilees to be authentic black performers in a way they didn't apply to the later Fisk groups (see Appendix 3), one of which happened also to be touring New Zealand at the same time. The *Waihi Daily Telegraph* (January 10, 1925) noted: "Over twenty-six years have passed since the public of this Dominion have had an opportunity to hear a genuine company of Jubilee singers, and it is an opportunity that no one should miss."

Nevertheless, the critic for the *Evening Post* (November 3, 1924) wanted even more "authentic" material: "It was a pity perhaps that the Dixie Jubilee Singers did not strictly confine themselves to negro, musical and other items.... If Saturday's performance, before a house packed in every part, may be taken as a guide it was made quite clear that the negro items were most popular."

Whether by accident or design, the Fisk and Dixie troupes did not clash or cross each other's paths. After two weeks in Wellington, the Dixies toured the major centers of Christchurch, Dunedin, Palmerston and Auckland, until January 6, 1925, after which they embarked on a fairly leisurely series of dates in Whangarei, Waihi, Stratford, Opunake, Levin, Horowhena, Temuka, Otautau, and finishing at Queenstown on March 26, 1925. They found enthusiastic audiences at all venues and the only media notice other than their performances were for the occasional charity event they supported.

They returned to Wellington on April 10 to participate in a Good Friday Easter music festival. They finished up their New Zealand tour with one last concert at Auckland's King's Theatre on June 10, 1925. They were apparently in no hurry to return home to the U.S., as the two ladies, Mrs. Neale Buckner and Helen Smallwood, departed for San Francisco on the RMS *Tahiti* on July 21, while the males—Buckner, Gauze, and Morris—didn't leave until August 18, 1925, on the SS *Maunganui*.

Back in the U.S., Buckner formed a second Sunset Four, but while they were fulfilling an engagement at the Union Square Theatre in San Francisco, he was struck and killed by a car.[9] By June 1926 Gauze and Morris had teamed as the Harmony Three, and according to the *Pittsburgh Courier* (June 5, 1926), had "played everything in California following their arrival in America from Australia and are headed East." So ended the Buckner Dixie Jubilee Singers.

Williams and Taylor

On November 18, 1924, the SS *Ventura* arrived from San Francisco with a large number of theatrical personnel for the Tivoli circuit, including another African American duo, a comedy dance act, (Robert) Williams and (Clinton) Taylor. Like the earlier Johnson and Wells, Williams and Taylor are an example of a high-profile black act that was largely missed by the conventional literature on African American entertainers because their career, since at least 1918, was almost entirely on the prestigious white Keith-Orpheum circuit. A report shortly before their arrival described their act as follows:

> Williams and Taylor are two colored funsters specializing in dance steps. One is corked to the deepest shade of black. The other sticks to his natural saddle-color. They are immaculately garbed in dinner-jacket fashion. The black fellow at times intones like the late Bert Williams…. These fellows are marvellous dancers in speedy soft-shoe steps, in somersaulting while keeping time with taps of their hands and feet, in splits, in nip-ups. They score a hit of riotous proportions.[10]

The scheduling of Williams and Taylor's appearance in Melbourne was complicated by the presence there already of Scott and Whaley. *Table Talk* (December 24, 1924) reported that the management deemed it "unwise to have two black-faced acts on the same bill." Scott and Whaley gave their farewell Australian appearance in early December, so Williams and Taylor were able to move to the Sydney Tivoli after only six nights in Melbourne. They had a three-week engagement in Sydney, then back to Melbourne for three weeks, followed by a week at the Wintergarden in Brisbane, opening January 26, 1925. Billed mainly as a support act on the vaudeville bill, they were generally well received without attracting any special attention. They wrapped up their Australian tour with another week in Sydney, from February 7 to 14, 1925. According to the Sydney *Sun*, "Williams and Taylor were also particularly well received by the large audience." They left Australia from Perth in late February after an overland rail trip. Although reported as returning to the U.S., they show up in 1926 in England, and by 1927 were a featured act in Lew Leslie's highly successful *Blackbirds of 1927*. They remained in England for several years.

The Versatile Three

With Scott and Whaley in Sydney, and Williams and Taylor in Melbourne, the next Tivoli circuit attraction, known as The Versatile Three, opened their Australian season in

Perth on December 6, 1924. They were Augustus (Gus) Haston (born ca. 1880), Anthony (Tony) Tuck (born ca. 1883), and Charles (Charlie) Wenzel Mills (born ca. 1880). Tuck and Mills had been members of the original string-band associated with James Reese Europe's Clef Club orchestra in 1910. When dancers Vernon and Irene Castle toured France during the summer of 1913 they were accompanied by the trio of Tuck, Mills, and drummer Charlie Johnson. Gus Haston was already in England, having toured Europe in 1905, playing mandolin with Ernest Hogan's Memphis Students. After the French tour he joined the other three to form the new Versatile Four. They soon established themselves as firm favorites in a 10-year engagement at London's fashionable Murray's Nightclub, the Pavilion theatre, and around the English music halls. The Versatile Four (and Three) recordings made between 1916 and 1920 are significant examples of pre- or early jazz. Some experts believe their 1916 "Down Home Rag" has a credible claim to pre-date the Original Dixieland Jazz Band's 1917 recordings as the first jazz record.[11]

Featured by

THE VERSATILE THREE.

(HARSTON, MILLS and TUCK)

FRANCIS, DAY & HUNTER.

The Versatile Three, from left to right: Augustus (Gus) Haston, Charles (Charlie) Wenzel Mills and Anthony (Tony) Tuck. From the sheet music cover. Author's collection.

Drummer Johnson had dropped out before the Australian tour, leaving them a Versatile Three again. By the time they arrived in Australia they were being billed as a jazz group, though audiences showed equal appreciation of their close harmony singing and spirituals. Mills was the pianist of the group, while Tuck played banjo, cello, and bandolin (his own invention), and Haston played banjo and saxophones. Before they had even landed in Australia on the SS *Mongolia* on November 26, 1924, the trio was already declared an Australian success. The *West Australian* reported:

> Just before the SS *Mongolia* arrived at Fremantle yesterday a presentation was made to The Versatile Three in acknowledgment of their services at the various functions held aboard during the trip. The presentation took the form of a large photograph of the ship signed by the captain and each passenger. The captain and others referred to the unselfish and wholehearted way in which they had come forward on every occasion, and stated that not a little of the success and pleasure of the social side of the trip was due to their efforts.

Their welcome onshore was equally warm. They opened at Perth's Prince of Wales Theatre on December 6 to enthusiastic reviews;

> They started off with a little harmony, then on to a finger stretching bout in which the pianist and the bandolist figured, and then the saxophone joined in. The Versatile Three are a wonderful turn— the saxophone just talks, and the bandolin patters out its melody as a set of speedy fingers pluck the strings, and the pianist is the goods, too.

In response to their "enormous success," their season was extended by a week, ending on December 26, 1924, followed by a week in Adelaide, beginning January 3, 1925. They finally reached Sydney on January 17 for a two-week Tivoli engagement. The positive reviews focused largely on the refinement of their act, by contrast with the conventional notion that jazz had to be noisy and discordant. The *Evening News* (January 28, 1925) enthused: "Harmony and refinement are the main features of their act, which is the most popular of its kind that has been here." A similarly warm welcome awaited them at the Melbourne Tivoli, from where after a three-week season, they departed for New Zealand on February 27, 1925.

Though short, their New Zealand visit was equally successful. They opened with a week at Auckland's His Majesty's theatre, prompting the NZ *Herald* (March 9, 1925) to comment: "Harmony and jazz, almost at express speed, kept the audience alert. Indeed, the sheer joyousness of the trio is infectious (why is it that negroes have the gift of looking happier when they are happy than white folks?) and disperses dullness." There followed two weeks at Wellington's Grand Opera House, one week at Theatre Royal, Christchurch, and finishing with a week at Dunedin's His Majesty's Theatre. They returned to Sydney via the SS *Ulimaroa* on May 1, 1925.

The Australian return season lasted two months, two weeks at the Melbourne Tivoli, followed by two weeks at Sydney Tivoli, co-starring with popular Scottish comedian Will Fyffe. By June they were back in Melbourne, "in response to hundreds of requests for a return season" (*Argus*, May 5). This time they were sharing the bill with a six-year-old white prodigy drummer billed as "Traps, the Drum Wonder, The world's youngest but greatest jazz musician." Traps was well known to jazz fans in later years as Buddy Rich, swing band leader, and sometime brawler with Frank Sinatra (despite a lifelong friendship).[12] The Versatile Three finished in Melbourne on June 18 and started the final leg of their Australian visit with a week at the Wintergarden Theatre in Brisbane. They were last recorded transiting through Fremantle on their way home to England via the SS *Maloja* on July 13, 1925. They returned to the U.S. in 1926 to tour the Orpheum circuit, but disbanded in England 1927 and went their separate ways.

18

The Jazz Age
(1926–1927)

The next candidates for African American visiting entertainers arrived simultaneously, both landing on the SS *Sonoma*, which docked at Sydney on July 20, 1926. It included the Tivoli bound Sheftell's Revue and the Fuller bound Grant, Bates, and Rogers acts, who opened on their respective circuits, Sheftell at the Sydney Tivoli, and the others at Fuller's Melbourne New Bijou, on July 24. The Sheftell revue was the larger and more significant of the two.

Sheftell's Southern Revue

Joe Sheftell's *Southern Revue* was a throwback to the days of the large touring troupes. It was a complete show, with 11 performers plus a wardrobe mistress. The troupe's membership was: Joe Sheftell, manager, patter and songs; Minta Cato (Mrs. Joe Sheftell), classical singer and pianist[1]; Ukulele Bob Williams, virtuoso ukulele player, pianist and tap dancer; the "Chocolate Ballet" dance troupe, Helen Wright, Dempsie Woodson, Elizabeth (Bee) Saunders, and Marie Wood; dancers Richard Saunders and Willard McConn; and A.B. (Racehorse) Williams, comedian.

As this only accounts for 10 of the reported 11 performers, and the wardrobe mistress did not perform, it can probably be assumed that Baby Minta Cato, who made a brief appearance in the show's finale, is included in the 11. The wardrobe mistress was actually Minta Cato's mother, so also a babysitter for Baby Minta, and general mother for the troupe.

Joe Sheftell was a veteran vaudeville performer, having led a predecessor troupe, the Eight Black Dots, since 1912. A WA interviewer admitted being surprised to find that the leader of the new show in town was "a full-blooded American negro," and a university educated man, who could discuss in a soft, musical, cultured voice, "from an intelligent angle, America's racial problems, and big world subjects."[2] The main featured stars of the show were Minta Cato and Ukulele Bob Williams.

Minta (Minto) Cato was born in Little Rock, Arkansas, in 1900. She was one of the most talented African American performers to visit Australia. A classically trained singer and musician, she was described by the *Pittsburgh Courier* (June 20, 1931) as a

dramatic soprano, who sings high notes up to D sharp or E flat above the staff and double C below the staff, all in mellow tones as clear as a bell. She compares favorably with Rosa Ponselle of the Metropolitan Opera Company. An accomplished pianist who plays skillfully difficult numbers as,

159

Romance in D flat, all movements of Beethoven's Sonata, Rustles of Spring by Seidlinger, Chaminade's Autumn, Rachmaninoff's Prelude in C sharp minor, etc.

Although she performed with distinction in grand opera, including *Aïda*, the lack of opportunity for black divas in her era meant that much of Cato's singing career was focused on show tunes and spirituals. In her *Southern Revue* performances she held "aloof from the frivolities of her compatriots."

Ukulele Bob Williams was an early black proponent of the ukulele. He has been compared to the more famous Ukulele Ike (Cliff Edwards, widely known as the voice of Jiminy Cricket in Walt Disney's *Pinocchio*). Ukulele Bob had a featured role in the great black musical *Shuffle Along* (1921). His recording of two blues tracks, "West Indies Blues" and "Go 'long Mule" can be found on Document Records' album "Hokum Blues 1924–1929."

Southern Revue opened at the Sydney Tivoli on July 24, 1926, advertised as "a Miniature Musical-Comedy, not a minstrel show." The basic show was about 30 minutes but performances usually ran closer to an hour. They were supported by a vaudeville bill, or in some cases by a movie. Critical reaction was highly positive, the July 25 *Sun* noting "It is a long time since the Tivoli has re-echoed to such applause as it did at yesterday's two performances." The *Sunday Times* reported:

Short turns, cleverly done, keep the whole cast in life throughout the turn, which is a whirlwind of movement. The dancing was excellent. The Charleston was presented in a dozen different guises; each one more diverting and entertaining than its predecessor. The ballet moves through a dozen sprightly numbers in many beautiful costumes, and added their melodious voices to the general tumult when the final dance number, in which most of the cast took part, was being staged.

The Sydney season, which lasted four weeks, was exceeded by Melbourne's almost six weeks, from August 23 to September 29. Artistically and commercially, the troupe was every bit as successful as in Sydney, with continuous full houses. However, in other respects their Melbourne visit was problematic. First, en route from Sydney, while changing at Albury, their stage props and clothes went astray, leaving them to play their opening matinee and night performances in street clothes. Further compounding this, Minta Cato was sidelined for the day by an asthma attack. Nevertheless, the September 2 *Table Talk*

Minta Cato in "A Real Plantation Revue" from *Tivoli Theatre Program and Magazine*, 21 May 1926. Author's collection.

reported: "They received a reception which falls to very few acts nowadays, and the oldest inhabitant of the Tivoli is still wondering how long it is since such applause shook the rafters."

Things ran smoothly again after the opening setback, but the next problem, two weeks later, was more embarrassing. Regional media throughout Australia seized eagerly on reports of "FIGHT WITH KNIVES. NEGRO COUPLE'S QUARREL." Following an all-night party, female dancer Bee Saunders reacted jealously at husband Richard Saunders's behavior and attacked him with a knife.

> With blood streaming from knife wounds in the face, hands and neck, Richard Saunders, 31 years, and his wife, B. Saunders, were brought to Melbourne Hospital early yesterday morning in a Civil ambulance. While on duty in Spring-Street, Constable Ebert was informed that a colored man and his wife had been seriously stabbed in a boarding house in the street. The constable went to the house, and found a well-dressed negro and a woman, both very weak from loss of blood. He summoned an ambulance and had them conveyed to the hospital.[3]

The report later said that "the wounds were not serious, and that the sufferers were only being detained for observation." Both parties were described as being "penitent," neither choosing to file any charges, and they soon resumed their performances. The couple apparently stayed together, at least for the Australian tour but sadly, in June 1927, the *Pittsburgh Courier* reported that "Mrs. Elizabeth Harris Saunders, aged 28, wife of Dick Saunders, died at the Tuberculosis Hospital at 4 a.m. Friday [10th]."

No further action appears to have been taken by the police at the time, and the media soon moved on. Nevertheless, for the other members of such an urbane and sophisticated troupe, it must have been galling that the incident fed into the old stereotypical image of the knife-wielding, chicken-stealing, watermelon-eating "coon." On the other hand, given the entrenched status of racial stereotypes in Australia, and the fact that their Melbourne opening performance had been advertised in the *Age* (August 18, 1926) with the words "Dem feet will shuffle soon. De culled folks am coming," perhaps the publicity did them no harm after all. The rest of the Melbourne season was highly successful and was followed by two well-received weeks in Adelaide. After a brief three-night run in Geelong, they next appeared in Brisbane, opening at the Wintergarden Theatre on October 25 for two weeks, finishing on November 6. The October 29 *Daily Standard* reported: "Larger and larger are the crowds which swarm the Wintergarden Theatre every day to see Sheftell's Southern Revue." A radio presentation by the troupe was described by the *Telegraph* (October 27, 1926) in typical stereotyped terms, announcing:

> For to-night's bedtime session ... they would entertain the children with coon lullabies and songs with ukulele accompaniment, and a real plantation 'Mammy' will give one or two delightful recipes, for making corncakes and waffles. All of the songs and the whole of the conversation carried on before the microphone will be in 'coon' language with a fascinating American accent.

After Brisbane, the Southern Revue gave a farewell season in Sydney, with two weeks at the Tivoli, then a week at the Haymarket Theatre. Their Australian tour wound up with two weeks in Perth, finishing December 31 before departing on the AMS *Sierra* for San Francisco on January 15, 1927. In view of events that would occur only a year later, it is worth noting that the *Southern Revue*'s Australian visit was an unqualified success. Despite the usual stereotypical reporting, there was no hint of racial prejudice in their reception.

Shortly after their return to the U.S., Minto Cato and Joe Sheftell appear to have gone their separate ways. She continued to pursue a successful career in opera and musical-comedy (*Aïda* and *Showboat*). She is best remembered today for her starring role in the Lew Leslie production *Blackbirds of 1930*, in which she introduced the evergreen song "Memories of You." The music for the show was written by the black collaborators Eubie Blake (composer) and Andy Razaf (lyricist). Cato was at the time involved in a romantic relationship with the married Razaf. "Memories of You" was tailored to her formidable range, including a high C. Even today, though popular as an instrumental piece, it is not tackled by many singers. Minto Cato died in 1979, aged 79.[4]

Grant and Bates and Frank Rogers

Grant and Bates were Archie Grant and Eva Bates, billed as "Two Bright Spots from Darktown, Doing their Stuff Dixie style." They had been working together since at least 1922 on the West Coast, when they were in the cast of a show called *Atta Boy* at the New Angeles Theatre, Los Angeles. Frank Rogers was something unusual, a black ventriloquist, reputed to be one of the best in the field. He had been performing to strong reviews since at least 1910.[5] They opened at Fuller's New Bijou Theatre, Melbourne on 24 July 1926.

Reactions were enthusiastic, the *Newcastle Sun* 14 September enthusing:

> King Jazz reigns supreme at the Victoria Theatre this week. No more devoted subject has he than Grant and Bates, two colored exponents of syncopation in its original and unadulterated form. There is no mistaking it when they sing "Pickaninny Blues" or "Alabama Shore." The feminine singer has a voice which can only be described as stentorian. At times she becomes positively deafening, yet the syncopated rhythm is never lost.... The eccentric dancing of her colored friend, who adds much burnt cork, and the proverbial dress suit, to his make-up, is decidedly original. Altogether Grant and Bates provide a particularly enjoyable and lively interlude.

Frank Rogers also gained positive attention, being viewed by the *Newcastle Sun* (September 14 and 16, 1926) as something out of the ordinary in the field of ventriloquism.

> He commences with the usual dolls, and after raising a good laugh at their expense, maintains the deception alone. In three distinct voices he relates a conversation between a mother, father and small girl [relating to the use of "cuss words"].... The little girl's piercing squeak is in marked contrast to the sepulchral rumble of her 'poppa.' It is an excellent turn of its kind, which should not be missed.

Other notable features were his imitations of everyday sounds, animals, and "the effect of distance in the impersonation of a raucous showman a quarter of a mile away."

Their Melbourne season lasted three weeks, followed by three weeks in Brisbane (Empire Theatre), a week in Newcastle (Victoria Theatre), three weeks in Adelaide (Majestic Theatre) and finally reaching Sydney (the Tivoli) for three more weeks, but with just Grant and Bates, Frank Rogers being temporarily off the scene. They would all soon reunite in New Zealand.

The trio opened at Wellington's His Majesty's Theatre on December 6, 1926, their season finishing on Christmas Eve. Grant and Bates then opened at Fuller's Princess Theatre in Dunedin on Boxing Day, but without Frank Rogers, who opened separately at the Prince Edward Theatre, Auckland, on December 28. Rogers was sharing a bill with, inter alia, a young Australian dancer of later fame, Neva Carr Glynn, and another African American duo, Stompy and Stella. Their season lasted until January 14, 1927, after which Rogers played at Dunedin's Princess Theatre, minus Stompy and Stella, from January 17 to February 5, followed by Fuller's Opera House, Christchurch from February 8 through the 25th. During the last week of the engagement, Bert Chadwick (see below) was also on the bill. Rogers then departed on the RMS *Makura* for San Francisco and home, where the *Pittsburgh Courier* (May 17, 1927) reported that he was working at the Princess Theatre, San Francisco. After Dunedin, Archie Grant and Eva Bates's itinerary was a variation on that of Rogers, Christchurch (January 17 through February 11, 1927), and finishing at Auckland's Prince Edward Theatre on March 12. They then also returned to the U.S. to resume their West Coast career.

Stompy and Stella

Albert L. Celestan and Stella Johnson, billed as Stompy and Stella, arrived in Wellington (NZ) on the RMS *Makura* on October 23, 1926. They had established a reputation for themselves in the Los Angeles region, the *Eagle* (December 21, 1928) noting: "Stompy is one of the greatest entertainers of the eccentric dance seen here. He has a very unique manner of stomping his feet in a loud and hard fashion that sets his audience wild."

Stompy and Stella opened at Fuller's His Majesty's Theatre on October 25. Apart from the perennial song and dance routines, their act included mini-revue items described as "funny playlets," parodies of well-known plays. A "burlesque of the Charleston," still a novelty in Australasia despite being old-hat in the U.S., proved popular. They also featured a sketch based on a topical popular song "Take Me for a Buggy Ride," a 1926 hit for white singer and vaudevillian Frank Crumit. The November 17 *Christchurch Press* praised them:

> On the vaudeville side of the bill Stompy and Stella, two real genuine coons, sang and danced and told stories in a thoroughly delightful manner. Stella sang 'Bye-Bye, Blackbird' very well, and she concluded this number by whistling through her hands in the manner of an ocarina.

They followed the usual New Zealand circuit, Wellington two weeks, then Christchurch, Dunedin and Auckland, three weeks each, finishing in Auckland on January 17, 1927. In Auckland, they shared the bill for some of the time with Frank Rogers. The *NZ Herald* declared that Stompy and Stella "excelled chiefly in burlesque dancing, which was really far more clever than they led the audience to believe." On January 21 they embarked on the SS *Marama* to cross the Tasman Sea to Sydney.

Stompy and Stella in Australia

Stompy and Stella opened their Australian season at Brisbane's Empire Theatre on January 29, 1927, to a warm welcome from the February 7 *Courier*:

> Stompy and Stella, the coloured comedians, and newcomers at the Empire, have the natural flair of their people for the broadly humorous. In a series of entertaining songs and dances they alternately charmed and convulsed the packed house. Stompy is an eccentric dancer of great ability, and his queer movements and body contortions established him immediately as a firm favourite. Stella has a telling voice which was heard to great advantage in a tuneful song number, "Blackbirds."

They finished in Brisbane on February 11 and opened at Sydney's Fuller's Theatre on February 19 for three weeks, then after a short gap, at Melbourne's Bijou Theatre for two weeks. Their final engagement was at Adelaide's Majestic Theatre, for two weeks ending on April

16, 1927, despite media reports stating they would be back for another week.

The next news of the team appears in a San Francisco report in the *Pittsburgh Courier* May 17, 1927, noting, "Stompy and Stella are just back from Australia and they say they are very glad to be back." The *Eagle* (December 21, 1928) reported Stompy as "appearing in an important role" in the movie *Hearts in Dixie*. Shortly after that, Stompy appears to have gone out on his own. He was reported performing around Los Angeles up to at least 1937. In January 1947, Stompy's mother listed him in the *Pittsburgh Courier* as a "Missing Person," not heard from since February 1946, but as she had done something similar in 1941, and again in 1949, it may just have been her way of making him write home!

The Ferris Jazzland Revue Company

During the same time (late 1926, early 1927) that Stompy and Stella, and Grant/Bates and Rogers were playing the rival Tivoli/Williamson and Fuller circuits in New Zealand, a new black troupe arrived, the Ferris Jazzland Revue Company. They were a throwback to the days of McAdoo and Curtis, an independent troupe negotiating bookings locally. They entered into some form of contractual arrangement with the Wellington Amusement Syndicate Company, whose theatrical manager, Alfred Linley, assumed the responsibility of arranging bookings.

Nobody who loves a laugh should miss Stompy at Fullers' Theatre. He is one of the funniest colored comedians America has sent us.

Stompy Celestan of Stompy and Stella, from *Sydney Sportsman*, 22 February 1927, artist unknown. Courtesy *Trove*, National Library of Australia.

They arrived at Wellington on September 27, 1926, on board the RMS *Tahiti*, and opened at the Paramount Theatre on October 1. The troupe was essentially a Ferris family business under patriarch Bismark Ferris (1881–1939). He had a long history in early jazz as a bandleader and clarinetist with traveling circuses and Wild West shows, including Buffalo Bill and Pawnee Bill's *Two Bills Circus*. By 1920 a widower with five dependent children, he had retired to Los Angeles to direct the Ferris Family Company. His three daughters were all musically trained in jazz and classical style, Theresa (20), violin and banjo, Lucille (19) saxophone and clarinet, and Amy (17) blues singer and trap drummer. Seeing them in 1922, a *Chicago Defender* columnist wrote, "This little family is a whole show in itself.... The Ferris family is good enough for any of the big-time houses back East."[6] Lucille did not join the others on the New Zealand trip, staying home in the U.S. to look after her younger brothers.

Apart from himself and his two talented daughters, the package that Ferris had organized included: Fanny Benjamin (pianist, accompanist); Clifford Duncan ("La Buster," female impersonator, dancer); Dudley Dickerson (comedian, dancer, end man); Ulysses Everly (trombonist)[7]; Leola Everly (pianist, interlocutor); Louis Godfrey (comedian, tenor, end man); Harry Montgomery (tenor); Robert "Jokey" Murray (comedian); and (Miss) Ron Thompson (singer).[8]

Ferris Jazzland Revue, ca. 1925, Los Angeles. Front row: A.M. Benjamin, Ulysses Everly, Theresa Ferris, Amy Ferris, Fanny Benjamin (*at piano*), Lucille Ferris (not on New Zealand tour), Bismark Ferris. Back row unidentified, includes Leota Everly and probably some of Clifford Duncan, Dudley Dickerson, Louis Godfrey, Harry Montgomery, Robert Murray. Photographer unknown, in the "Shades of L.A." Photo Collection, Los Angeles Public Library.

The show was a combination of old-style minstrelsy, cakewalk, jazz, and vaudeville, with lots of the trendy Charleston thrown in. While the publicity claims of "Greatest aggregation of coloured talent that has ever left the States" and "America's Greatest Aggregation of Coloured Entertainers" were clearly hyperbolic, the early reviews were strongly positive. The February 10 *Evening Post* enthused: "The whole company with plantation songs, cakewalking, and Charleston dancing, kept things going with a swing to the accompaniment of jazz music. If anyone thinks that they can dance the Charleston let them see this company." That the jazz band included "four lady players" attracted interest, as did Clifford Duncan's act, the October 30 *Manawatu Times* declaring: "The surprise of the evening was Clifford Duncan, who carried off his impersonations of a lady member of the party, till the last act. When he eventually revealed himself the audience gasped, and then the house shook with applause."

The Wellington season of seven nights could be considered a successful debut for the company. However, despite similar later seasons in Christchurch and Auckland, the ensuing itinerary consisted largely of scattered one- and two-night stands in small regional centers, such as Levin, Ashburton, Patea, Palmerston North, Tauranga, Te Puke, Rotorua, Waihi, at town halls and small theatres. While the critical and audience response at these was favorable, it was a financial disaster. To add to the company's woes, at Napier on December 5, Robert Murray was admitted to a hospital, seriously ill; he died the following day of heart failure resulting from peritonitis, aggravated by an anesthetic.

The final Auckland season of six nights at the Town Hall Concert Chamber, finishing on December 31, was hailed enthusiastically by the December 28 *Herald*:

From the first number to the last a high standard of work was noticeable and there was a happy, care-free spirit of abandon. The undoubted ability of the American negro to portray the spirit of jazz was displayed in every item. In a highly diverting programme the work of two comedians, Dudley Dickerson and Louis Godfrey, was particularly amusing.

However, it was too late to salvage the tour. Three months into the planned six-month engagement, the company disbanded in disarray. Bismark Ferris, his family, and most of the troupe departed for San Francisco on the RMS *Makura* on January 4, 1927. Two members, Louis Godfrey and Clifford Duncan, remained in New Zealand, locked in contractual dispute with Ferris and the Wellington Amusement Syndicate. Ferris had departed, leaving the syndicate to deal with outstanding commitments. Amid complex claims and counter-claims, the main area of dispute centered on the men's contractual right to have their return fares covered, including rail from San Francisco to Los Angeles. The unfortunate Clifford Duncan ended up derelict on the streets of Auckland, arrested as "being an idle and dis-orderly person with insufficient means of support." Funds were found for both sea and rail, and he sailed for San Francisco on the RMS *Makura* on April 26. Godfrey's case dragged on into May but he too sailed on June 7, on the SS *Maunganui* bound for Vancouver.

Back in Los Angeles, Bismark Ferris's own career seems to have faded out, but not so his daughters. A 1936 *Eagle* column (May 29), praising successful Los Angeles women, went on to say:

[The Ferris sisters] have been outstanding with their band for the past years, and playing in various famous places here. Amy (Ferris) Floyd is a very fine rhythm drummer, as well as a fine vocalist: Lucille (Ferris) Bonnereise, to my knowledge, is one of the finest saxophone players in the country, also she plays clarinet to the highest ability and will make many of the men musicians 'sit up and take notice.' Theresa (Ferris) Waters is a very fine banjoist and guitarist who deserves fine recogni-tion.

Perhaps the one clear message that can be found from the Jazzland Revue fiasco is that the time was past when entertainers could succeed without the backing of a major theatrical circuit.

Bert Chadwick

In 1927, the Fuller circuit was back in the business of importing African American talent, in the person of Bert Chadwick. Known as the "Eccentric Ethiopian," Chadwick had a long career in vaudeville, dating back before World War I, mostly as a single on the mainly white Pantages circuit. His act was described as singer, dancer, and story teller. The usual Australasian touring sequence was reversed, Chadwick starting in New Zealand, for a three-week season at Fuller's Opera House, Christchurch. Billed as "The Dixie Dandy," he shared a large "high-class" vaudeville program, which for a week included the African American ventriloquist Frank Rogers, who is covered earlier in this chapter. The local *Press* (March 1, 1927) gave favorable reviews to the show, though paying little attention to Chadwick— "Mr Bert Chadwick, an American coloured comedian, told some humorous stories and sang some songs, and also performed some dancing with agility."

If Chadwick had garnered little attention in his Christchurch season, things were to get even worse when he opened at the Sydney Fuller's Theatre on March 26. Obsessed with promoting the return of their local comedy favorites Stiffy and Mo (Nat Phillips and Roy Rene), Fuller didn't bother to advertise anyone else on the bill. The *SMH*'s lengthy review ended with "and Chadwick in a vaudeville turn." In his one favorable review, *Sydney Sun* on March 27, the reporter seems to have confused Chadwick with another Bert (Elliott) on the bill, a juggler.

It may have been with a sense of relief that Chadwick opened at Fuller's New Bijou Theatre in Melbourne on April 5. Even there, identity confusion was likely in the Australian Rules football-mad city. The captain and coach of the champion Melbourne team was one Albert (Bert) Chadwick, later Sir Albert. While Chadwick's name did at least appear on the advertised bill this time, he didn't gain any more attention than in Sydney. After two weeks in Melbourne he dropped from view for several weeks until he reappeared at Adelaide's Majestic Theatre. Here, at last, he found his feet and, over a three-week season, under his old styling "the Eccentric Ethiopian," became a local favorite, praised by the *Adelaide News* (June 6, 1927):

> Bert Chadwick. a negro comedian, was well received, and was recalled for further verses of 'In the Gaolhouse' ... Bert Chadwick, the Ethiopian comedian, showed how to hold an audience by the quietest possible manner and simple talk, with eccentric dancing and popular vocal numbers. His rendering of the famous 'Bird's Eye View of My Old Kentucky Home' was most original and unlike anything Adelaide has previously heard.

The Adelaide season was followed by further successful ones in Newcastle and Brisbane during July and August. The July 4 Newcastle *Sun* noted: "With light and airy movement, his feet hardly touching the ground, Bert Chadwick, the 'Black Diamond,' won further success at the Victoria Theatre on Saturday.... Many of his numbers from last week's programme were repeated by request. He also told many amusing stories in his own droll fashion."

By late August he was back in Sydney, again supporting Stiffy and Mo, and also featuring in a broadcast on radio 2BL. His Australian sojourn finished with a return visit to Melbourne's Bijou Theatre during early September. While Bert Chadwick cannot be said to have made a big impact in Australasia, the fact that he spent most of 1927 in the region might be considered a success of sorts. It may have been bad luck for him that he was on the Fuller circuit rather than the more ambitious Tivoli. On return to the U.S., he resumed his vaudeville career in 1928 but drops from public view after 1932.

The Colored Emperors of Harmony

While Bert Chadwick had been a fairly obscure vaudevillian, the same could not be said of the Tivoli's next imports. The Colored Emperors of Harmony, who arrived via the SS *Sonoma* in early August 1927, had a sparkling pedigree. Their leader, William A. Hann, had been leader of his own Hann's Jubilee Singers as early as 1910. Around 1916 he organized the Four Harmony Kings as an offshoot of his Jubilee Singers.[9] In 1919, they were employed by James Reese Europe as his resident harmony quartet, which also started them on a recording career. They went on to be a major success in the record-breaking 1921 black Broadway show *Shuffle Along*, touring with it until 1923. They then toured until 1925 with its successor, *Chocolate Dandies*, the show that gave Josephine Baker her first starring role.

After *Chocolate Dandies*, the Four Harmony Kings split. Tenor Ivan Harold Browning kept the name for his half of the group, while Hann promoted himself to "emperor" with a new quartet, the Emperors of Harmony.[10] Hann, a basso, was accompanied by George

Jones, Jr., a baritone, who had been a late replacement in the group. To complete his quartet, Hann recruited Farley Berry Graden as first tenor, and Edward Caldwell, second tenor. Caldwell also doubled as a solo dancer. Like the earlier Royal Southern Singers, Graden had been a member of the Southern Syncopated Orchestra in Europe. The quartet was also one of the first to make Hollywood Vitaphone short sound movies, just before their arrival in Australia.[11]

The Emperors presented a stylish image, with silk top hats and tuxedos. This wasn't enough to protect them from stereotypical characterizations. Billed, like the earlier Ernest Hogan, as "unbleached Americans," *Smiths Weekly* (August 27, 1927) described them as "two chocolate coloured coons, one chestnut, and a tar baby." They opened in Sydney at the Tivoli on August 7, sharing a bill with, inter alia, three chimpanzees and the white American comedienne Edith Clifford. Their run, which lasted until September 3, received good notices, albeit with somewhat more attention paid to Clifford. A week's engagement from September 10, at Newcastle's Theatre Royal, elicited more positive reviews from the September 12 *NMH*:

> Each is the possessor of a remarkably tuneful and well trained voice. The value of their work lies almost wholly in their harmonisation, which is delightfully quaint and original. Their opening number, "Swing Along," a negro chant, gave an indication of the quality and the effective combination of their voices, and the rich blend was again apparent in the lullaby "Angel Child," the true spirit of each theme being caught and held. A negro yodel was something distinctly new, and brought out alternating and captivating bits of melody.

After Newcastle, the Emperors opened at Brisbane's Tivoli Theatre on September 19, reportedly "at a big salary." The September 20 *Courier* review was equally enthusiastic, noting: "Perhaps the yodelling songs are the most popular—the voices are up in the sky one moment, around the trees, deep down under the ground—everywhere in fact, and always harmoniously beautiful." Following an additional week at the Tivoli, the Emperors rounded out their Brisbane season with an equally successful engagement at the Valley Theatre.

They surfaced next at Sydney's Haymarket Theatre for a brief sojourn before opening at Melbourne's Tivoli on October 17, billed as "Worthy Successors to The Versatile Three, Four Southern Singers etc." The October 18 *Age* declared them, despite "the somewhat pretentious title of the Colored Emperors of Harmony," an immediate success. Their participation in a charitable Hospital Sunday function at Wesley Church helped their public image. The Melbourne run lasted four weeks, including a short (three night) stay at Geelong.

Melbourne was followed by a tour of northern Queensland towns, Townsville, and Rockhampton, finishing at Ipswich in early December. A planned opening for Christmas in WA, at Perth's Prince of Wales theatre, was frustrated by travel problems and didn't happen until December 31. Again, they gained some kudos by performing for the local Methodist church, the Perth *Daily News* (January 7, 1928) reporting: "The Colored Emperors of Harmony will sing Negro Spirituals, 'Swing Low, Sweet Chariot,' 'The Lord's Going to Move This Wicked Race,' and 'Get on Board, Little Children.'" They finished in Perth on January 13, 1928, heading back to Sydney for a new phase of their Australian venture. At this stage, basking in public approval and respect, they could well have felt that their five months in Australia so far had been a resounding success. Little were they to know that they would soon be caught up in a controversy not of their own making (see Chapter 19).

19

Sonny Clay's Colored Idea
(White Australia's Darkest Hour)

On Wednesday, January 18, 1928, the *SMH* amusement columns announced the opening of a new Tivoli program on the following Saturday. Described as "The Great Event in the History of the Australian Theatre World," it included SONNY CLAY'S PLANTATION BAND, "together with 24 wonderful Negro Stars, including the Four Dancing Covans, Ivy Anderson, Dick Saunders, and the Coloured Emperors of Harmony" (who were already resident). The title for the package, the "Colored Idea" was intended to suggest that this was not merely a revue, but a new type of presentation, probably to distinguish it from the earlier Sheftell Revue.[1]

Sonny Clay was a Los Angeles–based jazz pianist (originally drummer) and sometimes bandleader who had played with Jelly Roll Morton and Kid Ory. His bands were in the genre referred to as "territory bands," with a high reputation in their region, though not nationally well known. Notable trumpeter Teddy Buckner, who played in Clay's band in the twenties, said, "Sonny Clay was a genius. He could walk down the street talking to you—having a conversation—and be writing an arrangement at the same time."[2]

The Clay band was the first full-scale African American jazz band to visit Australia. The personnel can be assumed to be the same as that given for their December 1927 Los Angeles recording session, which included the unissued Sonny Clay composition "Australian Stomp." That session had 10 musicians, identified as Ernest Coycault, Archie Lancaster (trumpet), Luther "Sonny" Craven (trombone), Leonard Davidson (clarinet, alto sax), Louis Dodd (alto sax), William Griffin (tenor saxophone), Sonny Clay (piano), Rupert Jordan (banjo), Herman Hoy (tuba), David Lewis (drums).[3] While many of these musicians are relatively obscure today, they were a powerful aggregation with strong early jazz credentials. Ernest Coycault had been a member of Bill Johnson's "Original Creole Band" in 1907; Luther Craven was a member of Louis Armstrong's New Cotton Club Orchestra in the early thirties.[4]

The Four Covans were a highly regarded tap and rhythm dancing team, led by Willie Covan since 1917. Although they were billed as the Four Covans, and travel records show four of that name arriving and departing Australia, the actual performing group consisted of Willie and his wife, Florence; as well as his brother Dewey and Elmer Turner, Dewey's female dancing partner (who would later have a stellar career as a dancer with Cab Calloway's orchestra). The fourth non-performing Covan was Dewey's wife, named Margarite.[5] Willie Covan had been in Florence Mills's early shows, including *Shuffle Along* (1921) and *Dover Street to Dixie* in England (1923), partnering Florence's husband, Ulysses "Slow Kid"

169

Thompson. He was the inventor of the acrobatic dance step known as "twice around the world, no hands." He would also be famous in later years as the tap dancing trainer of MGM's movie stars, including Debbie Reynolds in *Singin' in the Rain*.

Ivy (better known later as Ivie) Anderson had been building a reputation as a singer—and sometimes dancer—in the road version of *Shuffle Along*, and at the early Cotton Club in 1925, before the Duke Ellington era. She would later go on to fame as Ellington's greatest vocalist. In 1927, Ivie had been featured successfully in her own *Creole Revue* on the West Coast, with a cast that included Stompy and Stella, recently returned from New Zealand and Australia. Her repertoire in Australia included the racial protest theme song of the recently deceased Florence Mills, "I'm a Little Blackbird Looking for a Bluebird" (*Melbourne Herald*, February 21, 1928). She also featured two numbers associated with her favorite singer, Ethel Waters, and pleased audiences with a novelty number, "Henry Ford Has Made a Lady Out of Lizzie."

Dick Saunders, dancer and master of ceremonies, was the same Richard Saunders who had been stabbed by his wife during the Australian Sheftell Revue visit. He had also been part of Ivie's *Creole Revue* in Los Angeles.

Sonny Clay's band arrives in Sydney on SS *Sierra*. Back row: (Trumpet) Ernest Coycault, (Saxophone) probably William Griffin, (crouching) possibly Sonny Clay; center: (Trombone) Luther Craven, (Banjo) Rupert Jordan; front, from left, Florence Covan, Ivy Anderson and Herman Hoy (Tuba). By photographer Sam Hood. Courtesy Mitchell Library, State Library of New South Wales; Hood Collection.

Apart from the Emperors of Harmony, who were already in town, the main troupe arrived in Sydney on the SS *Sierra* on January 20, 1928, playing the "Australian Stomp" in the harbor as they landed. The show opened at the Sydney Tivoli on January 21 to an enthusiastic reception. Ironically, in view of what happened later, one of the most positive reviews was that of the January 22 Sydney *Truth*:

> Sonny Clay's Idea burst like a ray of colored sunshine on the patrons of the Tivoli yesterday afternoon. The band is all your dreams of jazz come true. Each player subordinates his part to the gen-

Opposite top: The Sonny Clay band arrives in Sydney on SS *Sierra*. Foreground dancers: Florence Covan, Willie Covan, by photographer Sam Hood. Courtesy Mitchell Library, State Library of New South Wales; Hood Collection. *Opposite bottom:* The Four Covans, ca. 1932; From left: Carita Harbert (replaced in Australia by Elmer Turner), Dewey Covan, Willie Covan and Florence Covan. Courtesy of the Rusty Frank Archive.

eral rhythm of the whole orchestra, and the result is perfect coordination. Sonny Clay himself is at the piano, and plays "Me and My Shadow," and "Rain" in a manner entirely new to Australian audiences.

Truth's entertainment columnist was not on the same wavelength as the paper's proprietor Ezra Norton, a staunch promoter of the White Australia policy. More in line with Norton's view was the same day's Brisbane edition of *Truth*, reporting an exposure of the "Inside Doings of Metropolitan Drinking Den Vice Vortex," noting, "There are the usual cheap nigger-sung jazz records to dance to."

The January 23 *SMH* was also enthusiastic: "Sonny Clay's Plantation Band was accorded an enthusiastic reception by a crowded house. Equally adept at rendering classical airs and weird Jazz effects, the bandsmen reigned supreme during nearly half of the programme, and appeared thoroughly to enjoy themselves."

Popular as the music was, Australian jazz historian Andrew Bisset suggested that

Tivoli Theatre poster for Sonny Clay's "Colored Idea." Author's collection.

"Clay's idea of jazz did not conform to the Australian idea which demanded a hot finish to each number with everyone blowing hard, instead of the fade-out affected by the *Colored Idea*. The hard-hitting finish is still favoured by Australian traditional jazz bands today."[6] *The Colored Idea* played to good houses for a month at the Sydney Tivoli before switching to the Melbourne Tivoli on February 20. The Melbourne opening was warmly welcomed by the *Age*: "Brightness and 'pep' characterise the turn given by Sonny Clay's colored artists, who opened at the Tivoli yesterday. From the time the show opens, with a blare of brass and a flash of white teeth, to the last hurricane step dance, everything moves at a decidedly quick step."

At this stage the troupe might well have felt that their season was proving a resounding success, but a number of factors were coming into alignment that would soon throw a different light on things. First of these was the attitude of the local musicians' union. It's normal practice in any country for the union to protect the jobs of its members by resisting or limiting the importation of foreign musicians. In Australia's case this was exacerbated by the very hard line taken by the U.S. towards Australian musicians being permitted to perform there. In 1927, the American Federation of Musicians had banned a concert tour by the Australian Commonwealth Band, a conventional military band, generating much resentment in Australia.[7] Jazz added a new element of complexity. There was much legitimate interest in having U.S. jazz musicians come, enabling local aspiring jazz and dance music performers to learn from the "experts." However, many of those experts were black, at a time when the White Australia Policy was being aggressively promoted.

In 1923, the Musicians Union of Australia had written into its rule book an objective:

"To uphold and maintain the White Australia policy, and prohibit the admission of coloured races as members." In 1924, Sir George Foster Pearce (1870–1952), the minister for home and territories (including immigration), came under pressure from the union to reject all American jazz bands. While sympathetic to union demands, he pointed out that immigration laws recognized a distinction between regular employees and those who could be characterized as "artists," such as actors and singers, and it was anomalous that this could be construed to include musicians. At the suggestion that this might even include "Negro jazz bands" he responded: "Senator Pearce: You have nothing to fear there. I have already refused two applications for permission to import negro bands. Coloured men will never be allowed to come in."[8]

Against this background, it's not surprising that the March 22 *Table Talk* reported: "There is said to be many heart burnings among musicians about the engagement of Sonny Clay's Negro Band at the Green Mill." The Green Mill was a popular dance hall. An advertisement in the *Age* had announced a "Sonny Clay's Midnight Dance" at the Green Mill on March 6, apparently part of a planned regular series.

If the Clay band had remained just a stage act they could probably have continued un-noticed but invading the secular home of dance musicians was a red rag to a bull, despite *Table Talk*'s supportive comment: "Had it not been for the enterprise of some of our dance hall managers in importing American bands, it is likely that we should be still dancing to the old-time music, but even musicians admit that they have learned a lot and still have much to learn from the musicians from overseas."

On its own, the musicians' resentment might not have led to anything drastic. By March 23, the *Age* announced: "Only a few More Nights Remain to See Them Prior to Their Return to America. LAST NIGHTS and FAREWELL." However, there was another hidden factor, fairly recently revealed by Australian investigative journalist, the late Richard Hall.[9] Trawling through National Archives records, Hall found that Inspector Longfield Lloyd of the Sydney office of the Commonwealth Investigation Branch (then equivalent of ASIO) had, on his own initiative, commissioned surveillance of the black musicians while they were in Sydney during February, on the grounds that they were consorting with white women (no crime under Australian law, despite what might apply in the Deep South of the U.S.).

The surveillance continued in Melbourne, aided by the fact that the musicians had moved from hotel accommodation to apartments, where their movements were more easily observed. On the evening of Saturday, March 24, accompanied by journalists from the *Truth*, the police set out to raid the apartments at Rowena Mansions, East Melbourne, where the Clay musicians were living. Around three o'clock on Sunday morning they arrested six black musicians and six young white women, and took them into custody.

Having achieved their objective, the police now found they had a problem. Despite allegations by *Truth* of drugs being present in the apartment nothing was found and, as there was no Australian law against mixed race relations, no charges could be filed against the musicians. The solution found was to charge the women with vagrancy, a charge typically made against prostitutes. The case was heard on the following Tuesday and soon collapsed. Aged between 19 and 23, the women were shown to be from respectable backgrounds and gainfully employed.

Nevertheless, the promoters of racial hatred had won the day. In modern terminology, the story went viral and a torrent of intemperate and vicious newspaper headlines appeared, most notably by *Truth* but with many normally respectable companions.

- SORDID STORY NEGRO NIGHT PARTY WITH WHITE GIRLS. MELBOURNE (*Sydney Sun*)
- NEGROES AND GIRLS. RAID ON A FLAT. Disgraceful Conduct Alleged. (*West Australian*)
- LUSTFUL ORGY. NEGROES AND WHITE WOMEN. DISGUSTING CONDUCT IN MELBOURNE FLAT. (*Courier*)

It was *Truth* that published the most virulent account, filled with vicious allegations and slanders, though being a weekly publication they were late off the mark. On April 1, under a banner headline, "A BLACK-OUT FOR SONNY CLAY'S NOISOME NIGGERS," it falsely reported it had "organised the raid." It claimed to have pursued the issue right back to the Sydney days, but nothing of the material quoted from *Truth* in numerous later accounts actually pre-dated the raid.

The tone of the media reports fanned a wave of public indignation. In Sydney, en route back to America, Sonny Clay claimed that "the raid on the flat at Rowena Mansions was a frame up from start to finish," and pointed out that the Musicians Union had been hostile ever since the unfriendly reception accorded the Commonwealth Band when it visited America; that detectives had followed the musicians all the time they had been in Australia (confirmed by Richard Hall's research); and that he could "see nothing wrong with the boys going round with the white girls, so long as they treated them as gentlemen should." Clay's comments were widely reported across many local newspapers around that time but despite some supporting remarks from the U.S. consul, his protestations of innocence and injustice were swept aside in the hysteria. Predictably, the public outrage was picked up by politicians. On March 27, the following exchange occurred in the Australian parliament (reported by *NMH*):

> MR JACKSON: BASS, TASMANIA: Has the attention of the Minister for Home and Territories been drawn to a newspaper report, published under the following heading: "Nude girls in Melbourne flat orgy; Negro comedians as partners; Raid by police." If so, has any action been taken in regard to the matter? Are any credentials required by the Home and Territories Department as to the moral character of negroes who arrive in Australia? Does the Minister not think that, in the interests of a White Australia and moral decency, permits to such persons should he refused?
>
> SIR NEVILLE HOWSE: MINISTER FOR HEALTH: My attention has been drawn to the report referred to by the honorable member, and action has been taken. The negroes will sail from Australia on Saturday next. I do not know whether credentials are required with regard to the moral character of such visitors, but certainly they are required in respect of general behaviour. I shall look very carefully into all such applications for admission in the future.

So, with summary justice on hearsay evidence, the six musicians caught up in the raid were sentenced to deportation. Worse was yet to come. The waspish Welsh-born former prime minister Billy Hughes, in a speech denouncing Italian migration (referring to them as "dagos") went on to say about the Melbourne incident, "We have some of her negroes—players of jazz music—here now, but if what happened in Melbourne the other day had taken place in a southern state of America those negroes would not be leaving our shores on Saturday."[10]

While Hughes's remarks on Italians brought strong criticism, his apparent approval of the Southern states practice of lynching went generally uncommented on, though a satirical piece in the April 7 *Smith's Weekly*, under the heading, "Billy Hughes Lights the Fiery Cross," noted of his speech to the Nationalist Party convention: "Staid, old Nationalist ladies enthusiastically cheered his pretty suggestions of nigger-lynching."

While the deportation order applied only to the six involved in the court case, all of Sonny Clay's band, accompanied by Ivy Anderson, left Australia on the SS *Sierra* on March 31, their contracts having been terminated by the theatrical management. Ironically the SS *Sierra* was advertised as providing "Novel Entertainment Features, including American Jazz Orchestra for Dancing and Concerts."

Understandably, the black press back in the U.S. was indignant at the treatment of the Clay troupe, picking up particularly on Hughes's endorsement of lynching. The West Coast *Eagle* (April 6; May 4, 11) carried several items noting the events. These also included an exculpatory message from the Tivoli management, explaining that they had no choice but to terminate the musicians' contract. They added: "There is more behind the case than meets the eye; and there is more than a suspicion that the whole affair was a frame-up against the Negroes." There was also a letter from the committee of the Masonic Club of Victoria, extending "sincerest sympathy" to Sonny Clay and assuring him that "during our various meetings … you at all times conducted yourself as a gentleman should."

Interviewed in 1960, Sonny Clay laid the blame for the unfortunate events squarely at the feet of the Musicians Union, saying, "If I'd listened to what was going to happen to me they'd never have got me out of the United States. Australian unions were waiting for us and had said what they were going to do to us when we got to Australia." He also mentioned that by the time he got back to the U.S. talking pictures had become the craze, vaudeville was declining and the West Coast had lost out to the East as a center of recording, making his opportunities more limited.[11]

Nevertheless he resumed his career in America, but with the Depression looming he soon switched to piano playing instead of leading orchestras, until he retired in 1940. After World War II he worked as a piano tuner but made a comeback in the 1960s, as a solo pianist in clubs and on records. He died in 1973.

On her return to the U.S., Ivy Anderson became a vocalist with the Earl Hines orchestra, and later was Duke Ellington's greatest vocalist, until ill health forced her retirement from show business in 1942 to run a popular restaurant, Ivie's Chicken Shack. Interviewed in the 1940s by Bill Hill, she avoided saying anything about the unsavory affair, mentioning only that she had used two of Ethel Waters' numbers successfully in the show. Ivy (Ivie) died in 1949.

The deportation and cancellation of contracts applied only to the Sonny Clay Orchestra members, the others having been on independent contractual agreements. The Covans, Richard Saunders, and the Emperors of Harmony were not considered part of the "problem" and continued performing for a while longer, including an engagement at the Geelong Theatre for the Covans up to April 3. The Emperors in particular were recipients of sympathy from the Hobart *Mercury* on April 2, 1928.

> With the farewell to the coloured Emperors of Harmony at Wesley Church this afternoon, we have rung down the curtain on one of the most painful public scandals in the history of Melbourne. These men, negro minstrels of the Fisk type, and of apparently exemplary life, have been regular contributors to the Sunday afternoon programmes at Wesley Church, as well as to the Tivoli performances of the Coloured Idea Company.

On April 21, the Covans (including Elmer Turner) and Richard Saunders sailed for San Francisco on the SS *Sonoma*. Reporting the event, the April 22 *Truth* added: "[The Colored Emperors] still remain. Originally engaged by the Tivoli management, they were some weeks ago 'sub-let' to Hoyts and are now doing the suburbs under an engagement that has about a fortnight to run." The Emperors continued performing around suburban Sydney for a time and were also widely heard on radio. There was even a brief return to the Tivoli on April 30. On May 3, they departed for America on the SS *Niagara* via Vancouver, and resumed their activities there until leader William Hann died of a heart attack in his dressing room in December 1930, after which the group faded out.

The repercussions of the Sonny Clay affair continued, like aftershocks from an earthquake, for many years. Even before the Clay musicians had left, the *Border Watch*, on March 31, 1928, reported:

> No more negro entertainers are to be admitted into Australia. This decision has been reached by Federal Cabinet as an outcome of the case in which negroes were found in East Melbourne flats with white girls.... The decision of Cabinet will not be hard and fast, as there may sometime be occasion to allow some special person to enter.

In practice there would be exceptions for stage performers but it would not be until 1954 that a full black jazz orchestra would be allowed to visit Australia, with the huge success of Louis Armstrong's All-Stars group. Perhaps the best summary of the issues involved is from Bisset (*Black Roots, White Flowers*, 45–46): "White society could accept the humble Christian aspirations of the spirituals which showed Negroes in a yielding, resigned light, but could not tolerate Negroes in the exuberant, confident and assured role that jazz gave them."

20

The Post-Clay Lean Years
(1928–1934)

While the aftermath of the Sonny Clay affair had a negative effect on the presence of African American entertainers in Australasia, there were other significant contributing factors. The Great Depression was looming, triggered by the collapse of the Wall Street markets in October 1929. The arrival of the "talkies" in Australian cinemas, starting with *The Jazz Singer* in 1928, undermined much of the appeal of live theatre. On the local Sydney scene, the Tivoli had been struggling for some time, being too small to be economic. In 1928, the proprietors, J.C. Williamson, finally sold the building to Hugh D. McIntosh, who wanted it for development purposes. The Sydney Tivoli staged its final performance on Saturday, September 28, 1929. Less than a week later, Charlie Pope, who had graced its stage for so many years, also took his last curtain call, dying on October 5, 1928, aged 60. Generally, for the next five years, performers of color who arrived either came from England, or as part of imported Broadway plays like *Show Boat*.

Janice Hart (a.k.a. Cassie Walmer) and Frank O'Brian (1928)

One colored performer did make a big splash on the Australasian scene in the immediate aftermath of the Clay affair. This was Janice Hart, who came with her husband, Dublin-born English dancer-comedian Frank O'Brian. Described as "a second Florence Mills," performing Josephine Baker's Casino de Paris routines, she was the previously popular Cassie Walmer under a new persona (see Chapter 13). The local media either failed to realize that Janice was actually Cassie or chose to ignore it. The connection was never mentioned in the Australian media until April 1935.[1] Hart and O'Brian arrived in Sydney on the SS *Mooltan* on June 16, 1928. They were shown on the passenger manifest as John Robson (O'Brian's actual name) and Cassandra Louisson, the latter being the surname of Cassie Walmer's first husband, who had accompanied her in 1913.[2]

For their opening at the Sydney Fuller's Theatre on Castlereagh Street, Hart and O'Brian recruited local members for their ballet troupe, known as the Eight Fuller Flappers. One of these was teenager Grace Boyd, already a trained dancer. She would be better known in later years as Gracie Le Brun, wife of Bobby Le Brun, and along with him a member (later co-manager) of the George Sorlie tent shows, and also early Australian TV pioneers. When Gracie handed over her first week's pay—£5.18—from the Hart and O'Brian show to her mother, she was sent back to explain that there must be a mistake; it was more than her father earned in a week! Janice Hart assured her, "That's right, that's the salary for this show." Gracie stayed with the show through the Sydney engagement, but was considered too young to go with them to New Zealand in November 1928.[3]

Unlike Cassie Walmer, who played over the Tivoli circuit, the Hart and O'Brian show played over the Fuller circuit. The longevity and popularity of their show, in both Australia and New Zealand, was more like a burlesque show than a vaudeville collection of discrete acts. Also, the show was frequently changed, with new routines and themes on a weekly basis. Apart from O'Brian, as a comedian and eccentric dancer, and Hart, as a singer and dancer, there was Bert Lee, an English comedy character actor. The rest of the cast members were locally established performers,

Portrait of Janice Hart and Frank O'Brian, from the English theater program, 1933. Author's collection.

including singers, dancers, and comedians, all carry-overs from *Band Box Revue*, a Fuller circuit production that had run since 1925. In addition, there were the previously mentioned Fuller Flappers ballet troupe, and seven local musicians, Vasco's Varsity Boys Jazz Band. The format was a fast-paced series of songs, dances, comedy routines, and musical numbers, the July 8 *Sydney Sun* noting, "No attempt was made to present continuous comedy, but revue items trod on each other's heels with riotous speed, and every piece was refreshing and spontaneous." The July 9 *SMH* agreed:

> The most lavish scene of the revue was apparently very acceptable to the audience. Janice Hart, supported by the whole company, who wore Chinese masks and Eastern garments, presented "Singapore Sorrows, a breath of the East." Miss Hart's low, compelling voice was well suited to the eerie minor tones of the song, whilst her Oriental supporters formed an effective background of writhing figures, bowing, twisting, brandishing daggers, and finally stealing away up winding mountain glades, above which they popped at intervals an augmented supply of Oriental heads.

As with Cassie Walmer, much attention was directed to Janice Hart's lavish costumes. The August 8 *World's News* announced: "Miss Janice Hart … has brought no fewer than 50 stage costumes to effectively dress song scenes and dancing specialties in the revue productions. They represent the last London and Paris words as elaborate stage toilettes." The Sydney season opened on July 7, 1928, under the title *Laffin' Thru*. It ran until August 10, closing under the title *Merry Moments*. They opened next at Adelaide's Majestic Theatre on August 13 for a lengthy season of more than 11 weeks, ending on November 2. The jazz band and the Fuller's Flappers were still with them. The August 20 Adelaide *News* enthused:

> Frank O'Brian is the life and soul of the party…. His patter is bright—and occasionally broad—and his dancing is a delight. Both he and the feminine lead of the new company, Janice Hart, shake a

remarkably agile pair of legs. Their step dancing ranks easily among the best seen at the Majestic for many moons.... Janice Hart had a finger in most of the pies, and gave them a rare flavor. She was at her best in the African novelty, "Zulu Wail," an eerie song and dance scene.

Hart and O'Brian in New Zealand

After the Adelaide season, the troupe headed off to New Zealand. They opened at the New Opera House, Christchurch, on November 15, 1928. Items that the *Press* considered as scoring well included a bright sketch, "A Wireless Episode," "which introduced a number of ingenious inventions, such as 'all weather' boots, a motor horn guaranteed not to disturb the lightest of sleepers, a flycatcher, a comb for baldheaded men ... and a revolution in Mexico with realistic effect."

If the length of the seasons is any indication, their popularity in New Zealand at least matched that in Australia. The Christchurch season lasted 10 weeks, ending January 26, 1929; Dunedin (Princess Theatre) had eight weeks, ending 23 March; Wellington (His Majesty's Theatre) lasted 11 weeks. Auckland (St. James Theatre) had the final run, lasting 11 weeks until September 5, 1929, at which time they were replaced by the musical-comedy *Rio Rita*, starring Australia's legendary Gladys Moncrieff. In total, they had spent nearly 10 months touring New Zealand's major cities, probably a record for an overseas company. Although they didn't visit many of the smaller towns that other companies favored with short stays, the length of the seasons in the main cities was more than enough to allow anyone who wanted to see them to do so.

Australia Again

Finally, more than a year after their original arrival, Melbourne got to see Frank O'Brian's Revellers in their new show *Dancing Thru*, opening at Fuller's Bijou Theatre on September 14, 1929. The jazz band was now known as Tiny's Varsity Boys, under leader Tiny Douglas. As usual, the program varied weekly, the *Advocate* noting for week two, "The main item of this week's programme consisted of an amusing army burlesque, entitled *All Smiles on the Western Front*, in which Frank O'Brian was seen to advantage as the raw recruit to the army. He has a whimsical style which is likely to prove very popular with Melbourne theatregoers."

The Melbourne season ran for a month, ending on October 15. It was then Sydney's time for a second season at Fuller's Theatre, which lasted seven weeks. After a holiday break, they opened to a great fanfare at Brisbane's newly reopened Empire Theatre on Boxing Day 1929. This was to be their longest and probably most successful run, lasting over three months, until March 29. The tone was set by this extract from the *Courier*'s review of the opening:

> They furnish the maddest, merriest, and gayest of entertainment, and seem to be absolutely tireless. Mr Frank O'Brian['s] ... inimitable dances, clever witticisms, and amazingly clever dancing were a sheer delight.... Miss Janice Hart won popularity without an effort. She has a distinct personality, and is a clever dancer.

The Brisbane *Truth* declared the show "A riot." Reviews continued in similar vein throughout the run, with new material regularly presented. A sense of the humor can be had from one sketch, "The Last Shot," a burlesque on the popular tales about the French Foreign Legion (*The Desert Song, Beau Geste*, etc.) in which Frank O'Brian as the general, and Janice Hart as his wife, are the sole survivors in an Arab attack on their outpost. As the victorious sheik arrives, the general instructs his wife to shoot herself with the last bullet rather than fall victim to the Arab. Having had a glance at the handsome attacking sheik, she shoots her husband and flings herself into the sheik's arms.

On March 30, 1930, they gave their farewell performance at the Empire, which was scheduled to close as a vaudeville house in favor of movies. In a sign of the enthusiasm the troupe had aroused, the final performance was broadcast live over radio, and before the curtain was rung down, the stage was a bower of streamers. Thus finished Hart and O'Brian's Australasian tour, after almost two years. However, it was not the last that would be seen of them.

Kentucky Jubilee Singers (1929)

After the Sonny Clay affair and the prejudice that followed, only one African American act would come directly from mainland U.S. to Australasia for the next five years. In mid–1929 there was a flush of newspaper reports about "a troupe of Negro entertainers seeking admittance." The June 12 *Argus* reported, "In view of the strict conditions under which negro performers are now admitted to Australia, it is likely that the Application before the Home Affairs Department will be granted. Definite evidence of their good repute and bonds of £100 in respect to each member of the party are required."

The group referred to were the fairly safe and wholesome Kentucky Jubilee Singers, who arrived in Wellington (NZ) without a need for bonds, to open at the Grand Opera House in mid–July 1929. Under the managership of a white entrepreneur, Forbes Randolph, they were a recreation of a notable 19th century group of the same name. The group consisted of eight male singers, Arthur Gaines and Robert Caver (first tenors), Hinton Jones and Augustus Simons (second tenors), Archie Cross and William Veasey (first basses), and Arthur Payne and E.D. Pierson (second basses). There was also a specialty Buck and Wing dancer, George Alfonzo. The most notable member was Arthur "Strut" Payne, whose long, illustrious career stretched back to playing in the Williams and Walker shows *Bandanna Land* (1908), and *Mr. Lode of Koal* (1909).[4]

Though the obvious comparison with the Fisk Jubilee Singers cropped up regularly in write-ups of the Kentucky Singers, their show had a quite different pattern of its own. Instead of loosely linked songs, it offered a dramatic structure with a strong narrative thread, particularly in the second act, which was a playlet dealing with the misfortunes of war. The *SMH* (September 2, 1929) approved:

> The entertainment as a whole was of quite a novel type. It reminded older members of the audience of the Jubilee Singers, who visited Sydney many years ago, yet the style of the Jubilee Singers had been much extended and enlarged upon. Instead of being linked together with some genial patter into a vaguely related series, the spirituals have been woven by Mr. Randolph into a play with a definite and strongly dramatic plot. The main scene takes place in a dug-out in France during the war period.

The musical material included such traditional spirituals as "Roll, Jordan, Roll," "Steal Away," "Swing Low, Sweet Chariot," and "Deep River," but also Stephen Foster favorites like "Swanee River," "Old Black Joe" and "Old Kentucky Home."

Their NZ engagements included Auckland (July 6–13), Wellington (July 15–22), a one-night stand in Levin (August 1) before heading to the South Island, starting at Christchurch (Lyttelton) for a week (August 3–8) and finishing at Dunedin (August 10–14). The response at all venues was enthusiastic: Auckland (*NZ Herald*) "Delightful performance"; Wellington (*Evening Post*) "The singers were applauded again and again last evening"; Christchurch (*Press*) "No lover of vocal music—indeed, no lover of any kind of music at all—can afford to miss the wonderful programme"; Dunedin (*Otago Daily Times*) "They succeeded completely in pleasing the audience."

The Singers opened their Australian season in Sydney on August 31 at the Palace Theatre, which was a temporary replacement for the soon-to-close Tivoli. Even *Truth* was lavish in praise: "The Kentucky singers, eight singing blackbirds at the Palace, are superbly harmonious people with dark brown voices that blend organ depths with lovely, flute-sweet heights." Despite the positive response, the Sydney season was to be a short one, ending on September 12, the Brisbane *Telegraph* noting: "The Kentucky Singers are able to make only a hurried tour of Australia as American engagements await them at the close of the year."

During the Sydney run the *SMH* reported: "Randolph's Kentucky singers, who are at present appearing at the Palace Theatre, have made two double-sided records, which should prove of considerable interest to anyone who heard their artistic singing." Adelaide was the next city to enjoy the Kentucky Singers, with a week at the Theatre Royal starting September 14. The *Advertiser* observed:

> When a negro opera is written, Arthur Payne's fine bass voice could be utilized. In 'Old Black Joe' he displayed an almost incredible depth and purity of tone with a breath control that was a lesson to every music student. At the other end of the scale is the haunting 'There's a Cradle in Caroline.' Arthur Gaines took a soaring tenor note that lasted so long his listeners involuntarily held their breath lest anything should mar its beauty.

The Melbourne season opened on September 21, back on Tivoli territory. Given that Melbourne had been the scene of the Sonny Clay debacle it might have been expected that there would be some reaction to the return of a black vaudeville act, even as wholesome as Jubilee singers. There was no such public reaction, only packed houses and a warm welcome. The only discordant note was from a lengthy letter by Nationalist Party Senator J.F. Guthrie, widely circulated in regional media, supporting the introduction of a 5 percent media tax by the government on foreign film distributors. Ranging widely, it took a sideswipe at black performers.

> Worse still, some of the amusement companies import nigger bands and nigger singers. The Commonwealth Band, which performed with marked success in Europe, was insulted in America, and not allowed to perform there. I saw a band of fat niggers arrive at Spencer-Street, last week. I asked who they were and who had imported them. They replied—"We are the Kentucky Singers, under engagement in Australia to the theatre people." Ye gods and little fishes! Foreign films, foreign 'talkies' teaching our children to mutilate in every way the English language, canned foreign music, imported nigger singers. Where do Australians stand with those who are making fortunes out of the public, and yet object to pay 5 per cent., or even part of 5 per cent., towards the funds of their own country.

The senator's letter didn't seem to have any effect on the Tivoli box office. The Melbourne season ended on October 12 and the Kentucky Singers sailed for North America on the liner *Niagara* on the 17th. They continued performing in Europe, where sometime in 1930, "Randolph [entrepreneur and manager] abruptly deserted his singers and ran off with the payroll."[5] Despite this, they reformed and continued touring in Europe until the outbreak of World War II, when they broke up.

Janice Hart and Frank O'Brian Return (1935)

Almost five years to the day after their departure, on March 26, 1935, Janice Hart and Frank O'Brian arrived back in Australia on the SS *Strathnaver*. With great fanfare, their new show *Birds of the Night* (*Oiseaux de la Nuit*), was declared to be their version of a long-running Casino de Paris revue, with Janice allegedly playing the roles originated by Josephine Baker. The publicity for the opening at Melbourne's Tivoli, on April 20, 1935, described it as "the show that made Josephine Baker famous." Advance reviews reported that Janice Hart planned to dance nude à la Baker, as she had done in London ("Paris shocks promised," April 1 Melbourne *Herald*). If Josephine had a leopard, then Janice had a pet monkey. The local media picked up on and amplified the hype, the June 30 *Truth* reporting:

Frank O'Brian purchased this glamorous variety revue—lock, stock and barrel, and adapted it into English. Its presentation in London and New York created an even greater furor than in Paris. In the original French production, the famous colored American Star Josephine Baker appeared in the leading role, which was subsequently taken over by Janice Hart to England.

Janice Hart, star of *"Birds of the Night,"* the startling show from the Casino de Paris. From the English theatre program, 1933. Author's collection.

They had been touring this show in England since 1931. There never was a Josephine Baker show of that title. Josephine had her first Casino de Paris revue during 1930, *Paris qui Remue* (*Paris which Bustles*), and after a year's interval, during which she was replaced by rival Mistinguett, a second revue in 1932, *La Joie de Paris*. There is no evidence in media reports of the time that the material presented in *Birds of the Night* included any of the songs associated with Josephine's Casino de Paris revues, such as "J'ai Deux Amours" or "Suppose." In fact, the material in *Birds* seems to have been a mélange of vaguely French-flavored items, along with original material, popular songs, and ballet scenes with elaborate costumes designed by Janice. In an Australia where few had ever been to France, except as cannon fodder in World War I, no one questioned the authenticity of the claims. Janice was seen in many parts—as a sinuous Chinese singing girl, as the untamed jungle flower "Anona," as a dapper chocolate soldier, and finally as a dazzling, iridescent bird of the night surrounded by fluttering white doves.

The show was again a comprehensive package, albeit this time more a collection of individual vaudeville acts than the integrated burlesque of last time. The company of 60 included the Kiraku Brothers (Japanese acrobats), the Three Loose Screws (knockabout comedians), the Broadway Boys and Brenda (eccentric dancers), Les Cyranos (Adagio dancers), the Can-Can Girls, a ballet of 24, and a Beauty Chorus of 16.

Under *Birds of the Night* as an umbrella title, the show went through weekly revisions with titles like *Women of the World* and *Why Go to Paris?*, finishing the Melbourne run on June 28 as *Au Revoir*. It opened at Sydney's New Tivoli Theatre on July 6, with the same format and cast, though the support acts would change over the course of the season. *Truth* approved: "'BIRDS OF THE NIGHT' unquestionably lived up to the hosannas of praise that had preceded this famous French revue from London and Paris, and yesterday more than five thousand people had their first real taste of a real Parisian revue, and found it an epicurean feast of fun. The dances were exhilarating, the songs beguiling and melodious, while the frocking was a revelation in Parisian creations."

Unscripted drama occurred in the Sydney season, on July 23, when, in a scene called "Jungle Love," Janice Hart made a Tarzan-like leap from the roof of a hut on to a bough of a tree which collapsed, dropping her to the stage with a fractured ankle. Her role was limited for a while to supervising the ballet troupe, one of whose members was the next subject of media interest. Little had been heard of Janice Hart's original promise (threat!) to do a Baker-style nude dance. However, perhaps as a replacement for the injured Janice, the version of the show that opened under the alternative title *Une Nuit Excitante* ("An Exciting Night") featured a fan dance by one of the ballerinas, Peggy Waddington, against a background of ballerinas in black costumes. The publicity proclaimed: "STARTLING FAN DANCE BAFFLES EVERYONE—IT'S A SENSATION." Seen by the *SMH* as "graceful," this was not so much a Josephine Baker–style nude dance (which French ballet critic André Levinson described as "an expression of primitive animality") but rather the more sedate fan dance made famous by Sally Rand at the 1933 Chicago World's Fair.[6]

Nevertheless, it was seen by one audience member as sufficiently a threat to public morals to warrant a report to the police, who seem to have taken little interest. Perhaps the police commissioner enjoyed his invitation from the management to view the next performance. At any rate, the dance continued to be featured strongly in the promotional material and the publicity helped swell audiences.[7]

By August 10, Janice was sufficiently recovered from her injury to rejoin the next variation of the show, called *A Night in Montmartre*. However, it was noticeable that later performances relied more on her singing, and there would be further problems with her ankle down the road. The Sydney

"A Bird of the Night—To Say Nothing of the Monkey." Janice Hart as seen by cartoonist Stanley Parker, Melbourne *Table Talk*, 16 May 1935. Courtesy *Trove*, National Library of Australia.

season finished on September 13. Janice and husband Frank took a break for a holiday in the Blue Mountains resort of Mount Victoria before opening again on November 2 at Newcastle's Victoria Theatre. This time they were on the Fuller circuit, with a new support troupe that included Queenie Paul, Mike Connors, and dancer Alma Aldous, familiar from their 1928 visit. The Newcastle engagement lasted more than a month, finishing on December 6.

Their next opening, in Brisbane on Boxing Day 1935, featured a curious coincidence. On the same date in 1929 Hart and O'Brian had been the featured show at the reopening of the old Empire Theatre as a vaudeville house. Now, exactly six years later, they were opening at the same theatre, under its new name, St. James Theatre, once again being relaunched as a vaudeville house. The show was still exuberantly, and misleadingly, advertised as "Direct from the Casino de Paris." As before, they were a big success in Brisbane, including via radio broadcasts. Janice became a recognized public figure for her flamboyant cream saloon car with an uncommon radiator mascot—a metal heart with the name Janice inscribed upon it. The Brisbane season lasted seven weeks before they set off, once again, for New Zealand.

New Zealand Once Again

Having finished at the St. James Theatre, Brisbane, the Hart and O'Brian show now opened at the St. James Theatre, Wellington, on March 6, 1936. They were again accompanied by a large supporting cast of over 30 artists. A featured item was the performance of the celebrated Sally Rand fan dance. As in Australia, Janice was featured in vocal numbers only, one of which incorporated clever costume changing. The Wellington season lasted a month, followed by four weeks at Christchurch (another St. James Theatre). After the Christchurch finale there was a gap covering the month of June, during which they relaxed on the South Island, judging by this statement credited to Janice in Dunedin.

> I like your New Zealand hotels better than those anywhere else in the world. They have a homely touch about them, and I think they are superior to Australian hotels. Central heating was lacking in many Australian hotels, although it could be very cold there in winter. We find in your best hotels that the proprietors personally supervise your comfort, and one feels that one is getting special attention.

Presumably refreshed, they resumed their tour at His Majesty's Theatre, Auckland, on July 6, with an unchanged cast. The Auckland season ended on August 1, and Hart and O'Brian sailed for Sydney via the SS *Aorangi* on August 4.

Australian Finale

Back in Australia, it became obvious that Janice Hart's problem with the earlier ankle injury was still troubling her. The October 31 *Australasian* reported: "Janice Hart will not be associated with Mr. O'Brian this season, owing to an accident to her foot, which has kept her idle for the past 10 months." Not quite true, though it had kept her from dancing. It was obvious that without Janice, its Princess of Dark Men, a diminished *Birds of the Night* would be like *Hamlet* without the Prince of Denmark, so Frank O'Brian opened without her, as "Frank O'Brian and his Travesty Entertainers" at Adelaide's Majestic Theatre on September 12.[8] After a successful four weeks, he replaced Roy Rene (Mo) at the Melbourne Tivoli on November 4, for a five-week season. He opened at the Sydney Tivoli in mid–December, where he played in the pantomime *Mother Goose* until mid–January, after which the pantomime alternated as a matinee with Frank O'Brian's revue *OKAY for Sound* in the evenings. This revue, which included a boxing kangaroo, ended on January 28, 1937. The last Australian public notice of Frank O'Brian was playing on stage as a support act for movies at Melbourne's St. Kilda Palais Pictures on January 30, presumably while awaiting a ship back to England.

While the long association of Cassie Walmer/Janice Hart with Australia and New Zealand petered out rather anticlimactically, it was not the end of her career. By mid–1937 Hart and O'Brian were back, touring their show in England. They would continue to do so until at least 1947, by which time Cassie was 59 years old. She lived to the grand old age of 92, dying in 1980 in Camden Town, in the same London Borough where she was born.

Walter Richardson, Show Boat, etc.

Another African American who arrived from the UK in 1928 was Walter Richardson. Richardson was a tenor with an impressively long record, including with the Black Patti troupe in 1898, and a role in Williams and Walker's *In Dahomey*, the show that was performed before the Royal Family at Buckingham Palace in 1903. Along the way he had been in many all-black revues, and in 1928 had made a name for himself in London singing "Roll Away, Cloud" in the musical-comedy *Virginia*. During July he had been widely reported in the Australian media as coming from London to take the role associated with Paul Robeson in the soon to open *Show Boat*, singing "Ole Man River." A large advertisement in the July 20 Melbourne *Age*, announcing the opening of *Show Boat* at His Majesty's Theatre on August 3, included his name with the caption "The Famous Coloured Singer and Tenor Whose Performance in the London Production of *Virginia* Created a Sensation. He Will Play Joe, and Will Sing 'Ole Man River.'" It also promised a "special ballet of colored dancing girls brought from the USA."

When *Show Boat* finally opened in Melbourne it was not Richardson who sang "Ole Man River" but a blacked-up local tenor, Colin Crane. Whatever dispute may have led to Richardson's replacement, J.C. Williamson presumably still had contractual obligations to him and he continued performing around the local Tivoli and J.C. Williamson's houses. This included a successful two weeks at Adelaide's Theatre Royal, followed by the Melbourne Tivoli for the first half of September. During early October he was featured as stage support for movies at Hoyt's Theatre Royal. From October 26, he appears on the bill at the Sydney Palace as a support for the main act, "Jerry and her Baby Grands," until late November.

He finished with a series of cabaret-style engagements at the Ambassadors and other local venues, where his accompanist was the half–African black jazz pianist Reginald Foresythe, who also came out with *Show Boat*.[9] Richardson's cabaret engagements finished around late November, one of them being an event for the Manly Amateur Athletics Club, at which a fellow performer was the young Barbara James, an early Australian jazz pioneer.[10] Despite losing his scheduled role in *Show Boat*, Richardson may have felt his Australian engagement was not entirely unprofitable. Back in America he continued his entertainment career at least into the mid–1930s.

The Show Boat Ballet Girls

Meanwhile, back at *Show Boat*, the eight "colored dancing girls" supported the black-face Colin Crane singing "Ole Man River," *Truth* noted, "The colored ballet get a good hand and earn it." The *Indianapolis Recorder* (July 13, 1929) reported: "A wonderful chance to sail the seven seas came to a group of Sunkist maids when they sailed Tuesday for Australia to play long engagements with a company from the states." The list supplied included nine names, but the August 4 *Sunday Times* correctly had eight. Using a variety of sources, including the passenger list from the SS *Ventura*, to reconcile conflicts between the two lists, it seems probable that the eight were: Eileen (Patsy) Hunter, Isabel Hodge, Palmere Jackson, Georgia Prestley (probably the same person as the Zenoria Preachley on the passenger list), Flora Washington, Dorothy Williams, Dorothea West, and Dorothy Yoes. They were all experienced performers, based on the West Coast. The *Sunday Times* mentioned that they had been "seen and heard" in the highly regarded all-black movie *Hearts in Dixie*. Flora's sister, Mildred Washington, had a featured role in that movie, which was showing in Australian cinemas while they were there. By the time *Show Boat* opened in Sydney, their ballet troupe had swelled to 10.

Though they were not U.S. national stars, the careers of several of these girls can be traced through the media during the 1930s onward. Hunter, Washington, and Yoes were featured in a Fanchon and Marco revue *Hi Yaller Idea* in 1928; Washington and her son Cliff played in a Valaida Snow revue at the Chicago Cotton Club in 1935; A San Diego historical website has a photograph of "Dorothy Yoes and her Creole Cuties" in the early thirties.[11] As late as 1956 Palmere Jackson portrayed Aunt Jemima at a commemorative event. A tantalizing possibility is that, as well as appearing in *Hearts in Dixie*, these girls may have appeared, or been heard, in the 1929 movie of *Show Boat*, which played in cinemas in Australia concurrently with the stage version. In that case they could have watched themselves on the screen in the same show.[12] *Show Boat* ended its Melbourne run after three months on October 11, and a two-month run in Sydney at His Majesty's Theatre ended on December 26, 1929.[13]

21

The Norman Thomas Quintette
and Ulysses S. Thompson

During the early thirties, theatres, including the Tivoli, struggled. Hugh D. McIntosh's efforts to revive the Melbourne Tivoli's vaudeville fortunes had bankrupted him in 1931–1932. Then, in 1934, Frank Neil entered the scene. An experienced manager recently returned from South Africa, Neil was managing director of the newly formed Tivoli circuit of Australia Ltd. The empire he inherited included Sydney's old Grand Opera House in Castlereagh Street, refurbished in 1932 by the team of Mike Connors and Queenie Paul, and renamed the New Tivoli. Neil was to follow a strong vaudeville policy for the revitalized Tivoli circuit. This was helped by the fact that the Fuller circuit left the field open for the Tivoli by switching their theatres to first-run cinema houses.

By 1935 memories of the post–Sonny Clay embargo on black acts, especially those featuring jazz, may have faded somewhat. In November 1935, the Melbourne Tivoli bill, titled *Lucky Stars*, featured the Norman Thomas Quintette, "Five Colored American High-speed Song and Dance Entertainers, the Last Word in Modern Syncopation." They headed a bill of 25 performers. The members of the quintet were leader Norman Thomas (pianist), Paul A. Smith (tenor), Freddy Crump (drummer), and two dancers, Norman Thomas Junior and Edward Chavers.

Table Talk (November 28) reported: "The outstanding turn [on the Tivoli bill] is that of the Norman Thomas Quintette of American negroes. This includes grand opera, dancing and comedy." The Quintette was not a conventional jazz group. Singer Smith performed opera (*Pagliacci*) as well as ballads and swing numbers. Thomas was a very capable trick pianist; Crump was a phenomenal show drummer who didn't sit at the drums but bounced and clowned around them in an acrobatic fashion. Their madcap style can be seen today on the Internet (YouTube) in the Vitaphone short movie *Harlem-Mania* (1929) and other items featuring Crump. *Table Talk* summed up their style:

> Their act is a little bit of everything. Do you want pianoforte? There is Norman Thomas himself, putting 'The Mocking Bird' through the most amazing and spectacular paces. Do you want a dash of opera? There is Paul Smith singing 'Vesti La Giubba' from Pagliacci, investing it with more than the clown's pathos, with the pathos of his Race. If you feel like some hot dancing, Eddie Chavers and Norman Thomas Junior turn on an act that leaves you breathless. And if you want buffoonery there is Freddie Crump, the drummer, the smallest, fastest, most mischievous black imp it's possible to imagine.

Their 10-week season at the Melbourne Tivoli closed on January 29, 1936. It was followed by an equally successful nine weeks at the New Tivoli in Sydney. While the close of the Sydney season was the last chance for Tivoli fans in both cities to see the Norman

Thomas show, it was the beginning for people in many small and large regional centers. Under an agreement with Frank Neil, the group went on the road with George Sorlie's roaming tent show, under his regular title of George Sorlie's *Crispies and Crackers*. They were now a quartette, Chavers having returned to America. George Sorlie (see Chapter 13) had for years been touring regional centers under canvas with his large marquee tent shows. The itinerary that the Norman Thomas group followed with Sorlie included Bathurst, Wellington, Narromine, Dubbo, Gilgandra, Maryborough, Rockhampton, Mackay, Bowen, Townsville, Condobolin, Forbes, West Wyalong, Young, Wagga Wagga, Albury, Hillston, Hay, Naranderra, Leeton, Cootamundra, and Goulburn. It was dictated by the various annual agricultural show-week dates for each town. The whole itinerary lasted more than six months (April 20 to the end of October 1936).

When the Thomas group left, Sorlie was about to start a whole new cycle in Tasmania, starting at Hobart. The Norman Thomas

The Norman Thomas Quintette; foreground: Norman Thomas Senior (pianist); back, from left; Edward Chavers (dancer), Paul A. Smith (tenor), Norman Thomas Junior (dancer), Freddy Crump (drummer). From Bobby and Gracie Le Brun collection (MS Acc11.137). Courtesy the Australian National Library.

Quartette went to England and Europe, where they played the music halls for many years. Freddy Crump was very popular in Europe, including England, Denmark, and Sweden.[1] Sorlie apologized to his Tasmanian audience for missing out on the Thomas Quartette but, in fact, he had a replacement up his sleeve, one highly recommended by Norman Thomas himself, Ulysses S. "Slow Kid" Thompson.

Ulysses S. "Slow Kid" Thompson

Kid Thompson, as his friends called him, was one of the top figures of the U.S. tap world, famous not only in his own right, but for a time even more so as the husband of the great Florence Mills, until her untimely death in 1927. Ulysses S. Thompson was born in Prescott, Arkansas, on August 28, 1888, to George Washington Thompson and Hannah Pandora Driver. He was christened simply Ulysses. An aunt who was also his schoolteacher added the "S" later because the other children couldn't manage Ulysses, and in this way he became U.S. Thompson. His mother died of typhoid when he was seven years of age.

At age 14 he left home to fend for himself. He had already developed entertainer skills while dancing on the street for nickels and dimes. He worked in various manual jobs, in a sawmill, a brickyard, a steelyard, a rock quarry, and as a grocery delivery boy, until his dancing skills got him a job helping a "high-pitch" doctor whose "pitch" was selling patent medicines on the streets. Kid Thompson's job was to dance, sing, and tell jokes to attract a crowd so the doctor could make his pitch and sell his brew. Medicine shows, common then, were a good source of work for black entertainers, giving them the opportunity to develop professional skills. Thompson claimed the medicines were mostly alcohol.

In 1904, at age 16, he discovered the world of carnivals and circuses. For several years he followed the big top to earn his living. Carnivals and circuses usually had a "plantation" that featured fast-paced black entertainment, an ideal setting for someone with his experience. Among the circuses he worked in were Mighty Hagg,

Ulysses S. "Slow Kid" Thompson. From the Johnny Nit collection, courtesy Evelyn Cynthia Williams and Debbi Williams.

Sells-Floto, Hagenback & Wallace, and Ringling Bros. He also worked in a host of other stock shows, medicine shows, and animal shows. Between 1911 and 1913, with Hagenback and Wallace, he was a minstrel end man for the P.G. Lowery orchestra, and in 1915 was "in the sideshow at Ringling Bros. entertaining on the stage by myself, singing, dancing and telling jokes."[2]

Besides his brilliant natural talent for dance, he could play music reasonably well on several instruments. He also clowned in a style he described as "hokum," fooling around and telling a few jokes. Following the circuses in summer, he had gravitated by 1912 to vaudeville during the winter season. There he earned the nickname "Slow Kid" for a remarkable slow-motion dance he performed, although he could also do fast tap and acrobatic routines. A contemporary description of his act in 1912 ran, "Unlike his name, he is not slow. The fact is, he is the fastest slow man you ever saw. He tells a few jokes that are old and new, but the way he tells them he gets the laughs."

By 1916 Thompson had become a member of a burlesque/vaudeville act known as The Tennessee Ten.[3] It was through this that he was to meet his future wife, Florence Mills, a featured singer and dancer with the troupe. The Ten comprised eight men and two women. It played the better-class burlesque theaters on the Keith circuit and included a full jazz band, a rival to Freddie Keppard's famous Creole Band.

Thompson's time with the Tennessee Ten was interrupted in 1918 by a stint in the U.S. Army, serving in Europe as a musician. "In the army I was a clown drummer, I used to do all the stuff, throw sticks up and catch 'em in time, you know. They had an army band, they gave a concert for the soldiers, and they have a big circle and I used to get in the circle and dance and bounce around and all that stuff. I was a big hit."

When the success of the show *Shuffle Along* opened up a new era for black entertainers in 1921, Thompson saw a new opportunity for his talented fiancée. They left the Tennessee Ten and moved to New York, where he subjugated his own career to managing and promoting her outstanding talent. This paid off when she replaced one of the *Shuffle Along* leads, Gertrude Saunders, becoming an even bigger hit. Florence Mills became a new kind of sensation on Broadway and in Europe, featured by entrepreneur Lew Leslie in a series of shows (*Planta-*

U.S. Thompson and Florence Mills, 1926, by photographer Claude Harris, London. Author's collection.

tion Revue, Dover Street to Dixie, and *Dixie to Broadway*), culminating in *Blackbirds of 1926* and *1927* in the UK, France, and Belgium. Kid Thompson was content to play a background role, sometimes in her shows, sometimes on his own. Her early death, aged 31 in 1927, from tuberculosis aggravated by overwork, left him alone to pursue his solo career again.

After the death of his wife and partner, Kid Thompson had stayed out of the American limelight, touring widely in Europe and Asia before his arrival in Australia in 1936. Part of the reason for this was the attempts made by well-meaning friends to be matchmakers for the eligible Thompson. Many years later he described to Delilah Jackson an attempt by Susie Edwards—of the vaudeville comedy team Butterbeans and Susie—to pair him with Ethel Waters, not long after Florence Mills had died. "We stayed for a night together and that was it. … Liked each other quite well but not really interested."

U.S. Thompson and George Sorlie

U.S. Thompson arrived in Sydney on the SS *Maunganui* on November 14, 1936. It's remarkable that throughout his lengthy sojourn in Australia, he was never identified as the great Florence Mills's husband, even though as late as October 1937, almost a year after his arrival, and nearly 10 years after her death, Australian media in the major cities was still advertising silk stockings in the "Florence Mills shade."[4] This silence was probably out of respect for his privacy by the many friends he made on his visit.

While in Australia, Thompson's act included the famous stair dance usually associated with Bojangles Robinson. Bojangles was notoriously aggressive to those who "stole his steps" but if anyone could get away with doing so, it was the husband of Bojangles's adored friend Florence Mills. In fact, Bojangles had presented him with a pair of dancing shoes when he heard Thompson was departing for Australia.[5]

U.S. Thompson opened with George Sorlie's *Crispies and Crackers* at Hobart's Theatre

Royal on Wednesday November 18, 1936. The Hobart *Voice* reported: "Foremost among the attractions is U S Thompson, the great American colored star, who was a headliner in London and New York with the Blackbirds Revue Company." It also mentioned that "quite a pleasant surprise is Australia's youngest and best comedian, Bob Le Brun. His natural humor and his contagious smile have made him quite a favorite on the mainland." Bobby Le Brun's real surname was Marshall. He took the name Le Brun from an American roller skating dancer Lew Le Brun, who had been an early mentor to Australian dancers during 1912 to 1914.

Bobby Le Brun's diary for November 17, 1936, noted, "Met new dance act U.S. Thompson—seems nice." Next day he commented, "U.S. Thompson a nice quiet fellow—so different to Daddy Thomas."[6] The meeting between Kid Thompson and Bobby Le Brun was to be the start of a lifelong friendship, also involving Bobby's fiancée and soon to be wife, the dancer and choreographer of the troupe, the same Grace Boyd, later Gracie Le Brun, who had been part of the Hart and O'Brian company. A strong bond between Ulysses and Bobby was their shared passion for golf. "We were so keen that we played 18 holes every day, sometimes 36 and on odd occasions Thompson would say 'Bobby, we got time for another round' and we'd play 45, then back to town and to work."[7]

From Hobart, after a short Queensland visit, the Sorlie troupe with Thompson worked its traditional way through the market weeks of NSW towns (Inverell, Glen Innes, Scone, Newcastle, Bathurst, Wellington, Dubbo, Gilgandra), then Queensland (Maryborough, Rockhampton, Bowen, Mackay, Townsville) and back to NSW again (Condobolin, Wagga Wagga, West Wyalong, Leeton, Lismore, Murwillumbah and Grafton) finishing in mid-November 1937. The reviews were invariably positive, the *Glen Innes Examiner* (March 2, 1937) reporting:

> None will doubt the claims of U.S. Thompson to championship honors as a whirlwind dancer. Thompson, whose whimsical manner makes his tapping wizardry the more appealing, went through a long turn without once ceasing to tap. His interpretive numbers, particularly that of the homing inebriate and the lady crossing through the traffic were excellent. It's so easy, he said, and made it appear so.

The November Grafton engagement marked the parting of the ways for Kid Thompson and the Sorlie caravan but it was not the end of his friendship with Bobby and Gracie Le

George Sorlie's "Silver King," a visiting golf team at the Gympie Golf Links in Queensland 1937. From left: Frank Perrin, Bill Bennett, Bobby Le Brun, U.S. Thompson, Doug Cameron, Jock Taylor, George Sorlie. Author's collection, courtesy of Gracie Le Brun.

Brun. They would remain in contact until Bobby's death in 1985. Bobby and Gracie visited U.S. Thompson in New York in the 1960s, at which time he presented them with a set of whimsical Parisian pictures bought by himself and Florence Mills in the 1920s. The pictures still had pride of place in Gracie's home up to the time of her death, aged 99, in 2011. In later years, Bobby Le Brun was famed for his performances as Sorlie's Pantomime Dame. Jim Sharman, director of both the theatre and film versions of *The Rocky Horror Show*, credited Le Brun's pantomime dance as the inspiration for the character of drag queen Frank-N-Furter in the play and film.[8]

U.S. Thompson: The Tivoli and New Zealand

Having parted company with the Sorlie show in Grafton, Kid Thompson appeared at the Melbourne Tivoli in November 1937, sharing a bill with veteran English music hall star and male impersonator Ella Shields (of "Burlington Bertie from Bow" fame) as well as notable Australian Neva Carr Glynn. Though featured relatively low on the bill, the November 16 *Argus* noted Thompson for "the cleverest and most artistic tap dancing routines seen for years." By December 23, the show had moved to the Sydney Tivoli, in conjunction with the Christmas pantomime *Cinderella*. On February 11, they opened at Brisbane's Regent Theatre, by which time Thompson was sharing equal billing with Ella Shields. Dance fans had a chance to compare his tap dancing with that of Fred Astaire, as by February 18 his show was supporting the Regent's showing of the Astaire movie *A Damsel in Distress*.

On March 7, the show, still with Ella Shields and U.S. Thompson, opened in New Zealand at Auckland's His Majesty's Theatre, this time as a full stage show, not supporting a film. After Auckland the show moved to Wellington (Grand Opera House) for two weeks, followed by Christchurch's Theatre Royal, where the *Press* noted: "The tap dancing of U.S. Thompson was sparkling and varied, especially in a number of imitations and in his cartwheels combined with taps." Thompson dropped out partway through the Christchurch season. He could have continued his successful engagements in Australasia but had another agenda that made him homesick for America.

Like many African Americans of the era, Kid Thompson was a fanatical follower of boxing—"I used to know the history of all of them"—but after his time in Australia, "I lost track of everything." This was the era of Joe Louis, the Brown Bomber, as big a hero as Jack Johnson but with a cleaner reputation. Louis had won the heavyweight crown from James Braddock in 1937 but, by June 1938, a rematch with Germany's Max Schmeling, who had sensationally defeated Louis in 1936, was a huge draw. Kid Thompson had returned to be part of it. More than 70,000 people crammed into New York's Yankee Stadium for the fight. It was widely seen as a showdown between Hitler's Nazi ideology and democracy, but for African Americans it had even deeper significance. Kid Thompson was driven to the stadium by his friend Will Vodery, formerly musical director of Florence Mills's shows. Thompson saw Louis knock Schmeling out before Round 1 was over, while Vodery was still parking his car!

In November 1938, the *Pittsburgh* Courier reported: "U.S. 'Slow Kid' Thompson, the nation's peerless dancer and husband of the late lamented Flo Mills, is back in town from Australia, riding down Central Avenue with his big limousine and liveried chauffeur." Though obviously comfortably off, Thompson would continue to perform in show business into the 1960s. In 1946, he married Dr. Gertrude Curtis, the first African American female dentist in New York, who was also the widow of songwriter Cecil Mack (R.C. McPherson), lyricist for many well-known songs including "The Charleston." Dr. Curtis died in 1973 at the age of 93, leaving Kid Thompson a part-owner of the copyright to the song Florence Mills had performed so popularly years before. U.S. Thompson lived to the advanced age of 101 years, dying in the home of a niece in Little Rock, Arkansas, in 1990.

22

Nina Mae McKinney

While Kid Thompson was wandering around outback NSW with the Sorlie tent show during August–September 1937, a friend of his from the U.S. was arriving in Australia. The SS *Mooltan* arrived at Fremantle on August 24, carrying on board the beautiful black film star Nina (pronounced Nine-ah) Mae McKinney, on her way to engagements at the Melbourne and Sydney Tivoli theatres. The local media was agog with interest, as Nina's reputation had traveled ahead via her role as a glamorous African queen opposite Paul Robeson in the popular 1935 movie *Sanders of the River*, which was still playing in some Australian cinemas. Her first major film role, aged 16, had been as the seductress "Chick" in *Hallelujah* (1929), the first all-black, all-sound musical film. She was selected for this role after producer King Vidor noticed her as a lively chorus girl in Lew Leslie's Broadway production *Blackbirds of 1928*.[1]

After *Hallelujah*, Nina Mae was disillusioned with the limited opportunities in Hollywood, complaining to the *Argus* interviewer that, though she had a contract with MGM, she was denied worthwhile roles because "the censor, who disliked scenes of white men making love to me, ordered the film to be cut." She moved to Europe in hope of better opportunities, and in England made several movies, including the aforementioned *Sanders of the River*, as well as being an early pioneer on BBC TV. Impresario C.B. Cochran, who featured her at his Trocadero cabaret, observed:

> Many new personalities were introduced to London at the Trocadero, and none more vivid than Nina Mae McKinney, a *café au lait* girl with dazzling teeth, enormous bright eyes, and tremulous hips, of a kind to re-invigorate any tired business man. Nina caught the town, and seemed to possess that something which compelled publicity. She was, however, a packet of mischief, and a constant anxiety.[2]

The media coverage that followed Nina Mae as the SS *Mooltan* made its way, from Fremantle to Adelaide, and eventually Melbourne on August 31, focused heavily on her starring role with Paul Robeson and she was eager to sing his praises:

> Robeson is a wonderful man and marvellous to work with. He is married and has a son aged nine years who has been brought up in Switzerland and who could speak German before he learnt English. Robeson himself speaks fluent Russian and loves Russia, spending all his holidays there. He also speaks the language of the South African negroes, in whom he is greatly interested. He loves Africa because he feels our forefathers came from there.

Her admiration for Robeson was undoubtedly genuine and reports of an affair between them during the filming had been enough to worry Robeson's wife, Eslanda Goode Robeson.[3]

"Hello Harlem" Sydney Tivoli theater program cover featuring Nina Mae McKinney, 1937. Frank Van Straten Collection.

Nina Mae's entourage on the sea voyage included two piano accompanists, Kirby Walker, a U.S. national, and Yorke de Sousa, a West Indian of British nationality. Her show opened in Melbourne on Monday, September 6, under the title *Hello Harlem*. Apart from Nina and her featured pianists, the bill included another colored act, Batie and Foster, a comedy tap dancing team. Batie and Foster had left England for Australia some time before Nina Mae's departure on the *Mooltan* and they had already been part of Frank Neil's preceding show, the Sydney version of *The World Looks Up* since August 5 (closed September 8). They had been based in the UK for some years, but jazz musician Mezz Mezzrow had also mentioned Batie and Foster as being among the outstanding acts featuring in Harlem's Lenox Club around 1931.[4] The Stearnses concurred, saying that, in their act, "the comedy often obscured the high quality of the dancing…. While Clarence Foster mugged, Walter Batie executed a walking tap pantomiming Harry Langdon."[5]

The Australian content of *Hello Harlem* included the perennial Roy Rene (Mo). Jealous of his status as Australia's leading comedian, Mo bitterly resented having to play second fiddle to an imported black American female. "I've been turned out of me room," he raged, "and for a black sheila."[6]

The September 7 *Argus* reported:

> Miss Nina Mae McKinney appeared before crowded houses at the Tivoli Theatre yesterday. Soft-spoken, with just a trace of that negro huskiness which can be so fascinating, Miss McKinney sings three songs, each stamped with the character expected of her, and performs two dances—one of them the African drum dance from *Sanders of the River*.

For the September 11 *Australasian*: "Her voice is of the honey type, with a perfect enunciation that makes every syllable audible." Predictably the gossip columns of the local media followed Nina Mae eagerly. At the Caulfield spring races she wore "a long sable stole over her deep beige cape, and her shallow crowned, brown felt hat had a band upstanding feather of pine green." The September 16 *Table Talk* reported at length her criteria for the "ideal man." However, not all the coverage focused on trivia, the September 25 *Age* noting:

> Off stage, Nina Mae McKinney, who is starring in an act at the Tivoli, is a very intelligent, sensitive and frank young woman, without any affectation. To hear her talk of the film stars is to realise that her life is among them. But to hear her talk of herself is to get the impression of a shy, self-depreciating, sentient trouper who yet, like all troupers, lives for the applause that makes the routine of stage appearances bearable.

By late September, Nina Mae was being heard regularly over Australian radio. By the time the Melbourne season was drawing to a close, Sydney was eagerly anticipating the prospect of seeing *Hello Harlem*. The October 5 *Labor Daily* reported: "Melbourne has simply gone wild over Nina Mae McKinney, the glamorous colored screen star so well

Top: Nina Mae McKinney as Chick in the film *Hallelujah* (1929), Metro Goldwyn Mayer (MGM). *Bottom:* Nina Mae McKinney in *Sanders of the River* (1935), London Film Productions.

remembered in *Sanders of the River* and other films. Day and night for the past five weeks Nina Mae McKinney with a celebrity entourage of 30 stars has packed the Tivoli to over-flowing."

The Sydney opening occurred on October 14, still with Roy Rene, but Batie and Foster were gone. The critical response was as enthusiastic as that in Melbourne. The *Sun* reported:

> In vaudeville there must be talent, style and personality. Nina Mae Mc-Kinney, who made her first appearance at the Tivoli last night, has them—the soft crooning voice, her modest air in contrast to the rowdy barbarity of the majority of colored entertainers, her elegant bearing and clothes, and her delightful charm.

The first hint of possible problems with the show came in a report from *Truth*, just three days after the opening, that "she is a little homesick, and rather dreading an operation for the extraction of her tonsils at the end of her Australian season, but looking forward to a long rest in Australian sunshine afterwards." Despite this ominous note, things progressed happily with the show for the next few weeks, the October 23 *Smith's Weekly* noting: "Her performance is somewhat brief—perhaps its very excellence makes it seem so—but there can be no question about her grace and charm. Slender, sepia-colored, and with large eyes, she moves with perfect dignity, in contrast to the general vaudeville-background."

On October 30, the *SMH* reported that Nina Mae had fainted during her performance at the Tivoli Theatre. "She had sung two songs, and was seen to stagger when leaving the stage, but she returned and gamely began her next number, a dance. She fell heavily in the middle of it, and was carried off. It was announced later that she had been temporarily indisposed, but had recovered." In the confusion following Nina Mae's collapse, Roy Rene was rushed on stage to fill the gap, and pleased the audience with some impromptu impersonations. Returning to be assured he had done well, he responded, "It's a pity that black sheila can't faint at every performance. It'd improve the show."[7]

On November 1, the *SMH* was advertising the "last 13 days" of *Hello Harlem* with Nina Mae but by November 3 her name was omitted and did not appear again, another clear case of Hamlet without the Prince (or Harlem without the princess). For the rest of the season, which ended on November 17, Roy Rene (Mo) was billed as the star. The media was sympathetic to Nina Mae, the November 7 *Truth* declaring, "The sympathy of Australians will go out to Nina Mae McKinney, brilliant little star of *Sanders of the River*. Miss McKinney has been in ill health since her arrival in Australia, but fought on pluckily with her engagement until at the Sydney Tivoli last week she was forced to abandon her performance." On November 17, the *Sun* reported, "Miss Nina Mae McKinney, the well-known colored actress, who recently appeared at the Tivoli, was operated upon yesterday for tonsillitis. Her condition to-day is satisfactory. When she recovers, she will be further operated upon for appendicitis."

On the surface there seems to be no reason to question the media accounts of the circumstances surrounding the end of Nina Mae's participation in *Hello Harlem*. Reports of her health problems had circulated for quite a time before her withdrawal. It's a historical fact that she was admitted to St. Luke's Hospital, Darlinghurst, on November 15, 1937, for a tonsillectomy. However, the private reminiscences of her friend Ulysses "Kid" Thompson cast a different light on some aspects of the events. Following his Melbourne Tivoli appearance, Thompson had played the Sydney Tivoli from December 19 and was in Sydney until his show departed to Brisbane in early February 1938, so he was in Sydney throughout the period of Nina Mae's convalescence.

Below is a partly edited transcript of Kid Thompson's words, from the tape of a private conversation with Delilah Jackson, recorded sometime in the 1970s and now in the author's possession.

> So anyhow, the man that was interested in her was the president of [names a large U.S. corporation]. So anyway, Nina Mae got in bad with the management because the management didn't want this man backstage during the performance, this man who was interested in Nina Mae, because nobody was allowed backstage during the show, and Nina Mae got hostile because the management wouldn't allow her boyfriend who was a millionaire, more than a millionaire…. The management of the theatre let Nina Mae go because the man couldn't stand backstage and watch the show.[8]

Thompson went on to relate how Nina Mae invited him out to meet the man at her seaside apartment.

> The man got her a mansion, out in a place in Sydney called [Watson's Bay], that's the part of Sydney where the aristocrats and the rich people live, out in Watson's Bay. So Nina Mae said, "Kid, come on out. This man, he's my friend and he's got plenty [of] everything." So I knew Nina Mae and I went out there and had breakfast with them.
>
> So the man told me, in front of Nina Mae, he said "Thompson, I want to ask you something. I want to buy Nina Mae a home in Honolulu and I'll come back in the plane from London to Honolulu and Nina Mae can come back in the plane from New York to Honolulu and that's the way we'll spend our time, and back and forwards like that. What do you think of that?"
>
> I said, "Well, I'm not concerned but I think it's wonderful, I think it's marvelous." Nina Mae said to me, "Kid … if he can't buy me a home on Riverside Drive I don't want no home in Honolulu, and going back and forwards from New York to Honolulu. I want a home on Riverside Drive."[9]

Thompson went on to say that Nina Mae got nothing from the man, noting also that she had had the best chance in Hollywood of any black actress of her time. His account of the events is broadly corroborated by official documents held in the Australian government's National Archives, which are quoted below.[10]

Following the closure of *Hello Harlem* and her medical procedures, Nina Mae's plans were to extend her Australian visit to six months, bringing her mother to Australia to help with her convalescence, while seeking to extend her career beyond variety and vaudeville, with roles in serious dramas like David Belasco's *Lulu Belle* or Somerset Maugham's *Rain*.[11] This naïve hope failed to take account of the Tivoli management's demand for the earliest possible cancellation of the bond by which they had sponsored her and manager Jack Evans's entry to Australia under strict contract to the Tivoli. At some point Nina Mae had confided to her hospital and convalescence nurse that Frank Neil, Tivoli manager, had "boasted that he would not let up until he had driven her from the country" (archives).

Faced with the intransigence of the Tivoli, Nina Mae sought the assistance of a Sydney solicitors' firm, Westgarth and Co. The principal, Dudley Westgarth, lodged an application on behalf of her and manager Jack Evans for a fresh bond in Westgarth's name. In return he offered to release the Tivoli of all obligations under their original bond, being under the impression the Tivoli had already booked a return passage for Evans, departing on November 20. Customs duly advised Solicitor Westgarth that a new bond had been issued for three months, from December 1, 1937 (archives).

Nina Mae had wanted Evans to stay on as support until her mother's hoped-for arrival but Evans decided he wanted to leave earlier. He did so, via SS *Niagara* on December 23, but not before Westgarth was advised that under the new bond it was he, not the Tivoli, who was now responsible for Evans's passage.

In the meantime, during December 1937 and January 1938, Nina Mae was seen around

Sydney. Her photograph was featured in the December 28 *Daily Telegraph*, enjoying the annual Summer Cup race season at Randwick racecourse. However, there were sinister machinations occurring in the background. On January 19, 1938, the Customs and Excise department requested Acting Detective Inspector C.J. Brossois to "please make very discreet enquiries as to Miss Nina Mae McKinney's mode of living. It has been confidentially stated that she is not behaving as she should and is also drinking."

The involvement of secret surveillance in this fashion seems ominously similar to the pursuit of Sonny Clay's troupe 10 years earlier. However, Inspector Brossois was a different proposition, carrying out his investigation quickly, thoroughly and without bias. He interviewed several people who had been in close contact with Nina Mae. Relevant extracts from his report include[12]:

> **Miss De Sallis** (lessor, King's Lynn apartments), asked about rumours of excessive drinking, or other irregular behaviour with members of the opposite sex, responded that "she had heard no rumours of that nature. In her opinion Miss McKinney behaves correctly. She has met the lady at social functions and has observed her bearing and found it to be above reproach."
>
> **Mrs. L. Kilduff** (caretaker, Mount Stewart Flats, Woolahra, Nina Mae's later residence) informed me that Miss McKinney's mode of living, i.e., sleeping by day and moving about and disturbing the other tenants at night is likely to cause friction. Up to the present no complaints have been lodged by the other tenants. The impression is forced upon one that Miss McKinney's colour is the main source of friction at this building.
>
> **Mrs. Chandler** (lessor, Mount Stewart Flats), "spoke in flattering terms about Miss McKinney.... The rent of the two flats ... and Miss McKinney's very heavy telephone bill, which has run to as much as £12 in one week, is paid without delay."
>
> **Sister Rudd** (nurse at St Luke's, and afterwards privately for Miss McKinney). "She also formed a high opinion of Miss McKinney. Speaking professionally, she stated that no one could be a habitual drug-taker or consumer of alcohol without showing signs of acute distress during a period of careful nursing and general supervision for over six weeks without such stimulants. Sister Rudd is emphatic that Miss McKinney leads a normal existence.... She is convinced that no reproach of any kind attaches to Miss McKinney's behaviour."

Inspector Brossois's own comments included: "From the information obtained at second hand I learned that Miss McKinney is a person of great charm and very cultured. Nothing was learned that could be construed as detrimental to her character.... Such objection to her presence in exclusive flat buildings as has been noted appears to be due primarily to the fact that she is coloured, and secondly to the fact that she keeps unusual hours."

It is clear from the above that Inspector Brossois's report gives an unequivocal vindication of Nina Mae's character, and clears her of any imputations of improper conduct. However, the Inspector of Customs cover note, forwarding the report to the Department of the Interior, reveals a secret treachery. When Nina Mae told her nurse about the Tivoli hounding her, she also told her that "malicious rumours regarding her alleged immoral conduct and her habit of taking drugs and alcohol were being circulated by someone with a grudge against her." Clearly she suspected Frank Neil and the Tivoli as being behind the rumors. However, the Inspector of Customs stated, "The enquiries were made as a result of certain information conveyed to the Boarding Inspector by *Mr. Westgarth, solicitor*, as to Miss McKinney's mode of living," going on to add,

> Mr. Westgarth informed the Boarding Inspector that Miss McKinney intended applying for the temporary admission of her mother and for further six months' extension of her present exemption which expires on 28/2/1938. He suggests that no further exemption be granted as he considers that it

is not desirable she should be permitted to remain in Australia on account of the way she is carrying on, drinking, etc.

For a solicitor to act secretly against his own client's interests and instructions is clearly unethical. One can only surmise that following his humiliation over the Jack Evans passage matter, and faced not only with a further six months responsibility for Nina Mae, but also her mother, Westgarth's mindset may have been similar to that of King Henry II of England when he declared about Archbishop Thomas Becket, "Will no one rid me of this turbulent priest [actress]." At any rate, with her own representative acting stealthily against her, Nina Mae's fate was sealed.

Her immediate reaction was to flee to Melbourne, accompanied by Nurse Rudd. Seeking information as to her whereabouts, a customs memorandum noted: "It is understood there is a man in the case who resides at Melbourne to whom Miss McKinney has gone. It is stated that she was in constant communication with him by 'phone night and day." It also commented, "Mr. Westgarth would deeply appreciate advice in writing that no further exemption will be granted to Miss McKinney, on receipt of which he will arrange for her to leave the Commonwealth by the first available steamer." Nina Mae was back in Sydney at the Hotel Australia by February 11, with passage booked on the SS *Niagara* sailing February 17. It was Inspector Brossois who confirmed, "Miss Nina Mae McKinney was on board the SS *Niagara* when that vessel sailed for Vancouver via Auckland."

By mid–March 1938, Nina Mae was back in the real Harlem, presumably with some regrets about her Australian experience. It had obviously been unwise of her to fall out so seriously with the Tivoli but she was a strong-willed 25-year-old displaying the same spirit of independence she showed in rejecting her admirer's offer of a home in Honolulu. It is also a fact that Tivoli manager Frank Neil could be a difficult person, as witness his ongoing feud with Roy Rene, whom he sacked, and a nasty temper tantrum insulting actress Anna May Wong.[13]

After her return to the U.S., Nina Mae's career was on a downwards trajectory. Hollywood had very few decent parts for black actors, as successors Lena Horne and Dorothy Dandridge would find out. Her opportunity for a lead role in a planned black (race) film, *The Duke is Tops*, went to Lena Horne because of Nina Mae's delayed return from Australia. She did have a strong performance in another well-made race movie, *Gang Smashers*, followed by some forgettable ones. Her later Hollywood appearances saw her in the traditional black roles of housemaids and menials. She pursued a declining theatrical career before fading into obscurity, dying at age 54 in 1967. In recent years her significance in black film and entertainment has been the subject of a positive reevaluation, including a 1978 posthumous award from America's Black Film-makers Hall of Fame for her "lifetime achievement." Her outstanding first film role as Chick in *Hallelujah* will stand the test of time.

23

1937:
The Harmony Kings
and Bob Parrish

Apart from the presence of the high-profile Ulysses Thompson and Nina Mae McKinney, there was a steady procession of top quality African American performers during 1937 to 1939. Frank Neil organized a regular series of Tivoli shows alternating between Sydney and Melbourne, typically running five weeks at each theatre. While most came via the Tivoli circuit, there was also a reemergence of vaudeville in the Fuller circuit via New Zealand, marking the return to active theatrical management of Sir Benjamin Fuller.

The Harmony Kings

The *West Australian* (May 10, 1937) reported: "A large theatrical party, bound for Melbourne under engagement to Tivoli Theatres Ltd., a party of 11 vaudeville artists, is travelling by the liner *Moreton Bay*, which reached Fremantle from Great Britain yesterday."

Their show, titled *The Talk of the Town*, opened in Melbourne on May 24. Included in the cast were the Three Harmony Kings (generally billed as just "The Harmony Kings"), whose names were William Howard Berry (tenor), George H. Dosher (bass), and Charles Exodus Drayton (baritone). We have seen (Chapter 18) that the original Harmony Kings quartet had split in 1925, into the Colored Emperors of Harmony (who had played in Australia successfully in 1927), and these newly arrived Harmony Kings, reduced to a trio in 1933 when the original leader, Ivan Harold Browning, returned to the U.S. from Europe, and Drayton took over as leader.[1] They followed the same sophisticated presentation that had typified the Colored Emperors of Harmony, top hats, canes, and refined elegance. Given their impeccable professional record, it's not surprising that the Harmony Kings were well received by audiences and reviewers in Melbourne. Described as "a symphony in color" by the May 25 *Age* 25, "[They] blended in spirituals and disagreed in an amusing version of a cat fight," and from the May 29 *Australasian*: "The Harmony Kings are three coloured vocalists who produce spirituals or a cat fight of amazing realism with equal facility and felicity." They were also featured widely on national radio. The Sydney season, starting on June 30, was initially equally well received, the *Sun* and the *Labor Daily* noting respectively, "The Harmony Kings, three negro vocalists, present concerted singing in unusual, but most attractive style," and "Of equally high standing in their sphere are the Harmony Kings, three splendid negro male songsters."

201

Offstage, things ran less smoothly. On Saturday July 10, the Sydney Tivoli was disrupted by an industrial dispute over wages for backstage staff, about 40 employees including ushers, stagehands, etc. The dispute was a result of Australia's unique Federal Arbitration Court, which had the power to decide when and by how much the national basic wage should be increased. In this case the court had concluded that employees of the Tivoli Theatre and the J.C. Williamson theatre company should not be awarded the basic wage increase, despite cinema workers being included. The employees union decided to fight the decision by calling a strike. "On Saturday night, when the management stated definitely that it would not pay, the employees walked out. The three American negro singers, billed on the programme as the Harmony Kings, offered to pay the sum out of their own pockets, but were refused permission to do so by the management."[2]

The Harmony Kings. From left: William Howard Berry (tenor), George H. Dosher (bass), Charles Exodus Drayton (baritone). "A Symphony in Song and Fun" at the Tivoli in *The Talk of the Town* (1937). Courtesy of the Australian National Library.

The dispute closed the Tivoli for a week, a sad case of "the show must not go on." It reopened on Saturday the 17th, with a change in format on July 22 to the alternate *Cavalcade of Variety* format, which would finish on August 4. "The Harmony Kings, from the London Palladium, hold the stage toward the end of the programme. The entertainment skips along without missing a beat from start to finish." During their last week, the Harmony Kings were also featured on a series of Sunday night harbor cruises. They departed for London via the SS *Orford* on August 18, with a parting shot at the racial profiling they had experienced at the hands of Australian immigration officials, reported by the August 19 *Argus*:

> Annoyance at Australian immigration laws was expressed yesterday by Mr Charles Drayton singer, and leader of the negro trio the Harmony Kings.... Mr Drayton said, "We are stage singers well known in many countries of the world. To judge from the action of Australian authorities, however, one would think that we were criminals. When we arrived at Fremantle more than two months ago … our passports were taken from us. During our stay we were left without identification papers, and our passports were not returned until we left Sydney a few days ago. We have travelled all over Europe and have never before had a similar experience. At least, we were always permitted to retain our passports. Australian regulations have puzzled and annoyed us."

The most unpleasant aspect of their experience was being assembled in the pursers office before the ship left so that immigration officials could make sure that they were leaving. Though Drayton's lament was prominently reported in local media, no official comment was forthcoming. This unsavory tale clearly illustrates that the legacy of the Sonny Clay incident had not passed by 1937. Any idea that the Harmony Kings' experience might have been exceptional is dispelled by Frankie Manning's account (see Chapter 25) of a similar experience of discrimination with the Lindy Hoppers, in the mixed-race show *Hollywood Hotel Revue* (1939), a few years later.

The Harmony Kings returned to London. In 1938, Berry and Dosher toured Sweden, replacing Drayton with pianist Henry Crowder, who had some notoriety as the black lover of socialite Nancy Cunard. The group stayed on, based in Brussels, until the Nazi invasion of Belgium caused their return to the U.S. in 1941. By then the Harmony Kings were finished performing as a group, Berry dying in 1942. From 1943 to 1945, Dosher performed on Broadway in the black musical *Carmen Jones*. Charles Drayton was reported performing in charity benefits as late as 1948 but by 1950 was reported seriously ill in Harlem Hospital.

Bob Parrish (1937–1940)

Bob (Robert Laurance) Parrish arrived in Melbourne on the SS *Mariposa* on May 20, 1937. In the early 1930s, as a teenager, he had established a strong local reputation around Los Angeles but struggled to promote his career further. While working as an elevator operator, a local theatre manager helped him get an audition on a major national radio talent contest, the Major Bowes Amateur Hour. Winning first prize in the Amateur Hour soon led to a regular feature spot on Eddie Cantor's national radio program. Cantor described Parrish as the "logical successor to Paul Robeson," with a similar high-range baritone voice. This helped assure his professional success, so it's not surprising his repertoire included "Ole Man River," so closely associated with Robeson. Before his departure for Australia he had announced his engagement to a prominent Los Angeles socialite, Jean Thompson, at a farewell party attended by Bill "Bojangles" Robinson.

Parrish opened in Frank Neil's new revue *Three Cheers for the Red, White and Blue* at the Sydney Tivoli on May 27, 1937. He was one of a large vaudeville cast, headlined by Con Colleano, tightrope walker, and Irene Vermillion, dancer, with her Famous Dart Trumpeters. Australian audiences, loving a good song well sung, took the handsome young Bob Parrish to their hearts. The June 5 *Labor Daily*, labeling him "Eddie Cantor's great find," declared him "already a furor at the Tivoli." Declaring it the Tivoli's "best show in its history," *Truth* described him as a "colored baritone, with a voice as smooth as chocolate cream." The Sydney season ran to record houses right up to the end on June 28, when Parrish moved on to join the Melbourne Tivoli's new show *The World Looks Up*.

Melbournians proved even more enthusiastic for Bob Parrish than Sydney-siders. The June 29 *Argus* reported: "Some of the items in the new programme at

Bob Parrish, "A rich baritone of equal range to Paul Robeson," at the Tivoli in *Three Cheers for the Red, White and Blue* (1937). Courtesy of the Australian National Library.

the Tivoli are so good that they virtually constitute a show in themselves. Pride of place is unhesitatingly given to the singing of the negro Bob Parrish, whose voice is wonderfully flexible, with a richly coloured texture and dramatic power. The crowded house gave him a rare ovation."

On July 19, a new version of the show, titled *Having a Wonderful Time*, was introduced. The *Argus* praised "the remarkable breath control of the negro baritone Bob Parrish who challenges comparison with Paul Robeson himself in a dramatic rendition of 'Ole Man River.'" The new version finished in late July, when Parrish disappeared from the Australian scene temporarily. In California, the *Eagle* reported that he had sent his languishing fiancée, Jean Thompson, a stuffed Koala bear.

Parrish's temporary absence from Australia was a result of Frank Neil taking his *Red, White and Blue* show to New Zealand. The New Zealand version, and Parrish in particular, was received every bit as enthusiastically as in Australia. They opened in Auckland's His Majesty's Theatre on August 2 for a two-week engagement, the August 12 *Evening Post* commenting, "There is a very high standard of singing, due to the presence in this galaxy of stars of Bob Parrish, a coloured singer who is brought back time and time again." Apart from the obligatory "Ole Man River," his repertoire included "Sweet Mystery of Life" and the popular 1937 hit "September in the Rain," which was then widely adopted by other singers in New Zealand.

After Auckland there was a three-week engagement at Wellington's New Opera House. The New Zealand tour ended on September 28 with two weeks at Christchurch's Theatre Royal, again with comparisons to Paul Robeson. By October 11, Parrish was back at the Melbourne Tivoli in the new *Laugh Show of 1937* with a new vaudeville cast, following Nina Mae McKinney's *Hello Harlem*. The welcome back after his absence was as warm as ever, the October 16 *Australasian* enthusing: "That baritone of his is worth going a long way to hear. He is the only artist I have known whom the audience has compelled to break the Tivoli law of no encores."

After a month *The Laugh Show* moved to Sydney on November 18, where once again it replaced *Hello Harlem*, this time following the debacle of Nina Mae's early collapse and departure. The Sydney edition finished just before the pantomime season on December 22, but by then Bob Parrish had been doubling since mid–November as onstage support for the Hoyts movies chain, with the Ronald Colman movie *The Prisoner of Zenda*. He followed the movie when it opened in Brisbane at Hoyts Regent cinema, and he stayed on to support successor movies, while singing on radio. By January 22, 1938, he was back in Sydney, supporting Hoyts suburban cinemas (Mosman, Neutral Bay, Balmain, North Sydney, Bondi), with two shows a day billed as "The Voice of the Southland." By early February, Parrish was back with *The Prisoner of Zenda* in Melbourne, his farewell appearance being announced on February 26, 1938.

Parrish sailed on the SS *Mariposa* on February 28, arriving in the U.S. on March 14, 1938. The March 17 *Eagle* proclaimed his arrival in a banner headline: "BOB PARRISH IN TRIUMPHANT RETURN FROM AUSTRALIAN CONCERT TOUR." They quoted his enthusiastic praise for his experiences: "Australia is the country if you want to get ahead on the basis of ability … if you've got something to give and they think you're okay they'll give you anything." A few months later he married his fiancée, Jean Thompson, who had waited faithfully for his return.

Still home in America, Parrish scored a career coup in March 1939 when he gained the plum role of Nanki-Poo, opposite Bill Robinson as the Mikado, in Mike Todd's Broadway production of the all-black cast *The Hot Mikado. The Hot Mikado* was a prominently featured attraction of the 1939 New York World's Fair. It ran for 85 performances on Broadway before going on the road.

Bob Parrish: Australia Again (1940)

By April 19, 1940, Parrish was back in Melbourne "under engagement to the Tivoli Theatres," which were now under Wallace Parnell instead of the recently deceased Frank Neil. This time Parrish was accompanied by his wife, described as a former stage artist but now preferring to be his partner in a round of golf. Initially, Parrish was back on the familiar Hoyts cinema rounds, plus radio broadcasts. However, it was soon obvious they had bigger plans for him, with the announcement of a new Tivoli vaudeville bill for Melbourne under the title *Radio Roundup*, opening May 13, 1940. The theme of the show was that the public was allowed to vote for the radio stars they most wanted to see featured on stage. The May 18 *Australasian* reported: "The overseas contingent is headed by Bob Parrish, who sustains the high opinion formed of his voice on his previous appearances." The show ran in Melbourne until June 15, followed by a Sydney opening on June 21.

The Sydney season ran until August 1, during which time Parrish also continued playing the local Hoyts cinemas. The show resurfaced as *Radio Revels* in Adelaide (SA) at the Majestic Theatre on August 7, 1940. Claiming there was a "tonic in every act," the August 8 *Adelaide News* declared the "Star performer undoubtedly was Bob Parrish, American colored baritone, who has personality plus, and a marvellous lilting voice. His singing of 'Blue Orchids' was given a wonderful reception." *Radio Revels* finished its Adelaide run on August 27, and it was back to the Melbourne Tivoli for Parrish, billed as "The return of Everybody's Favourite," on September 2.

His new vehicle was the Tivoli's *Our Anniversary Show* starring Roy Rene (Mo), and celebrating "50 Years of Glorious Entertainment." Noting that Parrish was suffering from a sore throat, the *Australasian* commented, "Bob can sing better with a sore throat than many vocalists can sing at their best." The Melbourne run lasted until October 12, reopening in Sydney on October 17; it ran until November 20. Parrish then reappeared briefly in Melbourne, supporting Hoyts cinemas again for a week starting December 21, 1940. He probably spent the intervening period with Australian friends, as he had endeared himself to various charities by presenting color movies of his travels in Australia and New Zealand. When, or how, Parrish left Australia is unclear but by 1942 he was back in America, described in the May 2, 1942, *Pittsburgh Courier* as "a sensation.... The music world's latest find" and about to lead his new Detroit orchestra on a 16-week tour of one-nighters. He would return to Australia once more in 1948, spending nearly six months playing the Tivoli circuit.

24

1938: Chris Gill,
the Edwards Sisters,
Chuck Richards and Peg Leg Bates

With the departure of Ulysses Thompson and Nina Mae McKinney in early 1938, the next African American performers to arrive were part of Frank Neil's new Tivoli production *Variety Show Boat*, commencing in Sydney on Monday July 18, 1938. Chris Gill was a singer and acrobatic dancer, who arrived from London on the P & O liner SS *Strathmore*. On the same bill, arriving from San Francisco via Honolulu on the SS *Monterey*, were the two Edwards Sisters, described as "rapidfire tap dancers."

Chris Gill had been an original member of the Four Flash Devils, pioneers of the dance style known as "acrobatic flash." They had performed successfully in black stage shows such as *Change Your Luck* (1930), *Singin' the Blues* (1931) and the 1933 revival of *Shuffle Along*. *Change Your Luck* was a flop but the Four Flash Devils were "the highlight of the show ... part of a new trend; teams instead of a solo dancer and hair-raising acrobatics such as slides, flips and splits in addition to tap."[1] In 1936, they were featured in the popular British musical film *Soft Lights and Sweet Music*, after which Chris Gill decided to become a single. He played cameo roles in several movies, including *Jericho*, which starred Paul Robeson.

The Edwards Sisters (Ruth Jay and Louise Eddie) had been trained by their father, Jay Eddie Edwards, owner of a Harlem dance studio and organizer of dances and beauty contests. Jeni Le Gon, who tapped with Bojangles Robinson in the movie *Hooray for Love* (1935), considered them among the greatest female tap dancers: "Alice Whitman was the best.... And there was a set of sisters, the Edwards Sisters, they were very, very good."[2] The sisters were accompanied by their father-manager and their mother.

The Melbourne run finished after a month, on August 19, and the show opened at Sydney's Tivoli on August 25. The Edwards Sisters were described in publicity as one of "the fastest girl tap dancers in the world." The September 11 *Sydney Sun* agreed: "A change in color is imparted by the two Edward Sisters, 'Harlem's High Speed Steppers,' who literally beat the band, and Chris Gill, who manages his voice as skillfully as he does his feet." Chris Gill's sophisticated presentation was noted by the *Truth*: "Talking of dressing, there's the perfectly tailored suit of Chris Gill, white as his teeth. This colored gentleman delights with 'That's Why Darkies Were Born,' and some very slick tap-dancing. Also from Harlem are the Edward sisters, lightning workers in dances of their own."

The Sydney run finished after a month on September 28. The Edwards Sisters returned to the U.S. to continue their careers. They featured later alongside many of the top U.S. big bands, including Tommy Dorsey, Gene Krupa, Charlie Barnet, and Duke Ellington. They remained active into the 1950s.

Chris Gill stayed on for a while in the increasingly common role of stage support for movies. Billed as "Vaudeville's most Versatile Entertainer," he provided "a very lively 20 minutes stage session." He finished in Brisbane around October 20, supporting the movie *The Rage of Paris*, which introduced "Danielle Darrieux, the new screen sensation." He was back performing in England by early 1939 and was a regular feature of UK show business into the 1950s, including frequent broadcasts on the BBC.

Chuck Richards

Frank Neil's next Tivoli offering, under the title *Why Be Serious*, featured a leading American vaudeville comedian Will Mahoney, and his American wife Evie Hayes. In the usual Neil style, the cast included an African American, baritone singer Chuck Richards, born in Baltimore Maryland in 1913. By the time he came to Australia Richards already had a distinguished career in jazz, having performed at the Harlem Cotton Club in 1933 and being a frequently recorded vocalist with such leading jazz bands as Chick Webb (1933), Mills Blue Rhythm band (1934–1937), and Fletcher Henderson (1937–1938). Richards doesn't feature notably in the jazz vocal pantheon today, mainly because he was more a ballad crooner than a jazz singer, patterning his style on Bing Crosby.

The Mahoney-Hayes show opened at the Melbourne Tivoli on August 22, 1938. It was highly praised in the media for its fast action comedy, with Richards mostly just seen as one of a good cast. The *Argus* referred to him as "the inevitable negro singer." Praising the high comedy content, the August 27 *Australasian* mentioned "Chuck Richards, a negro singer, is the only performer who strives for tears rather than laughter." The Melbourne show ran for a month and opened in Sydney on September 29 or five weeks, finishing on November 2. Again, the show in total was highly praised, with only vague references to Richards as one "who stuck out." Despite his Bing Crosby crooner style, perhaps there was too much jazz inflection in his delivery for the classically oriented Australian audiences, who liked their black baritones in the Robeson style à la Bob Parrish.

His Australian experience may have discouraged Richards, because he abandoned his singing career on his return to his native Baltimore. There he had a distinguished career as a disk jockey, radio announcer, and (later) a television presenter, being a pioneering African American in several of these capacities. All who knew him found him a friendly, likeable personality. He died in Baltimore in 1984, aged 71.[3]

Clayton Peg Leg Bates (and Jesse Cryor)

The next notable African American performer to arrive, in September 1938, was Clayton "Peg Leg" Bates, the one-legged tap dancer. Anyone who finds the concept of a one-legged tap dancer odd, or even humorous, knows nothing about this remarkable performer. Already dancing on the streets at age five, he didn't let the loss of a leg at age 12 in a cotton gin accident stop him. Instead, he worked out techniques to achieve unique percussion effects with his wooden peg, which were beyond the ability of two-legged dancers. He worked his way through the traditional ranks: minstrel shows, carnivals, black vaudeville.

In 1928, at Harlem's Lafayette Theatre, he was spotted by Lew Leslie, who was looking for talent for his next *Blackbirds* show in New York. His role in *Blackbirds of 1928*, the most successful of the *Blackbirds* shows, along with Bojangles Robinson and Adelaide Hall, brought Bates fame not only in America, but Europe as well. He was regularly featured on *The Ed Sullivan Show*.

Describing his Australian experience to Rusty Frank, Bates said:

> In 1938, I went to Australia and played the Tivoli circuit, their big-time vaudeville circuit. Unlike American vaudeville circuits, which only kept an act in a theater for one week or a split week, the Australians would keep a vaudeville show in one theater for five weeks at a time! I was in Australia for ten weeks; five weeks in Melbourne, and five weeks in Sydney. The Australians had no color barrier and were very fond of blacks. They showed strong appreciation for my talent, and I was always invited to their homes and to parties.[4]

Peg Leg Bates. Publicity still, photograph by Maurice Seymour, courtesy of Ronald Seymour.

Billed as the "The Monopedic Dancing Sensation," Bates made his Melbourne debut on September 26, 1938, a joint headliner in a bill of 15 acts titled *International Merry-Go-Round*, which also included the ubiquitous Roy "Mo" Rene. The *Argus* reviewer was suitably impressed:

> Peg Leg Bates … performs a dance which is unique in the theatre to-day. Mr Bates is a 'monopede,' in other words a one-legged dancer, and he can perform more timing and vigorous steps with one leg than most dancers can with two. With one foot and a wooden peg, he taps out the most complicated rhythms and finishes his act by an amazing display of acrobatics.

In an odd coincidence, the Tivoli bill that included a one-legged African American dancer and also had a one-eyed African American singer. Jesse Cryor, billed as the "Singing Bootblack," had lost an eye in a childhood accident. He enjoyed a long career in black vaudeville and jazz between 1927 and 1952. He is rumored to have been the uncredited singing voice of Brer Rabbit in the Disney movie *Song of the South*. He died in 2006.[5]

The Melbourne season finished on October 29, and the Sydney season opened on November 3. Once again, local audiences had the chance to see contrasting African American dance styles, with Whitey's Lindy Hoppers playing at the rival Theatre Royal. The *Sun* noted: "Peg-Leg Bates proved that a wooden leg can be an aid instead of a hindrance in strenuous dance effects. Other good turns [included] Jesse Cryor, Harlem crooner," and later (November 20):

> PEG LEG BATES, one of the top-liners at the Tivoli, as his stage-name indicates, has only one leg. But this deficiency is more than made up for by the remarkable uses to which he puts his wooden

substitute! With it he beats out a queer rhythm that provides an effective accompaniment to his intricate dance steps. He also uses it as a pivot for amazing balancing feats.

The Sydney season finished on December 7, 1938. Home in the U.S., Peg Leg Bates went on to continue his show business career until 1989. However, it's in a different sphere that he is most fondly remembered by African Americans today. In 1951, along with his wife, Alice E. Bates, he founded the Peg Leg Bates Country Club in the Catskill Mountains near New York. Until then, the Catskill resorts, popular with wealthy whites, had been effectively out of bounds for black people. For several generations of African Americans, affordable annual visits to the Bates Country Club were among their most cherished early memories. He leased out the resort after his wife's death in 1987. Active in many social and charitable activities to the end, Peg Leg Bates died in 1998, aged 91.[6]

25

Frankie Manning and the
Lindy Hoppers (1938–1939)

The day after *Variety Show Boat* opened in Sydney with Chris Gill and the Edwards Sisters, New Zealand got its next taste of whirlwind black entertainment in the form of eight members of Whitey's famous Lindy Hoppers from the iconic Savoy Ballroom in Harlem. They came as part of an elaborate New York show, *Hollywood Hotel Revue*, with over 70 performers, arriving in August 1938. Described as "one of the most spectacular shows ever to visit this country," glamour and comedy were its key themes, with 40 scantily—though tastefully—clad white "American Beauties." The principal stars were established Broadway and film performers, including the lead comedians, brothers Willie and Eugene Howard, who had a long history in major Broadway shows since 1912, including *Ziegfeld Follies of 1934*. The show presented a Hollywood-style extravaganza, with the opening part featuring a tribute to Florenz Ziegfeld, using his theme "Glorifying the American Girl." While the media was obsessed with the glamorous show girls, the presence of a Negro dance troupe also attracted interest.

Billed as "The Big Apple Dancers," the Lindy Hoppers represented a whole new genre of jazz dancing, associated with the Jitterbug and Swing Dancing. Their era is usually identified as starting at the Savoy Ballroom in Harlem in 1928, when during a dance marathon (like in the movie *They Shoot Horses, Don't They*), a dancer named George "Shorty" Snowden incorporated a fast breakaway solo hop step that fascinated watchers. Asked by a journalist to describe it, he called it the "Lindy Hop" in honor of Charles Lindbergh's recent famous Atlantic flight.[1]

The Savoy Ballroom was a thriving center for emerging swing bands like Chick Webb, Duke Ellington, and Count Basie, who competed with fierce rivalry in "cutting contests." The dancers interacted passionately with the bands, initially as participants rather than performers. As the skill of the Lindy Hoppers attracted increasing admiration, a Savoy bouncer called Herbert White, known as Whitey, saw an opportunity to form them into groups that could be marketed professionally. At one time Whitey was employing more than 70 swing dancers. By 1935, the Lindy repertoire had evolved to include "air steps" in which the dancers became airborne, unlike conventional tap, which was typically ground-based. Their skills are shown to good advantage in a wild scene in the 1937 Marx Brothers movie *A Day at the Races* and the Olsen and Johnson film *Hellzapoppin'* (1941).[2]

The group that came to New Zealand in 1938 had some of the greatest of Whitey's dancers, including the legendary Frankie Manning, who was credited (along with partner Frieda Washington) for the invention of air steps. The advance publicity proclaimed that

The Big Apple Dancers on tour with Hollywood Hotel Revue in New Zealand, summer 1938. Front row, from left: Willamae Ricker, Lucille Middleton. Middle row, from left: Billy Ricker, Eunice Callen, Frankie Manning. Back row, from left: Snookie Beasley, Jerome Williams, Esther Washington. Photograph credited to Steele. Courtesy of Chazz Young for Frankie Manning Collection.

they would perform the dances "The Big Apple" and "The Suzy Q." Though they were never individually named during their almost full year in the region (with one exception involving first names only), the group included: Frankie Manning; Billy Ricker; Willa Mae Ricker; Snookie Beasley; Eunice Callen; Jerome Williams; Lucille Middleton; and Esther Washington.

The *Hollywood Hotel Revue* opened with great ballyhoo on August 26, 1938, at His Majesty's Theatre, Auckland. In a style reminiscent of the Grand Parades of the earlier minstrel shows, the opening-night performance was preceded by the cast arriving at the theatre in an imitation of a typical Hollywood premiere at Grauman's Chinese Theatre. The leading members were dressed like, and wearing masks depicting, such well-known film stars as Norma Shearer, Clark Gable, Myrna Loy, and Joan Crawford. A crowd of 3,000 gathered to witness the spectacle, totally blocking access to the theatre. The August 27 NZ *Herald* reported: "Queen Street was blocked by crowds of people who attended for the spectacle, or who were drawn by the presence of others, and from about 7.45 to 8.5 p.m. all motor traffic was held up. A few tramcars managed to make their way slowly through the press as a result of the efforts of police and traffic officers." The *Herald* also described the show as "One of the most lavishly staged revues which Auckland has seen for a long time.... The costumes, although at times daringly brief, are charming in colour and design, and feature, among other effects, innumerable exotic and striking headdresses in which sweeping feathers, cobwebby lace in brilliant colourings, and glittering jewels alternately appear."

The Lindy Hoppers were seen as a popular feature:

> Having taken America by storm, the 'Big Apple' was introduced to Auckland. It is one of those wild dances, seemingly without any set rules to be followed, that only the negro can perform properly, and a team of eight of them, with the rhythm and abandon that they infuse into all their celebrations, gave last night's audience a taste of this speedy revel. Of all the orchestra, only the drummer seemed to have no trouble in keeping pace with the flying feet of this clever team, as they rose and shone in a mad whirl.

Discussing the reaction to the show, the *Auckland Star* considered that "the apple dance party's act in the Showboat finale to Ziegfeld's Tribute gave them pride of place with the audience." While the speed of the dancing impressed the audiences, it presented one practical problem. "It was hard to get the band to play at the right tempo. The revue's musical director had to hire local musicians, and the drummer wasn't used to playing as fast as we danced, so eventually he was replaced by someone they picked up in a nightclub, The other musicians also struggled."[3]

After a record-breaking five-week run in Auckland, the cast of *Hollywood Hotel Revue* sailed on the SS *Wanganella*, arriving in Sydney on September 19. They created some excitement on a Monday morning when members of the cast paraded from the side of the *Wanganella* in their rehearsal costumes, along with the Lindy Hoppers in full revue costume.

The *Hollywood Hotel Revue* opened in Sydney on 23 September at the Theatre Royal. This allowed a one-week overlap with *Variety Show Boat*, which was still playing at the Tivoli, thus enabling Sydneysiders the opportunity to compare high-class tap, via Chris Gill and the Edwards Sisters, with the latest of the Lindy Hop/Jitterbug sensation. The show was enthusiastically received, the September 28 *Mail* noting: "It moves at a breathless pace, and each ballet and stage picture (they are all exceedingly beautiful) is timed to the second."

Sydney was not as tolerant of the scanty female costumes as Auckland. George Gollan, who held the senior NSW government position of Chief Secretary, attended the show with his wife and took offense at the wedding scene in which "eight bridesmaids come forward to the footlights in elaborate gowns reaching to their toes. They then turn about and are shown to be naked from neck to heel, with a thin veil of net to the back of the dress." At Gollan's request, the scene was censored. The October 1 *Adelaide News* reported that at the next show each girl wore a small black card pinned to the net at the back. On each card was painted a letter, spelling out the word "Censored."

The Lindy Hop group faced no such problems; several reviews even complained that they should have appeared in more than one scene. Their only public attention, apart from the show, was a report of their charitable visit to Camperdown children's hospital. However, echoes of the White Australia discrimination did occur. On the last day of the Sydney season, November 19, Brisbane's local media carried two separate public advertisements, the first seeking "Board & residence accommodation wanted for Hollywood Hotel Revue company," and the second, "Accommodation wanted for the Eight Original Apple Dancers. Nine distinguished negroes of the Hollywood Hotel Revue company. Three married couples, one lady, and two single gentlemen."[4]

The Brisbane season opened at His Majesty's Theatre on November 2. The lesson of the crowd problem at the Auckland opening parade had been learned, the November 28 *Telegraph* reporting: "The negro big apple dancers, wearing pill-box caps and brass buttons before the show, formed a barrier by linking hands in an effort to hold back the insistent crowds which surged around the door of His Majesty's Theatre and overflowed on to the opposite footpath."

African Americans in bellboy uniforms protecting glamorous white actors seems rather stereotypical today but probably looked natural to an Australian crowd at that time. Reactions to the performance were generally enthusiastic, though some local critics found the high-energy intensity of the Apple Dancers a bit confronting: "The coloured dancers … seemed to go berserk once they got into full motion. There was no elegance here; merely hot-blooded frenzied action." (*Telegraph*); "The energetic interlude of the eight original negro apple dancers was like a football scrum. The dance has no grace, but it has action" (*Courier-Mail*).

Once again, the only media attention for the Lindy Hoppers outside the theatre came from their charity activities. A *Telegraph* journalist reported (December 2):

> I doubt if I ever saw a sharper contrast in my life than I saw yesterday afternoon, when the eight Apple Dancers from the Hollywood Hotel Revue company went out to Corinda to dance for the crippled children of Montrose Home; Along one side of a long room lay 65 children—some in prams, some in cots, some reclining on invalid chairs. A few were able to walk—after a fashion—but there was not one child present whose limbs were whole—whose arms or legs were not supported by splints, strapped to irons, or lying powerless of movement. On the other side of the room, eight coloured men and girls danced vigorously to the music of a portable gramophone.

The Brisbane season closed on December 14, and the show opened in Melbourne's Princess Theatre in time for Christmas on December 24. The Melbourne season was as successful as ever but was overshadowed by the occurrence in January 1939 of the infamous Black Friday bushfires, one of the worst natural disasters Australia had experienced. This was followed by a series of appeals, with fundraising concerts for the victims, in which the *Hollywood Hotel Revue* participated along with numerous other shows and stars. One appeal held at the Melbourne Tivoli included not only the *Hollywood Hotel* cast but also the Tivoli's own recently arrived African American stars Radcliffe and Rogers, and Ada Brown, of whom more later. In addition to stage performances, another successful fundraiser had the glamorous show girls of the revue selling bushfire buttons on the streets of Melbourne.

The *Hollywood Hotel Revue*'s Melbourne season ran for three months. It overlapped with the Dancing Chefs' season at the Melbourne Tivoli, where they also performed at a night club (see

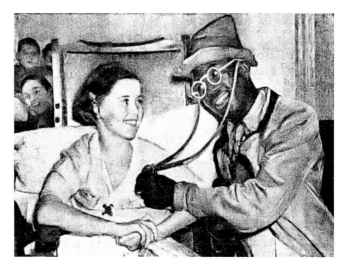

"Dr." Jerome, one of the eight Apple Dancers who entertained the crippled children at Montrose, "sounds" the reactions of one of the small patients. *Brisbane Telegraph*, 2 December 1938. Courtesy *Trove*, National Library of Australia.

Chapter 26). They and the Lindy Hoppers would go to see one another perform, but Frankie Manning recalled that he had to act as chaperone for 17-year-old Eunice Callen, when one of the Chefs tried to seduce her.[5]

As the show approached its final weeks in Melbourne, Sir Benjamin Fuller was reported to be in the West, negotiating for a season in Perth and Kalgoorlie (*West Australian*, February 8). Other reports suggested Sydney would be next. After it finally finished, on March 22, 1939, it was in New Zealand that it next surfaced. It opened on Easter Saturday, April 8, at His Majesty's Theatre, Dunedin, running until April 22. There followed St. James Theatre, Christchurch, for a week before opening a three-week season in the capital Wellington, at the Grand Opera House. The New Zealand welcome was every bit as warm as in the original Auckland season almost a year earlier, with *Christchurch Press* (May 4, 1939) noting: "This scene ends with a performance by the eight original apple dancers, a troupe of negro dancers who bring an enthusiasm, vividness, life, and colour such as have never before been seen in Christchurch. It is worth going to the show to see them alone."

Members of the local Wellington Swing Club were described by the May 15 *Post* as pleasantly surprised at one of their weekly dances by the arrival "at about 11 p.m. ... of the original Big Apple dancers of the *Hollywood Hotel Revue Company*, who joined in the dancing with zest. Mr. Snookie Beasley, on behalf of the American dancers, gave a short talk on swing dancing and complimented members of the Wellington Club on their enthusiasm."

The *Hollywood Hotel Revue* finished its Australasian venture with a one-week return engagement at its original venue at Auckland. The Lindy Hoppers, and presumably also most of the white cast of the show, sailed to Vancouver on the SS *Niagara* on June 4, 1939.

While the Lindy Hoppers' tour was a theatrical and commercial success, Frankie Manning made some interesting comments on the social side of their Australian experience. He praised the harmony that had existed between the white and black components of the Hollywood Hotel Revue troupe. While acknowledging being well-treated in Australia, he mentioned the racial profiling that had resulted from the Sonny Clay era: "I was bonded to leave by Australian regulations. Only the black performers were; the producers put the money up."[6]

He also observed the attitude of white Australians to the Aboriginal population.

> We were treated well in Australia, but I did see Aborigines being treated the same as we blacks were in America. They were excluded from places and all that kind of stuff. In fact, it seemed like white folks there didn't want us associating with the Aborigines.... I think it was to keep the Aborigines from getting ideas from us, because we were doing better than they were.[7]

Whitey's Lindy Hoppers and the associated troupes led by Frankie Manning and Norma Miller continued to be a major force in jazz dance into the 1950s and later. The Stearnses commented, "The Lindy caused a general revolution in the popular dance of the United States." Frankie Manning continued actively as a dancer and choreographer up to the time of his death in 2009, aged 94. He revisited Melbourne in 2002. His son, Charles "Chazz" Young, was also a talented Lindy Hopper and visited Australia in 1955 with Norma Miller's Dancers.

26

1939: Radcliffe and Rodgers,
Ada Brown, the Dancing Chefs,
Chuck and Chuckles,
the Mills Brothers

For the opening season of 1939, Frank Neil unveiled his new Tivoli offering, *The Big Fun Show of 1939*, advertised as including "twelve world variety acts, which constitutes the largest number of vaudeville specialties ever brought together in one bill at the Tivoli." Its headlining stars were the African American music and comedy duo (Frank) Radcliffe and (Gene) Rodgers, accompanied by blues singer Ada Brown, billed as "Harlem's Queen of Rhythm."[1]

Gene Rodgers was a jazz pianist, composer, and arranger, who played and recorded with many of the biggest names of jazz, "including King Oliver, Clarence Williams, Coleman Hawkins, and Benny Carter."[2] He teamed with Frank Radcliffe in the early thirties, touring as a popular vaudeville act in many shows, including a tour of European capitals. While in England, Rodgers made a number of records with Elisabeth Welch, who had been a star of *Blackbirds of 1928* and co-star with Paul Robeson in *Song of Freedom* (1936) and *Big Fella* (1937). Radcliffe and Rodgers's act involved clever musical items along with quickfire comedy patter as quoted in the *Australasian* on January 21, 1939.

> "Let's see now—one plus one makes 11."
> "You're *wrong*! One rabbit and one rabbit makes *two* rabbits. Boy, you don't know your *arithmetic*."
> "Boy, *you* don't know your *rabbits*!"

Born in 1890 in Kansas City into a musical family, Ada Brown had established herself as a blues singer in the classical mode as early as 1923 when she recorded with Bennie Moten's Kansas City Orchestra. She had been performing from an early age, since at least 1920 in Chicago at Mott's Pekin Theatre. She played in many black shows, including *Brown Buddies* (1930), starring Bojangles Robinson. Before coming to Australia she had been a featured act at the London Palladium in 1938.

The show opened to critical acclaim at Melbourne's Tivoli on January 16, 1939.

Argus commented: "Radcliffe and Rogers, coloured artists, are restrained in their offering. They sing well but it is in their lazy patter that they really excel. Ada Browne from Harlem gives a first-rate performance, her negro spirituals and old songs of Alabama being of a high standard." The "restrained" comment is probably in reference to the recently described frenetic activity of the Lindy Hoppers.

The media also took a strong interest in Frank Radcliffe's prowess as a champion amateur golfer, the January 20 *Argus* noting: "Frank Radcliffe, of Radcliffe and Rodgers, the new top liners at the Tivoli, is the former amateur coloured golf champion of America. He has been in Melbourne only four days and every morning has played at Albert Park. He is a splendid player as his round of 73 with a finish of four 3s yesterday morning proves."

(In the segregated world of U.S. golf in the thirties there was no place for African American golfers in the Professional Golf Association [PGA], whose bylaws stated it was "for members of the Caucasian race." Would-be black professional golfers founded their own association, The United States Colored Golfers Association, later renamed The United Golf Association. It was the amateur section of this that Frank Radcliffe had won in 1935.[3])

Radcliffe and Rodgers, with Ada Brown, were part of the special bill presented at the Tivoli to raise funds for the Black Friday

Ada Brown as she appeared in the film *Stormy Weather* (1943).

bushfires appeal. This included stars from other theatres, including the *Hollywood Hotel Revue* and its Lindy Hoppers. The event raised £205 for "The Argus" Bushfire Relief Fund, approximately $17,000 in today's terms. The Melbourne run of *The Big Fun Show of 1939* ended on February 18, after five weeks. The Sydney run opened at the Tivoli on February 23. The critical reaction was as positive as in Melbourne, as in *SMH* on February 24: "Ada Brown sang five songs and the mobile expressiveness of her face and eyes was almost as fascinating as her vocal method.... The bickerings of [Radcliffe and Rodgers] were particularly laughable." The Sydney engagement lasted five weeks, ending on March 30, 1939.

With the conclusion of the Australian engagement Ada Brown went back to her London Palladium engagements before returning to the U.S. in November 1939. She continued her successful career until her retirement in the late 1940s. Probably the peak was her exuberant singing performance with Fats Waller in the 1943 all-black movie *Stormy Weather*. In 1936, she was one of the founders of the Negro Actors Guild of America. She died in 1950.

After the Sydney engagement the partnership of Radcliffe and Rodgers split up, with Frank Radcliffe choosing to stay on in Australia. Gene Rodgers resumed his jazz career back in the U.S. He joined Coleman Hawkins's orchestra in 1939, just in time to achieve a measure of fame as the pianist on Hawkins's immortal 1940 recording of "Body and Soul," one of the most iconic jazz recordings of all time. He later worked with Fats Waller and Erskine Hawkins, and as a solo act for many years, including several film appearances. His last recording was made in 1986 with the Harlem Blues and Jazz Band. He died in 1987, aged 77.

Frank Radcliffe Solo

Frank Radcliffe's decision to stay on in Australia was probably as much to do with golf as with professional opportunities. His professional commitments dovetailed nicely with his personal interests. He opened on April 18 with George Sorlie's touring show in Bathurst (NSW), billed as "America's Kolored King of Komedy," known as "The Man with the Phenomenal Voice." We have already seen, through the friendship of U.S. Thompson and Bobby Le Brun, how golf was an integral part of the life of the Sorlie troupe. This gave Radcliffe the opportunity to play on many regional, integrated golf courses, challenging local records. By April 27 the *Wellington Times* was reporting: "Frank Radcliffe, recognised as one of the best coloured golfers of America, who will be visiting Wellington next week with George Sorlie's company, created a new course record for the Bathurst golf links this week. He beat the former record, established by Norman von Nida recently, by one stroke."

Acquiring Radcliffe, who was very popular with audiences, was a coup for Sorlie. When Radcliffe took a two-week break from the Sorlie tour to play at the Theatre Royal in Brisbane, from November 10 through the 25th, his act was described thusly by the Brisbane *Telegraph*:

> Frank Radcliffe, coloured entertainer, presents one of the highlights of the show in his 'staircase dance,' the dance made famous by Bill Robinson, the coloured film star. Radcliffe … brings down the house with his 'hot' trumpet playing in the Louis Armstrong manner.

Back with Sorlie in December, Radcliffe continued touring regional NSW, and making headlines with his golf prowess, until May 1940. He then switched to another traveling troupe, Coles New Varieties, opening with them in Bourke (NSW) on May 22. "Leading a brilliant cast of 40 performers is Frank Radcliffe, the colored comedian and dancer, a phenomenal performer whose voice ranges from soprano to basso." After NSW the Coles troupe played in Adelaide and other SA centers during June, July, and August, followed by four months around Perth and regional WA, Radcliffe's movements could as easily have been tracked by reports of the golf courses he played on as by the theatres he starred in.

Radcliffe's last Australian performance with Coles Varieties was at Katanning Town Hall in the southern corner of WA on December 31, 1940. Later, he was back in the U.S. performing with a new partner, Bud Harris. However, this was not the last Australia would see of Radcliffe, as he would be back in 1955 with fellow African Americans Bert Howell and Norma Miller and her dancers, in the Tivoli show *Colored Rhapsody*.

Frank Radcliffe's prowess on the golf course gained more attention than his entertainment activities. The *Telegraph* (Brisbane) 22 May 1939.

The Dancing Chefs

On January 12, 1939, the *Eagle* reported that a Mrs. Lillian Harris had thrown a Bon Voyage party for her dancing son, Julius "Happy" Mitchell, and his partners Smiles Woods and George McDaniel, to send them on their way to Australia. The trio, known as the Dancing Chefs, because they performed in chefs' attire, arrived in Australia as part of a company of vaudeville artists on February 11. Their show, *Young Bloods of Variety*, opened at the Melbourne Tivoli in February. The trio performed in a style known as "challenge tap dance." This was a variation on tap presentation, in which the routine would begin with unison tap, but then each member would present his or her specialty, attempting to "one up" the others. An example of their performance style can be seen in the 1940s short *Breakfast in Rhythm*.[4]

Perhaps Australia had already had a surfeit of tap dancers. The Dancing Chefs didn't make a big impact on critics, their notices being blandly polite; e.g., *Australasian*, February 25: "Dancing turns are given by the Dancing Chefs and Berrigan and Lashwood—both good teams." And the March 31 *SMH*: "The Dancing Chefs, three coloured dancers, figured in a presentation of high-speed tap dancing."

The Melbourne season ran until March 25, followed by an engagement in Sydney from March 30 to May 3, 1939. The Dancing Chefs group split up on their return to the U.S. By August 1942, Happy Mitchell had a new partner, while the Three Dancing Chefs, with several changes of personnel, like the legendary "grandfather's axe," continued performing into at least 1944, entertaining the troops.

Chuck and Chuckles

There was a gap of about three months after the Dancing Chefs before the next African American act arrived (though Frank Radcliffe was still touring regionally). The next one came on the SS *Monterey*, arriving in Melbourne on August 11, 1939, as part of a new Tivoli show that opened on August 21. The main feature of the show was white crooner Nick Lucas. Though largely forgotten today, Lucas was a major figure in his day, claiming to be the first "crooner," ahead of people like Rudy Vallee and Bing Crosby.

The African American component was the comedy dance team of Chuck and Chuckles, namely Charles Green (Chuck) and James Walker (Chuckles). Their name, like their act, was patterned after the famous team of Buck and Bubbles (Buck Washington and John "Bubbles" Sublett). Referring to Chuck and Chuckles as "one of the greatest [comedy tap] teams," the Stearnses described them thus: "Chuckles played a ragged set of vibes [vibraphone] and excelled at legomania, while Chuck performed graceful and breathtaking rhythm tap in the style of John Bubbles."[5] James Walker was tall and slim, while Charles Green was of stocky build, creating a contrast of styles. Part of Chuckles's act was to mimic the well-known "lazy" black film actor Stepin Fetchit.

The media coverage of the Melbourne season, which ran to September 30, focused on the lead artists, while noting Chuck and Chuckles as an effective support act. The one substantial reference in the August 26 *Australasian* seemed somewhat ambivalent: "There are also Chuck and Chuckles, two coloured dancers of the athletic type, who are the big noises of the show. The noise they make is so big that it sounds like a riot." During their run in Melbourne, war was declared between England and Germany, with Australia also immediately entering the war. Following the October 5 Sydney Tivoli, reviews still focused on the lead acts but were more positive about the pair, as in the October 6 *SMH*: "Chuck and Chuckles, two lively negroes presented 'Rhythm for Sale.' Both danced with superb boisterousness to which the absurdly lanky legs of one of them gave all the more value."

The Sydney engagement closed on November 15, but that was far from the end of Chuck and Chuckles in Australia. Despite the low-key media coverage, they had obviously made an impression in some quarters. The November 26 *Perth Sunday Times* 26 announced "Mr Jack Lester,

Chuck and Chuckles with vibraphone. Photographer James J. Kriegsmann, 1930s publicity still. Author's collection.

producer of the Ziegfeld Follies, which commences at His Majesty's Theatre on Friday week, signed up 'Chuck and Chuckles,' two American negroes who were stars in the original 'Follies' on Broadway. Mr Lester said that this dancing team would receive an enormous weekly figure. 'They are considered to be the fastest dancers on any stage in the world.'"

Though Chuck and Chuckles had played many leading vaudeville venues, the reference to the original Follies is probably attributable to Mr. Lester's hyperbolic style, also demonstrated in his promise the show would include jitterbugging, which "dates back to the jungle element and the savages of years ago. The gyrations and erratic movement are similar to the old war dances of the Pacific Isles."

The WA *Ziegfeld Follies* opened at His Majesty's Theatre on December 8, proclaimed as "the largest cast of imported artists ever presented on an Australian stage." The critics and audiences alike embraced the hype, including the *Daily News*:

> The ghost of Flo Ziegfeld strutted blithely across the footboards of His Majesty's Theatre last night. It could not have found more apt, more homely surroundings. There for it were over 50 glorified girls dancing and singing their way on and off stage as they were caught up in the rapid succession of events in a spectacular revue. … Applause greeted the first-class performances of negro fast-steppers Chuck and Chuckles.

The successful Perth season ended on January 4, 1940. On January 11, Chuck and Chuckles traveled to Adelaide by rail, entertaining passengers in the dining car en route. The Port Pirie *Recorder*'s reporter described Chuckles as "a real counterpart of the famous film coon comedian Stepin Fetchit…. He has the same lanky figure, high-pitched drawl, and drooping eyes." In Adelaide they joined the cast of an already running show *Frolics of 1940*, playing at the Canvas Theatre, which genuinely was a canvas structure.[6] One of the leading comedians of the show was the previously mentioned Bobby Le Brun, already well used to performing under canvas with the Sorlie tent show. No doubt he would have exchanged reminiscences of his recent fellow performer and golf partner Ulysses Thompson with Chuck and Chuckles.

Their run with *Frolics of 1940* lasted a month, closing on February 20. The show was disrupted for some days when a severe storm blew away part of the canvas, as reported by *Adelaide News* on January 25, 1940: "Bobby Le Brun and other artists, including Chuck and Chuckles, the American Negro comedy duo, worked with prop assistants to save lights, pianos, furniture, and other valuable equipment from damage by the rain. The Tivoli Theatre will be used while repairs are being carried out." In the best traditions of the business, the show continued, as described by the *Adelaide Sport* on January 26: "Chuck and Chuckles, the American negro comedy-tap team, took the audience by storm, and tapped and sang so many encores that the long-legged Chuckles finally mumbled, in his inimitable impersonation of Stepin Fetchit, 'Man, I'm tired, yeah man.'"

It may be that their success in WA and SA had added luster to the reputation of Chuck and Chuckles. At any rate, they were welcomed back to the east side of the country, opening at the Melbourne Tivoli on March 4, 1940, in a show called *Lucky Stars*. The Melbourne engagement closed on April 6, with the Sydney opening on April 12. While media coverage was low key, mostly noting them as effective support acts, the *SMH* commented: "Chuck and Chuckles, billed as 'America's greatest team of comedians and dancers,' are funny, but are more brilliant as dancers." The Sydney season ended on May 16, 1940, and the pair returned to the U.S.

They continued performing together until 1944, when Charles "Chuck" Green had a breakdown and spent 15 years in a mental institution. He recovered and resumed his career, performing into the 1970s and 1980s. He died in 1997, aged 77. In 2003, he was inducted into the Tap Dance Hall of Fame. After Chuck dropped out of the team, James "Chuckles" Walker found a new "Chuck," with whom he continued performing as Chuck and Chuckles until 1946—and probably later.[7]

The Mills Brothers

The Mills Brothers were the last African American act to arrive in Australia before Pearl Harbor, apart from the aforementioned return visit by Bob Parrish in 1940. They arrived at Fremantle from London on September 26, 1939. Coming from a long, successful engagement in England (including a Royal Command Performance), their arrival in Australia was out of necessity. "We left England for the last time just three days before war was declared on Germany [September 3] and the only boat we could get was to Australia."[8] The group comprised Donald (b. 1915), the lead; Harry (b. 1913), the baritone; Herbert (b. 1912), tenor; and John (b. 1882), bass. John was the father, John Senior, having replaced his son John Junior, who died in 1936. Apart from their vocal roles, the brothers' specialty was their ability to faithfully imitate the sounds of musical instruments, including tuba, trumpet, saxophone, clarinet and oboe, with a convincing orchestral sound.

Growing up in the town of Piqua, Ohio, the brothers were achieving local success in Cincinnati when the visiting Duke Ellington heard them in 1931 and recommended them for an OKeh recording contract in New York city. Their first recording, "Tiger Rag," was a nationwide best-seller and a number-one hit on the charts, and they soon became the leading vocal group in the U.S. The only actual musical instrument used in their recordings and performances was a guitar, originally played by John Junior, replaced after his death

Tivoli program cover of the Mills Brothers, from top: Herbert, Harry, John Sr., and Donald. Courtesy Frank Van Straten collection.

by Norman Brown, hence the billing "Four Boys and a Guitar." By the time they arrived in Australia they were already well known and popular from radio broadcasts and occasional film spots. The Australian Broadcasting Commission (ABC) obtained exclusive broadcasting rights for the duration of their Australian stay.

They made their Australian debut at the Tivoli Theatre, Melbourne, on Monday October 2, 1939. Under the headline "Clever Mills Brothers," the *Age* enthused:

> Sincerity and simplicity form the keynote of the art of the Mills brothers, the four famous harmonists and musical mimics who head the bill in *Business as Usual*, with George Wallace at the Tivoli. They infuse humor and the deeper note of serious emotion into their melodies and part songs. Donald, the tenor, is like the theme of a fugue. Harry begins with the tones of the trumpet, but emerges as the whimsically comic spirit of the troupe. Pop represents the mellow bass undertones in the score, and Herbert is the oboe, playing unobtrusively the reedy chants of Pan. True artists, they provide rare and novel entertainment.

The popular Melbourne engagement ran for six weeks, until November 11, though the media paid more attention to the Mills Brothers' national broadcast sessions than to their live performances. The Sydney Tivoli season started on 16 November, delayed by a week to extend the preceding Nick Lucas season. This also meant that the Mills Brothers replaced Chuck and Chuckles, who were bound for the Perth *Ziegfeld Follies*. The Sydney reaction to the Mills Brothers was predictably enthusiastic, e.g., this November 17 *SMH* review:

> The Mills Brothers were accorded an ovation at the end of their performance at the Tivoli last night. Shouts mingled with the clapping, and the singers had to give several encores. Within the limitations of their style, the brothers achieved some extraordinarily clever effects. They are masters of the clipped rhythm; the insistent, beating accent, the deliberate eccentricities of decoration in the swing mode.

There were some suggestions that they could have included more close harmony singing in preference to some of the "vocal gymnastics," but overall response for their unique effects was positive. In a curious coincidence, when the Mills Brothers opened at the Tivoli, a concert was being given at the Town Hall by the German Comedy Harmonists troupe of six, who had been touring Australia since June. The Comedy Harmonists had also pioneered a form of vocal imitation of musical instruments. The December 3 *Sydney Sun* reported: "Nice to see the Comedy Harmonists applauding [the Mills Brothers] at the Tivoli. No need for professional jealousy here. Both have a strong audience appeal but get their effects quite differently."[9]

The Sydney run ended on December 20, and the Mills Brothers sailed for America via the SS *Mariposa* on January 5, 1940. They spent two months in Hollywood and New York, then went on to South America, not returning until 1941. As they had already spent lengthy periods in Europe before Australia, Herbert Mills recalled, "In the meantime, the Ink Spots were coming up, and people had sort of forgotten us." By 1943 however, their careers were back on track with big hits like "Paper Doll" and "Glow Worm," as well as movie and television appearances. They would continue pleasing audiences for many more years.

Australian Postscript

There was an amusing Australian postscript to the Mills Brothers tale. Donald Mills and his English-born wife Sylvia had their young daughter Leola with them on the SS *Mariposa*. In a neighboring cabin there was the Australian Allen family, mum Violet, and her teenage daughters June and Joan. They were a dancing family who ran a dance studio and ballroom in the Sydney suburb of Stanmore.[10]

Joan's talent at classical dance had won her a scholarship to the English Royal Ballet School, but with the war on they did not consider it safe to travel to the UK, so Mum decided instead to use the money they had set aside for that on a trip to Hollywood on the *Mariposa*. On board, they became babysitters for young Leola Mills.

Further adventures awaited them on arrival in Hollywood. On a visit to the Pantages Hollywood theatre, for the premiere of the animated movie *Pinocchio*, they were approached by a distinguished-looking man who, noting from their accents that they were foreigners, asked where they came from. Learning they were from distant Australia, he enquired if they were there to see the film. On being told they didn't have any money with them, he handed them free tickets. June asked for his signature in her autograph book, which he duly signed "Walt Disney." Later on, June and Joan became friends with a girl of about

their own age, named Judy Gar-
land. As they had already done a
tour of one studio, Judy offered to
take them round hers (Metro-
Goldwyn-Mayer) but, alas, the SS
Monterey was waiting to take them

DANCING. Misses **VIOLET, JUNE, JOAN ALLEN.** Private or Class. **Correct style. Old-time or Jazz.** STUDIO. **CAMBRIDGE-ST. STANMORE.** L3131.

Advertisement for the Allen dance school, published in *Sydney Morning Herald*, 12 March 1937.

home. There was a sequel to their trip in 1963. When the Mills Brothers played the Sydney
Chevron Hilton that year, the Allen family took them to dinner.[11]

27

Epilogue:
1940–1941 and After

Despite the serendipitous gift of the Mills Brothers' visit to Australia, the start of World War II in 1939 made it difficult to import overseas stars, so the Tivoli, of necessity, began to rely more on resident local talent. The death of Frank Neil, in a traffic accident in January 1940, inevitably affected the Tivoli's vaudeville policy vis-à-vis African Americans, as his successor Wallace Parnell would not have had Neil's in-depth knowledge of the U.S. scene.

With the exception of boxers, the only African American entertainers playing in Australia during 1940 and 1941 (and none in New Zealand) were those who were already in the country, namely Bob Parrish, Frank Radcliffe, and Chuck and Chuckles. A planned 1940 visit by opera singer Marian Anderson was canceled and did not materialize until 1962.

Throughout the war years no imported African Americans played at the Tivoli (or elsewhere as far as the author can tell). Unlike the early years of the century, there were no resident African Americans like Charlie Pope and Irving Sayles to feature as Tivoli regulars.

Wartime fuel restrictions forced George Sorlie to close down his touring tent shows by November 1941, but he continued in variety performances around the country during the war, such as in J.C. Williamson's *Les Folies Bergère*, starring Roy Rene in Adelaide in late 1944. After his death in 1948, Sorlie's widow revived the tent show in 1949, with the support of Bobby and Gracie Le Brun, who continued it until the popularity of television caused its final closure in the early 1960s.

The entry of the U.S. into the war after Pearl Harbor in December 1941 changed the dynamic of African American entertainment culture in the Antipodes. Despite the lack of theatrical entertainers, the arrival of American troops brought large numbers of African Americans to Australia. Over the course of the war about a million American troops passed through Australia, of whom about 10 percent (100,000) were black. As in World War I, the American troops in Australia were strictly segregated on race lines. In Brisbane, which had the largest contingents, black soldiers were restricted to the south of the Brisbane river, white soldiers to the north. The Australian government sought to have black soldiers kept out of Australia.

On 29 March 1942, General Douglas MacArthur announced his support for the Australian Government's proposal that no more African-American soldiers be sent to Australia during World War Two. The proposal also suggested that those units that were already in Australia should be sent to New Caledonia or India. General Douglas MacArthur said: "I will do everything possible to prevent friction or resentment on the part of the Australian government and people at the presence of American colored troops.... Their policy of exclusion against everyone except the white race known locally as the White Australia plan is universally supported here."[1]

New Zealand does not appear to have had similar problems. It is unclear whether any black troops were stationed there, but there was some tension between racist white U.S. troops and Maori people.[2]

Despite the restrictions, social contact between African Americans and the local Australian population was widespread. In South Brisbane the black troops had their own Doctor Carver Service Club, named after a prominent black scientist. The Carver club was a center of attraction for jitterbug and swing dance enthusiasts. Sydney similarly had a Booker T. Washington club. The Australian jazz community was a beneficiary of the presence of both African American and white U.S. troops. Local jazz musicians at the Booker T. Washington club would enjoy having black musicians occasionally "sit in," and their dancing skills were appreciated.[3]

It wouldn't be until November 1954 that an imported African American act would play the Tivoli again. This was the returning Frank Radcliffe, teamed with violinist Bert Howell, at the Sydney Tivoli. The same pair would feature again in 1955 at the Melbourne Tivoli, in the show *Colored Rhapsody*, starring Norma Miller and her Lindy Hop dancers.

The year 1956 would see another black dance troupe, the Katherine Dunham Dancers, at the Tivoli, but more significant events also happened at the old Sydney Stadium, founded as a temporary structure so many years before by Hugh D. McIntosh. In July 1954, a jazz concert was held there featuring Ella Fitzgerald, Buddy Rich, and Artie Shaw. It was described as marking "the effective end of the de facto Australian ban on African American jazz performers," which had applied ever since the ill-starred 1928 Sonny Clay visit.[4]

That would be followed by Louis Armstrong in 1954 and in 1956 (the latter being also a return visit for Peg Leg Bates). Later, there would be a continuing stream of world-famous African American jazz musicians, bandleaders, singers, and entertainers: Nat King Cole (1955, 1956, 1957), Lionel Hampton (1957), Sammy Davis, Jr. (1959), Harry Belafonte, Sarah Vaughan, Dizzy Gillespie (1960).

An instance of reverse traffic

Tivoli Theatre program cover for 1955 show *Colored Rhapsody*. Inset: Norma Miller, the leader of Norma Miller Dancers. Author's collection.

occurred in 1950 when African American baritone Todd Duncan, the original Porgy in the 1935 premiere of George Gershwin's folk opera *Porgy and Bess*, invited Australian Aboriginal tenor Harold Blair to study in the U.S. While there, on March 18, 1951, Blair performed at a benefit concert in the New York Town Hall. In 1960, Paul Robeson would sing "Joe Hill" to the workers on the Sydney Opera House building site, and eventually the great Duke Ellington himself would arrive in 1970 (Ellington's dancer granddaughter, Mercedes Ellington, had preceded him by 10 years, playing in *West Side Story* in 1960).[5] The year 1970 also saw the arrival in the musical *Hair* of another long-term African American stayer, Marcia Hines. But that's all a topic for another book...

Appendix 1
African American Boxers Pre–World War I

In the late 1800s and into the early 20th century, Australia was a happy hunting ground for African American boxers, many from the West Indies. We have already noted the rivalry, promoted by Hugh D. McIntosh (See Chapter 14), between Sam Langford (The Boston Tar Baby) and Sam McVea, who fought each other in Australia six times between 1911 and 1913. Including their bouts with each other, Langford fought 11 bouts in Australia before leaving in 1913, while McVea fought 14 bouts before leaving in 1914. Their rivalry would continue in U.S. until 1920. Neither would lose to any Australian boxer, though Colin Bell did hold Langford to a draw in 1913. Other notable figures are covered below.

Jack Dowridge

After Black Perry (Chapter 1), the next significant figure was John Dowridge, better known later as Jack. Born in Barbados in 1848, he arrived in Australia in 1872. He acquired boxing skills during some years spent in London, known as the "Black Diamond." He settled in Brisbane, where he acquired a tobacconist store, and ran a hotel and Coffee Tavern, as well as a boxing school. His Dowridge's Athletic Hall became a focal point of Queensland boxing. He was the best-known public figure in Australian boxing in the late 19th century, primarily remembered as a trainer and promoter of other boxers.

Despite some early brushes with the law involving dubious property deals, Dowridge soon established a reputation as a popular, respected citizen. Among careers he helped progress were those of African Americans Peter Jackson and Edward "Starlight" Rollins. Dowridge's son, Jack Junior, won the Australian national featherweight title in 1903 and 1904. Jack Senior died in 1922, aged 74, at his Milton (Brisbane) home, and was buried at Lutwyche cemetery. Numerous obituaries credited him wrongly with having been the winner of his son's titles. On the other hand, when Jack Junior died in 1935, most of the obituaries wrote it up as Jack Senior's death. This was a tribute to how well remembered the "Black Diamond" still was in the minds of the sporting public.

Peter Jackson

The most notable Australian boxer of the late 19th century was Peter Jackson.[1] Born in 1861 of Jamaican parents in the Danish West Indies (later U.S. Virgin Islands), he came to Sydney as a seaman around 1880. Following a move to Brisbane, he came under the tutelage of trainer Larry Foley (a link to Black Perry) and started boxing in 1882. Known as "Peter the Great" and

"Black Prince," at 187 cm tall and 87 kg weight he was a heavyweight. "Jackson was more scientific than Jack Johnson, was faster and smoother than Joe Louis but hit just as hard, and possessed footwork similar to Muhammad Ali."[2]

He won the Australian heavyweight title by KO (after 30 rounds!) at Larry Foley's Hall in Sydney in 1886. Despite his West Indian ancestry, Peter Jackson was a much-loved Australian hero. The local media always reported his overseas exploits as Australian achievements. On one of his overseas departures, the *Referee* (December 3, 1890) wrote, under the heading "Our Loss America's Gain":

> Though all men admire him for his superb science as a boxer, it is not for that alone that we feel so proud of the negro gentleman, for a gentleman he is, and in my eyes he has a greater claim to the title than many a white skinned aristocrat with a pedigree dating back to the days of the Conquest. Peter Jackson is one of the very few men in existence whose word is as binding as his bond, and no man has ever yet questioned his truth.

After he had conquered the best in Australia, Jackson looked further afield, to the U.S. The world heavyweight championship was firmly in the hands of white champions who refused to face black contenders. Title holders John L. Sullivan, James Corbett, and James J. Jeffries happily fought black fighters on their way up but drew the color line once on the throne. For a black fighter the only game in town was the World Colored Heavyweight Championship. With that in mind, Peter Jackson traveled to San Francisco in August 1888. He successfully wrested the title from the holder, Canadian George Godfrey, with a hard-fought points win over 19 rounds and held the title unchallenged until 1896.

With another 13 straight wins in the U.S., Jackson's next target was England. A bout was arranged for the British Commonwealth title, sponsored by, among others, the Marquis of Queensberry and the Earl of Lonsdale (creator of the Lonsdale Belt),[3] against Jem Smith on November

Peter Jackson, "The Black Prince." World Colored Heavyweight Champion (1888-1896); Heavyweight Champion of Australia (1886) and of England and Australia (1892). From *Souvenir of the Tommy Burns–Jack Johnson, Boxing Contest* (1908). Courtesy Australian National Library.

11, 1899. Despite the high expectations of the British public for their champ, Jackson won by disqualification in two rounds, when it was already obvious Smith was outclassed. Jackson was lionized in England and America. Among many presents he received were a ruby and diamond pin from Lord Lonsdale, a ring from London friends, another handsome pin from Brighton friends, and a half-dozen gold-headed canes, as reported by the *San Francisco Chronicle* on January 31, 1890.

After a further succession of straight wins in England and the U.S., Jackson returned to Australia in August 1890. In May 1891, he was back in San Francisco for a bout with white future world champion James J. Corbett, for a $10,000 purse. Because the world champion, John L. Sullivan, had refused to fight either, the bout was promoted in some quarters as being for the "world's best heavyweight." After 61 rounds, both men were too exhausted to continue and the referee declared a draw. This was the high-water mark of Jackson's international career, though his KO win in England over fellow Australian Frank Slavin, in May 1892, probably pleased him more, as it gave him his second British Commonwealth heavyweight championship title.

Jackson suffered severe injuries in the Slavin fight and from then on it was all downhill. He toured the U.S. in 1893–94, giving exhibition bouts and playing Uncle Tom in a production of *Uncle Tom's Cabin*. In London during 1896–97, there were more exhibition bouts, including with future heavyweight champion Bob Fitzsimmons ("Jim Corbett said it was like a professor giving a pupil a lesson.").[4]

It was an out-of-condition Peter Jackson, after six years without a major fight and needing the money, who faced another future world champion, Jim Jeffries, in San Francisco on March 2, 1898. The result was predictable, the referee declaring a knockout in the third round, an inglorious end for Peter the Great's illustrious career.

Returning to Australia in 1900, he was soon diagnosed with TB and died at a sanatorium in Roma (Qld) on July 13, 1901, aged only 40 years. Fellow African American Jack "Black Diamond" Dowridge paid for his burial in Brisbane's Toowong Cemetery, with a white marble monument inscribed "This was a man."[5] Peter Jackson is considered to be one of the greatest fighters never to get a shot at the world heavyweight crown.

Edward "Starlight" Rollins

"In the day when I fought, boxing was not the pillow cushion stunt it is now."

Edward William Rollins was born in Georgetown (British), Guyana, probably on April 1, 1852. He claimed Zulu heritage, with some possible Spanish blood on his mother's side. His family was financially comfortable, but this was disrupted by his mother's death when he was nine. He left home soon after, for a wandering career as a sailor and ship's cook, plying between England, the U.S., and the West Indies. Shanghaied on a ship heading to Australia, he deserted in Sydney around 1880. With the help of fellow African American Peter Jackson, who was yet to start his own boxing career, Rollins found work as a diver on a pearling lugger at Thursday Island. After four years he made his way to Brisbane, toughened by hard living and well able to handle himself in a fight.

A dispute between Rollins and another black boxer, known as Charley "Moonlight" Martin, brought him to the attention of Jack Dowridge, who promoted a fight between the pair in June 1885. A drama based on Rolf Boldrewood's novel *Robbery Under Arms* (serialized in the *SMH* 1882–3) was popular at the time, so Dowridge billed Rollins as "Starlight," after the bushranger Captain Starlight in the book. Rollins won the bout, the name Starlight stuck, and at the ripe old age of 34 he embarked on a boxing career, trained and mentored by Dowridge, and later in Sydney by Larry Foley. Though six feet tall (183 cm), he was rangy and fought as a middleweight rather than heavyweight.

Despite his late start, Rollins's boxing career lasted more than 25 years. It finished at the grand old age of 60 in 1911, though he had a long gap after 1904, with other activities including seaman and theatrical entertainer. It was an up-and-down career, his Boxrec.com record showing 90 bouts, 30 wins (KO 16), 38 losses (KO 20), drawn 12. Although he challenged for the Australian Middleweight title three times, the closest he came was Victorian State champion in 1903. In 1890, he had a win against future world heavyweight champion Bob Fitzsimmons. He spent some time in New Zealand during 1895–96, with four fights, one win, two draws, and a no-contest. While there, he later told the *Sporting Globe* (Melbourne) on January 25, 1936: "I toured the music halls with my boxing, skipping, ball-punching and club-swinging act. It was a proud day for me when I was appointed boxing instructor at Wellington Government House."

In 1897, Starlight Rollins worked his way as a seaman to England, where he spent three years giving exhibition bouts, and again playing music halls with his act. His proudest moment came after a bout, when Peter Jackson introduced him to the Prince of Wales (later King Edward VII). The prince gave him a gold-headed Malacca walking cane as a memento of the visit and addressed him as Professor Starlight in recognition of his boxing expertise. For the rest of his life he reveled in the title "Professor" Starlight, and the gold-headed cane was a familiar sight on the streets of Melbourne.

After his final retirement, Edward Rollins lived a long life in Melbourne, a respected figure, and sought-after expert on the boxing scene. He died in 1939, aged 88 years. Australian actress, TV star, and popular singer Colleen Hewett is one of his descendants.

Peter Felix

The next noteworthy African American boxer of the era was three-time Australian heavyweight champion Peter Felix. He was born on July 17, 1866, in Saint Croix, U.S. Virgin Islands (like Peter Jackson, to whom he was reputed to be a cousin). At six feet three inches and 180 pounds, he was definitely a heavyweight.

Starting his professional career in Sydney in 1892, he had a meteoric rise. He suffered only one defeat up to 1900, in his first challenge for the Australian heavyweight title against veteran Mick Dooley. He won the title for the first time in July 1897 from the same Mick Dooley. He lost it to Tut Ryan in October 1898, then won it back by beating Bill Doherty in Kalgoorlie in December 1899, only to lose it again to Doherty in July 1900. He won it for the third and last time in September 1903, holding it for a year until he finally lost it for the last time to Arthur Cripps. After that, his career went into decline, with frequent losses, many by KO until his last major fight in 1911.

Along the way, in 1896, Peter Felix beat Starlight Rollins for the "Australian Coloured Heavyweight" title, one of the rare examples of Starlight in the heavy ranks. In 1907, Felix was matched with the great Jack Johnson, the fight being billed as for the "Coloured Championship of the world." The bout was scheduled to run 20 rounds but proved to be an ominous display of Johnson's power, the referee declaring him the winner by knockout before the first round had finished. One reporter described Johnson as "simply toying with his opponent."

Unlike Peter Jackson, Peter Felix was a flamboyant figure and fancy dresser, but mild mannered. "At all times he was courteous and obliging, and was a favourite with many whom he came across during his years as a private tutor, masseur, and actor." His death from heart failure on November 10, 1926, was widely reported throughout the Australian media. The comprehensive obituary in the *Referee* commented: "It can be said of Peter Felix that he lived his life without offence to a single person, and his death will be honestly regretted by many of the old-timers in all parts of the Commonwealth." He is buried in Sydney's Rookwood Cemetery. Hugh D. McIntosh led the funeral procession, accompanied by a large percentage of the boxing community.

Other Boxers of the Era

While it's hard to be sure just how many black boxers there were and how long they stayed, some of the most notable are listed below. Results follow the Boxrec.com practice of showing bout results in the numeric form "bouts, wins, losses, draws."[6]

- **James (Jimmy) Lawson**: Born U.S., arrived in Australia early 1880s; Middleweight, active 1885–1890, nineteen recorded bouts, 5, 4, 3. Queensland State champion 1887.
- **Raymond Burke**: Born Antigua, West Indies, 1876; Died May 19, 1940, in Burra, SA, where he had lived for twenty-two years. He straddles the entertainer categories, having reportedly come to Australia in 1896 to join one of McAdoo's troupes as a boy

baritone. Despite Boxrec.com showing only one bout, he had an extensive boxing career that ran from 1898 to 1918, including the SA lightweight championship.

- **Ike Stewart**: Born Kingston, Jamaica, 1863; Died Sydney 1914, buried Rookwood Cemetery; Middleweight, active 1899–1910. "Ike in six years figured in no fewer than 46 bouts, winning 28, losing 11, and 7 were drawn" (*Referee*, February 25, 1914).
- **Ted Savral**: (Known as The Cakewalker). Lightweight, active 1900–1912, twelve recorded bouts, 5, 7, 0.
- **Tom Mitchell**: Born?—Died July 1923, Brisbane. Welterweight, active 1900–1904, nine recorded bouts, 3, 6, 0.
- **Joe Thomas**: Lightweight, active 1885–1906, 6 Bouts 1, 3, 2.

Appendix 2

African American Boxers
Post–World War I

Grantlee Kieza labels 1920 to 1950 the "Golden Age" of Australian boxing, but compared to the earlier era it could not be considered so for African American boxers, with the exception of the great Archie Moore.[1] Because of his notability, Moore is dealt with first.

Archibald Lee Wright (a.k.a. Archie Moore)

Born 1916, Benoit, Mississippi, U.S.; Died 1998 (age 81). Classified Light-Heavyweight (Boxrec ID: 8995); The legendary Archie Moore ("Old Mongoose") was the longest reigning Light Heavyweight World Champion of all time (December 1952–May 1962). He had one of the longest professional careers in the history of the sport. The *Ring* magazine ranked Moore as the No. 1 contender in three different weight divisions: middleweight in 1942, light heavyweight in 1950, and heavyweight in 1955. He challenged unsuccessfully for the world heavyweight championship in bouts with Rocky Marciano (1955), and Floyd Patterson (1956). In 1962, aged 46, he lost a bout to future champion Muhammad Ali (Cassius Clay), being the only man to have boxed both Marciano and Ali.

Apart from his remarkable boxing career, Archie Moore was admired and respected for his commitment to social work on behalf of African Americans and the underprivileged.[2] Moore's Australian record was a clean sweep of seven wins in seven bouts, between March 30 and July 11, 1940, all by KO or TKO, except the last one, in which Aboriginal boxer Ron Richards held him to a 12-rounds points decision.

Australian record:	Wins: 7 (KO 6)		
Career record:	Wins: 185 (KO 131)	Losses: 23 (KO 7)	Drawn: 10

The remaining boxers identified are presented in chronological order of each boxer's first fight in Australia. The records given are based on the relevant Boxrec.com entries, which are acknowledged to be possibly incomplete. Minor differences between details and totals may be attributable to "No Contest" decisions and similar. Counts of KOs include TKOs, where relevant. One of the more successful locals to confront the imports was notable Aboriginal boxer Ron Richards. His wins record included Tommy Jones (two KOs), Deacon Kelly (two wins) and Roy de Gans (two KOs). He also "went the distance" with Archie Moore.

Tiger Jack Payne

Born Oklahoma, U.S., November 22, 1906, Died: Unknown; Classified Light Heavyweight but fought above (Boxrec Id: 35579). Tiger Payne was probably the most successful of all the

African American boxers who came post–1925. He spent two discrete periods in Australia—23 bouts between October 24, 1925, and April 14, 1928; six bouts between August 13, 1932, and March 11, 1933. At one stage he won eight successive local bouts by knockout. He was the last African American to hold the Australian Heavyweight title, following in the footsteps of Peter Jackson, Peter Felix, Sam McVea, and Sam Langford.

Australian record:	Wins: 19 (KO 16)	Losses: 9 (KO 1)	
Career record:	Wins: 55 (KO 33)	Losses: 33 (KO 2)	Drawn: 13

The Rest

Joe Hall (The Buffalo Bison)

Biographical details unknown. Classified Welterweight (Boxrec ID: 69090); 19 Australian bouts, between November 7, 1925, and July 16, 1927.

Australian record:	Wins: 8 (KO 4)	Losses: 10 (KO 1)	Drawn: 1
Career record:	Wins: 31 (KO 8)	Losses: 40 (KO 6)	Drawn: 13

Sunny Jim (Searcy) Williams

Born: 1896, Seguin, Texas, U.S.; Died: 1970 (Age: 73). Classified Light Heavyweight. (Boxrec ID: 52708); 24 Australian bouts, between January 9, 1926, and September 10, 1927. Probably the next most notable after his rival, Tiger Payne. They fought three times in Australia, one win each and a No Contest.

Australian record	Wins: 17 (KO 9)	Losses: 4	Drawn: 2
Career Record:	Wins: 68 (KO 25)	Losses: 18 (KO 2)	Drawn: 14

Dornett Joseph "Frisco" McGale

Born: 1901, Falmouth, Jamaica; Died: 1958; Classified middleweight (Boxrec ID: 68342); Seventeen Australian bouts between January 23, 1926, and August 31, 1927.

Australian record:	Wins: 9 (KO 4)	Losses: 7 (KO 1)	Drawn: 1
Career record:	Wins: 60 (KO 15)	Losses: 23 (KO 2)	Drawn: 18

Tommy Jones

Born 1916, Worcester, Massachusetts, U.S., Classified Middleweight (Boxrec ID: 75617); two periods in Australia and one in New Zealand. Sixteen Australian bouts between July 8, 1935, and September 14, 1936; 12 between November 30, 1937, and October 15, 1938, and two New Zealand, November 1938 (both wins). Challenged unsuccessfully for the Australian Middleweight title.

Australian record:	Wins: 15 (KO 8)	Losses: 10 (KO 4)	Drawn: 2
Career record:	Wins: 73 (KO 40)	Losses: 46 (KO 10)	Drawn: 10

Deacon Leo Kelly

Born: November 24, 1911, Vicksburg, Mississippi, U.S. Classified Light Heavyweight (Boxrec ID: 34975); 23 bouts (including two in NZ, both won by KO) between August 14, 1935, and March 29, 1938. The last was a return visit by a much-depleted Kelly after a year's lay-off with eye problems.

Australian record:	Wins: 16 (KO 11)	Losses: 5 (KO 1)	Drawn: 2
Career record:	Wins: 39 (KO 30)	Losses: 17 (KO 4)	Drawn: 7

David Rodger "Roy" de Gans

Born: 1914, Pocatello, Idaho, U.S. Died: 1963 (Suva, Fiji). Classified Middleweight (Boxrec ID: 72104); Roy de Gans is unusual, in that he divided his time almost evenly between Australia and New Zealand. The records suggest that he finished his career in New Zealand. Sixteen Australian bouts between June 19, 1935, and April 6, 1936. Eleven NZ bouts between May 7, 1936, and March 15, 1937.

Australian record:	Wins: 6	Losses: 6 (KO 3) Drawn: 4
New Zealand record:	Wins: 5	Losses: 6 (KO 2)
Career record:	Wins: 38 (KO 10)	Losses: 21 (KO 10) Drawn: 13

Clarence Oland Reeves (a.k.a. The Alabama Kid)

Born 1914, Concord, Georgia, U.S. Died: 1970, aged 56. Classified Middleweight (Boxrec ID: 12452); The most prolific import of the era, and one of the most successful. Career ran from 1928 to 1950. Stayed 10 years in Australia, 1938 to 1948, for a total of 73 bouts, 3 of them in New Zealand.

Australian record:	Wins: 50 (KO 26)	Losses: 16 (KO 4) Drawn: 4
New Zealand record:	Wins: 2 (KO 2)	Losses: 1
Career record:	Wins: 183 (KO 110)	Losses: 58 (KO 19) Drawn: 21

Johnny "Blackjack" Hutchinson

Born 1917, Philadelphia, U.S. Died: 1994, aged 76. Lightweight/featherweight (Boxrec ID: 13856). Fought 33 bouts in Australia/New Zealand between December 1938 and October 1940.

Australia/			
New Zealand record:	Wins: 20 (KO 8)	Losses: 10	Draws: 3
Career record:	Wins: 65 (KO 29)	Losses: 23 (KO 5)	Draws: 8

Jack Benjamin "Jackie" Wilson

Born 1909, Westminster, South Carolina, U.S. Died: 1966; Classified Featherweight (Boxrec ID: 11782); One of the few imports with world-ranking status, Wilson would go on later (1941) to hold the National Boxing Association (NBA) World Featherweight title, having failed in a challenge just before coming to Australia. He clearly outclassed his Australian opposition, with 13 straight victories in Australian bouts between February 4 1939, and August 3, 1939.

Australian record:	Wins: 13 (KO 1)	
Career record:	Wins: 101 (KO 20)	Losses: 45 (KO 6) Draws: 7

And Just for the Record

Fewer than 10 bouts or fewer than five wins in Australia/New Zealand have been considered too marginal to cover in detail, so the following are included just for the completists.

Buddy Saunders (a.k.a. Young Kid Norfolk): Welterweight. (Boxrec ID: 58179); Five Australian fights (three wins, two draws), between May 1, 1926, and November 13, 1926.

Young Sam Langford; Welterweight (Boxrec ID: 339881), two Australian fights, both losses, between December 1930 and January 1931.

Allen Matthews; Welterweight (Boxrec ID: 21662), four Australian fights, 3 wins, 1 loss between August and December 1938.

Walter Lee: Welterweight (Boxrec ID: 254264); Seven Australian bouts (6 losses, 1 win), between August and December 1938.

Ossie Stewart: Light-Heavyweight (Boxrec ID: 36933); seven Australian bouts (4 wins, -3 KO, 3 losses), between December 1938 and August 1939.

Appendix 3
The Later Fisk Jubilee Singers, 1902–1936

After the death of Orpheus McAdoo, his Jubilee troupe continued performing, initially still under his name as McAdoo's Jubilee Singers. When Orpheus's brother Eugene (Julius) took over as manager, he kept the name McAdoo's Jubilee Singers for a while. However, by April 1902, he had adopted the title McAdoo's Fisk Jubilee Singers. Eugene departed to England in 1904 to form an English offshoot of the Fisk Singers, with himself, Euna Mocara, and former member Laura Carr as the Fisk Jubilee Trio. By then the unqualified name Fisk Jubilee Singers had become an institutionalized Australasian brand name with little concern for its historical accuracy and only tenuous links with the U.S., though replacements might still occasionally be recruited from the that country.

When Frederick Loudin had originally brought his troupe to Australia in 1886 the singers were no longer formally affiliated with Fisk University, but Loudin did have the university's blessing on his venture. The claim of later groups to continue using the name was based on a tenuous idea of historical continuity. The strongest link in that chain was Belle Gibbons, whose continuing presence would sustain it over many years into the 1930s.

Following Eugene McAdoo's departure a core group was formed under the management of tenor R.H. Collins, and including Belle Gibbons and Professor C.A. White. Between 1904 and 1910, with these three as a nucleus, Fisk Jubilee troupes would tour extensively around Australia and New Zealand, with frequently changing personnel. With such volatile changes it would be pointless to attempt to trace variations in detail (but see endnote for names[1]). It is also difficult to establish with certainty which of the newcomers were African Americans or had possible African American ancestry. Like grandfather's axe, they would undergo many changes, while retaining an identity widely welcomed by audiences as familiar friends in regional towns all round Australia and New Zealand.

In 1910, the Singers spent a lengthy period in New Zealand, opening in Wellington on February 19 and finishing in mid–October.

Of these, only Gibbons, Collins, and White can be positively identified as U.S. born. The *Age* (March 19, 1917) commented: "Miss Bertha Miller and Miss Alice Baptiste, who are the most typical looking 'negresses' in the company' … by way of contrariness, were born in Melbourne." Sidney Haines is probably the only other who can be identified as "colored." Florence Dixie was a pseudonym for white Australian Bessie Campbell, whose association with Hosea Easton in the 1880s was mentioned in Chapter 2. After a tour of Tasmania in late 1910 this group broke up, various members appearing in other capacities elsewhere. By April 1914 they had reformed as the Fisk Jubilee Singers, touring regional centers large and small, under the leadership of Professor White, along with Belle Gibbons, R.H. Collins, Bertha Miller, Alice Baptiste, and Syd-

The Fisk Jubilee Singers on New Zealand tour, ca. March 1910. Back row from left: Beatrice Caire, Sydney Haines, Flo Dixie (Bessie Campbell); center from left: Bertha Haynes Miller, Professor C.A. White, Belle Gibbons, R.H. Collins, Alice Baptiste; front from left; E.R. Martin, Arthur Haynes. Courtesy of the Irene Cox Collection, Alexander Turnbull Library, Wellington, New Zealand (Ref: PA1-q-242-477).

ney Haynes. The missing previous members had been replaced by several local additions, including Leila Wyburd (soprano) and a "male soprano," Max Barber (ethnicity unknown). A slight change of their traditional emphasis was the presentation of ragtime items in which Bertha Miller was promoted as a specialist. They continued regional touring until early 1917.

The Marshall Palmer Era

A new phase began in March 1917 when Marshall Palmer, a white Australian actor/vocalist and "descriptive singer" became the new manager of the troupe. The *Queensland Times*, on February 8, 1917, recorded: "Mr Marshall Palmer, who has been introducing a number of popular singing competitions at the Olympia Theatre, has taken over the management of the Fisk Jubilee Singers, and will leave for Sydney on Tuesday, when he will reorganise the company to tour New Zealand and Tasmania." While there is little doubt that Palmer's arrival revitalized the success of the reorganized Fisk group, his approach took them away from the old Jubilee tradition towards a more commercial one, linked to the minstrel show. Palmer's approach was like that of a major corporation acquiring a local iconic brand to exploit its customer base. The Adelaide *Register* (September 10, 1923) described the troupe under his regime: "The old form of the nigger minstrel circle was adhered to even to the business of the interlocutor and the cornermen, though the bones and the extremely grotesque costumes were mercifully dispensed with."

The first results of Palmer's new initiatives came with a season opening at the Auditorium in Melbourne on March 17, 1917. The enlarged group, racially integrated and heavy in local Australian talent, included: Belle Gibbons (lady baritone); Davina Morrison (soprano); Bertha Miller (soprano); Alice Baptiste (mezzo-soprano); Harold Wilson (basso); Marshall Palmer (tenor); Sydney Haynes (tenor); Charles Callow (tenor) and Professor C.A. White (accompanist). The response was good, with Palmer himself being popular, the March 19 *Argus* noting: "Of the soloists, Mr Marshall Palmer was particularly successful."

After the close of the Melbourne season in mid–April, the Singers spent the rest of 1917 touring Melbourne suburbs and regional Vic, Adelaide, and regional SA, Perth and regional WA before departing for New Zealand via Adelaide, in early 1918. En route, they picked up the colored contralto Claire (also Clare and Clara) Solly, who had been making a reputation for herself at Adelaide's Majestic Theatre. Solly, born in Milparinka (NSW), has been described in several sources as Australian Aboriginal but was actually of part–African descent, through her Bermudan grandfather Frederick Christopher Bamess, stone mason and Milparinka resident, and her English grandmother. She would go on to have an illustrious career from about 1918 right into the 1950s, including theater and radio in Australia, Europe, and England.

New Zealand 1918–1919

The Palmer Fisk Singers opened their New Zealand tour on March 9, 1918, with a week in Dunedin. It would be over a year before they would return to Australia. The memory of the earlier Fisk troupes assured them of a warm welcome, though there was a mixed reaction from some, including the *Wellington Dominion* on April 22, 1918:

> The Fisk Jubilee Singers, which opened a season at the Concert Chamber on Saturday evening, before a packed audience ... follow on the lines of their predecessors up to a point. They sing many of the old-time jubilees with much of the old-time charm, but they scarcely reach the same average vocal standard, and as half of the company are not coloured people at all, there is hardly the same flair attaching to their efforts as formerly.

In addition to playing the major centers, the Fisk troupe exhaustively toured regional towns and villages on a grueling round of one- and two-night stands. By the end they had visited 170 towns and given 290 concerts (*Otago Witness*, April 9, 1919). Along the way, around June 1918, they were joined by African American tenor Huntley Spencer, who had come to New Zealand in 1912 with Billy Kersands (see Chapter 15) and stayed on in Australia afterwards. A discordant note was struck when the troupe played the town of Feilding, an agricultural outpost in the North Island. Belle Gibbons, having pre-booked accommodation for the group, was greeted on arrival by the landlady with "You had better try to find accommodation elsewhere; I do not accommodate coloured people." Gibbons' indignant letter to the editor of the May 31 Feilding *Star* was widely reprinted, with sympathy, throughout the New Zealand media.

As the result of a ban on public performances due to the outbreak of the influenza pandemic that killed more people than World War I, the troupe was quarantined in Christchurch throughout November and December 1918. Their actions during this difficult time earned them some kudos for their active participation in remedial activities, including placing Marshall Palmer's motor car at the disposal of the Central Depot every day, reported in the *Star* on December 2, 1918.

By early January 1919, the quarantine rules had been relaxed and the Singers resumed touring regionally, the April 2 *Poverty Bay Herald* noting: "After a very successful tour of the Coast district the Fisk Jubilee Singers returned to Gisborne yesterday.... The company remain in the district until after the hui [a Maori festival], which they desire to attend." Another report read: "They were treated like royalty by the Maoris in Gisborne, and entertained and made the recipients of valuable gifts by Sir James & Lady Carrol, the Maori member and his wife."[2] They sailed for Sydney on the SS *Manuka* on April 10, 1919.

Australia 1919–1925

Back in Australia, the singers opened at Sydney's Apollo Theatre, from May 31, 1919, until June 28. There followed a tour of regional NSW. In January 1920, a Tasmanian tour, delayed by a seamen's strike, broke a long theatrical drought for the isolated island state. The Tasmanian tour ended on May 17 and was followed by tours of regional Vic (May–July), Adelaide and SA (August–November), and finishing the year in Perth and regional WA. Again there were the usual changes of personnel, comings and goings with replacements typically filled from local talent. They were back east in Melbourne for an opening at the Athenaeum Hall on Christmas Day, minus Bertha Miller, who had joined the cast of the musical-comedy *Chu-Chin-Chow* at the Melbourne Tivoli, her absence being compensated by the return of Belle Gibbons. Despite reports of their imminent return to America at the end of the short Melbourne season, the Fisk Singers continued touring regional Vic up to late August 1921.

They reappeared in Sydney at the Haymarket Theatre in September and followed this with touring regional NSW, including Newcastle in February 1922. The lineup was probably the thinnest in terms of African American ancestry yet.[3] Nevertheless, audiences still accepted them as true successors to the original Fisks! The genuine African American component was to suffer a disastrous blow during the Newcastle season, when Professor C.A. White was taken ill and died in a Sydney hospital on February 6, 1922, aged 61. After a brief break to mourn their lost musical director, the Singers resumed touring in regional NSW. The tour wound down in late November 1922, and they didn't surface again until April 1923 in Geelong (Vic), in association with a modern film production of *Uncle Tom's Cabin*, with which they would tour Vic.

The revised company had a revitalized African American flavor, with the return of Belle Gibbons and Huntley Spencer, plus the recruitment of the evergreen Charles Pope, singing the new popular hit song "Dinah," and a new colored mezzo soprano, Elsa Carr, allegedly from the Carolinas but actually born in Bendigo, Australia, from Afro-Caribbean parents.[4] The April 13 *Ballarat Star* proclaimed them "an outstanding success," and Charlie Pope "literally rocked the house at every appearance."

Sometime in early November the Fisk troupe split into two units. There is no evidence this was a result of dissension in the camp. It may be that its purpose was to have two lots independently supporting the showing of the *Uncle Tom's Cabin* in both WA and SA. One group under Marshall Palmer, with himself, Charles Pope, Belle Pollard (soprano), Walter Whyte (lyric tenor and musical director), and Spencer Reynolds (tenor) stayed on playing in regional WA until late November. Pollard and Whyte were veteran white Australian vaudevillians, regulars with the Tivoli and J.C. Williamson Opera Company. Reynolds was a local Australian performer.

The second group comprised Belle Gibbons and Huntley Spencer (both African American), Cecile Stephano (NZ soprano) who had been part of an earlier Fisk tour in New Zealand, Marshall Lawrence, Vi James, and Dan Cash, a South Australian local. They continued playing around SA until mid–February 1924, after which silence descended on the Fisk front until May 1924.

A reunited group surfaced in Brisbane on May 5, 1924, and went on to an extensive tour of Queensland, as far north as Cairns. It included Charles Pope, Marshall Palmer, Vi James, Belle Pollard, Walter Whyte, Bertha Miller, Cecile Stephano, George Bentley, and Marshall Lawrence. While they attracted enthusiastic audiences and good reviews, there were signs that those with genuine memories of the old Fisks were not convinced of their legitimacy. A writer to the *Courier* (May 22, 1924) complained:

After hearing stories of the Fisk Jubilee Singers and their earlier visits to Queensland I was surprised when I heard the so called Fisk Singers recently at the Tivoli. No doubt the original singers have closed their careers by now but according to announcements we expected to see a group of their descendants, instead of three dark people and some half dozen white actresses.... Rather than allow these songs which are sacred to white people as well as dark people, to depreciate into a farce it would be better to drop them altogether and for the mixed company to change its name.

The complaint was legitimate. The uniquely African American intonations and delivery of the original Fisks, which had baffled and even amused audiences, could not be truly reproduced by classically trained white singers, however technically proficient. The absent Belle Gibbons had been the only legitimate claimant. Even the ragtime style of Bertha Miller was from a different African American tradition. The Queensland tour ended back in Brisbane on January 1, 1925, when Marshall Palmer embarked on a solo career for a time in drama and pantomime, portraying Ned Kelly.

New Zealand 1924–1927

On July 3, 1924, while the Palmer troupe was working its way through Queensland, a second Fisk troupe arrived to tour New Zealand, under the management of a notable NZ Maori entrepreneur, Gaetano J. Fama, popularly known as Tano Fama. While there were many personnel changes during the course of their NZ tour, the original group included Belle Gibbons, Miss Ron Thompson (soprano), Alice Baptiste (mezzo-soprano), Marjorie Alwyne, (contralto), Davina Morrison (coloratura soprano), Madeline Joyce (pianist), Herbert Maxwell (basso), Harry Franklin (baritone), Harry Penn (tenor), and Huntley Spencer (musical director). Of these, Belle Gibbons, Alice Baptiste, and Huntley Spencer had lengthy Fisk associations going back to the early 20th century. Gibbons, Spencer, Baptiste, and Thompson were the "colored" component, albeit only Gibbons and Spencer were U.S.-born. The tour lasted until July 10, 1925, with some breaks along the way, most notably from mid–February until mid–April 1925. It's not too great a stretch to speculate that this break, and the change of personnel, were linked to Tano Fama's divorce action against his wife on grounds of adultery with a member of the troupe, reported in NZ *Truth* on May 16, 1925.

After this break, the make-up changed noticeably. From late April onward the personnel was Belle Gibbons, Hartley Montgomery (tenor), Alice Baptiste (mezzo-soprano), Barbara Maxwell ("Scottish Nightingale"), Ron Thompson (soprano), Herbert Maxwell (basso), James Haydock (pianist and musical director), and the Maxwell Trio. For a while, Huntley Spencer, Marjorie Alwyne, Davina Morrison, and Harry Penn were playing as the Kentucky Four, which continued with changing personnel until mid–1927, by which time Spencer was the only ex–Fisk member.

Australia 1927–1930

The next Fisk appearance in Australia didn't occur until September 1927, when Marshall Palmer again lead a troupe that included Sid Haynes, Leila Wyburd, Bertha Miller, Vi James, and accompanist Doreen Hurst, supporting the movie *Uncle Tom's Cabin*. In what can be considered the final degradation of a once time-honored brand, they were billed along with what was called Marshall Palmer's *Ye Ole Nigger Minstrels* show. They toured regional NSW until December 1927, when Marshall Palmer went back to his dramatic promotions, including Christmas pantomime and running children's singing competitions.

In May 1928, Palmer revived the minstrel show, including the Fisk team, in Brisbane. After Brisbane they toured regional Queensland north up to Cairns and back, billed as "THE FISK JUBILEE SINGERS & NIGGER MINSTRELS." A date at Dalby, near Brisbane, on December

21, appears to have been their final engagement. This marks the last live public appearance of the Fisk Singers in Australia, though some individual members would crop up in vaudeville shows from time to time afterwards. They were in the public eye, or at least ear, throughout the thirties, through a long series of broadcasts about the history of the early Fisk Jubilee Singers. The last public performance of any kind in Australia came in December 1930, when radio station 2BL (Sydney) made several broadcasts of "the Fisk Singers," featuring a quartet of Belle Gibbons, Leila Wyburd, Syd Haynes, and Bill Kenney.

New Zealand 1936

A last dying gasp of the Fisk Jubilee Singers in Australasia came in July 1936, when Huntley Spencer arrived in Christchurch to assemble a Fisk Singers team for a New Zealand tour. The group included five men and five women who, apart from Spencer himself, appeared to be all locally recruited, with no familiar Fisk past performers. They opened in Christchurch on July 13. Following a moderately successful week, they played a poorly attended performance in nearby Leeston and then appear to have folded, thereby finishing the Fisk saga in New Zealand and Australia.

Appendix 4
Miscellanea

Given the frequently confusing usage of the terms *black* and *blackface* in the media of the era, it often required careful examination to determine which acts were genuine African Americans as opposed to white imitators. Some marginal cases, which didn't warrant inclusion in the main part of the book are dealt with here.

Dan Barry Dramatic Company

Dan Barry (1851–1908) was an Irish-born dramatic producer and entrepreneur whose company toured widely in regional Australia, from his Melbourne base, the Alexandra Theatre. He is probably best remembered today as a producer of the world's first feature film, *The Story of the Kelly Gang*. Between 1898 and 1902 his melodramatic productions occasionally included *Uncle Tom's Cabin*. This was advertised as including "real colored jubilee singers" as well as buck dancers, and two of the cast, Jake Nobbo and Tom Nubba, were described as having once been "real slaves." No other trace of these two can be found. Except for a brief period in 1898 when the role of Uncle Tom was played by long-term resident John Matlock, there is no evidence that any genuine African Americans were involved. Examination of the rest of the full cast list from the *Lorgnette* (June 2, 1898) suggests they were all white. A reference to Moody and Sankey hymns, usually associated with white evangelism, also casts doubt on the genuineness of the alleged Jubilee singers.

Edmunds and Lavelle

Around the time the Ferris Jazzland Revue was playing out its ultimately unhappy New Zealand tour, the Sydney Tivoli was presenting an act, Edmunds and Lavelle (Glen Edmunds and Rena La Velle), described as "blackface" or "colored," under the title "Two Shades in One." The act was apparently two males but at the end the lighter skinned "male" was revealed to be a female, while according to the Sydney *Sun* (October 26, 1926): "Edmunds and Lavelle, the negro and white comedians, also hoaxed the audience, and were discovered to be a white man and his wife." The November 18 *Table Talk* added: "GLENN EDMUNDS, of Edmunds and Lavelle, now appearing at the Tivoli Theatre, first got the idea of working in blackface when he was in the American Navy. He entertained his sailor pals with various stories of the Southern States, and so successful was he that he was known as the Entertainer in Chief of the American Navy."

Edmunds and Lavelle played seasons in Sydney, Melbourne, Brisbane, and possibly a short season in Wellington (NZ) before arriving back in the U.S. in early February 1927. No conclusive evidence has been found to indicate whether this was a white "blackface" rather than an African American act. The above quotations would normally seem to be sufficient evidence that they were white, except there was a passing reference in the Baltimore *Afro-American*, on January 17, 1927, to their presence in Australia. This is often an indication that an act is recognized as black. No other references can be found in the usual specialist black sources, everything found being in general sources like *Variety* and *Billboard*. Rena La Velle was listed by the New York *Dramatic Mirror* (October 26 1907) as playing in Sam Devere's white minstrel company in 1907. Glen Edmunds and Rena la Velle advertised their availability for work in *Billboard* (October 16, 1914), an unlikely place at that time for black acts. Given these facts, it would seem on balance probable they were not African American.

Chapter Notes

Chapter 1

1. Cassandra Pybus, *Black Founders: The Unknown Story of Australia's First Black Settlers.*
2. *Ibid.*, p. 4.
3. *Ibid.*, p. 24.
4. *Ibid.*, p. 144.
5. The most useful source for information on Perry's activities in Australia can be found in the pages of *Bell's Life in Sydney* and *Sporting Reviewer*, available via the Australian National Library's *Trove* facilities. Particularly useful was the issue of October 20, 1849, which contains a "biographical sketch" of Perry's life, and the account of the Perry-Hough fight in the issue of October 13. Other material is available in Kevin Smith, *Black Genesis: The History of the Black Prizefighter, 1760–1870,* and Richard Fotheringham, *Sport in Australian Drama*, and Peter Fryer, *Staying Power: The History of Black People in Britain.*
6. See http://www.phrases.org.uk/meanings/as-happy-as-larry.html (Viewed January 11, 2018).
7. Coulthurst's movements were traced through the *Argus*, April 24, 1867, and the *Ballarat Star*, May 18, 27, 30, and June 14, 1867.
8. Ira Frederick Aldridge (1807–1867) was born in New York, but spent most of his career in England and Europe. He was the first African-American actor to make his name on the professional stage in Europe. See: https://en.wikipedia.org/w/index.php?title=Ira_Aldridge&oldid=878427672 (Viewed January 16, 2019), and Peterson, *Profiles of African American Stage Performers and Theatre People, 1816–1960*, pp. 4–5.
9. The author is indebted to Jeffrey Green, *Black Americans in Victorian Britain* (141) for drawing attention to Ira Aldridge Junior's presence in Australia. The sad, detailed story of Aldridge's life can be followed in two articles by Bernth Lindfors from the online journal Text Matters: A Journal of Literature, Theory and Culture (ISSN 2083–2931). See: https://content.sciendo.com/view/journals/texmat/2/2/article-p194.xml and https://content.sciendo.com/view/journals/texmat/3/3/article-p234.xml (Viewed January 17, 2019).
10. Robert C. Toll, Blacking Up: The Minstrel Show in Nineteenth-Century America.
11. *Ibid.*, pp. 3–4.
12. *Ibid.*, p. 31.
13. Useful general discussions of minstrelsy in Australia can be found in John Whiteoak and Aline Scott Maxwell (editors), *Currency Companion to Music and Dance in Australia*, 415; and Philip Parsons (editor), *Concise Companion to Theatre in Australia*, 181. The Pacific region, including Australia and New Zealand, are comprehensively surveyed in Matthew W. Wittmann, *Empire of Culture: U.S. Entertainers and the Making of the Pacific Circuit, 1850–1890* (a dissertation submitted in partial fulfillment of the requirements for the degree of Doctor of Philosophy (American Culture) in the University of Michigan, 2010).
14. Tom Fletcher, *100 Years of the Negro in Show Business*, p. 37.
15. David Krasner, *Resistance, Parody and Double Consciousness in African-American Theatre, 1895–1910*, p. 25.
16. Henry T. Sampson, *The Ghost Walks*, p. 4.
17. See Charles Dickens, *American Notes*, Vol. 1, p. 218.
18. Buck and Wing dancing: "A style of step dance featuring energetic leg and arm movements and typically performed in wooden-soled shoes, popular in the 19th-century United States and considered an early form of tap dance." Courtesy www.yourdictionary.com/buck-and-wing (Viewed January 11, 2019).
19. The emergence of black minstrelsy in the United States is well covered in Toll, Chapter 7: "Black Men Take the Stage."

Chapter 2

1. Disentangling the complex sequence of Hicks's troupes was aided (and sometimes complicated) by the information supplied in Henry T. Sampson, *The Ghost Walks*; Richard Waterhouse, *From Minstrel Show to Vaudeville*; and Robert C. Toll, *Blacking Up: The Minstrel Show in Nineteenth-Century America.*
2. The humorous "stump speech" full of malapropisms and pseudo-scientific jargon was a staple of minstrelsy, described, with an example, in Toll, pp. 55–56.
3. *Mornington Journal*, May 19, 1880.

4. Waterhouse, 76; Extensive details on Hicks and the Georgias' activities are provided in Chapter 5.

5. Henry T. Sampson, *The Ghost Walks*, p. 30.

6. Establishing the practice of using a capital "N" for Negro was a battle yet to be won by Lester Walton in the United States.

7. Waterhouse, p. 148.

8. John W. Frick, Uncle Tom's Cabin *on the American Stage and Screen*, 121; Easton's Uncle Tom role was advertised in the *Argus* as opening on June 8, 1878. Frick makes it clear that Gustave Frohman, who cast Sam Lucas in the role, did not take over the Stoddard Comedy Company until sometime after July 1878; he cast Lucas later in the year. So Easton's claim to be the first black man to play Uncle Tom, as in the *Argus* advertisement, is vindicated, while leaving Lucas as the first on United States soil.

9. http://contentdm6.hamilton.edu/cdm/ compoundobject/collection/spe-ban/id/3406/rec/6 (S. S. Stewart Catalogue and Price List) (Viewed January 11, 2019) Easton's testimonial can be seen at Image 35, on page 29 of the catalogue.

10. "Before 1900, when minstrelsy and circus carnivals merged, and more specifically, when the popularity of the Cakewalk persuaded circuses to hire Negro performers, dancers and acrobats were thrown together and began to learn from each other…. The earliest and best-known Negro acrobats were tumblers, who worked on the ground performing somersaults, cartwheels, flips, and spins." Marshall Stearns, and Jean Stearns, *Jazz Dance: The Story of American Vernacular Dance*, p. 262.

Chapter 3

1. Quotation from the website of Fisk University https://www.fisk.edu/about/history (viewed January 11, 2019).

2. The origin of this story is unclear. It is not mentioned in Andrew Ward, *Dark Midnight When I Rise*, which documents the Fisks' performances for Queen Victoria. The story has many internet hits and is quoted, inter alia, in Angela Grant, *Rita's Saga: A Young Woman's Journey Through the Seedy Side of Nashville*.

3. Ward, *Dark Midnight When I Rise*, p. 378.

4. *Ibid.*, p. 269.

5. *Ibid.*, pp. 274–275.

6. Loudin's earlier career with the Fisk Singers is well covered in Ward.

7. Leota Henson's impressions of Australia and New Zealand are quoted by permission of Nina Gamble Kennedy, from letters Leota Henson wrote to Kennedy's grandmother, Nina Clinton Gamble. The strange cherry tree mentioned was the native Cherry Ballart (*Exocarpos cupressiformis*).

8. Copy held at Alexander Turnbull Library (New Zealand).

9. *Age* 2 May 1889; article "THE FISK JUBILEE SINGERS: A PROFITABLE TOUR."

10. *SMH*, "An Interesting Slave Story," June 30,

1886. The cited reference is to Marsh, *The Story of the Jubilee Singers*, p. 100.

11. *West Australian*, July 13, 1886: "MELBOURNE TEA-TABLE TALK," *Melbourne*, June 28, 1886.

12. Lynn Abbott and Doug Seroff, *Out of Sight: The Rise of African-American Popular Music, 1889–1895*, includes an excellent survey of this topic, under "Australasian Music Appreciation," 13–19, and "The Slippery Slope of Variety and Comedy," pp. 21–24. The author is indebted to them for several quoted comments.

13. Modern musicologist Marcello Piras confirmed this interpretation for the author, with the qualifying comment: "Early liturgical chant was monodic, not part singing; instead, the Chapel singers had 16th-century music in their book, e.g. Palestrina. Hence this—not Gregorian plainchant—would be the correct term of comparison, and is actually what the journalist had in mind. For him—most likely coming from the Protestant world—all Catholic liturgical music was conflated in a single category."

14. The Choctaw freedmen were formerly enslaved African Americans who became part of the Choctaw Nation with emancipation after the American Civil War, a requirement of the 1866 treaty the U.S. made with the Choctaw. See Wikipedia; http://en.wikipedia.org/wiki/Steal_Away (Viewed January 11, 2019).

15. Private email to the author from Nina Gamble Kennedy.

Chapter 4

1. The following list is not guaranteed to be exhaustive, and many centers were visited more than once: New South Wales (includes Sydney): Armadale, Ashfield, Bathurst, Broken Hill, Burwood, Camden, Goulburn, Kiama, Lithgow, Maitland, Manly, Moss Vale, Murrurundi, Newcastle, Newtown, Orange, Paddington, Parramatta, Penrith, Petersham, Randwick, Singleton, St Leonards, Tamworth, Wagga Wagga, Waverley, West Maitland, Yass.

New Zealand: Amberley, Ashburton, Auckland, Balclutha, Blenheim, Brunnerton, Cambridge, Christchurch, Dunedin, Feilding, Foxton, Gisborne, Gore, Greymouth, Greytown, Hamilton, Hastings, Hawera, Hokitika, Invercargill, Lawrence, Littleton, Masterton, Milton, Mosgiel, Napier, Nelson, New Plymouth, Oamaru, Ohnehunga, Palmerston, Patea, Port Chalmers, Poverty Bay, Rangiora, Te Aroha, Thames, Timaru, Waipawa, Waipukurau, Wanganui, Wellington, West Oxford, Woodville.

Queensland (includes Brisbane): Cairns, Charters Towers, Ipswich, Rockhampton, Sandgate, Toowoomba, Townsville, Warwick South Australia (includes Adelaide): Burra, Glenelg, Gawler, Kapunda, Kadina, Mount Barker, Mount Gambier, Narracoorte, Petersburg, Port Adelaide, Strathalbyn Tasmania (includes Hobart, Launceston): Beaconsfield, Campbelltown, Deloraine, Glenorchy, Latrobe, Longford, New Norfolk, Oatlands, Perth, Westbury Victoria (includes Melbourne): Bairnsdale, Benalla,

Bendigo (Sandhurst), Brunswick, Chiltern, Coburg, Colac, Collingwood, Echuca, Eaglehawk, Euroa, Footscray, Gippsland, Hawksburn, Hawthorn, Horsham, Portland, Prahran, Sale, Sandhurst (aka Bendigo), Shepparton, Traralgon, Warragul, Williamstown.

2. The Maloga Mission was replaced later by the nearby Cummeragunja Reserve in 1888, though Matthews continued his activities separately for a number of years. Maloga Mission and Cummeragunja played a major role, through education and lobbying, in the history of the Yorta Yorta Aboriginal nation, recognized in *First Australians*, Perkins, Rachel, and Langton, Marcia, editors. (Based on an award-winning SBS television series).

3. Nancy Cato, *Mister Maloga*, pp. 81–83.

4. See *Riverina Herald*, October 5, 1938, and also: https://en.wikipedia.org/wiki/Jimmy_Little and http://www.smh.com.au/it-pro/the-soul-source-of-inspiration-20120804-23m3i.html (Viewed January 11, 2019).

5. For details, see: http://www.abc.net.au/news/2018-07-21/indigenous-australian-music-influenced-by-black-american-music/10016962 (Viewed January 11, 2019).

6. *SMH*, October 19, 1886. While there are many versions of the John Brown song, the version performed by the Fisk Singers, as published in their book, seems to adhere closely to that by William Weston Patton, who wrote his influential version in October 1861, published in the *Chicago Tribune* on December 16 of that year.

7. Andrew Ward, *Dark Midnight When I Rise*, 154. "Porter" refers to Maggie L. Porter, one of the original Fisk Singers.

8. "The Ladies Column," *Euroa Advertiser*, November 11, 1887.

9. The account given here is summarized from a report in the *Argus*, December 18, 1888.

10. This is a tongue-in-cheek reference to the transportation of convicts to Australia.

11. The account of the legal battle between Loudin and Price, and its consequences, has been compiled from several reports, including *South Australian Register*, April 29, 1889; *Age,* May 2, 1889; *Launceston Examiner*, May 4, 1889; "Peripatetic Musings," *Williamstown Chronicle*, May 4, 1889; *Maitland Mercury*, May 7, 1889; and *The Star* (Canterbury, New Zealand), May 7, 1889.

12. http://en.wikipedia.org/wiki/Johnstown_Flood (Viewed January 11, 2019).

13. John P. Green, *Fact Stranger Than Fiction: Seventy-Five Years of a Busy Life with Reminiscences of Many Great and Good Men and Women*, p. 234.

14. Details of Loudin's later career can be found in Ward, pp. 391–393.

15. Details of R. B. Williams's life can be found at: http://www.wcl.govt.nz/heritage/robertbradfordwilliams.html; see also: https://bluesmokebook.wordpress.com/2015/12/12/he-came-he-sang-he-stayed/ (Chris Bourke blog) (Viewed January 11, 2019).

Chapter 5

1. The troupe that he arrived with was known as the Hicks-Sawyer Minstrels. The Sawyer part referred to a U.S. partnership, since dissolved. Although that name continued to be used, for simplicity's sake I will just refer to them as Hicks' Minstrels.

2. The first nationally known black professional baseball team had just been founded in 1885. http://en.wikipedia.org/wiki/Negro_league_baseball#Professional_baseball (Viewed January 11, 2019).

3. The full lineup, apart from Hicks himself (manager, interlocutor), was: Charles Bruce (band leader), the Connor Brothers, George, John and Eddie (acrobats), Horace Copeland (end man, comedian, dancer), Little Dixie (mascot, musician, drummer), W. H. Downs (tenor), Frank Duprez/Duprey (trombonist), Jack Evans (singer, dancer), A. Flores (musician), W. J. Harris (treasurer), Will Johnson (singer, bass), Dick Johnson (musician, drummer), Wallace King (singer, tenor), William Nunn (musician), Charles Pope (end man, comedian), Irving Sayles (end man, comedian), William "Billy" Speed (musician, drum major, stage manager), John H. Taylor (musician), Harry Thomas (singer, interlocutor), Charles "Chas" Washington (singer, musician, drummer).

4. Richard Waterhouse, *From Minstrel Show to Vaudeville*, p. 91.

5. *Evening News*, June 2, 1890; September 10, 1888.

6. For some obscure reason, from the Goulburn engagement on, they had taken to calling themselves the Gewaugady Minstrels, a title invariably misspelled by the media.

7. *New York Clipper*, June 21, 1890. Article entitled, "VAUDEVILLES AND THE MINSTRELS."

Chapter 6

1. Excellent detailed coverage of McAdoo's background and full career can be found in Lynn Abbott and Doug Seroff, *Out of Sight*, pp. 119–143.

2. A fascinating story of the McAdoo Jubilee Singers' influence on South African music, leading up to a modern tale of the song "The Lion Sleeps Tonight," is told in the article "The Lion Sleeps in Sydney Grave," Robert Messenger, *Canberra Times*, July 9, 2004.

3. "THE JUBILEE SINGERS," quoted from *Christian World*, *Singleton Argus* (August 10, 1892): 4. http://nla.gov.au/nla.news-article82449976 (Viewed January 24, 2019).

4. Australia, New Zealand locations (In alphabetical order, by state):

New South Wales: Armadale, Ashfield, Balmain, Bathurst, Ballina, Berry, Bourke, Bowral, Broadwater, Bulli, Burwood, Carrathool, Casino, Cooma, Cootamundra, Coraki, Dubbo, Goulburn, Glen Ines, Granville, Gunning, Hay, Katoomba, Kiama, Leichhardt, Lismore, Manly, Molong, Narrandera, Newcastle, Newtown, North Shore, North Sydney, Nowra, Parramatta, Penrith, Petersham, Queanbeyan, Richmond, Scone, Singleton, Sydney, Tenterfield, Ulladulla, Wagga Wagga, West Maitland, Whitton, Wollongong, Woodburn.

New Zealand: Ashburton, Blenheim, Cambridge, Carterton, Christchurch [Lyttelton], Clutha, Dannevirke, Dunedin, Eketahuna, Feilding, Gisborne, Gore, Greytown, Hastings, Hawera, Invercargill, Masterton, Napier, Nelson, Oamaru, Pahiatua, Picton, Taranaki, Te Aroha, Thames, Timaru, Waipawa, Waipukurau, Wanganui, Wellington.

Queensland: Brisbane, Bundaberg, Charleville, Charters Towers, Gatton, Gympie, Ipswich, Maryborough, Rockhampton, Roma, Townsville, Warwick.

South Australia: Adelaide, Auburn, Bordertown, Broken Hill, Burra, Carrieton, Clare, Fort Victor, Gawler, Glenelg, Goolwa, Hawker, Kadina, Kapunda, Moonta, Mount Barker, Mount Gambier, Murray Bridge, Norwood, Penola, Petersburg, Port Adelaide, Port Augusta, Port Wakefield, Portland, Quorn, Semaphore, Strathalbyn, Wallaroo, Yongala.

Tasmania: Burnie, Campbelltown, Devonport, Dundas, Evansdale, Hobart, Latrobe, Launceston, Oatlands, Ross, Strahan, Waratah, Zeehan.

Victoria: Bacchus Marsh, Bairnsdale, Ballarat, Benalla, Bendigo, Broadford, Camperdown, Colac, Collingwood, Drysdale, Eaglehawk, Echuca, Euroa, Geelong, Gippsland, Kilmore, Kyabram, Melbourne, Morwell, Prahran, Queenscliff, Tatura, Traralgon, Warragul, Yackandandah, Yea.

Western Australia: Albany, Beverley, Bunbury, Fremantle, Geraldton, Guildford, Katanning, Newcastle, Northam, Perth, Pinjarrah, York.

5. "The Color Line Is Costly," *Camperdown Chronicle*, February 14, 1895.

6. The discovery of gold near Coolgardie (WA) in mid-1893 would soon alleviate the worst effects of the recession.

7. This was an early forerunner of a genre that includes such items as the Rev. A. W. Nix's "Black Diamond Express" (1927) and Zeke's revival sermon, "The Cannonball Express" in the all-black 1929 King Vidor film *Hallelujah*.

8. Julia Wormley was variously referred to as Julie Wormley or Wormlie. As the 1880 U.S. Census gives her as Julia Wormley, born 1868, and as she was so named in later life, that form is used for consistency throughout.

9. "Trouble in the Amen Corner" by Thomas Chalmers Harbaugh (1849–1924) is still popular today in Country and Western circles, recorded by Jim Reeves and Porter Wagoner.

10. For W. H. Jude's career, see: http://en.wikipedia.org/wiki/W._H._Jude (Viewed January 11, 2019).

11. *Queenslander*, September 3, 1892, and *Illawara Mercury*, July 3, 1892; not to be confused with several other similarly titled songs, "The Swallow Song" was composed by Geibel; see http://www.loc.gov/search/?fa=contributor%3Ageibel (Viewed January 11, 2019).

12. *Referee*, June 18, 1892, and *Evening News*, July 5, 1892.

13. Gossip column, *New Zealand Observer*, January 7, 1893.

14. Confirmation of Miss Wormsley's later marital status can be found in *Crisis Magazine* for July 1912, which reported, "The Washington Dramatic Club recently gave Shakespeare's 'Midsummer Night's Dream' at the Howard Theatre. Mrs. Julia Wormley McAdoo and Miss Louise Europe helped in the production." However, Julia Wormley McAdoo and Eugene (Julius) McAdoo seem later to have gone their separate ways, as Eugene spent most of his later life out of the United States, much of it in England.

15. Abbott and Seroff, 126, quoting the Cleveland *Gazette* May 27, 1893. The birth was officially recorded on February 28.

Chapter 7

1. Much detailed information on the various groups and sub-groups that emerged in this period can be found at Djubal Clay's "Australian Variety Theatre Archive" website (https://ozvta.com/) (Viewed January 11, 2019).

2. The full story of the Tivoli, in all its glory, is told in the wonderful book by Frank Van Straten, titled simply *Tivoli*.

3. Frank Van Straten. *Huge Deal: The Fortunes and Follies of Hugh D. McIntosh*, p. 89.

4. The author is indebted to the Australian National Film and Sound Archive for permission to access the Tivoli index cards collection.

5. See Terry Waldo, *This is Ragtime*, p. 21, an excellent general history of ragtime. See also: Rudi Blesh and Harriet Janis, *They All Played Ragtime*.

6. Waldo, *This is Ragtime*, pp. 4–5.

7. Much of what is said here could equally apply to vaudeville's companion format, burlesque. Although today there is a tendency to associate burlesque with risqué performers, like striptease artists such as Sally Rand and Gypsy Rose Lee, most of it was "clean burlesque," suitable for family entertainment. The main dissimilarity was that burlesque usually offered a complete package show, rather than a string of disparate acts. Burlesque circuits were known as "wheels."

8. Benjamin Franklin Keith (1846–1914) and Edwin Franklin Albee (1857–1930). For details of their roles, see Frank Wertheim, *Vaudeville Wars*.

9. For comprehensive coverage of black theatre organizations, see Bernard L. Peterson, Jr., *The African American Theatre Directory, 1816–1960*, especially Appendix B 215+.

Chapter 8

1. See Lynn Abbott and Doug Seroff, *Out of Sight*, p. 127, for a summary of the new South African venture.

2. Henderson Smith (solo cornet), Jessie E. Smith (solo cornet), James P. Jones (solo clarinet), Oscar Lindsey (solo alto), John Brewer (first alto), James Harris (first trombone), Alonzo Edwards (second trombone), Pete Woods (baritone), Edward Tol-

liver (tuba), Turner Jones (bass drum), Frank Poole (snare drums), Jackson Hearde (cymbals), George Henry (drum major), John Pramplin (lightning gun driller). Abbott and Seroff, p. 464.

3. From obituary notice, "Death of Flora Batson," *Indianapolis Freeman*, December 15, 1906.

4. A detailed description of the Cakewalk can be found in Lynn Emery Fauley, *Black Dance: From 1619 to Today*, p. 33.

5. David Krasner, *A Beautiful Pageant: African American Theatre, Drama, and Performance in the Harlem Renaissance, 1910–1927*, p. 63.

6. A comprehensive summary of Curtis's career can be found at: http://berkeleyheritage.com/eastbay_then-now/peralta_park2.html (Viewed January 11, 2019).

7. The list is based on my gleaning from the *New York Clipper*, augmented with information from Abbott and Seroff, *Out of Sight*. There was no separate identification of the members of Professor N. Clark Smiths Pickaninny Band (of which there were sixteen members), but they are assumed to be included in the full listing here, based on supporting evidence.

M. B. Curtis (proprietor), Harry S. Stafford (business manager), Billy McClain (The Black Buffalo) (stage manager), Tom Logan (character artist, assistant stage manager), Chas. F. Alexander (musical director), Nathaniel Clark Smith (bandmaster, pickaninny band), Enrique Stefano (electrician), Amon Davis (Criterion Quartette, property master), Harry Thompson (assistant property master), Madame Ladson R. Alston (costumer), Ernest Hogan (The Unbleached American), Blutch Jones, George Jones (Criterion Quartette), William Jones (Criterion Quartette), Irving Jones (Criterion Quartette), Lewis H. Saulsbury (tenor robusto), Lawrence Chenault (lyric tenor and female impersonator), Robert C. Logan (America's eminent basso), Madah A. Hyer (Bronze Patti, The Californian Nightingale), Laura Moss (Boston's favorite soprano), Carrie Carter (comedienne), Jennie (Miss Vincent) Bradley (character artist), Marion Blake (greatest female baritone), Luella Price (dainty soubrette), Muriel Ringgold (Kentucky Four), Katie Carter (Kentucky Four), Siren Nevarro (The Creole Contortion Danseuse), Black Carl (Black Dante, "the original Dante the Great"), Ed Johnson, Jerry Chorn, Aaron Taylor (Master Levers), Frank Watts, Harry Hull, Harry Thyers, Ernest Thyers, Frank Sanford, Will Lawson, Tom Stirman, James Sprangles, Turner Baskett, Oree Locke, Will Counter, Needham Wright, Duke Kennedy, George Taylor, Harry St. Clair, Percy Denton, Palmer H. Locke.

8. The two reference books by Bernard Peterson were used: *Profiles of African American Stage Performers and Theatre People, 1816–1960* and *The African American Theatre Directory, 1816–1960*. Most of the scores came from the former but, for Madah Hyer, the latter was used. In the case of Siren Nevarro, the extensive material on her under the primary entry for her sometime partner Tom Brown, was treated as an effective secondary entry.

9. Tom Fletcher, *100 Years of the Negro in Show Business*, p. 138.

10. Will Marion Cook was one of the great geniuses of black music in the late 19th and early 20th centuries, classically trained in Germany and with Antonin Dvorak. Despite the training, Cook preferred to work in the black music idiom. He is renowned in jazz circles for bringing his Southern Syncopated Orchestra to Europe in 1919, including the great Sydney Bechet.

11. No explanation has been found for the curious "Black Buffalo" billing, but it may have something to do with the famous black regiments, the Ninth and Tenth Cavalry, who were known as the Buffalo Soldiers. McClain does not seem to have served with them but did feature the Ninth Cavalry Band in *Black America*; also, judging by his fraternal greetings to "buffaloes" back home, he may have been a member of a black Masonic lodge named after the Buffalo Soldiers.

12. Thomas L. Riis, *Just Before Jazz: Black Musical Theater in New York, 1890–1915*, p. 22.

13. Bernard L. Peterson, Jr., *A Century of Musicals in Black and White*, 23. A detailed description of the scale of the show can be found in Bill Reed, *Hot from Harlem*, pp. 46–48.

14. For additional details, see Eileen Southern, *The Music of Black Americans: A History* (Third edition), p. 244.

15. *Ibid.*, p. 254.

16. Siren Nevarro was sometimes called "Navarro" but much more commonly "Nevarro." Therefore, the more common, and likely correct, usage has been maintained.

17. Though he was billed as a female impersonator, this was a fairly minor facet of Chenault's long career on stage and in film.

Chapter 9

1. This, and following material, is paraphrased from the Sydney *Sunday Times*, July 2, 1899.

2. Henderson Smith letter, *Indianapolis Freeman*, September 9, 1899.

3. The Kelly Gang was the bushranger gang led by outlaw Ned Kelly, even today an iconic hero for some Australians, and a villainous ruffian to others. Ned Kelly was hanged at Pentridge Jail in 1880.

4. *Indianapolis Freeman*, letters that touch on the subject of the dissension in Curtis ranks include: 1899, (July 29, September, 2, September 9, September 23, October 14, October 21, November 25), and 1900 (January 6, March 17, the latter being the Hogan apology).

5. Quoted in *Wanganui Chronicle*, August 29, 1899.

6. "M. B. Curtis and the Making of the American Stage Jew," Harley Erdman, *Journal of American Ethnic History* 15 (Fall 1995): 28–45.

7. The Paul referred to is Paul Kruger, president of the South African Republic.

8. Bernard L. Peterson, *A Century of Musicals in*

Black and White, pp. 359–361. Henry T. Sampson, *Blacks in Blackface*, 9.

Chapter 10

1. For example, see *Wanganui Chronicle*, June 14, 1902, p. 7.

2. See *New Zealand Observer*, February 21, 1920, and *Wellington Evening Post*, August 19, 1924, and March 13, 1930.

3. Australian National Museum: https://www.nma.gov.au/defining-moments/resources/bubonic-plague

4. Abbott and Seroff, *Out of Sight*, p. 140, report that McAdoo's death certificate states the cause of death as "Pernicious anemia; Dilation of the heart; Cerebral anaemia syncope." In non-medical terms this probably simplifies to "heart failure."

5. A good summary of the later events can be found in Abbott and Seroff, pp. 140–143.

6. On October 1, 1900, Madame McAdoo was listed in advertisements as the lessee. Opera House, Auckland, and (similarly) of the Princess Theatre, Dunedin, in December.

7. Information about Madame McAdoo's later years is from the "Orpheus M. and Mattie Allen McAdoo Papers," held at Yale University Beinecke Rare Books & Manuscript Library.

8. Australian-born Percy Reginald Dix settled in New Zealand in 1891. In 1899, he established Dix's Gaiety Company at the Auckland City Hall, expanding soon into other New Zealand centers, including Wellington, and later Christchurch and Dunedin. He formed an alliance with Harry Rickards to bring over Australian-based acts. Competition from the rival Fuller Company forced him to shut down in New Zealand in 1905. He continued in Australia as a partner in the Dix-Baker vaudeville company until his death in 1917.

9. Tom Fletcher, *100 Years of the Negro in Show Business: A History*, 101.

10. *Camperdown Chronicle*, June 28, 1946 (Wrongly identifies Ferry as David Mitchell, another "Human Frog").

11. See Jeffrey Green, *Black Edwardians: Black People in Britain 1901–1914*, p. 98, and Abbott and Seroff, p. 127.

12. Although Ida May's name doesn't seem to appear in advertisements until August 1899, the passenger list on the *Moana* included a "Mr. and Mrs. Walker."

Chapter 11

1. For more on Williamson and his role in Australian theatre, see John West, *Theatre in Australia*, 52–54, and extensive other references therein. See also https://en.wikipedia.org/wiki/J._C._Williamson (Viewed January 11, 2019).

2. Usage of the time commonly employed the two variations: "Pickaninny" and "Picaninny."

3. Tom Fletcher, *100 Years of the Negro in Show Business: A History*, p. 157.

4. See Bill Egan, *Florence Mills: Harlem Jazz Queen*, p. 7.

5. "Looking Back with Eva: Early Days," *Storyville* magazine, Vol. 14, December 1967.

6. *Ibid.*

7. The only birthdate found quoted for Gassman was 1882, but the date given (1877) from an 1880 U.S. Census record, is more likely to be true. Had she been born in 1882, she would have been only nineteen years of age on arriving in Australia, and only sixteen when she was leading her first picks troupe in the United States.

8. Quotes from, respectively, *Evening News* (August 27, 1901), and *Courier* (March 24, 1902).

9. *Storyville*, Vol. 14.

10. Constance Valis Hill, *Tap Dancing America: A Cultural History*, p. 56.

11. Josephine's opening number was the popular 1913 James Monaco, Joseph McCarthy, song "You Made Me Love You." It was also sometimes performed by "Little Kathleen."

12. *Brisbane Telegraph*, June 6, 1914. By performing in formal male attire, Irene was following a tradition started by the great Aida Overton Walker, Cakewalk popularizer, when she performed the Cecil Mack, Ford Dabney song, "That's Why they Call Me 'Shine,'" wearing top hat, white tie, and tails, in the 1910 show *His Honor the Barber*.

13. Apart from the obvious internet sources, no trace of Sumner other than this Australia and New Zealand visit can be found in any of the authoritative black entertainment reference works.

14. *Evening Post*, May 16, 1914; Redfern and Worth appear to be two separate contemporary Haute Couture establishments, English-founded but Paris-based. Perhaps both were involved, as Worth specialized in evening wear; Redfern, day wear.

15. *Storyville*, Vol. 14.

16. Leeann Richards's full coverage of Daisy Jerome's career is at: http://hat-archive.blogspot.com.au/2013/12/daisy-jerome-red-headed-spark.html (Viewed January 11, 2019).

17. *Storyville*, Vol. 14.

18. Centers visited include: Ashburton, Timaru, Oamaru, Gore, Invercargill, Dunedin, Christchurch, Wellington, Masterton, Gisborne finishing at Auckland on May 15.

19. *Poverty Bay Herald*, May 19, 1915, and *Age*, May 20, 1915.

20. Tom Lord, *Clarence Williams*, p. 13.

21. In Sweden in 1976, shortly before she died, Eva gave a rousing performance at The Pawnshop, a famous jazz pub in the heart of Stockholm. Her numbers included the two Florence Mills songs "I'm a Little Blackbird" and "Mandy, Make Up Your Mind." The occasion was captured for posterity on CD "Live at The Pawnshop" from Opus3 Records. http://www.opus3records.com http://www.opus3records.com/artists/jazz/sacd22071.html (Viewed January 11, 2019).

Chapter 12

1. The story of Major Taylor's life, and his Australian adventures, are comprehensively covered in the following works, to which much of the coverage here is indebted: Jim Fitzpatrick, *Major Taylor in Australia* (Ebook available in Kindle format).

Also dramatized as TV mini-series *Tracks of Glory* (Umbrella Entertainment, DVD 2012). The TV series depicts the major public events reasonably accurately but adds fictionalized drama for personal events.

Andrew Ritchie, *Major Taylor: The Extraordinary Career of a Champion Bicycle Racer*.

"Major" Marshall Taylor, *The Fastest Bicycle Rider in The World: The Story of a Colored Boy's Indomitable Courage and Success Against Great Odds*.

2. McIntosh's career is comprehensively covered in Frank Van Straten, *Huge Deal: The Fortunes and Follies of Hugh D. McIntosh*.

3. The Immigration Restriction Act of 1901, generally considered the official start of the White Australia policy, had recently been enacted. While no visas were necessary to enter Australia, arriving passengers could be disbarred at point of entry under the draconian provisions of the act.

4. Wowser is an Australian term for killjoys who wants to impose their own standards on others. In the words of poet C. J. Dennis, "An ineffably pious person [is someone] who mistakes this world for a penitentiary and himself for a warder." In fairness to Taylor, he didn't seek to prevent people from drinking and enjoying lay pursuits on Sunday. He merely sought to persuade them by his own example.

5. Fitzpatrick, Kindle Location 382.

6. *Ibid.*, Kindle Locations 489–492.

7. *Ibid.*, Kindle Locations 510–511.

8. Taylor, 300.

9. Fitzpatrick, Kindle Locations 981–984.

10. For a fully detailed account of all the events involved in the 1904 season, Taylor's autobiography is comprehensive.

11. Taylor, p. 365.

12. *Ibid.*, p. 366.

13. Sydney Taylor-Brown lived to the ripe old age of 101, dying in 2005. She had an illustrious career, was "active in the YWCA, the National Association for the Advancement of Colored People, the United Way and the Urban League…. She missed few chances to talk about her father's racing career, including appearances on an NBC television special during the 1996 Olympics." [Obituary, *Pittsburgh Post-Gazette*, May 18, 2005]. She never revisited the city of her birth.

14. Taylor, p. 401.

15. See: http://www.majortaylorassociation.org/ (Viewed January 11, 2019).

Chapter 13

1. J. C. Bain (1870–1946) had worked for James Brennan until 1911, when he formed his own vaudeville company; years later, he resumed his earlier career as a comedian.

2. Detailed descriptions of the tent theatre and its facilities can be found in Bobby Le Brun and Bill Stephens, *Bobby Le Brun Interviewed by Bill Stephens* (1985), National Library of Australia (online audio available).

3. Spearritt, Peter (editor), "Sorlie, George Brown (1885–1948)," *Australian Dictionary of Biography*, National Centre of Biography, Australian National University, http://adb.anu.edu.au/biography/sorlie-george-brown-8585/text14989, initially published in hardcopy 1990 (Viewed January 11, 2019).

4. Le Brun, Stephens, *Interview.*

5. While Cassie always claimed her mother was French, census return information (provided by researcher Howard Rye) show different birth countries for her mother at three English censuses, in Germany, Belgium, and France, respectively. The original German location, Ettlingen, was very close to the French border, and she bore a son in Boulogne, France, in 1870, and may genuinely have identified as French.

6. See, for example, Brisbane, *Telegraph*, May 1, 1907, p. 6; Brisbane, *Truth*, March 23, 1913, p. 12; Adelaide *Register*, April 8, 1913, p. 9.

7. See *Truth* reference details re: Johnson send-off in Chapter 14.

8. *NMH*, April 25 and 29, 1907.

9. A scratchy version of Cassie's 1907 recording of the song can be heard at: http://www.library.ucsb.edu/OBJID/Cylinder15967 courtesy of Allen G. Debus collection; (Viewed January 11, 2019).

10. Adelaide *Critic* interview, April 16, 1913.

11. Written and composed by A. J. Mills and Bennett Scott in 1913. For the complete lyrics, see: http://monologues.co.uk/musichall/Songs-A/Anna-Maria.htm (Viewed January 11, 2019).

Chapter 14

1. Geoffrey C. Ward, *Unforgivable Blackness: The Rise and Fall of Jack Johnson*, p. 8. Much of the biographical detail on Johnson's early life is sourced from this book.

2. John Wren had a finger in many pies, including horseracing and illegal gambling, through his totalizator (tote) and City Tattersalls Club. He was notorious in later years through the publication of the novel *Power Without Glory* by Frank Hardy, which was the subject of a sensational court case. A summary of Wren's life can be found at: James Griffin, "Wren, John (1871–1953)," *Australian Dictionary of Biography*, National Centre of Biography, Australian National University, http://adb.anu.edu.au/biography/wren-john-9198/text16247 (Viewed January 11, 2019).

3. For information on Fred Maynard see *Australian Dictionary of Biography*, Volume 15 (Melbourne: University Press, 1996).

4. Ward, 91.

5. For the description of the CPA, and *Truth's* report, a valuable source was Theresa Runstedtler, *Jack Johnson: Rebel Sojourner*, pp. 39–40 was valuable; A *corroboree* is an Australian Aboriginal dance

ceremony, which is sometimes part of a sacred ritual.

6. As reported in the *Australian Star* on May 22, 1907. The *Newcastle Herald* of May 24, referred to her, more circumspectly, as "an Australian lady."

7. The *Referee*, June 26, 1907, quoting an Oakland California newspaper report of May

8. Hundredweight is a unit of measure, representing 112 Pounds in the British Imperial system, and 100 Pounds in the U.S. system.

9. The Australian media carried numerous lengthy reports of the proceedings, including the *Age* (Melbourne, March 17, 1908), and *Truth* (Brisbane, March 29, 1908). It is also covered in some detail in Ward.

10. Ernest Toy returned to Australia in 1949 as director of the Royal Philharmonic Society of Australia, a position he held until 1954.

11. Frank Van Straten, *Huge Deal: The Fortunes and Follies of Hugh D. McIntosh*, p.19.

12. *Ibid.*, pp. 30–31.

13. Quoted in Ward, p. 118.

14. Van Straten, p. 32.

15. *New York Herald*, December 27, 1908 (Quoted in Van Straten, p. 33).

16. Lawson wrote a poem titled, "The Great Fight," which includes the lines: "But O my people take heed. For the time may be near for the mating of the Black and the White to breed." Running against the popular tide, the *Southern Times* (Bunbury, Western Australia, January 5, 1909) ran an "obituary" for the White Australia Policy, quoting Peter Jackson, Major Taylor, English cricketer Ranjitsinhji, and now Jack Johnson, as evidence of the equal capabilities of coloured people, summing up: "The coloured man is not necessarily a Friday, an organ grinder, or a cannibal, any more than the white man is the sole heir to the royal gifts of Nature."

17. Percy Crawford, *The Tivoli Story*, p. 4, as quoted in Van Straten, p. 37.

18. The later colorful, controversial, career of Jack Johnson can be followed in Ward, *Unforgiveable Blackness*. Johnson had an important role in the world of black entertainment beyond the boxing ring. His Café de Champion on Chicago's South Side, founded in 1910, spawned a host of imitators, known as Black and Tan cafes. They were notorious for promoting liaisons across the race line. They also nurtured the early careers of many notable performers, including Ada "Bricktop" Smith, Florence Mills, and Alberta Hunter. As late as 1920, Johnson opened his Club Deluxe in Harlem, which would later become the famous Cotton Club.

Chapter 15

1. With apologies to Sir Walter Scott, whose poem of that title was "intended to illustrate the customs and manners which anciently prevailed on the Borders of England and Scotland," but might equally do so for Billy Kersands's world of minstrelsy.

2. Tom Fletcher, *100 Years of the Negro in Show Business: A History*, p. 62.

3. Mel Watkins, *On the Real Side: Laughing, Lying, and Signifying—the Underground Tradition of African-American Humor that Transformed American Culture, From Slavery to Richard Pryor*, p. 114.

4. From the *Mail* (Adelaide), "Minstrel Monologues: Billy Kersands's Brightest," November 30, 1912.

5. My copy of the sheet music, published in England, gives Kersands as the author of the song, with Jacob J. Sawyer as the composer. However, the Library of Congress version credits James E Stewart as composer. There were several composers by that name. Jacob J. Sawyer (1856–1885) was a pianist, composer, teacher, and arranger, and was the pianist for the Hyers Sisters Troupe. The mystery remains!

6. Fletcher, p. 61.

7. There is no connection with the earlier "Hugo's Buffalo Minstrels," founded by the Australian-based brothers Charles, William, and James Hugo; the Kersands troupe was organized by the American brothers Victor and Charles Hugo, of Hugo Brothers American Amusement Company, who did not accompany it overseas. The troupe was generally referred to as "Hugo Brother's Minstrels," or "Hugo's American Minstrels."

8. By prolific composer Edgar Leslie, whose best-known song was "For Me and My Gal."

9. *Darktown Follies* went through several versions under various names including *My Friend from Kentucky* and *My Friend from Dixie*.

10. Marshall Stearns, and Jean Stearns *Jazz Dance*, p. 129.

11. Lawrence Gushee, *Pioneers of Jazz: The Story of the Creole Band*, pp. 50–53. By 1918 the pair was reportedly on the States' West Coast, associated with Jelly Roll Morton, Bricktop, et al.

12. Bendigo *Advertiser*, October 21, 1912. Currency calculation from Reserve Bank of Australia's Pre-Decimal Inflation Calculator: http://www.rba.gov.au/calculator/annualPreDecimal.html (Viewed January 11, 2019).

13. *New York Clipper*, March 8, 1913; *Indianapolis Freeman*, March 13, April 26, 1913.

14. Sampson, Henry T. *Blacks in Blackface*, edition 1, p. 4.

15. *Oakland Sunshine* (California), March 27, 1915. Le Protti was also at the time the leader of one of the earliest jazz bands, The So Different Jazz Band, which included Reb Spikes, an important associate of Jelly Roll Morton. It's credited by some as the first to use the word *jazz* in the name of a band.

16. Frank Van Straten, *Tivoli*, p. 9.

Chapter 16

1. With apologies to former Australian prime minister Paul Keating, who was a master at doing it.

2. Later references are to a similarly named Irish comedian, known as "The fellow with the fiddle."

3. Details of Tisdale's later career can be found

in Tim Brooks, *Lost Sounds: Blacks and the Birth of the Recording Industry, 1890–1919*, pp. 327–333.

4. *New York Clipper*, January 1, 1898 ("Gun juggler" reference).

5. Nothing has been found to track Johnson beyond a last English theatrical engagement in November 1917, after which he drops from the public record, possibly having returned to the United States.

6. Henry T. Sampson, *Blacks in Blackface* (First edition), p. 63.

7. See *Indianapolis* Freeman article of September 11, 1909 for the biographical information on the pair. It shows that in 1909 the Sunny South Company included one of Duke's former colleagues from the Georgia Up To Date Minstrels, Allie Gilliam.

8. Sampson, p. 381.

9. Details sourced from Sampson, pp. 381–382.

10. The exact timing of the Cora Miskel engagement is difficult to pin down. The pages of the *New York Clipper* do not show Cora Miskel and her Gold Dust Twins until 1904 (e.g., October 22 issue), though with a reference to her "picaninnies" in May 1903. The term "Gold Dust Twins" was used by more than one act. No independent verification of the English tour has been found. More generally, although the major events of Moore's early career have been widely documented, dates given for particular events vary widely. This is probably because most reports are from a time after his fame as TV's Kingfish, and are difficult to verify from primary sources.

11. *West Australian*, April 23, 1917, *Sunday Times* (Perth), May 6, 1917.

12. Although both versions crop up interchangeably in the media, the form "Larkins" is preferred in this book as that was how he signed his letters to his Australian partner Rachel (Rae) Anderson.

13. The Internet Movie database (IMDB.com), gives alternative birth info as 25 November 25, 1877, in Wilmington, North Carolina. My information, including a report of his mother's death and his funeral notices, supports Norfolk, Virginia, in 1882. Ref. *Eagle* and 27 March 20, 27, 1936, and *New York Age*, February 3, 1910.

14. The story of James Reese Europe's full career can be found in Reid Badger, *A Life in Ragtime*.

15. For copy of the sheet music, see https://www.loc.gov/item/ihas.100005951/ (Viewed January 11, 2019).

16. *New York Age* advert, April 2, 1914, and Lester Walton report, April 16, 1914.

17. See entry "Clay, Harry" in Philip Parsons (editor), *Concise Companion to Theatre in Australia*, p. 67.

18. Details of Larkin's Australian relationship can be found at Steve Goldstein's Facebook posting: https://www.facebook.com/notes/steve-goldstein/jolly-john-reunion/10150314627962649 and http://www.beneathlosangeles.com/bla/Detailed/819.html (both viewed January 11, 2019). Goldstein is the author of *L.A.'s Graveside Companion: Where the V.I.P.s R.I.P.*

Chapter 17

1. The earliest jazz reference found in the National Library of Australia's *Trove* site is for June 8, 1917, *Graphic of Australia* article "Lounge Lizards."

2. *Sydney Sun*, June 21, 1918. Details of the early development of jazz in Australia can be found in Andrew Bisset, *Black Roots, White Flowers*, and Bruce Johnson, *The Oxford Companion to Australian Jazz*.

3. Tim Brooks, *Lost Sounds: Blacks and the Birth of the Recording Industry 1890–1919*, p. 295.

4. Details of Scott and Whaley's careers can be found in Stephen Bourne, *Black in the British Frame*.

5. The Australian pound was still on par with the pound sterling in 1924–1925. Salary details courtesy Tivoli index cards held at the Australian National Film and Sound Archive (Canberra).

6. While Buckner's association with the title Dixie Jubilee Singers can certainly be traced back to at least 1909, his group is only one of many who have claimed that name. Probably the best known is the notable choral conductor Eva Jessye, whose famous Eva Jessye Choir was originally called the Original Dixie Jubilee Singers. It's also unlikely that any of the many recordings made under the Dixie Jubilee name are by the Buckner troupe, and they are definitely not the group featured with that name on the soundtrack of the 1929 movies *Hallelujah* and *Show Boat*, which was the Eva Jessye Choir (billed under their earlier name).

7. Jennie Robinson, who came to Australasia with McAdoo's Jubilee Singers in 1898 as Mrs. Hamilton Hodges, and settled in New Zealand until her death in 1920, had been a member of Donavin's Original Tennesseeans in 1878.

8. See the New York *Clipper* of July 20 and August 10, 1895, and *Duluth Evening Herald* of September 9, 1909.

9. Lynn Abbott, and Doug Seroff, *To Do This, You Must Know How: Music Pedagogy in the Black Gospel Quartet Tradition*, pp. 259–260.

10. (New York) *Morning Telegraph*, March 7, 1922. A *nip-up* is an acrobatic spring from a supine to standing position. It is executed by propelling the body away from the floor so that the performer is momentarily airborne, and typically ends with the performer standing in a squatting position (Source: Wikipedia).

11. The recordings made between 1916 and 1920 are by a mixture of Versatile Threes and Fours with minor personnel variations. "Down Home Rag" (1926) is considered an important example of early (pre-) jazz. See Mark Miller, *Some Hustling This!* pp. 28–29.

12. The Buddy Rich story has been told in Mel Tormé, *Traps—The Drum Wonder: The Life of Buddy Rich*.

Chapter 18

1. Although she was billed as Minta Cato throughout the Australian engagement, she was

more generally known in later years as Minto Cato.

2. *Daily News* (Perth), December 18, 1926, article "Bell-Boy to Producer."

3. *New York Age*, September 13, 1926. Dozens of similar reports can be found across regional media.

4. An excellent survey of Minto Cato's life and career can be found in Henry Louis Gates, Jr., and Evelyn Brooks Higginbotham, *Harlem Renaissance Lives: From the African American National Biography*, pp. 109–111.

5. No earlier black ventriloquist in Australia has been found. Though Hicks' Georgia Minstrels shared a bill with a ventriloquist known as Voltaire (a.k.a. Frank Lay, Ernest Voltaire), it is clear that he was white.

6. Quoted in Abbott and Seroff, *Ragged but Right*, p. 185. This has a large amount of detailed material on Bismark Ferris's career.

7. Ulysses and Leola Everly already had the name Jazzland in their CV before joining Ferris, as they had been part of the house band "Jazz Maniacs" at Charlie Turpin's St. Louis dance palace Jazzland, a significant venue in the history of ragtime and jazz.

8. Ron Thompson was locally recruited, having been part of the Fisk Jubilee Singers New Zealand tour in 1924. It's possible she was of Maori ancestry rather than African American.

9. The original Four Harmony Kings were Hann, Ivan Harold Browning, William Howard Berry, and Charles Exodus Drayton.

10. A useful account of the career of William Hann, the Four Harmony Kings, and the origins of the Emperors of Harmony, including the recording history of both groups, can be found in Tim Brooks, *Lost Sounds: Blacks and the Birth of the Recording Industry, 1890–1919*, especially pp. 452–463.

11. The Emperors of Harmony (African American Quartet) in *Those Pullman Porters*, Vitaphone 2101,One reel, copyrighted August 8 1927. See Edwin M. Bradley, *The First Hollywood Sound Shorts, 1926–1931*, p. 371.

Chapter 19

1. The Sonny Clay events were among the most widely documented in Australian entertainment history. For those who want to pursue more detail, the following sources offer a variety of perspectives: Richard Hall, *Black Armband Days*; Andrew Bisset, *Black Roots, White Flowers: A History of Jazz in Australia*; Bruce Johnson, "Deportation Blues: Black Jazz and White Australia in the 1920s," in *Journal of the International Association for the Study of Popular Music*, Vol. 1 No. 1 (2010); Liner notes for Sonny Clay CD *Deportation Blues* (CL103) CD; Kay Dreyfus, "The Foreigner, the Musicians' Union, and the State in 1920s Australia: A Nexus of Conflict," *Music and Politics* Volume III, Issue 1, Winter 2009 is good on the legal background; Deirde O'Connell "Contesting White Australia: Black Jazz Musicians in a White Man's Country," *Australian Historical Studies* (2016)

47:2, 241–258 covers the political conspiracy aspects well.

2. John Bentley, "Sonny Clay: A Veritable Giant (Part 2), from *Jazz Research* (November/December 1962), quoted in Jacqueline Cogdell DjeDje, and Eddie S. Meadows, *California Soul: Music of African Americans in the West*, p. 47.

3. The personnel as listed in Tom Lord, *The Jazz Discography*, CD edition 11.0. It is safe to assume that the Leo Davis mentioned in shipping lists is, in fact, Leonard Davidson. Reconciling these names with those shown on arriving and departing shipping lists presented a bit of a challenge. The main problem was that some of the musicians chose (on occasion) to identify their names as "Black," understandable in the context of later circumstances but less so before arrival. The musicians so affected appear to be Rupert Jordan (banjo) and William Griffin (tenor sax), but both were identified in reports, Griffin's name appearing on the departure list and Jordan being identified as one of the six caught up in the raid. Otherwise, all the names mentioned appear on the list of those who arrived on the *Sierra* in January and departed on it in March. The only contemporary photographs show ten musicians in each case.

4. Further information on Clay, his career and his musicians can be found in *Pioneers of Jazz: The Story of the Creole Band*.

5. Pinning down precise information about the composition of the four performing Covans has been difficult. Consistent with the account given is that four Covans and a Turner were on the passenger list for the *Sierra*. Melbourne *Table Talk* (March 8, 1928) carried a photo of Elmer Turner, identified as Elmer Covan. However, to confuse the issue, the *Sydney Sun* (January 28, 1928) carried a photo captioned "Dorothy Covan." No trace of a Dorothy Covan has been found in *any* source, and it can be assumed that this is a misidentification of either Willie's wife, Florence, or Elmer Turner. A *New York Eagle* report (June 16, 1955) names Margarite, later deceased, as Dewey Covan's non-performing wife on the Australia trip.

6. Bisset, p. 45.

7. *Ibid.*, 44.

8. The debate in parliament was covered at length in the *Argus* on September 2, 1924, among several other sources.

9. Hall, chapter titled "Black Arms on White Shoulders," beginning on p. 171.

10. *Lithgow Mercury*, March 29, 1928, among others.

11. Hogan Jazz Archive (Tulane University, New Orleans, LA). Sonny Clay interviewed by John Bentley (1960).

Chapter 20

1. *Sporting Globe*, April 20, 1935 "First sung coon songs in spangles under Cassie Walmer moniker."

2. The author is indebted to the redoubtable En-

glish researcher Howard Rye for this, and sundry other, Cassie Walmer information.

3. Gracie told the author in a private interview (given in her nineties) that she was thirteen at the time, but given her birth date of July 19, 1912, it's likely she was fifteen. That also seems more compatible with her relating that she was allowed to leave school to become a performer. Salary details are from "Grace Le Brun, interviewed by Bill Stephens (1985)," National Library of Australia Oral History collection.

4. Tracking the movements of the Kentucky Singers was complicated by the fact that throughout their time in New Zealand and Australia they could have gone to see their shadow selves, in one of the popular Movietone short "talkies," playing at numerous cinemas in both countries.

5. Tim Brooks, *Lost Sounds: Blacks and the Birth of the Recording Industry 1890–1919*, p. 104.

6. Levinson, André. "The Negro Dance: Under European Eyes," *Theatre Arts Monthly*, April 1927, 282.

7. Coverage of the fan dance and related issues can be found at *SMH*, July 27; *Truth*, July 28 and August 4; *The Labor Daily*, August 8.

8. The author has shamelessly pilfered the Hamlet pun from Edwin Adele's *Performer* (September 28, 1927) review of *Blackbirds of 1927* without Florence Mills.

9. Whether Foresythe fits within our African-American scope is a marginal call. He was born in England to an English mother and an African father of Sierra Leone Creole stock. Sierra Leone Creoles were descendants of freed African American, West Indian, and liberated African slaves who settled in the western area of Sierra Leone between 1787 and about 1885.

10. Barbara James's story can be found in Bruce Johnson, *The Inaudible Music: Jazz, Gender and Australian Modernity* (Chapter 5).

11. See http://www.sandiegohistory.org/journal/1978/july/women16/ (Viewed January 11, 2019).

12. Both *Hearts in Dixie* and *Show Boat* included the Billbrew Chorus, a large choir which might have incorporated the girls.

13. The eight California ballet girls provided the only identified (and advertised) African American contribution to *Show Boat*. Though the playbill for the large cast—printed well ahead of the opening performance—listed "Ladies and Gentlemen of the Mississippi Chorus," and "Ladies of the Mississippi Ballet" these were obviously local recruits. There were a few Australian-born colored performers with some claim to African American connections among them. These included several who had performed with the later Fisk Jubilee troupe, including Bertha Haynes Millar, Sydney Haynes and Elsie May (of whom more in Appendix 3). While the playbill includes names of five African Americans who had been in the original New York Broadway production (1927), exhaustive checking of contemporary media and Australian National Archives shipping records found no evidence that any of them came to Aus-

tralia. One, Alma Smith, is known to have been in a U.S. production long before the end of the Melbourne run. On balance it seems unlikely that any of them were part of the Australian show

Chapter 21

1. Information about Crump can be found at https://drumz4sale.blogspot.com.au/2012/05/freddie-crump-another-forgotten-genius.html (Viewed January 11, 2019).

2. Unattributed quotations from Thompson are all from the Delilah Jackson interview tapes (Bill Egan Collection).

3. This was the black Tennessee Ten, which was unrecorded, and is not to be confused with the later white group of the same name, which made some records under that title in 1923.

4. The *Herald* (Melbourne) October 2, 1937, seems to be the last. For those who couldn't afford genuine silk stockings it was possible to buy "Winner Home Dye," which included the Florence Mills shade.

5. Bobby Le Brun, "Tales of the Tent Shows," *Outdoor Showman*, June–July 1980.

6. Bobby Le Brun diaries, in Papers of Bobby and Gracie Le Brun, 1924–2004, NLA.

7. Le Brun, "Tales of the Tent Shows."

8. Jim Sharman, *In The Realm of the Imagination: An Individual View of Theatre*. (The inaugural Rex Cramphorn Memorial Lecture). The text can be seen at: http://www.currency.com.au/resources/1/Speeches%20Online%20-%20JS%20In%20the%20Realm.pdf (viewed January 25, 2019).

Chapter 22

1. Details of Nina Mae's biography, with emphasis on her movie career, can be found in Stephen Bourne, *Nina Mae McKinney: The Black Garbo*.

2. Charles B. Cochran, *Cock-A-Doodle-Do*, 281–282.

3. Bourne, 42.

4. Mezzrow, Milton "Mezz," and Bernard Wolfe, *Really the Blues*, p. 234.

5. Marshall Stearns, and Jean Stearns, *Jazz Dance*, p. 245. Harry Langdon was a silent screen comedian.

6. Fred Parsons, *A Man Called Mo*, p. 68. *Sheila* is rough Australian slang for a female.

7. Parsons, pp. 68–69.

8. Kid Thompson was recalling events from about forty years back, and some details on the tape are vague or unclear. He gave some information about the man involved, but not his name. The reference to Watson's Bay should actually be to Elizabeth Bay, Nina Mae's residence at the time being an apartment block there named "King's Lynn, Ithaca Road … a very exclusive structure."

9. Riverside Drive is a fashionable boulevard that runs along the Upper West Side of Manhattan, New York, parallel with the Hudson River.

10. National Archives of Australia; Series number: SP42/1; Control symbol: C1938/1574; Barcode: 31099866. Quotations from these documents are hereinafter referred to as "Archives."

11. *SMH* 16 October 1937 re: drama hopes; Archives, Director of Customs document, January 20, 1938, re: possible mother's visit.

12. The inspector's report from the Archive's documents extends over three single-spaced typed pages.

13. Parsons, pp. 62, 64.

Chapter 23

1. For the history of the groups that evolved out of the original Hann's Jubilee Singers, see Tim Brooks, *Lost Sounds: Blacks and the Birth of the Recording Industry 1890–1919*, particularly Chapter 31. Brooks's coverage does not include the later trio's Australian visit.

2. A comprehensive account of the dispute was given in *Labor Daily*, July 12, 1937, p.1.

Chapter 24

1. Stearns, and Stearns, *Jazz Dance*, p. 157.

2. Rusty Frank, *TAP! The Greatest Tap Dance Stars and Their Stories 1900–1955.* See Jeni Le Gon interview, p. 126.

3. "Chuck Richards Gave Up the Big Bands for Baltimore Media," *Baltimore Sun*, February 8, 2009.

4. Frank, p. 50. Curiously, when this author spoke with Bates in 1996 he was keen to tell about his 1956 visit down-under with the Louis Armstrong All-Stars, but made no mention of the 1938 visit.

5. Biographical details for Jesse Cryor can be seen at: https://web.archive.org/web/20130404161246/http://hubcap.clemson.edu/~campber/premium.html (Search "Cryor" to find relevant location) (Viewed January 11, 2019).

6. While information on Clayton "Peg Leg" Bates can be found in many sources, one of the best is a documentary by Hudson West Films *The Dancing Man—Peg Leg Bates*: http://hudsonwest.org/our-films/peglegbates/ (Viewed January 11, 2019). A nice book for children is Lynne Barasch, *Knockin' on Wood: Starring Peg Leg Bates.*

Chapter 25

1. There are other version of of how the name originated but this is as likely as any. A good account of the events involved in the origin of the Lindy Hop and swing dancing can be found in Stearns, Marshall, and Stearns, Jean. *Jazz Dance* Chapters 39 and 40; Other excellent sources include Manning, Frankie, and Millman, Cynthia, *Frankie Manning: Ambassador of Lindy* Hop, and Miller, Norma with Jensen, Evette. *Swingin' at the Savoy: The Memoir of a Jazz Dancer.* While the legendary Norma Miller, who is approaching 100 years at the time of this writing (2019), was not part of the 1938–1939 Lindy Hoppers group, she did make it to Australia with her Norma Miller Dancers as a main feature of the 1955 Tivoli show *Colored Rhapsody.*

2. The scene from *A Day at the Races* scene can be easily found on YouTube, e.g., https://www.youtube.com/watch?v=WwKFALb6Vw8 (Viewed January 11, 2019). Some versions also include Ivy Anderson, who was part of the Sonny Clay troupe's 1928 visit. The *Hellzapoppin'* sequence can also be readily found on YouTube and similar internet sites. It is considered the greatest recorded example of swing dancing, and includes Frankie Manning and Norma Miller, as well as Billy and Willa Mae Ricker of the Australia/New Zealand troupe.

3. Manning and Millman, p. 156.

4. *Courier*, November 19, 1938. The identity of the ninth person is unknown; it is known that the individual was not a dancer.

5. Manning and Millman, p. 154.

6. Ibid., p. 159.

7. Ibid., 157–158.

Chapter 26

1. For much of the time in Australia, Rodgers was incorrectly spelt *Rogers*, and Brown incorrectly spelled *Browne*. I have stayed with the correct versions.

2. A summary of Rodgers's jazz career can be found in John Chilton, *Who's Who of Jazz* (Fourth edition) 282–283. Examples of his amusing boogie-style piano can be found on the internet (YouTube or similar) by searching "Gene Rodgers."

3. Lane Demas, *Game of Privilege: An African-American History of Golf*, pp. 96–97.

4. The author is indebted to jazz movie and "soundie" expert Mark Cantor for clarifying (and correcting) details about the Dancing Chefs and their style. *Breakfast in Rhythm* was probably filmed in 1943, by which time only George McDaniel of the earlier trio was still a member, but it gives a fair indication of the style and skill level of the trio.

5. Stearns, and Stearns, *Jazz Dance*, 245–246. The "ragged set of vibes" (vibraphone) are not mentioned as part of their act in Australia.

6. The historic Adelaide canvas theatre was demolished to make way for a new building, sometime later in 1940.

7. "Sparking Show at Smalls," *Pittsburgh Courier*, June 15, 1946, p. 19.

8. Quoted in Mills Brothers Wikipedia entry https://en.wikipedia.org/w/index.php?title=The_Mills_Brothers&oldid=826506298 (Viewed January 11, 2019).

9. The Comedy Harmonists who toured Australia would have been a later version of the breakaway group that fled Nazi Germany after 1934.

10. *SMH*, March 12, 1937, p. 2.

11. The author was told this entertaining story by June (Allen) Strike herself, who was then in her mid-nineties, in 2015. The *Pinocchio* premiere was held on February 9, 1940.

Chapter 27

1. See http://www.ozatwar.com/usarmy/african american.htm (Viewed January 11, 2019).

2. See "Americans and Maori," *Ministry for Culture and Heritage*, https://nzhistory.govt.nz/war/us-forces-in-new-zealand/americans-and-maori (Viewed January 11, 2019).

3. Andrew Bisset, *Black Roots, White Flowers*, p. 85, and, more generally, the chapter titled, "Aussies on Parade."

4. https://en.wikipedia.org/wiki/Lee_Gordon_(promoter)#1954 (Viewed January 11, 2019).

5. *Australian Women's Weekly*, November 30, 1960, p. 11.

Appendix 1

1. Details of Peter Jackson's career can be found at his Boxrec.com and Wikipedia entries.

2. Boxing historian Tracy Callis quoted in Jackson's Boxrec.com biography.

3. The Lonsdale belt is still awarded to British boxing champions.

4. Quoted in Jackson's Boxrec.com biography.

5. *Referee*, February 14, 1935. The epitaph is a quotation from Shakespeare's *Julius Caesar*, Mark Antony's tribute on the death of Brutus, which begins, "This was the noblest Roman of them all."

6. Information about careers is drawn from the invaluable records on the website Boxrec.com, but it should be noted that these are often an understatement, either because of difficulty in finding details, particularly for early times, or because much of the boxing activity of the time was informal, such as tent shows, or illegal bare-knuckle fights.

Appendix 2

1. Kieza, Grantlee. *Boxing in Australia*, Chapter 3.

2. For details of Archie Moore's public and social life, see his Wikipedia entry.

Appendix 3

1. Names passing through the ranks included Beatrice Mercer, a white New Zealand contralto; Melbournite Harry C. Newton, filling the basso role of McAdoo; Alice Baptiste, mezzo-soprano; Elizabeth Cleva M'Clain, soprano; Minnie Cooper, mezzo-soprano; Walter Williams, tenor: Beatrice Caire, contralto; Sydney Haynes baritone; Bertha Haynes-Miller, soprano; Alaba Bailey, mezzo-soprano; Cecile Stephano, white New Zealand soprano; Mrs. Hamilton Hodges, soprano; Florence Dixie, banjo (actually white Australian Bessie Campbell), and notable young African-American tenor Clarence Tisdale.

2. The "hui" was a major Maori gathering. "The Gisborne hui promises to be of historic significance, constituting one of the largest 'native gatherings' held on the East Coast for many years. Considerable interest, of course, is added to the meeting in consequence of 'the arrival of the Maori soldiers,' and … steps are being taken by the Government authorities to secure phonographic and photographic records of Maori songs and customs." (*Poverty Bay Herald*, April 4, 1919).

The story of the Maori gifts is as reported in Abbott, and Seroff, *Out of Sight*, p. 142, quoting an article from Australian *Theatre* magazine, September 2, 1918.

3. The lineup included Vi James (mezzo-soprano, Australian), Leila Wyburd (soprano, Australian), Frank Allanson (baritone, English—no mention of African-American ancestry), Sid Haynes (baritone, African American), George Bentley (tenor, Australian), Violet McAdoo (lady baritone, part-African American), Marjorie Alwyne (contralto, Australian), Harry Penn (tenor, Australian), Professor A. C. Whyte (accompanist and musical director, African American), Marshall Palmer (tenor, Australian).

4. Variously known as Elsa Carr, Elsie May, Elsie Williams and just Black Elsie, she had some early success in several stage productions, as well as with the Jubilee Singers, before declining into a life of alcoholism and petty criminality in a rough area of Melbourne. A colorful figure, well known on the streets during the Depression years, the sad story of her later years and tragic end is told in David Sornig, *Blue Lake: Finding Dudley Flats and the West Melbourne swamp* (Brunswick, Victoria: Scribe Publications, 2018), and Brian Hansen, *The Jack Dyer Story: The Legend of Captain Blood* (Mount Waverley, Victoria: Brian Hansen Nominees, 1996). Thanks to David Sornig and David Jones for information on Black Elsie.

Bibliography

Abbott, Lynn, and Doug Seroff. *Out of Sight: The Rise of African American Popular Music, 1889–1895.* Jackson: University Press of Mississippi, 2002.

_____. *Ragged but Right: Black Traveling Shows, Coon Songs, and the Dark Pathway to Blues and Jazz.* Jackson: University Press of Mississippi, 2007.

_____. *To Do This, You Must Know How: Music Pedagogy in the Black Gospel Quartet Tradition.* Jackson: University Press of Mississippi, 2013.

Badger, Reid. *A Life in Ragtime.* New York: Oxford: University Press, 1995.

Barasch, Lynne. *Knockin' on Wood: Starring Peg Leg Bates.* New York: Lee & Low Books, 2004.

Bisset, Andrew. *Black Roots, White Flowers: A History of Jazz in Australia.* Sydney: Australian Broadcasting Corporation, 1979.

Blesh, Rudi, and Janis, Harriet. *They All Played Ragtime.* New York: Oak Publications, 1966.

Bourne, Stephen. *Black in the British Frame: Black People in British Film and Television 1896–1996* (First edition). London: Bloomsbury Academic, 2001.

_____. *Nina Mae McKinney: The Black Garbo.* Duncan, OK: BearManor Media, 2011.

Bradley, Edwin M. *The First Hollywood Sound Shorts 1926–1931.* Jefferson, NC: McFarland, 2009.

Brooks, Tim. *Lost Sounds: Blacks and the Birth of the Recording Industry 1890–1919.* Chicago: University of Illinois Press, 2005.

Cato, Nancy. *Mister Maloga.* St. Lucia: University of Queensland Press, 1993.

Chilton, John. *Who's Who of Jazz* (Fourth edition). London: Macmillan, 1985.

Cochran, Charles B. *Cock-A-Doodle-Do.* London: J M Dent & Sons, 1941.

Crawford, Percy. *The Tivoli Story: 55 Years of Variety.* Melbourne: Tivoli Theatre, 1956.

Demas, Lane. *Game of Privilege: An African American History of Golf.* Chapel Hill: University of North Carolina Press, 2017.

Dickens, Charles. *American Notes for General Circulation.* London: Chapman and Hall, 1842.

DjeDje, Jacqueline Cogdell, and Eddie S. Meadows. *California Soul: Music of African Americans in the West.* Berkeley: University of California Press, 1998.

Egan, Bill. *Florence Mills: Harlem Jazz Queen.* Lanham, MD: Scarecrow Press, 2004.

Emery, Lynn Fauley. *Black Dance From 1619 to Today* (Second edition). Princeton, NJ: Princeton Book Company, 1988.

Fitzpatrick, Jim. *Major Taylor in Australia.* Kilcoy, Queensland: Star Hill Studio, 2011.

Fletcher, Tom. *100 Years of the Negro in Show Business.* New York: Burdge & Company, 1954.

Fotheringham, Richard. *Sport in Australian Drama.* Cambridge: Cambridge University Press, 1992.

Frank, Rusty. *TAP! The Greatest Tap Dance Stars and Their Stories 1900–1955.* New York: Da Capo Press, 1900.

Frick, John W. *Uncle Tom's Cabin on the American Stage and Screen.* New York: Palgrave Macmillan, 2012.

Fryer, Peter. *Staying Power: The History of Black People in Britain.* (Second edition). London: Pluto Press, 2010.

Gates Jr., Henry Louis, and Evelyn Brooks Higginbotham (editors). *Harlem Renaissance Lives from the African American National Biography.* New York: Oxford University Press, 2009.

Goldstein, Steve. *L.A.'s Graveside Companion: Where the V.I.P.s R.I.P.* Atglen, PA: Schiffer Publishing, 2009.

Grant, Angela, *Rita's Saga: A Young Woman's Journey Through the Seedy Side of Nashville.* Bloomington, IN: AuthorHouse, 2012.

Green, Jeffrey. *Black Americans in Victorian Britain.* Barnsley, South Yorkshire: Pen and Sword Books Ltd., 2018.

_____. *Black Edwardians: Black People in Britain 1901–1914.* London: Frank Cass, 1998.

Green, John P. *Fact Stranger Than Fiction: Seventy-Five Years of a Busy Life with Reminiscences of Many Great and Good Men and Women.* Cleveland, OH: Roehl Printing Company, 1920.

Gushee, Lawrence. *Pioneers of Jazz; the Story of the Creole Band.* New York: Oxford University Press, 2005.

Hall, Richard. *Black Armband Days.* Sydney: Random House Australia, 1998.

Johnson, Bruce. *The Inaudible Music: Jazz, Gender and Australian Modernity.* Sydney: Currency Press, 2000.

_____. *The Oxford Companion to Australian Jazz.* Melbourne: Oxford University Press, 1987.

Kieza, Grantlee. *Boxing in Australia.* Canberra: National Library of Australia, 2015.

Krasner, David. *A Beautiful Pageant: African American Theatre, Drama, and Performance in the Harlem Renaissance, 1910–1927.* New York: Palgrave Macmillan, 2002.

_____. *Resistance, Parody and Double Consciousness in African American Theatre, 1895–1910.* New York: St. Martin's Press, 1997.

Lord, Tom. *Clarence Williams.* Chigwell, UK: Storyville Publications, 1976.

Malone, Jacqui. *Steppin' on the Blues: The Visible Rhythms of African American Dance.* Chicago: University of Illinois Press, 1996.

Manning, Frankie, and Cynthia Millman. *Frankie Manning: Ambassador of Lindy Hop.* Philadelphia: Temple University Press, 2007.

Marsh, J. B. T. *The Story of the Jubilee Singers; With Their Songs.* London: Hodder and Stoughton, 1887.

Mezzrow, Milton "Mezz," and Bernard Wolfe. *Really the Blues.* London: Corgi Books, 1961.

Miller, Mark, *Some Hustling This! Taking Jazz to the World 1914–1929.* Ontario, Canada: The Mercury Press, 2005.

Miller, Norma, with Evette Jensen. *Swingin' at the Savoy: The Memoir of a Jazz Dancer.* Philadelphia: Temple University Press, 1996.

Nolan, Melanie (editor). *Australian Dictionary of Biography (Volume 18).* Canberra: National Centre of Biography, Australian National University, 2012.

O'Meally, Robert (editor). *The Jazz Cadence of American Culture.* New York: Columbia University Press, 1998.

Parsons, Fred. *A Man Called Mo.* Melbourne: Heinemann, 1973.

Parsons, Philip (editor). *Concise Companion to Theatre in Australia.* Sydney: Currency House Inc., 1997.

Perkins, Rachel, and Marcia Langton (editors). *First Australians.* Melbourne: Miegunyah Press, 2010.

Peterson, Bernard L., Jr. *The African American Theatre Directory 1816–1960.* Westport, CT: Greenwood Press, 1997.

_____. *A Century of Musicals in Black and White.* Westport, CT: Greenwood Press, 1993.

_____. *Profiles of African American Stage Performers and Theatre People, 1816–1960.* Westport, CT: Greenwood Press, 2001.

Pybus, Cassandra. *Black Founders: The Unknown Story of Australia's First Black Settlers.* Sydney: UNSW Press, 2006.

_____. *Epic Journeys of Freedom: Runaway Slaves of the American Revolution and Their Global Quest for Liberty.* Boston: Beacon Press, 2006.

Reed, Bill. *Hot from Harlem.* Los Angeles: Cellar Door Press, 1998.

Riis, Thomas L. *Just Before Jazz: Black Musical Theater in New York, 1890 to 1915.* Washington, D.C.: Smithsonian Institution Press, 1989.

Ritchie, Andrew. *Major Taylor: The Extraordinary Career of a Champion Bicycle Racer.* Baltimore, MD: Johns Hopkins University Press, 1996.

Ritchie, John (editor) *Australian Dictionary of Biography: Volume 15.* Melbourne: Melbourne University Press, 1996.

Runstedtler, Theresa. *Jack Johnson: Rebel Sojourner.* Oakland: University of California Press, 2013.

Sampson, Henry T. *Blacks in Blackface: A Source Book on Early Black Musical Shows* (First edition). Metuchen, NJ: Scarecrow Press, 1980.

_____. *The Ghost Walks: A Chronological History of Blacks in Show Business, 1865–1910.* Metuchen, NJ: Scarecrow Press, 1988.

Smith, Kevin R. *Black Genesis: The History of the Black Prizefighter 1760–1870.* Lincoln, NE: iUniverse Inc., 2003.

Southern, Eileen. *The Music of Black Americans: A History* (Third edition). New York: W. W. Norton, 1997.

Stearns, Marshall, and Jean Stearns. *Jazz Dance: The Story of American Vernacular Dance.* London: Collier Macmillan, 1968.

Taylor, Marshall W. "Major." *The Fastest Bicycle Rider in The World.* Worcester: Wormley Publishing Company, 1928.

Toll, Robert C. *Blacking Up: The Minstrel Show in Nineteenth-Century America.* London: Oxford University Press, 1974.

Tormé, Mel. *Traps—The Drum Wonder: The Life of Buddy Rich.* Alma, MI: Rebeats Press, 1997.

Valis Hill, Constance. *Tap Dancing America: A Cultural History.* New York: Oxford University Press, 2010.

Van Straten, Frank. *Huge Deal: The Fortunes and Follies of Hugh D. McIntosh.* Melbourne: Lothian Books, 2004.

_____. *Tivoli.* Melbourne: Lothian Books, 2003.

Waldo, Terry. *This Is Ragtime.* New York: Da Capo Press, 1991.

Ward, Andrew. *Dark Midnight When I Rise: The Story of the Jubilee Singers Who Introduced the World to the Music of Black America.* New York: Farrar, Strauss and Giroux, 2000.

Ward, Geoffrey C. *Unforgivable Blackness: The Rise and Fall of Jack Johnson.* New York: Alfred A. Knopf, 2004.

Waterhouse, Richard. *From Minstrel Show to Vaudeville: The Australian Popular Stage 1788–1914.* Sydney: NSW University Press, 1990.

Watkins, Mel. *On the Real Side: Laughing, Lying, and Signifying—The Underground Tradition of African-American Humor That Transformed American Culture, From Slavery to Richard Pryor.* New York: Touchstone [Simon & Schuster], 1994.

Wertheim, Frank. *Vaudeville Wars.* New York: Palgrave Macmillan, 2006.

West, John. *Theatre in Australia.* Stanmore, NSW: Cassell Australia, 1978.

Whiteoak, John, and Aline Scott-Maxwell (editors). *Currency Companion to Music and Dance in Australia.* Sydney: Currency House Inc., 2003.

Index

Numbers in ***bold italics*** indicate pages with illustrations